Slap Shots and Snapshots
50 Seasons of Pro Hockey in Johnstown

The Tribune-Democrat
JOHNSTOWN magazine

Copyright (C) 2007

by The Tribune-Democrat and Johnstown Magazine,
subsidiaries of Community First Holdings,
a division of Community Newspaper Holdings Inc. of Birmingham, Alabama.

Printed by Jostens Printing and Publishing,
State College, Pennsylvania.

All rights reserved. No part of this book can be reproduced or transmitted
in any form or by any means, electronic or mechanical, including
photocopying, recording, or through any
information or retrieval system, without
permission from the publisher.

ISBN: 978-0-9796044-1-6
The Tribune-Democrat
Johnstown Magazine
425 Locust Street, P.O. Box 340
Johnstown, PA 15907-0340

Slap Shots and Snapshots — 50 Seasons of Pro Hockey in Johnstown

Editor:
Chip Minemyer, Editor, The Tribune-Democrat

Contributing Editors:
Angela Berzonski, Editor, Johnstown Magazine
Kimberly Williams, Design Editor,
Johnstown Magazine
Matt Jordan, Sports Copy Editor, The Tribune-Democrat

Business Manager:
Lou Gjurich, The Tribune-Democrat

Classified Sales Manager:
Christine Pringle, The Tribune-Democrat

Lead Writer:
Mike Mastovich, Sports Writer, The Tribune-Democrat

Contributors:
Dana Heinze
Mike Piskuric
Lou DeFazio
Mike Starchok
Dave Zeigler
John P. James
John Tanish

Photographs are from The Tribune-Democrat and team archives.
Select "Slap Shot" photos are courtesy of www.slapshotfan.com

contents

Introductions	5
Overview	11
War Memorial Arena	15
Slap Shot	18
Era 1: Blue Birds	42
Era 2: Jets in the '50s	54
Era 3: Jets in the '60s	102
Era 4: Jets in the '70s	156
Era 5: Wings and Red Wings	200
Era 6: Chiefs in the '80s	210
Era 7: Chiefs in the '90s	232
Era 8: Chiefs in the 2000s	282
Miscellaneous Statistics	331

SLAP SHOTS AND SNAPSHOTS

foreword

Johnstown Shares Long Love Affair With Hockey

By John P. James

A chilling, wind-driven rain pelted the western Pennsylvania city nestled between the Allegheny Mountains on this Friday morning, Nov. 4, 1950.

On a brighter note, Johnstown's newspaper predicted that by suppertime, the temperatures would reach a comfortable 55 degrees.

Johnstown is one of William Penn's more castigated communities. Stubborn to the umpteenth degree, the city had rebounded from two devastating floods — an 1889 disaster that still today claims a page in most American History textbooks, and again in 1936, which claimed fewer lives but left much of the downtown section floating in a sea of mud and surrounded by soggy, broken dreams.

Johnstown, rather than the beloved basketball coach Jim Valvano, could have invented the popular rally cry, "Never give up. No. Never give up."

But on this particular Friday, nothing was out of the ordinary. The nearby rivers — Little Conemaugh and Stonycreek — were behaving themselves. Women bustled around their homes, preparing their children for the week's final school day. The ladies were especially hurried, because downtown's Glosser Brothers Department Store was offering rib roast at 49 cents a pound.

Earlier, steelworkers had arrived home to wipe off the red dust — a by-product of belching blast furnaces — from cars, porches and windows.

Barber shops opened to renewed discussions of the foiled assassination attempt on President Harry S. Truman just two days earlier. And there was the city's 150th anniversary the following day.

Left: Johnstown Jets defenseman Dave Lucas has his eyes on the puck as it heads to the net during a 1960s-era game at Cambria County War Memorial Arena.

The Tribune-Democrat had reported five births at the city's three hospitals in its late editions. Nothing was out of the ordinary. Yet, in reality, this was a very special day. That evening, more than 3,000 persons would stream downtown for a birthday party — a reunion of sorts.

They would plunk down $2 for reserved seats and a buck for general admission to welcome back ice hockey to the brand new Cambria County War Memorial Arena.

The city had been briefly introduced to the rough-and-tumble sport in the 1940s, when the Johnstown Blue Birds occupied the old Shaffer Ice Palace located in the nearby neighborhood of Hornerstown.

But on this night, the home team would not be wearing a less-threatening bird on its new jerseys.

On this night, and for many years to come, the team would be sporting a fighter plane on its uniforms as the Johnstown Jets. The nickname was the brainchild of a 71-year-old who picked up a pair of free season tickets as the winner of a contest to name the team.

Approximately 2½ hours after the first regular-season face-off, Jets fans marched out of the city's newest sports mecca — the War Memorial. No one seemed to care that the visiting New York Rovers had defeated coach Wally Kilrea's Jets team, 7-5.

Johnstown once again had a hockey team — and that's all that mattered.

Johnstown relished its reputation as a "shot-and-a-beer" town. There seemed to be a church and bar on each street corner. Residents were used to working, praying, partying and playing hard.

The community never expected less from its hockey team. And seldom did the skaters fail to deliver. There have been numerous celebratory championships. Seldom did the franchise fail to at least secure a playoff berth.

Players wearing the Jets logo were a tough and talented bunch, on one occasion chasing the visiting team off the ice before the first face-off. That team from Buffalo, N.Y., never returned, and disbanded a year later.

And the fans had their moments before the War Memorial was encased in Plexiglas and the visiting teams and officials dressing rooms had security personnel present.

There were a number of unscheduled "fan participation night" gatherings that usually sent police cruisers scurrying to the Napoleon Street building, and had Jets General Manager Johnny Mitchell sporting a red face.

As popular cable television cooking guru Emerill Legassi would say, "Can't you feel the love?"

Similar to any love affair, there have been highs and lows. Another flood gutted the War Memorial and the City of Johnstown in 1977. But, once again, hockey and its fans bounced off the canvas following a one-year hiatus. And every season brings unfounded rumors of a franchise shift.

But also, as in any marriage, the fun is making up.

So, now sit down, prop up your feet and thoroughly enjoy "Slap Shots and Snapshots" — The Tribune-Democrat's chronicle of the love of a city and its hockey team.

It is one of minor-league sports most written-about, talked-about and filmed phenomenon.

It can be argued that hockey belongs to this city.

But, maybe, just maybe, hockey is this city.

The Story Behind the Story

By Dana Heinze

This project probably started in 1995, during my second tenure as the equipment manager with the Johnstown Chiefs, when I was hanging Johnstown Chiefs team pictures in the new locker room. At the time, I thought, "Boy, wouldn't it be neat to have all the team pictures from Johnstown history on these walls?" Then, I realized how many there were and wondered where I could get those pictures.

So it began. I set out on this quest to try to collect every team picture in Johnstown professional hockey history. This was not an easy task.

About 2½ years later, the team asked me to decorate a holiday window at the Glosser Brothers building on the corner of Franklin and Locust streets in downtown Johnstown. We put together a display of historic material concerning the Chiefs. From there, I was asked to come up with a display on the hockey history of Johnstown at the Bottle Works Ethnic Arts Center in Johnstown, so I did that. That collection probably had about 400 pieces in it of all the things I collected over the years. Like the holiday window, this display was a very big hit.

Eventually, I was introduced to a Mike Piskuric, who had an interest in working on the goalie statistics for Johnstown's professional hockey history. One thing led to another, and we came up with the idea of a book. Neither of us realized how difficult it is, or would be, to actually publish a book. We had the ideas, but how do we get this project to really happen?

I called Mike Mastovich, a sports writer with The Tribune-Democrat who has been the Chiefs beat writer for 17 seasons, and pitched our idea. Mastovich is known as a local sports historian, especially on the subject of Johnstown professional hockey, scholastic athletics and the AAABA Tournament. He previously wrote history-of-the-ECHL pieces for the league's 10th and 15th anniversaries, and won a statewide award for a magazine article on the history of hockey in Johnstown. After being approached several times by players and coaches about documenting a historical account of Johnstown hockey, Mastovich also had tinkered with the idea of a book.

The timing was right. Mastovich thought it was a great idea and was very interested in pulling the two camps together. After making sure there would be no conflict of interest with The Tribune-Democrat, he decided to contribute to the project.

About this time, an avid Johnstown hockey fan from Philadelphia, Steve Soltice, met my parents at a Chiefs game. Steve was the guy that was always encouraging Mike

(From left to right) Mike Mastovich, Mike Piskuric, Lou DeFazio, Dave Zeigler, Dana Heinze and Mike Starchok make up the Johnstown Hockey Company.

Piskuric and I to keep this project alive, pitching ideas for making it work.

Piskuric and I started working on all the stats, gathering memorabilia and writing an outline. We'd meet at the library or my parents' house and work on this project in our free time. It became evident how imposing this task was, since we had professional careers and personal lives of our own. Also, we realized how monumental a job it would be to try to capture the entire history of professional hockey in Johnstown. It wasn't like you could just go to the library and pull out a stat book that had all the information and copy, or go online and find it all with one click of a button.

Along the way, we've added some important members to our team — Johnstown natives Lou DeFazio and Mike Starchok, along with Dave Zeigler, who had worked for the Johnstown Jets and had insight on the team.

We came up with a new plan and the wheels were put in motion. We worked on this as a group for probably three years. We researched the statistics, the personnel, the history — no stone was left unturned.

Still, after much searching, we didn't have anyone with the financial resources to help us get this book published. Then in a conversation with Chip Minemyer, the editor of The Tribune-Democrat, I mentioned what we were doing. He said that he was working on a project, but when he was finished, he would contact us and we'd meet.

As it turned out, he and The Tribune-Democrat were producing an incredible book — "Disaster's Wake: A Retrospective of the 1977 Johnstown Flood." When that book was published, Chip met with Mike Piskuric and Mike Mastovich to lay the groundwork for a potential hockey book. Early in the summer of 2007, our group pitched our idea. The newspaper decided to make it happen.

Now the pressure was really on. We basically had two months to complete what we had been working on for the last few years. In crunch-time mode with the tireless efforts of our group — especially Lou DeFazio and Mike Starchok surgically dissecting game-by-game results and Mike Mastovich writing stories at a sometimes frantic pace — we have assembled the most comprehensive, accurate and — we believe — best compilation of the history of professional hockey in Johnstown.

There were challenges. We sometimes found discrepancies in our information, such as different statistics for various items. This was hard to grasp, because you are taught that when something is put down on paper, it is history. Yet, we were finding facts that didn't match.

We were like archaeologists, piecing together the accurate historical record, while painstakingly uncovering the factual information. It was frustrating at times because we were dealing with stats and information from the 1950s and '60s. There were no computers back then, and human error came into play. In one instance, instead of typing a "9" someone had typed a "7."

We all had our specialties. Mike Mastovich's writing and expression are a huge part of telling the story that is the history of professional hockey in Johnstown.

He interviewed dozens of former and current players, coaches and front-office people while writing 18 profiles and overviews of decades. Since 1991, he had written many historical pieces on subjects such as "Slap Shot," the 1960s-era Jets and the 1974-75 NAHL champs. Minemyer suggested that rather than attempt to rewrite these in-depth features, why not reprint the articles exactly as they originally appeared in The Tribune-Democrat? So, our book also includes 15 reprinted Mastovich articles that cover 60 years of hockey.

The tireless efforts of everyone else involved raised this project to the highest of standards. I was honored to be able to work with a group of people who are so passionate. That passion for the history of hockey in Johnstown has carried us.

It's easy to say, "We'll write a book." But to see how monumental of a task it was makes the final product even more significant. And, to have The Tribune-Democrat get on board with us is what made the production of this book possible.

What a journey it's been. We hope you enjoy the ride as much as we did, and we hope it only continues in the future.

"Johnstown Hockey Company"

Mike Mastovich

A member of The Tribune-Democrat sports staff for 21 years, Mastovich has been the Johnstown Chiefs beat writer since 1991-92. He also is a regular contributor to The Hockey News and Hockey Business News, and has been published in numerous newspapers and magazines.

Mastovich received the ECHL's Outstanding Media Award in 2004-05 and won a Golden Quill Award in 2006 for a Westsylvania Magazine package on the history of pro hockey in Johnstown. His work earned Sports Story of the Year for the entire company in 2003.

He thanks his wife, Terry, and children, Shelby, Michael and Ryan, for their patience and understanding, his parents Mike and Kathy, and brother, Dave Mastovich of MASSolutions, who provided guidance on the project. Mastovich also acknowledges editor Chip Minemyer of The Tribune-Democrat for making this book a reality. Thanks also goes to the Johnstown Chiefs, Johnstown's loyal hockey fans and the book team.

Dana Heinze

A Johnstown native and graduate of Westmont Hilltop High School, Heinze currently is the head equipment manager of the NHL's Pittsburgh Penguins. He spent eight seasons working for the ECHL's Johnstown Chiefs before moving onto the IHL with the Detroit Vipers and moving up to the NHL with the Tampa Bay Lightning. Heinze was with Tampa Bay for six years and won a Stanley Cup in 2004.

Dana has the distinction of being a local product who played a game for the Johnstown Chiefs. On Jan. 4, 1989, Heinze was a goaltender for coach Steve Carlson in a game against rival Erie. The Chiefs' regular goalie had been ejected after a brawl, and Heinze, the Chiefs' trainer, was called into service.

Heinze thanks his wife, Kathy, for her patience and support during this book project. He also recognizes his parents, Lou and Judy Heinze of Westmont; his brother, Eric and his wife, Jill. He thanks Joe Sager of the Penguins; Matt Polk, Pens' team photographer; Chuck Mamula Photography; Steve Soltice, Barbara Kent, Jim Brazill, Kevin McGeehan and the Johnstown Chiefs staff; the Cambria County War Memorial Arena staff; and The Tribune-Democrat, for their support.

Lou DeFazio

DeFazio is a graduate of Greater Johnstown High School who attended his first Johnstown Jets game on a Sunday afternoon in 1957. He played outfield and first base on Johnstown's 1966 AAABA Tournament baseball team. For 12 years, DeFazio has been a statistician and off-ice official for the ECHL's Chiefs. A history buff, Lou began researching Johnstown hockey at the Cambria County Library microfilm center 20 years ago. He has created an in-depth timeline for Johnstown pro hockey dating to the 1941-42 Blue Birds season. A true fan, DeFazio has visited 114 hockey arenas in the United States and Canada.

He thanks the Cambria County Library's periodicals department, as he made many trips up to the third-floor microfilm center.

Mike Piskuric

An area hockey historian, Piskuric is a graduate of Greater Johnstown High School. He became interested in hockey during the 1960s and continued to follow and research the sport for four decades. During this book project, Piskuric dug up statistics and verified many facts, unearthing discrepancies along the way.

Piskuric thanks his wife, Joanne, and children, Michael and Katie, for their support during the past five years. He appreciates the insight of Triangle Collectibles owner Joe Magistro, who gave Mike his first scrapbooks and information for this project. He also thanks, "Dana, Lou, the two other Mikes and Ziggy for all the fun that we had compiling this book."

Mike Starchok

Starchok began compiling statistics during the 1969-70 hockey season and has continued crunching numbers since then. Starchok has collected a database that includes every player drafted or signed by NHL teams dating to the 1964-65 season. For this book project, he and Lou DeFazio researched and compiled all the yearly statistics and records.

Starchok thanks his parents for always encouraging him; his son, Philip, for scanning photographs and programs for this book; his son, Mike, for his support; Ernie Fitzsimmons of the Society of International Hockey Research for advice and encouragement.

He thanks The Tribune-Democrat for making the publication of this book possible. Starchok is grateful for the efforts of all the other members of "Johnstown Hockey Co."

Dave Zeigler

Zeigler has been a fixture in Johnstown hockey for decades. He served as assistant general manager of Cambria County War Memorial Arena for 15 years and had first worked at the arena in 1971 as a 17-year-old "rink rat." He has supplied equipment and uniforms to hockey players from the pro ranks through high school and youth leagues as owner of Ziggy's Sports, adjacent to the War Memorial.

Zeigler has put his art degree to good use over the years, designing logos and uniforms. In this book, his collage depicting Johnstown hockey uniforms and former players provides a bit of nostalgia for the readers.

overview

Something Special for Hockey Fanatics

By Mike Mastovich

So, you're a diehard Johnstown pro hockey fan, right?

Did you know that the city's first professional team, the Blue Birds, indeed did migrate to Johnstown from Baltimore?

Or that the Johnstown Jets really were supposed to be named the Johnstown Steel Kings until it was learned that another team in a different league already had registered that nickname?

How about the fact that the Chiefs could have been called the Jets had it not been for some similar legal issues regarding who actually possessed the rights to the Johnstown Jets name?

Do you remember the exploits of Johnstown favorites such as Don Hall, Dick Roberge, Ed Johnston, Galen Head, Reg Kent, Dave Hanson, Rick Boyd, Frederic Deschenes, Bruce Coles, Perry Florio and the Carlson brothers?

Would you believe it if someone told you the Montreal Canadiens actually played the Johnstown Jets in an exhibition game in 1951 and Maurice "Rocket" Richard scored six goals?

"Slap Shots and Snapshots: 50 Seasons of Pro Hockey in Johnstown" examines these subjects and many more. The book project team and The Tribune-Democrat believe it's the most comprehensive and accurate collection of stories, statistics and photographs of a sport that has been part of the city since the 1941-42 Blue Birds first skated at the Shaffer Ice Palace in the Hornerstown neighborhood.

The Blue Birds, Jets, Wings, Red Wings and Chiefs all have created a colorful and memorable collection of talented and tough players, winning teams and devoted fans during 50 seasons played throughout six decades.

The Eastern League and North American League included rival teams such as Syracuse and Clinton. The East Coast Hockey League — now known simply as the coast-to-coast ECHL — has grown from five teams in 1988-89 to 25 members located in 17 states and British Columbia as the league celebrates its 20th anniversary.

Johnstown, the smallest market with the smallest arena, has been there since the start.

"Slap Shots and Snapshots" spotlights a city and a sport that have made the icy, cold western Pennsylvania winters just a bit warmer over the years.

The stories include overviews on each decade of hockey in Johnstown. Player features related to specific decades as well as a profile on former Jets General Manager John "Big Daddy" Mitchell and a history of Cambria County War Memorial Arena also are included.

There are 18 such stories, as well as 15 articles reprinted just as they appeared in The Tribune-Democrat. These historical reprints include detailed features on the 25th and 30th anniversaries of the Paul Newman motion picture "Slap Shot," filmed in Johnstown in 1976.

There is an in-depth look at the 1974-75 NAHL championship Jets squad that actually inspired "Slap Shot." Other reprinted newspaper stories focus on former Chiefs-Jets General Manager John Daley, Chiefs wing Mark Green's 50th goal in his 50th game, Art Dorrington's breaking the color barrier as the first black hockey player in North America, and NHL all-star goaltender Arturs Irbe's season with Johnstown.

The statistical portion of the book is comprehensive and includes every player in Johnstown pro hockey history. Goals, assists, points, penalty minutes, saves, jersey numbers — you name it, it's in here.

Each season has its own pages with team pictures, league standings, game-by-game results and individual player statistics. There's even a "what-if" Charlestown Chiefs statistical page with Federal League standings and game-by-game listings based on the movie.

The photographs are simply amazing, thanks to The Tribune-Democrat's talented staff and other team photographers. Black-and-white and color shots from various eras grace these pages.

Finally, a collage that includes every uniform worn by Johnstown's pro teams details the various "threads" the local players wore during hockey seasons. Stars from each era are depicted wearing those uniforms, making this the ultimate Johnstown all-star squad.

SLAP SHOTS AND SNAPSHOTS

Above: A capacity crowd of 4,074 attended the Chiefs' 1,000th ECHL game on February 22, 2003.

Below: Jets Dave Hanson and Galen Head prepare for take-off at the Richland Mall in 1975.

A panoramic view of the site where Cambria County War Memorial Arena eventually would be built. This photo was taken around the turn of the 20th Century.

Above: The War Memorial marquee lists a 1960s era schedule.

Right: The arena's first Zamboni ice-resurfacing machine.

14

War Memorial Arena

A Tribute to Military Service, Survival

By Mike Mastovich

Thirty years have passed, but in his mind Ed Neisner still can smell the "flood mud."

The former Johnstown Jets trainer vividly relives the mental image of what "looked like a tractor-pull gone horribly awry."

Layer after layer of brown muck and pools of contaminated water covered the floor and extended up several rows of seats at Cambria County War Memorial Arena. A distinctive stench emanated from inside a building that only two years earlier had been filled to capacity with fans celebrating the Jets' Lockhart Cup championship.

Neisner was among the first people inside the arena after a devastating flood struck Johnstown — the city's third such disaster — on July 19-20, 1977. "It took me a couple days to get down there because there were police and National Guardsmen everywhere," said Neisner, who lived in Ferndale Borough in '77. "A constable I knew got me through so I could check out our goods at the War Memorial. All I can remember is muck and mud up to my knees. I walked through muck and mud.

"We stored a lot of our stuff under the steps of the stands in the offseason," added Neisner, 50, now a Milwaukee, Wisc., physical therapist. "We kept all the jerseys and pants under there. I opened that up and it was just full of mud. Everything was ruined. The surface was just all mud. There was mud over the dasher boards and probably up three or four rows into the seats."

Ice-making equipment and other concessions equipment and heating units were lost. The additional strain and uncertainty provided yet another blow to the already financially-strapped Johnstown Jets organization. There was no professional hockey during the 1977-78 season, and it took Herculean efforts by John Mitchell and civic-minded businessmen to briefly bring back the sport in 1978-79 and 1979-80.

"There was all this devastation," Neisner said.

"Two years earlier we're celebrating a championship there. The next year we're making a movie, 'Slap Shot.' The third year it's wrecked," he said.

'Steeped in history'

Through the tough times in the post-flood Johnstown, the War Memorial Arena gradually came back to life. Eventually, the Johnstown Chiefs made the arena their home in 1988. The organization celebrates its 20th season in the now 25-team ECHL in 2007-08.

Johnstown is the only remaining member of the East Coast Hockey League's Original Five still playing in the same city.

Latrobe attorney Ned Nakles Jr. said the War Memorial's allure was one of the reasons he, his father, Ned. Sr., and law partner Leonard Reeves owned the Chiefs from 1993-95. The small-town atmosphere later brought Nakles and Reeves back as minority owners of the team.

"The thing that sealed it for me was the War Memorial. What a great, absolutely fabulous arena," Nakles Jr. said. "Every seat is a good seat. It's steeped in history with the photos and the feeling that you get there."

The War Memorial honors those men and women who served their country during conflicts around the world. There are plaques and photos honoring veterans from the Civil War, World War I, World War II, Korea, Vietnam and the Gulf War. A small veterans museum is located adjacent to the lobby, and hundreds of hockey fans visit the memorial before games.

The Chiefs traditionally host a Veterans Day game. Local vets participate in pregame events. The War Memorial has served its purpose well since its inception. The arena has been in operation since Oct. 16, 1950, but the concept was an outgrowth of a Johnstown Lions Club initiative in which about 50 civic organizations supported a war memorial.

After much discussion and debate, a decision to erect a practical memorial "with a useful purpose" won support. The War Memorial of Greater Johnstown was chartered in May 1943 as a non-profit corporation. The name was changed in March 1946 to Cambria County War Memorial Inc. to reflect the broadening of its field of operation.

"After the war, there was a lot of arguing about what kind of a thing we were going to build," said Charles Kunkle, long-time president of War Memorial Inc. "A couple of other guys from the Junior Chamber of Commerce had been in the service and were back. We went to (Tribune-Democrat Publisher) Walter Krebs and started to talk about a hockey rink, a sports arena. We stressed the fact that primarily it is a war memorial, and that's what it is. Every once in a while it seems to get characterized more as a sports arena than a war memorial."

Kunkle and Howard M. Picking Jr., chairman of the building committee, were key figures in establishing the War Memorial Arena as a respected venue. In 1947, the first of two financial campaigns was held. A second fund-raiser was necessary three years later.

"After it was the War Memorial, first we created the Cambria County War Memorial Inc. and then the Cambria County War Memorial Authority so we could borrow money," said

Kunkle, 92, at the time of a June 2006 interview. "We had a fund-raising campaign and I think we raised three-quarters of a million dollars, which would be the equivalent of several million dollars now. We didn't have enough money to pay the bills, so we had a second fund-raiser and raised $250,000."

Ground-breaking was held on Oct. 31, 1949. Construction was completed and the Ice Capades performed to three capacity crowds on Oct. 16-17, 1950.

'The right people'

An arena fact sheet provided to The Tribune-Democrat in February 1951 listed the cost of the completed project at $1.5 million. "Tom Lockhart plus many other people from Madison Square Garden gave us the benefit of experience when we built the War Memorial," Kunkle said of the Madison Square Garden assistant general manager, Lockhart, who also was president of the Eastern Hockey League.

"We asked Tom Lockhart to come here and also Phil Thompson, who was the head of the Atlantic City arena and the head of the Miss America Pageant," Kunkle added. "They were both arena people. They both loved the arena business and they were delighted to come here. They made many suggestions to us."

In nearly 60 years, the War Memorial has played host to scholastic and professional basketball games, ice skating programs, high school hockey, truck pulls, wrestling, graduation ceremonies, outdoor shows and boxing, among many other sports and entertainment events. The War Memorial's most storied history involves the 50 professional hockey seasons played by the Blue Birds, Jets, Wings, Red Wings and Chiefs.

The arena hosted six Jets championship teams through 1975 and was the site of much of the movie "Slap Shot" filming in 1976.

Resilience and rebirth

After an eight-season absence, the Chiefs came to Johnstown in January 1988 and were a huge hit with local hockey fans. Partly through the Chiefs' popularity and a resurgence in high school hockey, the arena underwent $800,000 in renovations in 1993. Two new locker rooms, a coach's office, meeting rooms and a hallway were added to the existing structure. The original locker rooms were renovated and divided into four rooms for student hockey and high school teams. Tile flooring was installed in the concourse and other cosmetic work was completed.

Ten years later, an $8.5 million renovation project concluded. The two years of work included new heating and air conditioning, upgraded restrooms, replacement boards and glass. The most noticeable improvement for fans was the new seating that replaced the original wooden seats. But only a few months later, heavy snow, ice and rain combined to deliver another potentially devastating blow to the then-54-year-old venue.

Rain had loosened the snow and ice, creating a snow slide that caused the roof to shift from its rafters, cracking an interior concrete block wall on one side of the building and collapsing a retaining wall on the Stonycreek River side. Initially, the Chiefs' ECHL season appeared to be in jeopardy after the Feb. 6, 2004 mishap.

Once again, the resilience of the city — and in some ways, the venue — showed.

Engineers declared the arena structurally sound and the Chiefs' season eventually resumed, despite areas closed by the damage and pending repair work.

The War Memorial continues to host hockey and other events as patrons pay homage to the region's veterans.

REPRINT

To commemorate the 25th anniversary of the release of "Slap Shot," The Tribune-Democrat interviewed former players, actors and local fans who had roles as extras in the movie. The following article was published on March 10, 2002:

They're back ... Sequel marks 25 years of 'Slap Shot'

By Mike Mastovich

No one will confuse the movie "Slap Shot" with "Citizen Kane" or "Gone with the Wind." Director George Roy Hill's often hilarious and sometimes dark comedy certainly won't pass for "Rudy." Who cares?

"Slap Shot" undoubtedly is one of the most popular sports movies of all time. The brutally honest Paul Newman flick about life in a minor-league hockey steel town in the 1970s was filmed in Johnstown, which makes "Slap Shot" even more significant here.

For better or worse, "Slap Shot," released 25 years ago this month, put Johnstown on the international hockey map. Probably forever. "Slap Shot" has been labeled a cult classic. But in hockey circles, the movie has taken on a life of its own. Lines from the film are memorized and recited by people either playing or watching hockey, from the minors to the National Hockey League — in Los Angeles, New York, or anywhere in between.

"It just flat-out is a great film," said former Johnstown Jets forward Dave Hanson, who played Jack, one of the Charlestown Chiefs' three bespectacled, fighting Hanson Brothers in the movie.

"It has withstood the test of time. At the time we did it, it was pretty much ahead of its time as far as it being a comedy but still being realistic," said Hanson, 47, who now is general manager of Neville Island Sports Center in Pittsburgh. "They were able to follow the fast action of hockey with certain camera angles and still made it look like the real thing.

"It had Paul Newman's credibility and talents. It

> "It had Paul Newman's credibility and talents ... It was just a great, funny hockey movie."
>
> — *Dave Hanson, former Johnstown Jets forward and one of the Hanson Brothers in the movie.*

"Slap Shot" filming in the War Memorial Arena dressing room.

had a great actor like Strother Martin. It had the Hanson Brothers. It was just a great, funny hockey movie."

Inspired by the Johnstown Jets team that won the 1974-75 Lockhart Cup title, Nancy Dowd wrote the screenplay after spending part of the championship season living with her brother, Ned Dowd, a Jets player. When Universal decided to make the movie, Henry Bumstead, art director for "Slap Shot," had recommended Johnstown to Hill over potential sites such as Duluth and Minneapolis, and Utica and Syracuse in New York.

"I recommended to George that he do it here because this seemed to be the best," Bumstead said during a 1976 interview. "It's amazing, but in these other cities there are no parks in the center of town. We wanted the park and that dog."

Bumstead referred to the historic statue of Morley's Dog, now at the corner of Main and Market streets. In the movie, Newman's character, Reg Dunlop, tells Lily Braden, played by Lindsay Crouse, that the dog saved Charlestown during one of its floods.

Rumors about the movie being shot here circulated in February 1976, as the Jets tried to defend their North American League championship. Speculation still lingers that the Hollywood hoopla led to Johnstown's upset playoff loss to the Philadelphia Firebirds.

"That was a bit of a bone of contention," Hanson said. "We were looking to repeat as Lockhart champions. We had a pretty good hockey team. I feel that the distraction of the movie with all the stuff going on didn't allow us to stay focused."

A four-man movie crew visited the city jail in the Public Safety Building on Washington Street. Ned Dowd, then a production assistant for Universal, was with a group from the studio that met with War Memorial arena representatives the next day.

When Newman watched a Jets game from the Cambria County War Memorial press box on Feb. 22, 1976, the rumors became reality.

In March 1976, Universal announced "Slap Shot" and Johnstown were a match.

Universal Studios estimated that $1.5 million was spent in Johnstown by the time the company wrapped up 60 days of production from March to May 1976.

The money was spent on hotel rooms for 115 cast members and crew, food, location rentals and transportation. About $30,000 was used to renovate a vacant store overlooking Central Park for the Big King Drugs store set.

The studio said 5,100 area people worked as extras, most earning $2.30 an hour. Those with speaking roles received much more, some of them several hundred dollars a day.

'A family atmosphere'

"Slap Shot" opened locally at Westwood Plaza Theater on March 25, 1977. It played in the area for at least seven weeks, probably longer, according to newspaper reports at the time. Newman's character was an aging player-coach who manipulated and motivated his players by concocting a tale that the soon-to-be dismantled franchise instead would be sold to an ownership group from a retirement community in Florida.

The Charlestown Chiefs stunk at the movie's outset. But fortunes gradually changed when Dunlop incorporated the rough-and-tumble play of the Hanson Brothers, played by Dave Hanson and Steve and Jeff Carlson, three Johnstown Jets.

"What I look at in the first 'Slap Shot' is the companionship of everyone that was there: The actors, the cameramen, the sound people, the management," said Steve Carlson, who reprises his role in "Slap Shot II: Breaking the Ice" (released that year.) "It was a family atmosphere. The people who were involved, the Newmans, the Jerry Housers, they helped us along. George Roy Hill gave us the freedom pretty much to be what we wanted to be. We didn't have to follow the script like most other people had to do."

In the movie, the more the team fought, the more it won. Fans began to fill the once-empty seats at the War Memorial. Fan club buses accompanied the Chiefs on road trips. Ambulances circled the arena, adding to a ghoulish atmosphere.

In the meantime, Dunlop gradually lost his already thin ties to his estranged wife, played by Jennifer Warren. His star player, Ned Braden, played by Michael Ontkean of "The Rookies" fame, almost suffered a similar fate in his relationship.

The supporting cast was strong, with Martin as General Manager Joe McGrath, Jerry Houser as Dave "Killer" Carlson, Yvon Barrette as goalie Denis Lemieux, Brad Sullivan as foul-mouthed Morris Wanchuk, M. Emmet Walsh as sportswriter Dickie Dunn, and Crouse. "We had a huge advantage over all the actors," said Dave Hanson, in a telephone interview from Pittsburgh. "The obvious advantage was that we were hockey players. Putting the skates on and the hockey scenes were easy for us. But for the acting scenes, we were 20-year-old kids who didn't have a care in the world. We all had kind of wacky personalities. George Roy Hill came to the conclusion that these guys are better off naturally trying to be themselves rather than telling us what we should be doing. They kind of let us run with the reins free."

Reminders abound

The Charlestown Chiefs won the Federal League championship in bizarre fashion, thanks to Ned Braden's striptease skate.

The spoils of that movie championship have lasted 25 years, especially when players, coaches or hockey fans walk into the War Memorial. For instance, Peter Laviolette, the current coach of the NHL New York Islanders, was visibly excited during his first trip to Johnstown as coach of the ECHL Wheeling (W.Va.) Nailers in 1997.

Standing at a pay phone near the arena lobby, Laviolette could be overheard placing a long-distance call. "Guess where I'm at?" Laviolette said. "The War Memorial, where they made 'Slap Shot.' " The arena often seems to elicit such a response.

When Chicago Blackhawks coach Brian Sutter attended two Chiefs games last month during the NHL's break for the Salt Lake City Olympics, Sutter spoke of the War Memorial's mystique and its history. The longtime NHL coach and former player said he stressed those intangibles to his son, Shaun, a rookie with the ECHL Chiefs.

Out-of-town fans from Wheeling; Trenton, N.J.; Peoria, Ill.; and Toledo, Ohio, occasionally attend Chiefs games during bus trips from their respective cities. The visitors typically stroll through the hallways, glancing at old photos and looking for reminders of the film in the arena that doubles as home of both the Johnstown and Charlestown Chiefs.

'What we did in real life'

Steve Carlson began to comprehend the magnitude of the Hansons' popularity during the 1992-93 season, when he coached the Memphis (Tenn.) RiverKings in the Central Hockey League. Almost on a whim, Steve asked Jeff Carlson and Dave Hanson to join him for a Hanson Brothers promotion coinciding with a RiverKings game.

Fans lined up for autographs. The Hansons signed for four hours.

Eventually, the Hansons incorporated zany routines, including Zamboni ice skiing, tossing hot dogs, tripping goaltenders and taunting the opponents. They've played NHL rinks nationwide and dozens of minor league venues throughout North America.

The brothers were featured in USA Today and many major-market newspapers. They have their own Web site: Hansonbrothers.net. The Hanson Brothers also did Bud Ice beer commercials several years ago. The Hansons struck a chord because, in addition to being funny, their characters were frighteningly the real deal.

"Everything we did in the film was pretty much us re-enacting what we did in real life, going into the stands in Utica, jumping a team in warm-ups against the Buffalo Norsemen," said Steve Carlson, who has done Hansons promotional appearances for almost 10 years. "That actually happened. Dropping our gloves every time we got a chance ... well, at least Jeff, Dave and Jack dropped their gloves every chance they got."

'So slick and easy'

None of the other Jets capitalized on the "Slap Shot" roles as successfully as the Hansons. But those 15 minutes of fame still are priceless to those playing minor roles in the film. Like John Gofton. Gofton remembers the crunching check into the boards. How could he forget? After 13 takes, Gofton was all wet.

The Johnstown Jets forward played Nick Brophy, a center on the Hyannisport Presidents. Gofton's character was on the ice for the opening of a game against the Charlestown Chiefs at the War Memorial.

"I remember it just like it was yesterday. It was very interesting, really fun to do,"

SLAP SHOTS AND SNAPSHOTS

Paul Newman accepts a Johnstown Jets jersey from Jets President Ed Hoke as Johnstown General Manager John Mitchell and NAHL Commissioner Jack Timmons look on at the War Memorial Arena.

said Gofton, 58, who rents out heavy equipment in Tillsonburg, Ontario. "It took a long time to get into the parts once you were there, and it took a long time to do the parts."

Gofton's character showed up drunk for the game, complaining to Newman's Reg Dunlop that his wife had left him and his coach refused to bench him even though he had been drinking. Dunlop relayed the story to the players on the Charlestown bench, noting that Gofton might wet himself if someone checked him.

On the next shift, Ned Braden smashed Gofton into the boards. "The opening face-off was very interesting. Newman did it so slick and easy," Gofton said. "I was nervous. I tried to be perfect. The real big part was when I got rammed into the boards and came off the boards crossing my legs like I peed my pants. We did that about 13 times.

"It turned out to be so popular," said Gofton, a member of the 1975 champion Jets.

Extras and unknowns

Not all of the area people in the film were hockey players. Thousands of extras appeared in the stands at Charlestown Chiefs games. Others rode the fan club bus that greeted the Chiefs on the highway. Some appeared in the bar scenes or at the drugstore.

Mickey McQuillan was 9 years old when he was cast as sportswriter Dickie Dunn's

Top: The Hanson Brothers always brought their toys on road trips.

Bottom: The referee (Larry Block) stands in front of the Hansons during the playing of the national anthem.

young son. McQuillan and his movie sister got into a verbal tiff as Reggie Dunlop leaked a rumor that the Chiefs would be moving to a Florida retirement community to reporter Dickie Dunn. "It was a relatively short scene," said McQuillan, 34, general manager of the Ground Round restaurant in The Galleria, Richland Township. "The final count was 29 times they had to shoot the scene because I kept smiling. I was supposed to be mad and I kept smiling. I still remember that day to this day, vividly, and I was only 9."

The scene was shot in the McQuillan family home on Coon Ridge Road in Upper Yoder Township. "At the time, my dad was a part owner of the Johnstown Jets and he would rent an apartment to players for the Jets," McQuillan said. "One of the players was Ned Dowd. One summer his sister, Nancy Dowd, came to live with him. She wrote the script. When it came time to cast the parts and she needed two little kids, all she had to do was look across the street at the driveway."

'Really great experience'

Gracie Head was a natural for her role. Head played Pam, a player's wife. In real life, Gracie married prolific Johnstown Jets scorer Galen Head, a captain on the 1975 championship team the Charlestown Chiefs mirrored. Early in "Slap Shot," Gracie Head sat near then-unknown actress Swoosie Kurtz and Nancy Dowd in the sparsely filled arena. All three portrayed players wives or girlfriends. Crouse, as Lily Braden, also appeared in the seats, then rose as The Star-Spangled Banner played and the movie title rolled. "It was a really great experience, but I don't think I'd ever do it again," Gracie Head said. "We were in makeup at 3 o'clock in the morning. You would sit there all day. Sometimes they'd take you and you'd be on only for an hour, but you had to be there all day waiting."

The pain eased on payday. "I remember picking up my first paycheck," Head said. "We were supposed to get paid $600 or $700 a week, and our first paycheck was $1,300. Paul Newman was coming down the hall and we joked that we thought we got his paycheck. He looked at it and said, 'No, I got more than that.'"

Like others who had speaking roles in the movie, Head still is compensated when "Slap Shot" airs. "I get paid $52 after taxes every time it's on television," she said. "I had to join the Screen Actors Guild because I had a speaking role. It's done now in other languages, too, so I get paid every time it's on in another country."

Her brief role in "Slap Shot" almost led to more work in the business for Head back in 1976. "They wanted me to do a commercial for Sure Deodorant in New York," Head said. "I didn't want to do it. I was in love with Galen. Swoosie Kurtz took it instead of me."

'I just showed up'

Dee Dee (Fresh) Jartin was one of the anonymous fans in the stands at the War Memorial during the filming. Then a 16-year-old sophomore at Greater Johnstown High School, formerly located adjacent to the arena, Jartin skipped classes to be part of the movie. When she won a free "Slap Shot" T-shirt as part of a drawing at the arena, Jartin didn't think it was that big of a deal. At least not until her name was picked from a pool of T-shirt winners eligible for Universal Studio's grand prize, a three-day trip for two to Hollywood.

"I just showed up at the War Memorial when they were filming people in the crowd," said Jartin, 41, a senior account executive with WCCP television in Richland

Township. "I put a ticket in the big barrel. Every day they drew a name. I initially won a T-shirt. My name was thrown back in and I won the grand prize.

"I won the grand prize — for skipping school. It was fun, a Universal Studios tour."

Of course, there was a downside to all the fame. A story in The Tribune-Democrat accompanied by a photo of Jartin and her mother broke her cover.

"After I won a trip, my teachers found out I skipped school," Jartin said. "When my dad found out, he was kind of mad."

"She had to tell us about her not going to school," said James Fresh, Dee Dee's father.

'A unique place'

The Johnstown Chiefs of the East Coast Hockey League walk a fine line with the "Slap Shot" image. The Chiefs took their name from their movie counterparts in January 1988, when legal red tape prevented the franchise from using the former Johnstown Jets name.

"Slap Shot" gives the team, the city and the War Memorial instant recognition among potential recruits, a fact embraced by the current Chiefs. But the developmental league favors a much more tame environment than the fictional, violent Federal League.

"The movie 'Slap Shot' being a cult hockey movie here in Johnstown, I think it's a great thing for our city," Chiefs General Manager Toby O'Brien said. "It's something that absolutely everybody in the hockey world knows when we pick up the phone (to recruit players). Visiting teams come in and you see them with cameras. It makes Johnstown a unique place in the world of minor league hockey."

Carlson coached the ECHL Chiefs for five seasons. He wore his hair short and the team seemed to distance itself from the rowdy "Slap Shot" persona in order to develop strong affiliations with National Hockey League organizations anxious to protect prospects.

There's no reason the team should avoid embracing the "Slap Shot" phenomenon. In fact, downplaying the movie's ties to Johnstown might be a missed opportunity.

The last time the Chiefs had a sellout was during the Hanson Brothers' only promotional appearance here on New Year's Eve 1998. Steve Carlson said the Hansons would love to return if all the financial details could be worked out.

"The movie very much is a positive. It gives us instant name recognition in the hockey world," O'Brien said. "We all know how great Johnstown is. The movie might not have made it look as great as it could be because the movie was about a dying town and a dying economy. We know Johnstown is more of a resilient place than that."

Like Johnstown, "Slap Shot" is resilient. And, unforgettable.

Top left: Charlestown Chiefs bus driver Walt Comisky (Cliff Thompson) uses a sledge hammer to make the bus look mean.

Middle left: Andre Bergeron (Jean Tetreault).

Top right: Johnstown Jets tough guy Dave Birch was a Hyannisport Presidents player in the movie.

Bottom: Tim "Dr. Hook" McCracken (Paul D'Amato) could "carve a man's eye out."

SLAP SHOTS AND SNAPSHOTS

Top left: Barclay Donaldson (Ross Smith) hurls an insult at Charlestown Chiefs player-coach Reg Dunlop (Paul Newman) prior to a face-off.

Middle left: Dave "Killer" Carlson (Jerry Houser) is stitched up after rising to Dunlop's defense.

Bottom: "Killer" Carlson, Denis Lemieux (Yvon Barrette), Steve Hanson (Steve Carlson), Yvon Lebrun (Ron Docken) and captain Johnny Upton (Allan Nicholls) watch in disbelief during the famous striptease-skate scene.

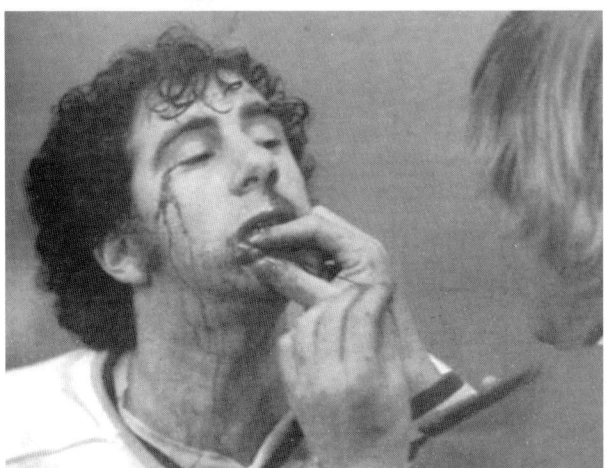

SLAP SHOTS AND SNAPSHOTS

Top: Ned Braden (Michael Ontkean), Reg Dunlop (Paul Newman) and Ogie Ogilthorpe (Ned Dowd) take a break during filming at Cambria County War Memorial Arena.

Left: The Sparkle Twins (Janet and Louise Arters) were among the Charlestown Chiefs' most enthusiastic supporters.

Bottom: Billy Charlesbois (Guido Tenesi) checks out his black eye.

29

CHIEFS

REPRINT

To commemorate the 30th anniversary of the release of "Slap Shot," The Tribune-Democrat produced a package of stories and photographs about the movie. The following article was published on Feb. 25, 2007:

Capturing the spirit of the thing ...

By Mike Mastovich

    A group of police officers prepared to contend with a large crowd and perhaps a traffic jam. The marquee, in capital letters, stated: "Filmed in Johnstown, Paul Newman, Slap Shot." But the anticipation and hype didn't translate into a packed theater for the "Slap Shot" premiere in Johnstown 30 years ago.
    The Westwood Plaza Theatre was a little more than half full, even though hundreds of movie goers were expected to attend — many of those hoping to catch a glimpse of their town or maybe even themselves as extras in the movie that had been filmed here a year earlier. After a slow start, "Slap Shot" has aged well. In three decades, its following has grown, even reaching cult status in some parts.
    Released by Universal Studios exactly 30 years ago today, "Slap Shot" is one of the most rented sports movies ever. Sports fans recite lines. The story of the foul-mouthed but likable hockey players who went from worst to first put Johnstown on the international map.
    "It's amazing how it took to people," said Allan Nicholls, who played Charlestown Chiefs captain Johnny Upton. "I think it's because it was one of those films that didn't talk down. It talked to people. People could involve themselves and relate a lot better.
    "There are so many big-budget films that are done for mass entertainment," added Nicholls, a video producer from Burlington, Vermont. "They achieve that and that's fine. People would never think of getting in touch with the former actors in those films. Because this one was so down to earth, gritty and real, it made itself available for that."
    In the movie, Paul Newman's character, aging Charlestown player-coach Reg Dunlop, brings the zany, bespectacled Hanson Brothers on board to reinvigorate the Chiefs and their fans with a rowdy brand of hockey and fighting.

Paul Newman during a locker-room scene.

Director George Roy Hill paired established performers such as Newman, Michael Ontkean — the skilled scorer and college graduate Ned Braden — and Strother Martin — stingy Chiefs GM Joe McGrath — with a group of up-and-coming actors and hockey players. "It was a great script. It was so close to reality," said actor Yvon Barrette, the Charlestown Chiefs goaltender, Denis Lemieux, perhaps best known for the line, "Who own da' Chiefs?"

"It was almost a documentary," said Barrette, a native of Quebec. "For the Hanson Brothers, that movie was almost like their life story. It was what happened to the Johnstown Jets hockey team. I think that's what made the movie so popular. It was a good mix of athletes and actors. Both helped each other."

Home sweet home

Nancy Dowd wrote "Slap Shot" after spending part of the 1974-75 season with the Johnstown Jets. Her brother, Ned, played for the North American Hockey League championship team that captured Johnstown's last professional hockey title.

Ned Dowd portrays Syracuse Bulldogs thug Ogie Ogilthorpe in the movie.

The Jets inspired the movie, so it was only fitting that Johnstown provide the setting.

"Nancy Dowd was insistent to Universal Studios that the film be shot here," said Johnstown's Denny Grenell, a retired bank executive and well-known promoter of the city. "That was one of her wishes. There was really no 'ifs', 'ands' or 'buts' that that movie was going to be filmed here. Once they got here, John Rubal, who was executive director of the Chamber of Commerce, got me involved. We promised Universal Studios everything under the sun and we hadn't even talked to anybody."

Johnstown delivered. Most of the hockey scenes were filmed at Cambria County War Memorial Arena. Central Park, downtown streets, bars and hotels were used for various shots, and Bethlehem Steel's mills in Franklin Borough provided a backdrop for a movie in which 10,000 steelworkers "were about to be put on waivers" after layoffs.

"The town struck me at first. ... I saw a lot of drug stores, bars and churches, and I spent a lot of time walking around," said actor Andrew Duncan, who as Chiefs broadcaster Jim Carr, used sports banter to provide viewers important background information in a natural manner. "We would walk to work. It was like a dream. There was camaraderie. Everyone was paid the same except the big stars. The rink, they had 750 extras, local townspeople, and they were having as much fun as we were. It was a great shoot. I think the town was overwhelmed by us. We had a great time. People invited us in."

Role players

Filming opened on March 22, 1976, and continued through June 9 that year. In addition to the actors, Johnstown Jets players participated in many of the hockey scenes.

Some of the filming occurred during a Jets' playoff run that ended early in an upset by Philadelphia. Some questioned whether the Jets were distracted by the movie.

But the hockey players filled a void.

"They had guys like Donnie Most (Happy Days), Peter Strauss (Rich Man, Poor Man) and Nick Nolte (48 Hours), a variety of professional actors who could not fill the role to make it as authentic as they wanted it to be," said Dave Hanson, who still reprises his Hanson Brothers act with Jeff and Steve Carlson during dozens of appearances each year.

"I think at the time it wasn't a big deal to us. We were just kind of going with the flow of things and didn't realize what it all was or how important it was."

Actors took the hockey serious. Practices and skating sessions preceded filming. One practice nearly ended Barrette's part in the film.

"We were just about to start the shooting of the movie. It was the last Saturday that we were rehearsing our hockey lines and we were on the ice," Barrette said. "We were missing some equipment for my knee. Someone came through the blue line and took a slap shot. I made the save but my knee was badly injured. I had to go to the hospital. I was laying on the ice and there were tears in my eyes. I told myself it was all done and they were going to pick somebody else. The doctor told me I would have to be on crutches for three weeks. (The actors) all came to the room, and George Roy Hill came too, just to tell me that Denis Lemieux was my part and they changed the order of shooting. I was on crutches 1½ weeks instead of three. I saw what a team it was and I knew it was special."

Hooked on ice

After playing Tim "Dr. Hook" McCracken in "Slap Shot," actor Paul D'Amato later had roles in "The Deer Hunter," "Suspect" and "F/X" as well as multiple guest appearances on "Law & Order." But "Slap Shot" was his first film, and his first line was an unprintable, vulgar insult to Newman's Dunlop, who had put a bounty on "Dr. Hook's" head.

"Part of the reason that 'Slap Shot' has lasted this long and has gotten the notoriety is that we had a great script and everybody worked as hard as they could," said D'Amato, who works in Manhattan. "Most of all, we did our own stunts, our own skating. There were no special effects. That's part of the reason that it's stuck around. There was nothing flashy. We weren't trying to outdo the last action movie. It's a beautiful story. It's an action film, but a real human-action film, not a car-chase film."

While most who followed the rough-and-tumble Jets of the 1970s agree that "Slap Shot" is a mostly accurate portrayal, some of the outlandish scenes were more fiction than fact.

Former Jets forward John Gofton, 63, a construction equipment rental manager from Tillsonburg, Ontario, offered a first-hand perspective. Gofton played Hyannisport player Nick Brophy.

"It's exaggerated. Some of the stuff happened, but not quite as severe as they said," Gofton said. "Some of it was made up. Some of the scenes were real, like the guys fighting in the stands. That really happened.

"Nobody shows up on the ice drunk," said Gofton, whose movie character was tipsy and wet himself after being checked into the boards by the Chiefs' Braden. "That was made up. The brawls at the end were a little exaggerated but we had fights that naturally happened. You can't make that up."

Brothers in arms

For the Hanson Brothers, the game continues. Steve and Jeff Carlson and Dave Hanson appeared in "Slap Shot II: Breaking the Ice," a 2002 sequel that couldn't equal the original. But the Hansons have an even better gig. The trio makes numerous promotional and charity appearances. They had an advertising deal with Budweiser. Their act has played throughout the United States and Canada, and more recently, Europe.

"It's even bigger now. It's growing constantly," Carlson said. "With the Web site, merchandise is just storming out of the office. We're getting calls constantly for appearances. It's not slowing down. We tapped into the European market. We've been to Germany twice in the last two years and just south of London, England, we played a game. In St. Louis we helped raise over $500,000 for charity in a one-night event with other celebrities."

A group of other "Slap Shot" alumni has tapped into their hockey past to raise money. Ken "Toe" Blake of Orange County, Calif., has helped assemble cast members to play in golf tournaments or sign autographs. The appearances have generated more than $50,000 in four years.

"It's terrific that people are willing to take these old photographs and have me sign it, and these guys sell them and all the profits go to charity," said actor Christopher Murney, who played Long Island Ducks goalie Tommy Hanrahan. "It's an amazing thing that 30 years later these things still have an effect. This isn't just a movie we did 30 years ago. This can be a good thing. It's a two-way street. It makes you feel like you've accomplished something. You give something, it gives back."

"Slap Shot" debuted exactly 30 years ago, but ironically didn't open in Johnstown until March 25, 1977. The opening night crowd might have been thin, but the movie aged well.

By May 1977, in its seventh week in Johnstown, "Slap Shot" averaged three times the theater's normal business. In Canada, "Slap Shot" out-earned the year's biggest movie, "Jaws." Decades later, "Slap Shot" is probably even more popular. Most professional hockey players have seen it. DVDs and VHS tapes replay the movie during long bus rides in the minors.

Even ESPN's Reel Classics has featured "Slap Shot."

"The short answer is no, we didn't see it coming," D'Amato said. "The long answer is we worked so hard on it. Everybody cared about the game. I'm not surprised, but at the same time I'm floored by it."

REPRINT

Part of The Tribune-Democrat's Feb. 25, 2007 package on the 30th anniversary of the release of the movie "Slap Shot," the following story was about some of the actors' favorite memories of the filming.

Snapshots from 'Slap Shot'

By Mike Mastovich
Photos courtesy of www.slapshotfan.com

    Thirty years later, players and actors who appeared in "Slap Shot" recall their time in Johnstown as if it happened this hockey season.
    They now work and live in places such as New York City, Pittsburgh, Quebec, Kenosha, Wisc., Burlington, Vt., and Tillsonburg, Ontario.
    But for one season in the movies, they were a part of Johnstown.
    Here are their stories — tidbits to ponder the next time you pop "Slap Shot" in the VCR or DVD player:

Andrew Duncan
Character: Charlestown Chiefs broadcaster Jim Carr

    On a bad hair day: "I remember watching the local sportscaster in Johnstown and studying him. That was the guy I was playing. When I went for the wig, (director) George Roy Hill said, 'I don't care what you get, just get something outrageous.'
    "I went to Glosser's and went to the wig department. The stylist started showing me wigs that made it look like you didn't have a wig. I said, 'No.' Then I saw one she pushed aside and I said, 'That's the one.' I stuck it on my head and looked in the mirror and started laughing. George looked at me and started laughing. He said, 'If you dare, I dare.'"

Yvon Barrette

Character: Denis Lemieux

On how he landed the role of the likeable Chiefs goalie: "I played hockey for fun as an amateur, but I am an actor (not a hockey player). I had to audition in Montreal. There was something like five other people. They were looking for a short French Canadian.

"We had a lot of fun doing that. The character was funny. It was fantastic for a young actor, 29, to work with an actor like Paul Newman and a great director like George Roy Hill."

Paul D'Amato

Character: Tim "Dr. Hook" McCracken

On acting with Newman and hockey players: "That set was so comfortable between the actors and the hockey players. We had all gone to hockey practice, we had all played for many years. It was second nature. The acting, I had studied for years and had gone to college for it.

"While I was in college studying acting, I played hockey. It was taking some of the things I did best and putting them together. I wasn't the only one. Everybody else was like that.

"It was not intimidating. It could have been intimidating, but Paul Newman was such a good guy, Strother Martin was such a good guy."

John Gofton

Character: Presidents forward Nick Brophy

On getting wet in the famous boarding scene: "That's 30 years ago. It was a once-in-a-lifetime experience for people like us who never get that opportunity. The scene — you just tried to let it happen. The boarding scene, we did it 13 times before they picked what they needed. The real big part was when I got rammed into the boards and came off the boards crossing my legs like I peed my pants."

Christopher Murney

Character: Long Island Ducks goaltender Tommy Hanrahan

On an impromptu college reunion: "I grew up in New England and I played pond hockey. I went to the University of New Hampshire with ('Slap Shot' actor) Mike Ontkean. He used to watch me do plays in the Theater Deptartment and I used to watch him play."

Allan Nicholls

Character: Chiefs captain Johnny Upton

On saying good-bye to Johnstown: "I got to know a lot of the people in Johnstown. We had created kind of a mini 'Slap Shot' society and we formed bonds with a lot of the citizens there.

"It was a celebration of a style of hockey and some hockey renegades, but also was a celebration of small-town minor league hockey. I remember when we left town, we left in a bus. People were standing outside the hotel and waving good-bye. It was a nice little send off. On those little signs at the hotel it said, 'Good bye, Slap Shot.' "

Steve Carlson

Character: Steve Hanson

On a hockey player's approach to filmmaking: "That's when I was 19 or 20. I got a nice paycheck. You look at it that way. They offer for you to do a film. You don't realize how big it is until 10, 20, 30 years later. You don't realize that as you're making the film. You're saying, 'We'll do it. Why not?' "

Dave Hanson

Character: Jack Hanson

On life in the movies: "We didn't think it was going to be huge at all. That wasn't even a thought in our mind when we were filming.

"At the time it was a fun summer thing to do. They offered us a seven-year movie contract after that. We said, 'We're not movie actors, we're hockey players.' We turned them down."

(Front, from left) Yvon Lebrun, Jean-Guy Drouin, captain Johnny Upton, general manager Joe McGrath, player/coach Reggie Dunlop, Jim Ahern, Denis Lemieux. (Back) Trainer Charlie Kischel, Dave Carlson, Billy Charlebois, Jeff Hanson, Steve Hanson, Jack Hanson, Ned Braden, Andre Bergeron, Morris Wanchuk, stickboy Woody Espey.

1976 FINAL FEDERAL HOCKEY LEAGUE STANDINGS

Team	Games played	Win	Loss	Tie	Points	Goals for	Goals against
Syracuse Bulldogs	48	28	17	3	59	219	177
Peterboro Patriots	48	26	21	1	53	222	193
Charlestown Chiefs	48	24	21	3	53	202	195
Hyannisport Presidents	48	23	21	4	50	174	164
Broome County Blades	48	22	23	3	47	181	182
Long Island Ducks	48	20	25	3	43	179	207
Lancaster Gears	48	13	30	5	31	171	230

Charlestown won Federal Cup as playoff champion.

Charlestown Chiefs
Owner - Anita McCambridge
General Manager - Joe McGrath
Player/Head Coach - Reggie (Reg) Dunlop
Trainer - Charlie Kischel
Stickboy - Woody Espey
Team Bus Driver - Walt Comisky
Broadcaster - Jim Carr
Team Colors - Blue, White and Gold

Note: *These three pages contain fictitious information based on results of games in the movie "Slap Shot" and the imaginations of our researchers!*

SLAP SHOTS AND SNAPSHOTS

Preseason Results
No preseason games played.
Regular Season Results

Day	Date	Opponent	Score Charlestown	Opponent	Attendance	Record
Fri.	31-Oct	Broome County	2	6		0-1-0
Sat.	1-Nov	Peterboro	3	5	2598	0-2-0
Wed.	5-Nov	Long Island	3	6		0-3-0
Fri.	7-Nov	Lancaster	5	5	2107	0-3-1
Sun.	9-Nov	Syracuse	2	8		0-4-1
Fri.	14-Nov	Long Island	6	5	1982	1-4-1
Sat.	15-Nov	Broome County	1	8		1-5-1
Wed.	19-Nov	Syracuse	0	5		1-6-1
Fri.	21-Nov	Peterboro	2	6		1-7-1
Sat.	22-Nov	Hyannisport	3	4		1-8-1
Sun.	23-Nov	Hyannisport	4	2	1189	2-8-1
Fri.	28-Nov	Broome County	2	7	1554	2-9-1
Sat.	29-Nov	Lancaster	6	3	1892	3-9-1
Fri.	5-Dec	Lancaster	4	4		3-9-2
Sat.	6-Dec	Syracuse	2	6	1749	3-10-2
Sun.	7-Dec	Hyannisport	1	5	983	3-11-2
Wed.	10-Dec	Long Island	3	8		3-12-2
Fri.	12-Dec	Peterboro	5	10		3-13-2
Sat.	13-Dec	Peterboro	4	5	1812	3-14-2
Wed.	17-Dec	Broome County	5	7	1016	3-15-2
Sat.	20-Dec	Hyannisport	3	8	1550	3-16-2
Sun.	21-Dec	Lancaster	1	3		3-17-2
Fri.	26-Dec	Syracuse	1	6	798	3-18-2

* Note: Hanson Brothers acquired via waivers – placed on roster.

Day	Date	Opponent	Charlestown	Opponent	Attendance	Record
Sat.	27-Dec	Long Island	0	2	1192	3-19-2
Wed.	31-Dec	Lancaster	0	5		3-20-2
Sat.	3-Jan	Long Island	6	2	1985	4-20-2
Sun.	4-Jan	Broome County	6	3	2164	5-20-2
Fri.	9-Jan	Peterboro	5	3		6-20-2
Sat.	10-Jan	Hyannisport	6	3		7-20-2
Fri.	16-Jan	Long Island	7	2	2371	8-20-2
Sat.	17-Jan	Broome County	5	1		9-20-2
Wed.	21-Jan	Hyannisport	7	3	2586	10-20-2
Fri.	23-Jan	Long Island	4	4		10-20-3
Sat.	24-Jan	Lancaster	8	3	2993	11-20-3
Wed.	28-Jan	Syracuse	4	1	3088	12-20-3
Sat.	31-Jan	Syracuse	5	2		13-20-3
Sun.	1-Feb	Hyannisport	6	3		14-20-3
Fri.	6-Feb	Peterboro	8	3	3355	15-20-3
Sat.	7-Feb	Lancaster	11	3	3526	16-20-3
Sat.	14-Feb	Syracuse	2	3		16-21-3
Sun.	15-Feb	Broome County	5	0		17-21-3
Fri.	20-Feb	Broome County	7	1	3608	18-21-3
Sat.	21-Feb	Long Island	6	2		19-21-3
Sun.	22-Feb	Lancaster	4	1		20-21-3
Sat.	28-Feb	Peterboro	7	3	3779	21-21-3
Fri.	5-Mar	Peterboro	5	3		22-21-3
Sat.	6-Mar	Hyannisport	6	4		23-21-3
Sun.	7-Mar	Syracuse	4	3	3259	24-21-3

Playoffs

Day	Date	Opponent	Charlestown	Opponent	Attendance	Record
Wed.	10-Mar	Peterboro	3	1		1-0
Fri.	12-Mar	Peterboro	5	1	3514	2-0

* – Charlestown wins best-of-3 semifinal, 2-0

Sat.	20-Mar	Syracuse*	1	0	4343	1-0

* – Charlestown awarded Federal Cup after uncontrollable brawl and Syracuse player/coach Tim (Dr. Hook) McCracken punched the referee.

Attendance Figures

	Dates	Totals	Average
Regular Season	24	53,136	2214
Playoff	2	7857	3929
TOTAL	26	60,993	2346

39

1976 Player Statistics

		Regular Season Scoring					Playoff Scoring			
	Games	G	A	Pts	PIM	Games	G	A	Pts	PIM
10 Ned Braden	42	37	37	74	6					
7 Reg Dunlop	48	30	38	68	124	2	2	1	3	4
12 Johnny Upton "C"	47	33	25	58	40	2	0	3	3	0
6 Jim Ahern "A"	48	15	37	52	66	2	1	1	2	2
14 Jean-Guy Drouin "A"	48	25	26	51	48	2	2	0	2	0
5 Billy Charlebois	48	9	33	42	26	2	1	2	3	2
8 Andre Bergeron	48	21	19	40	30	2	2	1	3	2
3 Dave "Killer" Carlson	44	8	22	30	108	2	0	2	2	2
2 Morris "Mo" Wanchuk	48	5	19	24	76	2	0	0	0	2
17 Steve Hanson	25	4	9	13	208	2	0	1	1	24
16 Jeff Hanson	25	8	4	12	229	2	0	1	1	15
18 Jack Hanson	25	2	8	10	242	2	0	0	0	20
19 Reggie Silk	23	2	5	7	14					
15 Charles Leblanc	23	2	4	6	8					
4 Archie McLeod	23	1	1	2	14					
30 Yvon Lebrun (g)	14	0	0	0	4					
1 Denis Lemieux (g)	36	0	0	0	0	2	0	0	0	0
Bench					12					0
TOTALS	48	202	287	489	1255	2	8	12	20	73

Regular Season Goaltending

	G	Min	GA	ENG	SO	GAA	W	L	T
1 Denis Lemieux	36	2103	122	3	1	3.48	21	12	1
30 Yvon Lebrun	14	777	70	0	0	5.41	3	9	2
TOTALS	48	2880	192	3	1	4.06	24	21	3

Playoff Goaltending

	G	Min	GA	ENG	SO	GAA	W	L
1 Denis Lemieux	2	120	2	0	0	1.00	2	0
TOTALS	2	120	2	0	0	1.00	2	0

* Note: No statistics for individual players included for Syracuse championship game.

All statistics compiled by Dickie Dunn. (Just trying to capture the spirit of the thing!!)

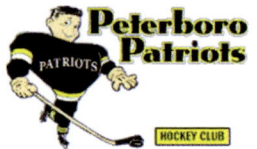

SLAP SHOTS AND SNAPSHOTS

Top: The Hanson Brothers (Jeff and Steve Carlson, and Dave Hanson) hoist hockey's biggest prize, the Stanley Cup.

Bottom: The movie Hansons participate in the Charlestown Chiefs' championship parade, riding in style with the big nose and black glasses, during "Slap Shot" filming in downtown Johnstown in 1976.

Duncan Galbraith played on the 1941-42 Johnstown Blue Birds.

Blue Birds:
Hockey comes to Johnstown — briefly

By Mike Mastovich

The Johnstown Blue Birds' existence in the Eastern Amateur Hockey League lasted a mere five months. But in many ways, the impact of that 1941-42 team still is felt today. The Blue Birds struggled financially, yet still managed to set a firm foundation for professional hockey in the city. In fact, eight years after the team's demise, memories of the Blue Birds partly inspired organizers of a fledgling arena to push for the building to honor those who served their country.

A sequence of events that brought pro hockey to Johnstown started when Frank Shaffer, president of Shaffer Ice Company, made a business decision in an attempt to keep pace in a changing market.

For generations, the Shaffer Ice Company, located at Horner and Cherry streets in the city's Hornerstown section, was the area's largest maker and distributor of ice.

With horse-drawn wagons, and later trucks, Shaffer delivered bags of ice to customers who needed to preserve food and milk. There also were industrial and commercial customers in need of large blocks of ice. In the 1930s, electric refrigeration at first cut into Shaffer's market, then virtually eliminated the need for most of his services. Shaffer had the expertise to remain in the "ice" business. He constructed an indoor ice-skating rink near the end of McMillen Street in Hornerstown. The Shaffer Ice Palace provided public skating and skating lessons.

Fate 'Picks' Johnstown

Early in the fall of 1941, Memorial Hospital's Junior Auxiliary hosted a hockey game between the University of Pittsburgh and Penn State. Neither school had an official ice hockey team. The game between two hastily assembled squads was not hockey at its finest level. The auxiliary had, however, sold 1,100 seats, and the Ice Palace was filled to capacity.

Fate intervened. A Canadian native, Pick Hines, was among those who attended the game. "Pick was a horse player," Johnstown's Charles Kunkle, long-time head of the War Memorial Inc., wrote in a 1999 profile on the Blue Birds. "He spent most of each year in Baltimore betting 'the nags' as they moved from Pimlico to Havre de Grace to Laurel and back. Pick's real hope in life as a Canadian was someday to make a killing at the track so that he could fulfill his dream of owning a hockey team. It happened. As told by Pick, one day in September he had a bundle on a long shot at Pimlico. The horse came in and Pick picked up in excess of $10,000."

Hines contacted Eastern Amateur Hockey League President Tom Lockhart, who also was assistant general manager of New York City's Madison Square Garden. Hines applied for membership in the league, hoping to put a franchise in Baltimore.

Lockhart approved the request. The Baltimore Orioles were solid on the ice, but because of the team's late addition to the league and little advance publicity, fans didn't flock to see the Birds play.

At about the same time, Hines happened to be in Johnstown for that Pitt-Penn State exhibition.

"Pick Hines came here and saw a full house at the old Shaffer Ice Palace," Kunkle said during a June 2006 interview. "... He was struggling down in Baltimore with the hockey team he had bought. He moved it up here because he struggled down there."

Hines mistakenly thought the Blue Birds would be a big draw in Johnstown, based on what he saw during that college game. He didn't know that the hospital auxiliary promotion was responsible for the sellout crowd at the Ice Palace that night.

Hines once again summoned Lockhart, asking for permission to move the Orioles from Baltimore to Johnstown. Eastern League officers Lockhart and Phillip E.M. Thompson visited Johnstown within a week.

Thompson was general manager of the Atlantic City Boardwalk Hall and founder of the Miss America Pageant held in that New Jersey city. He joined Lockhart during a visit to Johnstown Tribune Sports Editor George "Chick" Cooper, who in turn introduced them to Publisher Walter Krebs, a well-known supporter of Johnstown sports and civic events. Krebs promised to provide publicity. He also steered the men to a newly formed Johnstown Junior Chamber of Commerce. Kunkle was president of the Junior Chamber of Commerce.

> "The Blue Birds gave hockey a start in Johnstown, eight years before the coming of the Jets."
>
> — Charles Kunkle, head of the War Memorial Inc.

Pearl Harbor and war

The Jaycees, as they were known, sponsored a Blue Birds home game in December. Attendance during the several games prior to the Jaycees Night was light. Hines was disappointed. Whitey Kowalsky netted the first goal in Johnstown professional hockey history on Nov. 11, 1941. Kowalsky scored 5 minutes into the second period against New York at the Ice Palace in a 2-2 tie.

Less than a month later, during the 14th date of the season, the Junior Chamber-sponsored game was the best gate the Blue Birds had that season. But Hines and his team didn't have a chance to celebrate much on that Sunday afternoon.

Even before the conclusion of a 2-1 loss to visiting

BLUE BIRDS 1941-1942

Baltimore on Dec. 7, 1941 word began to spread that the Japanese had attacked Pearl Harbor. President Franklin D. Roosevelt declared war on Japan the next day.

As the economic situation worsened for Hines, he contacted Lockhart, informing him that he was broke, Johnstown's players hadn't been paid for two weeks, and the Blue Birds were about to be grounded. On the morning after an announcement that the Blue Birds would fold, a man named Harry Crichton entered Lockhart's Madison Square Garden office and plopped $2,000 on his desk.

Crichton said he wanted the Blue Birds to survive in Johnstown and was willing to cover expenses to finish the season. "Harry Crichton put up the $2,000 and that was a lot of money in those days," Kunkle said.

A football legend at Lehigh University, and also known for his prowess in volleyball and golf, Crichton was vice president of sales for the Johnstown Coal & Coke Co. founded by Johnstown native A.B. Crichton. In addition to having family in Johnstown, Crichton, who resided in New Jersey, had married Frank Shaffer's daughter. With Crichton's contribution and a spirited community effort, the Blue Birds finished the season. Johnstown and the New York Rovers tied for first place in the Eastern League but New York won the tiebreaker by scoring more goals.

Soon after the hockey season, the Ice Palace was converted for use as a manufacturing plant, and winning a war, rather than hockey games, was the priority.

The Blue Birds were history. Still, the team left an important legacy — one that helped foster the concept of a War Memorial Arena, home of the city's next hockey team — the Jets.

Kunkle recognized those local figures who helped bring the Blue Birds to Johnstown for that one memorable, and challenging, season.

He listed newspapermen Krebs, Cooper, Pat Malloy, Ben Coll and Jack Spielman. Kunkle also credited the original Jaycees: Jack Henderson, Marlin Stephens, Frank Reiter, Bruce McCordell, Curt Owen, Clem Harris, Elvin Overdorff, Alvin Schrott, John Werry and Bob Hoadley. Ernie DuPont and, especially, Crichton, also were men who made that season possible, Kunkle said.

"I want to tell you about the benefits this community gained from the Blue Birds other than the fact that they were greatly enjoyed and they broke even after we started running them locally," Kunkle said.

"The Blue Birds gave hockey a start in Johnstown," he said, "eight years before the coming of the Jets."

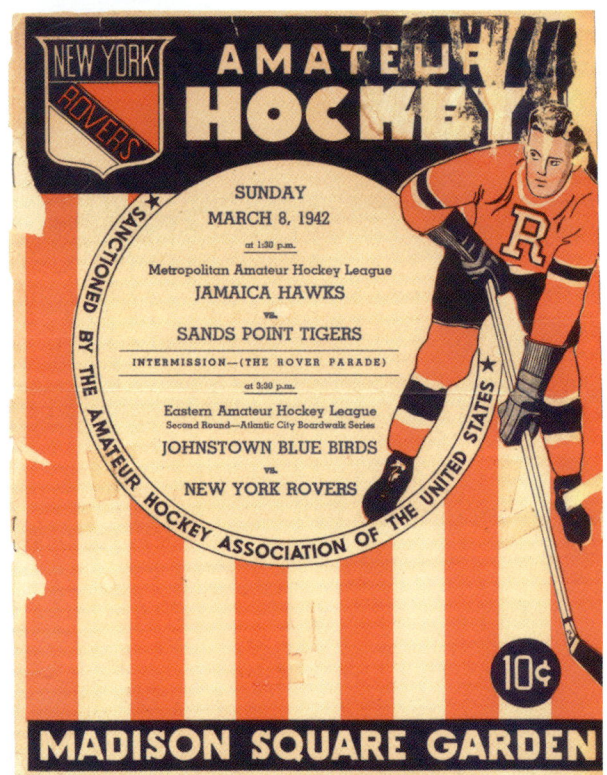

Top: The Baltimore Orioles and Johnstown Blue Birds prepare for a game at the Shaffer Ice Palace in Hornerstown.

Left: The Blue Birds played at Madison Square Garden in 1942.

Bottom: An official Blue Birds program.

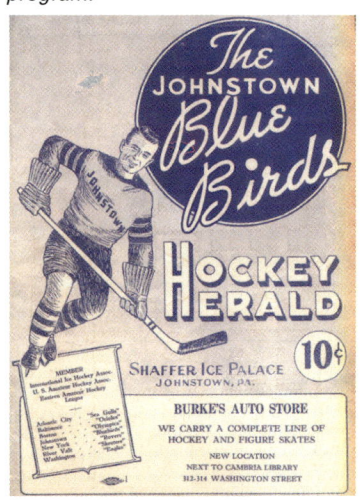

REPRINT

BLUE BIRDS 1941-1942

The Blue Birds were Johnstown's first professional hockey team, debuting on Nov. 11, 1941 and playing one season at the Shaffer Ice Palace in the Hornerstown section of the city. Even though the team played only one season, the Blue Birds created a foundation for pro hockey in Johnstown. The Blue Birds were collectively inducted into the Johnstown Hockey Hall of Fame. The Jan. 30, 1999 Tribune-Democrat story on the induction follows:

Blue Birds fly into hockey hall

By Mike Mastovich

After almost 57 years, the Johnstown Blue Birds are back.

Johnstown's original organized hockey franchise will be honored tonight, during the second intermission of the ECHL Johnstown Chiefs game against the Roanoke Express at the War Memorial Arena.

The Blue Birds debuted on Nov. 11, 1941 against the New York Rovers at the Shaffer Ice Palace in the Seventh Ward. The Birds flew to a 34-20-6 record in the Eastern Amateur Hockey League.

"That one season played by the Blue Birds was the foundation for the professional hockey we have in the city of Johnstown today," Chiefs general manager Toby O'Brien said. "They deserve to be enshrined in the Hall of Fame for their contributions to this city and this sport."

Then-Johnstown Mayor John A. Conway dropped the ceremonial first puck as a large crowd watched the Blue Birds and Rovers play the first game at the Ice Palace. But support wasn't always so strong.

The first local team ran into many difficulties usually associated with starting up a franchise. Financial troubles plagued the team, and a fans' booster committee helped in the operations. Despite the setbacks, Johnstown hockey might have returned after that inaugural 1941-42 season.

"If the present rink and its seating capacity are enlarged, the Blue Birds probably will be here again next season," Johnstown player-coach Hank Dyck said during a Feb. 19, 1942 interview in The Johnstown Tribune.

> **"They deserve to be enshrined in the Hall of Fame for their contributions to this city and this sport."**
>
> *— Toby O'Brien, Chiefs general manager*

"It would cost about $30,000 to operate a team here next year," Dyck said, noting that total would cover all expenses and 14 to 15 player salaries. "We would play about 30 home games, and that means we would have to take in about $1,000 a game to finance the team. If we had about 2,500 or 3,000 seats, we could lower the prices, and if we averaged 2,000 fans a game at an average seat price of 60 or 70 cents, that would take care of everything." Dyck also felt the Ice Palace playing surface should have been enlarged from 156 feet to at least 185.

Dyck's plan made sense. But the city had to turn its attention to other matters. Less than a month after the Blue Birds' first game, the Japanese bombed Pearl Harbor, and the United States entered World War II. Wartime restrictions eventually put the Blue Birds out of business, and the Shaffer Ice Palace was converted into an industrial facility to help the war efforts.

The Blue Birds weren't alone. The Army took over the Atlantic City Sea Gulls' arena, and the River Vale Skeeters also dropped out of the Eastern Amateur League after the 1941-42 season. Other teams in the league that year were Boston, Baltimore, River Vale, N.J., and Washington, D.C.

For one season, the Blue Birds — brought here by owner Pick Hines of Toronto — were Johnstown's hockey team. The Blue Birds earned 74 points and tied the New York Rovers for first place during the regular season. But the Rovers were awarded the league title because they scored more goals than Johnstown (272-249). The Blue Birds entered the prestigious Amateur Hockey Association of the United States playoffs, where they finished 5-3 among the top contenders.

A crowd of 1,076 attended the AHAUS finale on March 29, 1942, at the Ice Palace. Dyck scored three goals and Johnstown defeated the Atlantic City Sea Gulls 7-4.

For their efforts, the Blue Birds made big news locally. But a day after concluding its season with a big victory, the hockey team shared the local headlines with Heck's Store, which captured a basketball championship, and local teams winning the Serb bowling and basketball tournaments.

Members of the 1941-42 Johnstown Blue Birds were: Pick Hines; Hank Dyck; Red Anderson; Frank Ceryance; Jack Dyte; Duncan Galbraith; Whitey Kowalski; George Coombs; Ned Vitarelli; Len McCartney; Sammy Gigliotti; Ilio Marzo; George Boll; Jack McKinnon; and Ed Boiteau.

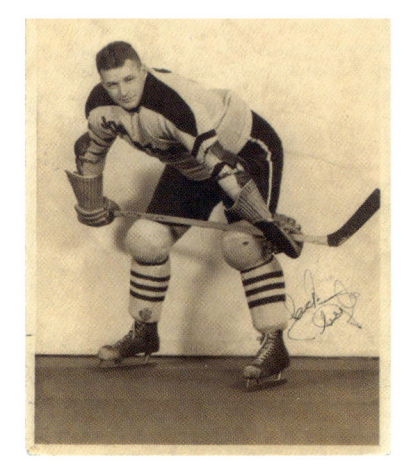

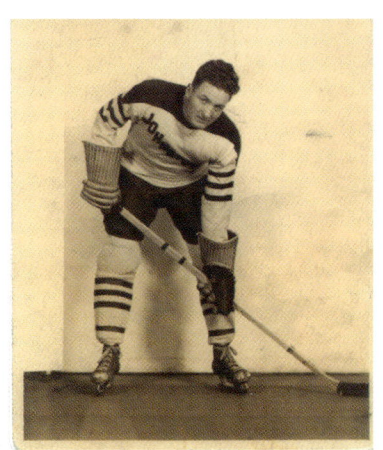

Top: Blue Birds Jack Dyte.

Bottom: Blue Birds George "Shorty" Coombs.

BLUE BIRDS 1941-1942

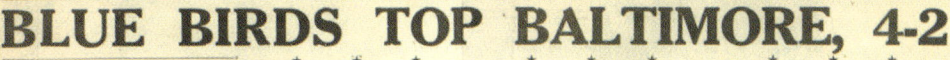

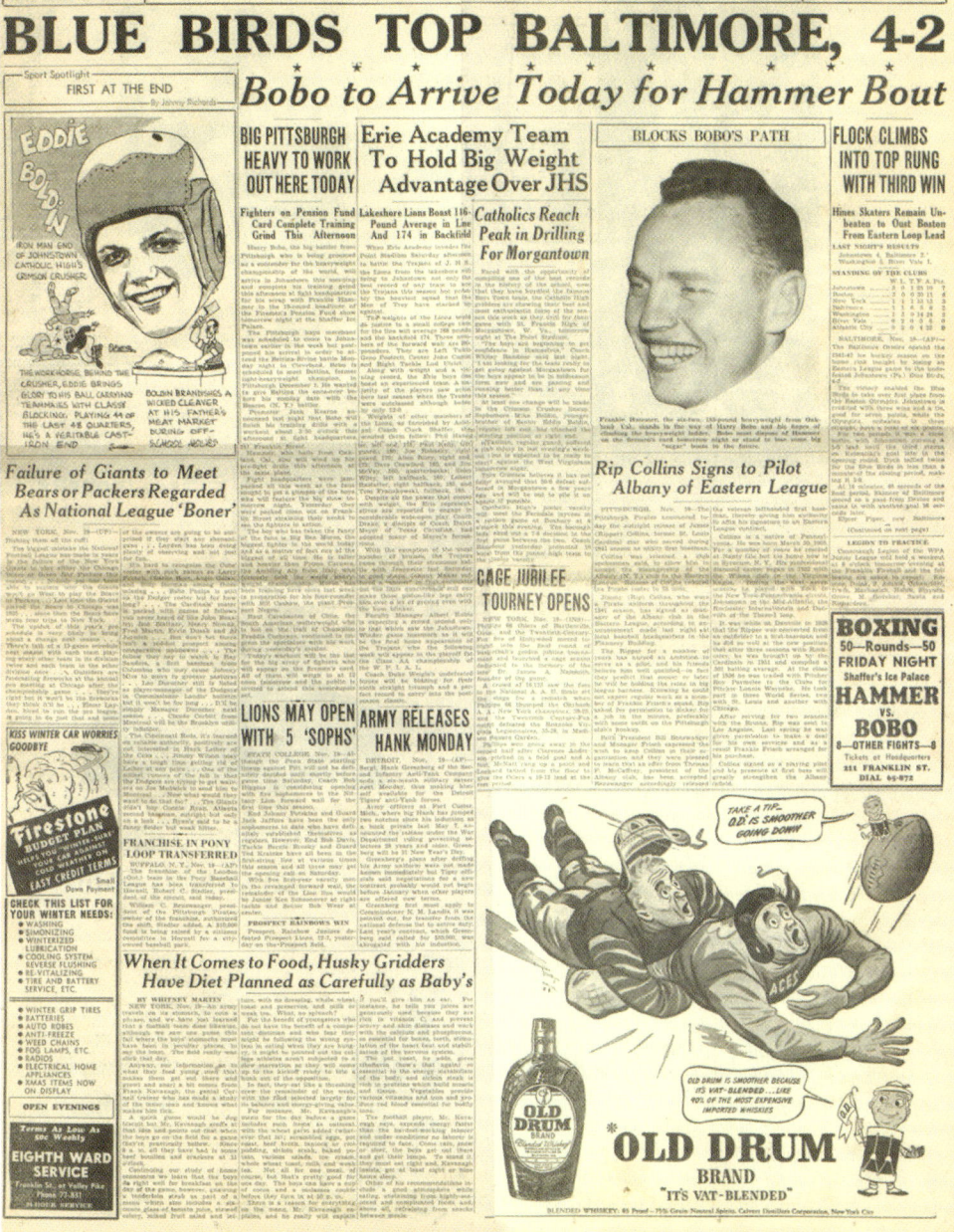

Early-season newspaper coverage of the Blue Birds appeared in The Johnstown Democrat.

49

1941-42 Johnstown Blue Birds

(Front, from left) Len McCartney, Ilio Marzo, George "Shorty" Coombs, Sammy Gigliotti, player-coach Hank Dyck. (Back) George Boll, Bill "Red" Anderson, Jack Dyte, Frank Ceryance, Duncan Galbraith, Whitey Kowalski.

1941-42 FINAL EASTERN AMATEUR HOCKEY LEAGUE STANDINGS

	Games played	Won	Lost	Tied	Points	Goals for	Goals against
New York Rovers	60	34	20	6	74	272	197
Boston Olympics	60	34	20	6	74	263	218
Johnstown Blue Birds	60	34	20	6	74	248	215
Washington Eagles	60	28	27	5	61	261	253
Baltimore Orioles	60	26	30	4	56	252	262
Atlantic City Sea Gulls	60	20	39	1	41	239	316
River Vale Skeeters	60	18	38	4	40	191	265

Johnstown Blue Birds
Manager - Pick Hines, Hank Dyck
Coach - Pick Hines, Jack McKinnon, Henry Dyck
Trainer - "Pop" Saunders
Team Doctors - Dr. Joseph R. Replogle, Dr. W.J. Reddy
Colors - Powder Blue, Black and White

BLUE BIRDS 1941-1942

1941-42 Game Results

Preseason Results

Day	Date	Opponent	Johnstown	Opponent	Attendance	Record
Sat.	1-Nov	New York Tigers (NYMHL)	11	0		
Sat.	8-Nov	Akron Clippers (MOHL)	3	1		

Note: NYMHL is New York Metropolitan Hockey League; MOHL is Michigan-Ontario Hockey League

Regular Season Results

Day	Date	Opponent	Johnstown	Opponent	Attendance	Record
Tues.	11-Nov	New York	2	2 (ot)		0-0-1
Wed.	12-Nov	at Baltimore	1	3		Exhibition
Sat.	15-Nov	Washington	9	4		1-0-1
Sun.	16-Nov	Washington	10	2		2-0-1
Wed.	19-Nov	at Baltimore	4	2		3-0-1
Fri.	21-Nov	at Washington	3	3 (ot)		3-0-2
Sat.	22-Nov	at New York	1	6		3-1-2
Sun.	23-Nov	at Boston	3	11		3-2-2
Tues.	25-Nov	Atlantic City	5	3		4-2-2
Thur.	27-Nov	Boston	4	3		5-2-2
Sat.	29-Nov	at Atlantic City	5	4		6-2-2
Tues.	2-Dec	New York	3	2		7-2-2
Thur.	4-Dec	River Vale	5	1		8-2-2
Sat.	6-Dec	at Atlantic City	5	2		9-2-2
Sun.	7-Dec	at Baltimore	1	2		9-3-2
Tues.	9-Dec	Atlantic City	5	2		10-3-2
Thur.	11-Dec	Baltimore	3	3 (ot)		10-3-3
Fri.	12-Dec	at Washington	4	5		10-4-3
Sun.	14-Dec	at New York	4	5		10-5-3
Tues.	16-Dec	New York	4	1		11-5-3
Wed.	17-Dec	at River Vale	3	0		12-5-3
Fri.	19-Dec	at Washington	3	2		13-5-3
Thur.	25-Dec	River Vale	3	1		14-5-3
Sat.	27-Dec	Baltimore	4	4 (ot)		14-5-4
Sun.	28-Dec	Washington	6	2		15-5-4
Thur.	1-Jan	Boston	6	5		16-5-4
Sun.	4-Jan	Akron Clippers (MOHL)	7	3		Exhibition
Tues.	6-Jan	Atlantic City	4	7 (ot)		16-6-4
Wed.	7-Jan	at River Vale	3	5		16-7-4
Sat.	10-Jan	at Boston	2	3 (ot)		16-8-4
Sun.	11-Jan	at Boston	1	8		16-9-4
Tues.	13-Jan	Baltimore	8	2		17-9-4
Wed.	14-Jan	at Baltimore	3	4 (ot)		17-10-4
Fri.	16-Jan	at Atlantic City	0	4		17-11-4
Sat.	17-Jan	at River Vale	3	2		18-11-4
Tues.	20-Jan	Boston	3	6		18-12-4
Thur.	22-Jan	Washington	4	1		19-12-4
Fri.	23-Jan	at Boston	0	10		19-13-4
Sat.	24-Jan	at Atlantic City	4	1		20-13-4
Sun.	25-Jan	at Baltimore	1	0		21-13-4
Tues.	27-Jan	Atlantic City	11	7		22-13-4
Fri.	30-Jan	at Washington	4	6		22-14-4
Sat.	31-Jan	Washington	5	1		23-14-4
Tues.	3-Feb	New York	5	3		24-14-4
Wed.	4-Feb	at River Vale	2	3		24-15-4
Fri.	6-Feb	at Boston	3	2		25-15-4
Sun.	8-Feb	at New York	2	2 (ot)		25-15-5
Wed.	11-Feb	at Baltimore	7	4 (ot)		26-15-5
Sat.	14-Feb	Boston	9	2		27-15-5
Sun.	15-Feb	Boston	6	1		28-15-5
Thur.	19-Feb	River Vale	6	4		29-15-5
Sat.	21-Feb	Baltimore	2	5		29-16-5
Tues.	24-Feb	River Vale	6	4		30-16-5
Fri.	27-Feb	at Washington	5	12		30-17-5
Sat.	28-Feb	at Atlantic City	1	7		30-18-5
Tues.	3-Mar	New York	4	0		31-18-5
Thur.	5-Mar	Baltimore	6	1		32-18-5
Sat.	7-Mar	at River Vale	1	3		32-19-5
Sun.	8-Mar	at New York	3	3 (ot)		32-19-6

Day	Date	Opponent				Record
Tues.	10-Mar	Atlantic City	6	1		33-19-6
Thur.	12-Mar	River Vale	12	3		34-19-6
Sun.	15-Mar	at New York *	1	11		34-20-6

* Game vs. New York on March 15 also counted as Game 2 of playoffs

Playoff Results

			Score			
Day	Date	Opponent	Johnstown	Opponent	Attendance	Record
Fri.	13-Mar	at Washington	0	3		0-1
Sat.	15-Mar	at New York *	1	11		0-2
Wed.	18-Mar	Washington	9	6		1-2
Fri.	20-Mar	Boston	6	4		2-2
Sat.	21-Mar	at Boston	5	2		3-2
Tues.	24-Mar	New York	6	1		4-2
Sat.	28-Mar	at Atlantic City	1	6		4-3
Sun.	29-Mar	Atlantic City	7	4		5-3

Attendance Figures

Game by game attendance figures were not available.
Shaffer Ice Palace had a capacity of 1,527.
On more than one occasion, games were sold out.
Total attendance for the year was more than 25,000.

1941-42 Player Statistics

	Regular Season Scoring					Playoff Scoring				
	Games	G	A	Pts	PIM	Games	G	A	Pts	PIM
16 Hank Dyck	58	47	40	87	38	8	10	5	15	2
11 Duncan Galbraith	60	35	35	70	68	8	3	3	6	15
5 George "Shorty" Coombs	58	31	35	66	15	7	8	7	15	0
8 Ilio Marzo	60	31	31	62	57	8	4	10	14	14
4 Bill "Red" Anderson	59	10	31	41	112	4	1	1	2	6
7 Whitey Kowalski	50	19	20	39	8	8	1	1	2	4
9 Sam Gigliotti	60	20	15	35	12	8	2	2	4	2
6 Len McCartney	60	13	19	32	22	8	0	3	3	0
2 Jack Dyte	60	12	20	32	105	8	5	3	8	12
15 Ned Vitarelli	28	10	22	32	28					
3 George Boll	60	10	16	26	59	8	1	4	5	2
10 Ed Boileau	31	10	4	14	36					
4 Jack McKinnon	17	0	2	2	2					
1 Frank Ceryance (g)	60	0	0	0	0	8	0	0	0	0
Bench										
TOTALS	60	248	290	538	562	8	35	39	74	57

Regular Season Goaltending

	G	Min	GA	ENG	SO	GAA	W	L	T
1 Frank Ceryance	60	3,700	215	0	3	3.49	34	20	6
TOTALS	60	3,700	215	0	3	3.49	34	20	6

Playoff Goaltending

	G	Min	GA	ENG	SO	GAA	W	L
1 Frank Ceryance	8	480	37	0	0	4.63	5	3

Anderson wore No. 12 until McKinnon left team.

Early-season newspaper coverage of the Blue Birds appeared in The Johnstown Democrat.

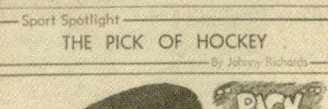

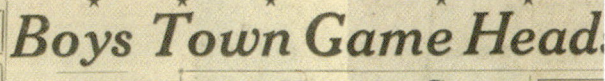

The Toledo Mercurys confronted War Memorial Arena fans during an ugly scene in the 1953 USAHA playoffs.

JETS in the 50s

By Mike Mastovich

The arena was brand new. While it might be unthinkable more than 50 years later, the home team wore red uniforms with white trim and letters.

The Johnstown Jets were a novelty on Nov. 3, 1950 as the first Eastern Hockey League game was played at Cambria County War Memorial Arena.

The city hadn't fielded a professional hockey team since the 1941-42 Blue Birds played at Shaffer Ice Palace in the neighborhood of Hornerstown. The sport was so unfamiliar that the 3,061 fans attending the home-opening 7-5 loss to the New York Rovers were tutored on the subject of hockey.

"Appreciating the fact that many Johnstown sports fans are not yet familiar with the rules of hockey, War Memorial officials have arranged for an extra player of the Jets to sit with the public address system operator," a preview story in The Johnstown Tribune reported. "Different points of the rules will be explained during the game. When the officials halt action on account of the rule violations, the announcer will explain the rule and how it was violated."

Beginning of it all

Johnstown hockey enthusiasts took the lessons to heart.

The Jets and their fans enjoyed a long skate that lasted from that 1950-51 season through the 1976-77 campaign. The Wings, Red Wings and Chiefs followed, as Johnstown teams have played 50 professional hockey seasons through 2006-07.

That first Jets team helped set the foundation. Forward John Horvath was 21 years old when he joined the Jets in 1950-51. He migrated to Johnstown after spending a season with the Pacific Coast Hockey League's Portland Eagles and another year with the Eastern League's Grand Rapids Rockets.

"I was in Portland, Ore., on the West Coast, and I asked them if I could come East,"

Horvath said. "I went to Grand Rapids the next year and played there for a year. The Jets coach raided the whole Grand Rapids team and brought us over to Johnstown. It was the first year in Johnstown and a brand new arena."

The coach was Wally Kilrea, a former National Hockey League player — mostly with the Detroit Red Wings — and American Hockey League coach in Philadelphia.

In addition to Horvath, former Grand Rapids players Wilfred Gorman and Randy Ellis joined the Jets. Orville "Crash" Kelly, Harry "Spook" Frost, Guy Leclerc and 10-year veteran Joe Desson were some other names on the first roster.

"It was new. The hockey fans were pretty well new, too," said Horvath, now 80 and living in Port Colborne, Ontario. "It was a struggle. But we had a lot of fun. It was a great city and still is. It was a brand new arena and we were all overjoyed."

That first Jets team won the Mayor Walker Cup as the regular-season champion in the four-team EHL.

Triple crown

Johnstown only got better the next two seasons. The Jets claimed minor hockey's triple crown in 1951-52, winning the Walker Cup as regular-season champions, the Atlantic City Boardwalk Trophy as EHL playoff champ, and the Amateur Hockey Association of the United States Cup for beating IHL champion Toledo. "We had a great team in our second year because the Montreal Canadiens sent us a couple players," said Charles Kunkle, an area civic leader who served as president of both the War Memorial Authority and the Johnstown Hockey Co. "We won everything."

Goaltender Ivan "The Terrific" Walmsley, center Fred "Skippy" Burchell and defenseman Larry Archambeault were EHL first-team all-stars in 1952. Walmsley led the league in every goaltending category and was named first on 30 ballots.

On March 6, 1952, Walmsley had his sixth shutout of the season in a 3-0 win over Boston. The teams were tied for first place prior to the game, and a then-record 4,139 fans crammed into the War Memorial. In the playoffs, the Jets withstood the New Haven Tomahawks and 3,700 rowdy fans at New Haven Arena to win 4-1 and take a 3-1 lead in the best-of-7 series. But that only was part of the story.

Referee Mickey Slowik was knocked out after being hit twice by Hawks players. The game was stopped several times after debris filled the ice. A part of the boards and an angle iron were tossed at one ugly point of the contest.

"The game had to be stopped several times to allow attendants to clear the ice of paper, peanut shells, Crackerjack boxes and beer cans," the April 11, 1952 edition of The Johnstown Tribune reported. "The near-riot reached its climax late in the game when a board and angle iron were tossed on the rink and a huge firecracker was exploded dangerously close to Walmsley. Showering of debris around Walmsley became so deep that New Haven's Nick Pidsodny switched goals with him. But Walmsley was given no better treatment at the opposite end of the rink as the downpour of garbage continued. When the game ended the red lines could not be seen, so heavy was

> "It was new. The hockey fans were pretty well new, too. It was a struggle. But we had a lot of fun. It was a great city and still is."
>
> — John Horvath, former Jets forward.

the shower." League president Tom Lockhart said New Haven's Joe Desson, a former Jet, would "draw a life ban."

Fan support

Despite the mayhem, the Jets had some support. Twenty-four hometown fans chartered an All-American Airways plane to New Haven. The Jets clinched the Broadwalk Trophy playoff title with a 5-3 win at New Haven three days later. Kilrea's team wasn't through. In those days, the EHL and IHL champs met to determine the U.S. Amateur title. The Jets defeated the IHL's Toledo Mercurys 4-1 in a best-of-7 series, with a 7-1 victory in front of 3,568 fans on home ice in the series clincher.

"An extraordinary scene on War Memorial ice followed the final buzzer," The Johnstown Tribune reported on April 25, 1952. "First, the Jets and Mercurys, who had completed a spirited if somewhat one-sided series, shook hands all around. Then the Johnstown players pulled coach Kilrea off his seat on the Jet bench, raised him to their shoulders and paraded around the ice."

In 1952-53, Johnstown repeated as Boardwalk Trophy playoff champions.

Unlike the previous season, when he had six shutouts, Walmsley didn't blank the opposition until it counted most. Walmsley and the Jets shut out Springfield 2-0 at the War Memorial to win the EHL playoff championship series 4-2. The shutout came after Springfield routed the Jets 7-2 in front of 4,909 fans at Eastern States Coliseum.

Jets wing Art Dorrington, who was the first black pro hockey player in the United States, netted the game-winner at 13:45 of the first period. Johnstown's Larry Regan hit the empty net from the right side of the blue line with only seven seconds left.

"Regan's championship-clinching goal brought a deafening roar from the 2,273 fans who were treated to a he-man brand of hockey," The Tribune-Democrat reported.

IHL champ Cincinnati swept Johnstown in three games for the U.S. Amateur crown.

Changing leagues

The Jets entered the International Hockey League for the 1953-54 and 1954-55 seasons. Left wing Don Hall and right wing Arnie Schmaultz were Jets on the first-team IHL all-star squad in 1954. Johnstown was the only club with two first-team picks.

The 1954-55 team ended with six consecutive losses and had the worst season in five years.

In June 1955, a local group attempted to secure transfer of the Jets ownership from Cambria County War Memorial Inc. to the Johnstown Hockey Co. But the IHL denied the transfer at the annual league meetings.

The arena "indicated it was disposed to discontinue its hockey sponsorship." A group of local hockey enthusiasts bought into the new company for $1,000 a share.

The Jets eventually bolted the IHL and returned to the Eastern League, and the ownership transfer was granted.

Jets captain Don Hall played 11 seasons in Johnstown, including 1956-57, when this photo was taken.

JETS IN THE FIFTIES

Don Hall

'Just a Great Hockey Player'

By Mike Mastovich

Former Johnstown Jets coach Wally Kilrea persuaded Don Hall to migrate from Toledo to the new Cambria County War Memorial Arena in the fall of 1951.

Once in Johnstown, Hall never really left. His 11-year career with the Jets, including nine consecutive seasons as an all-star, reveal the impact the player known simply as "Jet 9" had in Johnstown. The Toronto, Ontario, native appeared in 667 regular-season games with the Jets, scoring 393 goals and 585 assists for 978 points. That's an average of 89 points a year.

After his retirement in 1962, Hall's No. 9 jersey also was retired by the Jets. Only Hall's No. 9, Dick Roberge's No. 11, and Galen Head's No. 8 are retired uniforms in a city with pro hockey roots extending back to 1941.

"I'm sure Don could have made the majors if he wanted to," said Hall's long-time teammate and prolific scorer Roberge. "Don was just a great hockey player. He was a left winger and he was tough. He didn't back down from anybody. He was always there helping the line out and helping the team out. He'd have made the NHL teams now, as many teams as there are in the league. There were six teams in the majors when we played."

Hall still resides in Johnstown. He married a native, Jean Bendek, and the couple raised a family in the city.

As his hockey career progressed, Hall began working locally as a salesman for Janey, Dulles and E.W. Clark, a Philadelphia-based investment firm. The business changed names over the years, but Hall was a constant. He is a managing director for Wachovia Securities, headquartered in the Pasquerilla Plaza in Johnstown.

"I got into the business in 1958 or 1959. The New York Stock Exchange had a rule you couldn't be in two businesses at one time," Hall said. "They never really went after the athletes because the athletes had seasonal work.

59

"I took the position that once I made more money in the investment business than I did in hockey, I'd quit playing. This happened in 1962."

'Huge enthusiasm'

Prior to his retirement, Hall was money in the bank for the Jets.

His path to Johnstown, however, was a bit unconventional.

Hall began playing hockey in Toronto at age 10 and eventually skated for Oshawa in a top Junior A league. Ironically, Hall was a defenseman during his formative years.

"It was during this period that Conn Smythe, then the supreme ruler of the National Hockey League dynasty in Toronto, evaluated Hall as 'having the ability to become a good hockey player but is too lazy,' " The Tribune-Democrat reported on Nov. 6, 1965 — prior to Hall's joining the inaugural class of the Cambria County Sports Hall of Fame.

Smythe's assessment frequently provided motivation.

Hall entered the pros with the Toledo Mercurys in 1950-51 and scored 59 points for the International League squad. The next season, Hall made a move that ultimately changed his life and Johnstown hockey history.

The winger joined Toledo teammates Ivan Walmsley, a goaltender, and Norm Grinke, a defenseman, at the Jets' training camp under Johnstown coach Wally Kilrea.

The trio didn't have the Mercurys' blessings. The players eventually were suspended until the two clubs cleared the paperwork. Once on the roster, Hall, Walmsley and Grinke helped the Jets claim three titles during that 1951-52 season. Johnstown won the Mayor Walker Cup as the Eastern League's regular-season champion, the Atlantic City Boardwalk Trophy as EHL playoff champ, and the Amateur Hockey Association of the United States Cup. Ironically, the Jets beat Toledo to claim the latter Cup in a meeting of EHL and IHL champions. "We had a very good team that year," Hall said. "There was huge enthusiasm from the fans. The building was filled every night. The fans were noisy and very supportive.

"I had played in Toledo the year before with Ivan Walmsley and Norm Grinke. They were both friends of Wally Kilrea, the coach in Johnstown. He convinced us to play in Johnstown. We played a practice game the year before in Johnstown. We knew a little bit about the community. Wally convinced us this was a good place to play."

'The right decision'

Johnstown repeated as EHL playoff champion in 1953. Hall also was part of three straight championship Jets teams from 1960 through '62.

At the time of his retirement, Hall was Johnstown's only 10-year player and an all-star both in the EHL and IHL. He posted 119 points (regular-season and playoffs) in both 1953-54 in the IHL and 1955-56 when the Jets returned to the EHL after a two-season absence. Hall held four Jets records when he stepped down and still ranks second all-time in points.

Certainly his controversial move from Toledo to Johnstown in 1951 left Hall with no regrets. Decades later, he explained why he stayed.

"The Original Six were in the National Hockey League, and I had belonged to Toronto," Hall said. "I signed when I was 16 years old. I played defense. At that time, there was no big money in the National Hockey League. The salaries were $4,000. I could make more money playing in the Eastern League and going to school.

"Toronto wanted to send me to Los Angeles. At that time, L.A. was the end of the world. They then traded me to Montreal. Every time Montreal wanted me to turn pro, they wanted to send me to communities where nobody spoke English. I had a new bride. I felt it would be better over the long run to stay in Johnstown. Looking back on it, this community has treated me well. I think I made the right decision."

Hall traveled a great distance from Johnstown in 1963-64, when he briefly abandoned retirement to coach a United States team that toured Russia and other Iron Curtain countries at the height of the Cold War.

"We played in seven or eight cities in the Soviet Union and Czechoslovakia," Hall said. "We were supposed to play all the local teams, but every city we went, they flew the National Team in. Anytime we got close to winning, they'd put the National Team in. Back in those days, the Soviet National Team was equally as good as the National Hockey League teams. We were the first American team to ever go outside of Moscow in a sporting event. We had sellouts wherever we went. The building would completely sell out. A couple cities, they wanted us to stay and play extra games."

Hall remained active in Johnstown hockey as an administrator and investor with the Jets through the early 1970s. Also an avid golfer, he served 35 years on the Sunnehanna Amateur Tournament for Champions Committee and was named President of the Pennsylvania Golf Association.

Even though he hasn't competed on the ice for 45 years, Hall always will be linked to Johnstown hockey. His status in the sport was evident on that November 1965 night when Hall was inducted into the Cambria County Sports Hall of Fame.

His presenter also wore the jersey No. 9. The man who introduced Hall was none other than NHL great Gordie Howe.

Jets center John Horvath was one of Johnstown's early stars of the 1950s and a fan favorite.

REPRINT

JETS IN THE FIFTIES

John Horvath was a popular and productive forward with the Johnstown Jets in the 1950s. Five decades later, Horvath received a surprise birthday present when a member of the Hockey Hall of Fame showed up at his Port Colborne, Ontario, home with the Boardwalk Trophy won by the Jets. A Dec. 7, 2004 Tribune-Democrat article on the visit follows:

Hall of Fame lets former Jet relive shining moment

By Mike Mastovich

John Horvath watched his wife, Beryl, place a fancy tablecloth on the dining room table and wondered if perhaps company was about to arrive at their Port Colborne, Ontario, home. After all, the former Johnstown Jets star's 77th birthday was only a few days away. He figured that Beryl might have planned a small surprise party.

Horvath was wrong on that count. Instead, a piece of hockey history with strong ties to Johnstown made its way to the Horvath living room. A representative of the Hockey Hall of Fame accompanied the Atlantic City Boardwalk Trophy — a tall, brass prize featuring meticulous detail and craftsmanship.

The last time Horvath had seen the Boardwalk Trophy was in April 1953, when it was presented to the Johnstown Jets after the team won the Eastern Hockey League playoff title for a second straight year. Fifty-one years later, the trophy — once lost, and then rediscovered a decade ago in a Syracuse, N.Y., storage shed — awakened a variety of emotions for Horvath, a high-scoring center with the championship-winning Jets.

"It was a total surprise. I couldn't believe it," Horvath said in a telephone interview. "I was dumbfounded. I just about broke down in front of 25 people. I gathered myself. It was something else. It's long and slender. Beautiful."

Of course, the Hockey Hall of Fame doesn't make house calls bearing trophies for just anyone. Among Horvath's friends is hockey historian Fred Addis, whose daughter, Miragh, works at the Hockey Hall of Fame in Toronto.

Fred Addis asked his daughter if it would be possible to borrow the trophy for a day to honor an old friend. "All I really had to do is ask for it, and explained I had a family connection, and really wanted it presented to John," Miragh Addis told the Welland Tribune. "I just needed to have it back there first thing on Monday."

Beryl did her part by inviting friends and family while keeping her husband out of the loop. "A month before his birthday, I got a phone call from Fred Addis," Beryl Horvath said. "Fred said, 'How about we come down? My daughter works at the Hockey Hall of Fame in Toronto. We could bring the trophy and surprise him.'

"I'm thinking, John doesn't like surprises. But all of our friends said, 'Go for it.' "

A few days before Horvath's Oct. 28 birthday, the plan went into motion.

"That morning, John saw me putting a fancy tablecloth on the dining room table and wondered what was going on," Beryl said. "I told him we were having a few friends over for lunch."

Wearing special white gloves, Miragh Addis brought the Boardwalk Trophy into the living room, and Horvath's jaw dropped.

"She was holding this beautiful cup that was 4 feet high," Beryl said. "John was sitting on the couch. You should have seen his face."

Horvath certainly earned his special day with the trophy. He made his mark on Johnstown hockey history during his five seasons with the Jets from 1950-55. Horvath scored 102 goals and 328 points with the Jets and was part of coach Wally Kilrea's championship clubs in 1952 and '53. He led the EHL with 68 assists during that memorable 1951-52 season. He was part of three Jets teams in the EHL and was on Johnstown's only two International Hockey League squads in 1953-54 and 1954-55.

A friendly, colorful character, Horvath was well-liked by teammates and Johnstown fans. He still occasionally returns to the city and plans an outing this season.

"I was in Johnstown in 1954, when they gave him a John Horvath Night at the War Memorial," Beryl said. "It was a surprise. They announced his name and he was on the ice. The next night he was on television at 6 o'clock. All the stores in Johnstown gave us gifts. They just loved John in Johnstown."

Horvath's linemates included John Bobenic, George Harrison, Wilf Gorman and Art Dorrington. "The camaraderie was excellent," he said. "Our coach, (Wally) Kilrea, kept us going and happy. He was one of those guys who said, 'You do the work for me, and I'll do the rest for you.' "

His day with the Boardwalk Trophy commemorated a part of Horvath's — and inadvertently this city's — past. Although his career here concluded almost 50 years ago, Horvath still considers Johnstown a special place. "I had a ball," he said. "People treated me like royalty. People invited me for dinner at their homes. It was a real good city. I played in quite a few towns. Nothing compared to Johnstown. It was a beautiful city. They were real friendly there, more friendly than people in my hometown."

Next page, top left: Jets all-star Larry Archambeault in a March 13, 1952 photo.

Top middle: The Hockey Hall of Fame surprised former Jets forward John Horvath, taking the Boardwalk Trophy to his home in Port Colborne, Ontario, for his 77th birthday. Horvath last had seen the trophy, now housed in the Hall of Fame, when the Jets won the 1953 Eastern League championship.

Top right: Jets all-star and leading-scorer Fred "Skippy" Burchell in a March 13, 1952 photo.

Bottom: The Jets' locker room celebration after winning the 1952-53 championship. Don Hall messed up coach Wally Kilrea's hair in the center of the photo.

JETS IN THE FIFTIES

Jets right wing Art Dorrington broke down racial barriers, including playing for Johnstown from 1952 to 1954.

JETS IN THE FIFTIES

REPRINT

As one of the first black professional hockey players, Art Dorrington broke down racial barriers during his two seasons with the Johnstown Jets in the 1950s. The forward helped the Jets win the 1952-53 Boardwalk Trophy. In 2002, Dorrington visited Johnstown in an administrative role with the ECHL's Atlantic City Boardwalk Bullies, who played the Chiefs. An article on Dorrington's return that appeared in The Tribune-Democrat on Feb. 24, 2002 follows:

Dorrington was 'Jackie Robinson of hockey'

By Mike Mastovich

Art Dorrington returned to a Cambria County War Memorial Arena that really hadn't changed much since he played for the Johnstown Jets the early 1950s.

The venerable arena might have looked the same. The crowd's cheers might have had a familiar ring during Friday night's East Coast Hockey League game between the Johnstown Chiefs and Atlantic City (N.J.) Boardwalk Bullies.

But times certainly have changed. The 71-year-old Dorrington would know. Once labeled "the Jackie Robinson of hockey" for his role as the first black to play professional hockey in the United States, Dorrington is considered a pioneer in the sport.

"Back when I first started, there were a lot of cities that you went into where I couldn't stay with the team," said Dorrington, who was honored at center ice prior to the Chiefs' 2-1 overtime victory over Atlantic City. "I had to go to a different hotel. I couldn't eat with the team. I had to go to different restaurants. "But things like that, eventually, they got broken down. At first, it was real bad. I always had the desire to keep going and keep at it. I never had any problem at sticking at it. My teammates were pretty good. They helped out a lot. There was no segregation among the teammates. It was more or less the hotels and the restaurants and a few fans here and there."

The National Hockey League's New York Rangers recruited Dorrington in 1950. The Truro,

> "There were a lot of cities that you went into where I couldn't stay with the team ... I couldn't eat with the team. I had to go to different restaurants. But things like that, eventually, they got broken down."
>
> — *Art Dorrington*

Nova Scotia, native spent his first professional season with the Atlantic City Sea Gulls in the former Eastern Hockey League in 1950-51. During his third season, in 1952-53, Dorrington joined coach Wally Kilrea's Johnstown Jets. The left wing was part of a Boardwalk Trophy championship team that included former Jets stars such as Don Hall, John Horvath and goaltender Ivan Walmsley.

He spent two seasons in Johnstown, including 1953-54 — when the Jets played in the International Hockey League. Dorrington scored 25 goals and tallied 47 points on the EHL championship team and had 30 goals and 48 points with the IHL Jets.

On Friday, the Atlantic City resident returned to the arena as part of the Boardwalk Bullies community development department. Dorrington, who was joined by his wife, Dorothy, also was in a nostalgic mood. He received an honorary Chiefs jersey and dropped the ceremonial first puck. Dorrington reciprocated the Chiefs' generosity by presenting Johnstown General Manager Toby O'Brien a large framed reproduction of a 1953 Tribune-Democrat ad that included autographed photos of the Jets.

Dorrington keeps the original in his New Jersey home. A sports memorabilia collector once offered him $300 for the framed newspaper page, but he turned down the money. "I've had that poster since 1953," Dorrington said. "The sentimental value is worth much more to me."

Longtime Johnstown hockey fans remembered Dorrington, who smiled as he shook hands and chatted with people approaching him outside the Stars and Stripes Room.

"It's bringing back a lot of memories from the old times," Dorrington said. "From when I was here, the building hasn't changed too much. It still has the same hockey mystique to it. But the crowd is into the game a lot more now. I had so many good memories here in Johnstown."

Dorrington netted the game-winning goal against the Springfield (Mass.) Indians in the decisive sixth game of the 1953 championship series. On a line with center Fern LaPointe and right wing Milt Pridham, Dorrington took a long, cross-ice pass from Pridham and beat Springfield goalie "Nippy" O'Hearn for the first goal in a 2-0 road victory. After Johnstown, Dorrington played three more EHL seasons, one with the Washington Lions and two with the Philadelphia Ramblers, before an injury cut short his career in 1958.

In addition to his involvement with the Boardwalk Bullies, he helps Atlantic City youths play through the Art Dorrington Ice Hockey Foundation.

"I have 35 kids in my program," Dorrington said. "I raise money for them to play. I buy all the equipment and pay for ice time. We take them on field trips. That keeps me busy. I skate with them two or three times a week."

Fifty years ago, Dorrington broke down barriers resulting from racism and discrimination. Today, he introduces inner city youth to the excitement of playing hockey.

That's quite a legacy.

JETS IN THE FIFTIES

Jets in action during the 1950s.

Reggie Grigg (left), Fred "Skippy" Burchell (middle) and Don Hall (right) formed the EHL's highest-scoring line in 1951-52.

69

70

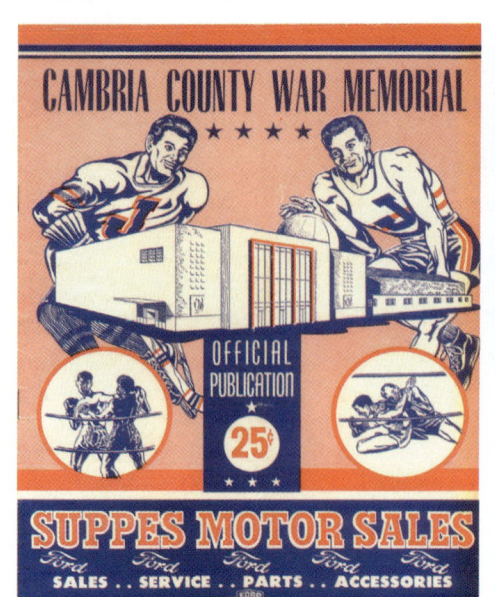

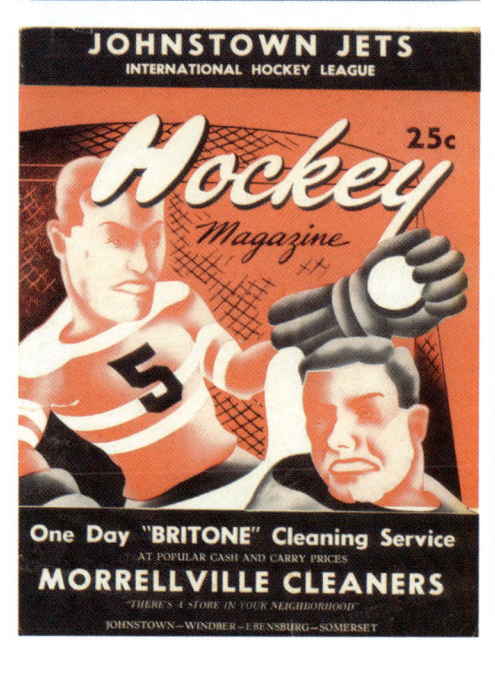

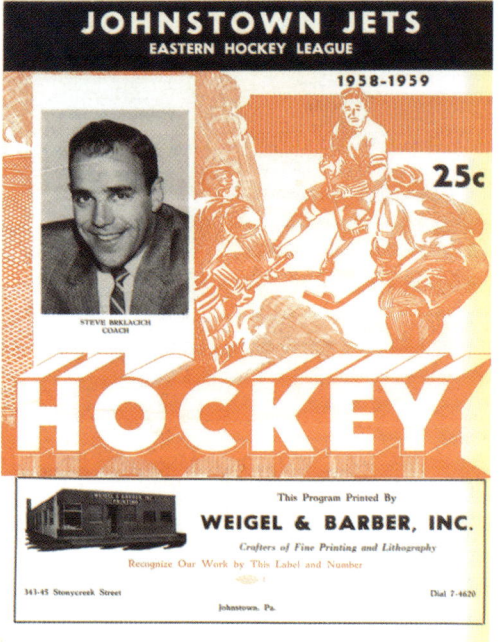

JETS IN THE FIFTIES

Top left: Jets goaltender Ivan Walmsley was a two-time All-Star who helped Johnstown win back-to-back Boardwalk Trophy championships in 1952 and 1953.

Top right: Walmsley accepts a handshake and recognition for his success in net during this March 16, 1952 photo.

Bottom left: The Jets faced the New York Rovers in 1951-52 at the War Memorial Arena.

Bottom right: Jets coach Wally Kilrea led Johnstown to two playoff championships in the 1950s.

71

1950-51 Johnstown Jets

(Front, from left) Edgar Blondin, Nick Phillips, Nick D'Amore, Wayne Stephenson, John Savicky. (Middle) Manager Len Black, George Harrison, Archie Richardson, Wilf Gorman, Orville Kelly, Randy Ellis, coach Wally Kilrea. (Back) Ken McNally, Ken Kilrea, John Horvath, Harry Frost, Robert Burns, Joe Desson.

1950-51 FINAL EASTERN AMATEUR HOCKEY LEAGUE STANDINGS

	Games played	Won	Lost	Tied	Points	Goals for	Goals against
Johnstown Jets	54	26	25	3	55	195	194
Boston Olympics	54	25	24	5	55	287	191
Atlantic City Seagulls	54	23	24	7	53	231	218
New York Rovers	54	22	23	9	53	168	178

Johnstown won Mayor Walker Cup as regular-season champion.

Johnstown Jets
Manager - Leonard Black
Coach - Wally Kilrea
Trainer/Utility Player - Edgar "Chirp" Brenchley
Colors - Red and White

JETS IN THE FIFTIES

1950-51 Game Results

Preseason Results
No Preseason Games

Regular Season Results

Day	Date	Opponent	Score Johnstown	Opponent	Attendance	Record
Sat.	28-Oct	at Boston	5	1		1-0-0
Fri.	3-Nov	New York	5	7	3,061	1-1-0
Sun.	5-Nov	New York	4	2	2,680	2-1-0
Wed.	8-Nov	Atlantic City	11	4	2,672	3-1-0
Fri.	10-Nov	at Atlantic City	2	2		3-1-1
Sat.	11-Nov	at Atlantic City	4	2		4-1-1
Sun.	12-Nov	Atlantic City	6	1	3,117	5-1-1
Wed.	15-Nov	at Boston	0	2		5-2-1
Fri.	17-Nov	at Boston	4	4		5-2-2
Sat.	18-Nov	Boston	5	2	3,687	6-2-2
Sun.	19-Nov	Boston	1	3	3,235	6-3-2
Wed.	22-Nov	Toledo (IHL)	4	3	1,994	Exhibition
Sat.	25-Nov	at Atlantic City	6	4		7-3-2
Sun.	26-Nov	at New York	2	3		7-4-2
Tues.	28-Nov	at New York *	6	2		8-4-2
Fri.	1-Dec	at Boston	3	4		8-5-2
Sat.	2-Dec	Atlantic City	4	9	2,042	8-6-2
Sun.	3-Dec	Atlantic City	5	3	1,710	9-6-2
Wed.	6-Dec	New York	4	3	1,363	10-6-2
Fri.	8-Dec	at Atlantic City	4	2		11-6-2
Sun.	10-Dec	Boston	3	1	2,693	12-6-2
Wed.	13-Dec	Boston	3	2	1,790	13-6-2
Fri.	15-Dec	at Atlantic City	2	4		13-7-2
Sun.	17-Dec	at New York	1	3		13-8-2
Wed.	20-Dec	New York	2	7	2,594	13-9-2
Fri.	22-Dec	at Boston	4	6		13-10-2
Sat.	30-Dec	at Atlantic City	4	1		14-10-2
Wed.	3-Jan	Atlantic City	7	4	1,886	15-10-2
Fri.	5-Jan	at Atlantic City	1	5		15-11-2
Sat.	6-Jan	New York	3	2	2,775	16-11-2
Sun.	7-Jan	at New York	1	4		16-12-2
Tues.	9-Jan	at New York *	2	4		16-13-2
Sun.	14-Jan	Boston	4	0	2,330	17-13-2
Wed.	17-Jan	New York	1	1	2,483	17-13-3
Fri.	19-Jan	at Atlantic City	2	3		17-14-3
Sun.	21-Jan	at New York *	2	6		17-15-3
Wed.	24-Jan	New York	4	0	3,469	18-15-3
Fri.	26-Jan	at Boston	1	2		18-16-3
Sun.	28-Jan	Boston	5	4	2,780	19-16-3
Tues.	30-Jan	at Troy (IHL)	5	3		Exhibition
Fri.	2-Feb	at Troy (IHL)	3	3		Exhibition
Sun.	4-Feb	Atlantic City	5	3	3,342	20-16-3
Wed.	7-Feb	New York	6	2	1,889	21-16-3
Sat.	10-Feb	New York	1	3	3,591	21-17-3
Sun.	11-Feb	at New York	3	4		21-18-3
Wed.	14-Feb	Atlantic City	4	12	2,337	21-19-3
Sat.	17-Feb	at Atlantic City **	4	9		21-20-3
Sun.	18-Feb	Atlantic City	5	2	2,387	22-20-3
Mon.	19-Feb	Atlantic City	4	3	1,644	23-20-3
Thur.	22-Feb	Royal Canadian Air Force	0	6	2,023	Exhibition
Sat.	24-Feb	at Boston	1	4		23-21-3
Sun.	25-Feb	at New York	4	8		23-22-3
Wed.	28-Feb	New York	4	1	2,579	24-22-3
Fri.	2-Mar	at Boston	2	7		24-23-3
Sun.	4-Mar	Boston	8	3	3,633	25-23-3
Tues.	6-Mar	Boston	5	4	3,587	26-23-3
Wed.	7-Mar	Boston	3	4	3,595	26-24-3
Sat.	10-Mar	at Boston	3	6		26-25-3

Playoff Results

Day	Date	Opponent	Score Johnstown	Opponent	Attendance	Record
Sun.	11-Mar	at Boston	2	5		0-1
Sat.	17-Mar	New York	2	1	3,529	1-1

73

Day	Date	Opponent			Attendance	Result
Sun.	18-Mar	at New York	2	6		1-2
Tues.	20-Mar	Boston	6	2	2,710	2-2
Thur.	22-Mar	Atlantic City	3	6	3,009	2-3
Sat.	24-Mar	at Atlantic City	5	7		2-4
Sun.	1-Apr	Cleveland Barons (AHL)	5	7	2,082	Exhibition

* Games were played in Troy, N.Y.
** Game was played in Philadelphia, Pa.

Attendance Figures

	Dates	Totals	Average
Regular Season Attendance Totals	27	74,951	2,776
Playoff Attendance Totals	3	9,248	3,083
Exhibition Attendance Totals	3	6,099	2,033
TOTAL ATTENDANCE	33	90,298	2,736

1950-51 Player Statistics

	Regular Season Scoring					Playoff Scoring				
	Games	G	A	Pts	PIM	Games	G	A	Pts	PIM
14 Wilf Gorman	54	25	47	75	8	6	3	2	5	2
12 John Horvath	42	26	33	59	86	6	3	5	8	4
9 Harry Frost	54	16	36	52	10	6	0	1	1	0
3 George Harrison	51	20	28	48	30	6	4	0	4	0
8 Archie Richardson	53	22	20	42	41	6	2	2	4	2
11 John Savicky	45	21	18	39	16	6	3	5	8	5
5 Randy Ellis	46	15	21	36	15	4	1	2	3	2
2 Joe Desson	53	9	27	36	121	6	0	3	3	24
7 Nick Phillips	45	17	14	31	62	3	0	0	0	14
15 Bob Burns	52	5	13	18	73	6	0	2	2	2
10 Edgar Brenchley	49	5	11	16	20					
4 Orville Kelly	49	6	9	15	196	6	0	1	1	10
3 Wayne Stephenson	53	1	9	10	53	6	0	2	2	7
16 Ken McNally	23	4	5	9	39					
6 Joe Kilbey	22	3	3	6	29					
5 Ken Kilrea	1	0	0	0	10	6	3	4	7	2
1 Nick D'Amore (g)	23	0	0	0	0	6	0	0	0	0
1 Guy Leclerc (g)	31	0	0	0	0					
16 Edgar Blondin						5	1	2	3	11
TOTALS	54	195	294	492	809	6	20	31	51	85

Regular Season Goaltending

	G	Min	GA	ENG	SO	GA	W	L	T
1 Guy Leclerc	31	1,867	102	3	0	3.28	16	14	2
1 Nick D'Amore	23	1,368	88	1	2	3.86	10	11	1
TOTALS	54	3,240	190	4	2	3.59	26	25	3

Playoff Goaltending

	G	Min	GA	ENG	SO	GA	W	L
1 Nick D'Amore	6	360	27	0	0	4.50	2	4
TOTALS	6	360	27	0	0	4.50	2	4

Harrison also wore Nos. 7 and 12
Stephenson also wore No. 12

JETS IN THE FIFTIES

1951-52 Johnstown Jets

(Front, from left) Reggie Grigg, Don Hall, Ivan Walmsley, John Bobenic, Fred Burchell. (Back) Norm Grinke, Orville Kelly, Ken McNally, George Harrison, John Horvath, Ed Montigny, Larry Archambeault, Wilf Gorman, Joe Krahulec, Edgar Blondin, head coach Wally Kilrea.

1951-52 FINAL EASTERN AMATEUR HOCKEY LEAGUE STANDINGS

	Games played	Won	Lost	Tied	Points	Goals for	Goals against
Johnstown Jets	65	39	21	5	83	264	186
Boston Olympics	66	38	27	1	77	246	240
New Haven Tomahawks	66	37	27	2	76	256	241
Springfield Indians	66	33	29	4	70	247	235
Atlantic City Seagulls	65	26	36	6	55	255	281
New York Rovers	61	25	34	2	52	233	231
Washington Lions *	36	9	24	3	21	124	155
Philadelphia Falcons **	25	8	17	0	16	68	124

* Washington Lions folded - January 25, 1952.
** Philadelphia Falcons folded - December 17, 1951.
Johnstown won Mayor Walker Cup as regular-season champion.
Johnstown won Atlantic City Boardwalk Trophy as playoff champion.
Johnstown won Amateur Hockey Association of the United States Cup with playoff victory against Toledo (IHL).

Johnstown Jets
Manager - Leonard Black, Charles Kunkle Jr.
Coach - Wally Kilrea
Trainer/Utility Player - Edgar "Chirp" Brenchley
Colors - Red and White

1951-52 Game Results

Preseason Results

Day	Date	Opponent	Johnstown	Opponent	Attendance	Record
Wed.	17-Oct	Atlantic City	5	6	1,926	
Fri.	19-Oct	at Washington	4	2		

75

Regular Season Results

Day	Date	Opponent	Score Johnstown	Opponent	Attendance	Record
Fri.	26-Oct	New York	8	1	2,932	1-0-0
Sun.	28-Oct	Washington	4	1	1,889	2-0-0
Tues.	30-Oct	at Washington	3	2		3-0-0
Wed.	31-Oct	at New Haven	4	6		3-1-0
Sat.	3-Nov	Springfield	2	5	3,580	3-2-0
Wed.	7-Nov	at Philadelphia	4	5 (ot)		3-3-0
Fri.	9-Nov	New York	2	3	2,232	3-4-0
Sun.	11-Nov	Philadelphia	11	1	1,953	4-4-0
Wed.	14-Nov	Atlantic City	4	2	2,121	5-4-0
Fri.	16-Nov	at Atlantic City	2	5		5-5-0
Sat.	17-Nov	at Boston	3	2 (ot)		6-5-0
Sun.	18-Nov	at New York	5	2		7-5-0
Tues.	20-Nov	Montreal (NHL)	2	10	1,638	Exhibition
Fri.	23-Nov	at Washington	7	5		8-5-0
Sat.	24-Nov	Washington	5	1	2,682	9-5-0
Sun.	25-Nov	Springfield	5	3	2,189	10-5-0
Sat.	1-Dec	New Haven	8	2	3,747	11-5-0
Sun.	2-Dec	New Haven	2	2	1,975	11-5-1
Wed.	5-Dec	New York	5	5	1,611	11-5-2
Sat.	8-Dec	at Atlantic City	0	6		11-6-2
Sun.	9-Dec	Philadelphia	10	0	1,823	12-6-2
Wed.	12-Dec	at Atlantic City	5	6		12-7-2
Sat.	15-Dec	at Philadelphia	9	3		13-7-2
Sun.	16-Dec	at New Haven	2	4		13-8-2
Tues.	18-Dec	at New York *	Postponed - Weather			
Wed.	19-Dec	at Boston	3	4 (ot)		13-9-2
Fri.	21-Dec	at Boston	2	6		13-10-2
Sun.	23-Dec	Atlantic City	10	6	1,285	14-10-2
Sat.	29-Dec	at Springfield	1	1		14-10-3
Sun.	30-Dec	at New Haven	3	4 (ot)		14-11-3
Wed.	2-Jan	Boston	7	1	1,552	15-11-3
Sat.	5-Jan	New York	4	3	3,334	16-11-3
Sun.	6-Jan	at Springfield	2	6		16-12-3
Wed.	9-Jan	at New Haven	6	3		17-12-3
Fri.	11-Jan	at Atlantic City	3	5		17-13-3
Sat.	12-Jan	New Haven	2	1	3,144	18-13-3
Sun.	13-Jan	at New York	5	2		19-13-3
Wed.	16-Jan	Atlantic City	8	2	1,980	20-13-3
Sat.	19-Jan	New Haven	3	3	3,916	20-13-4
Sun.	20-Jan	at New Haven	0	4		20-14-4
Sat.	26-Jan	New York	5	4	2,581	21-14-4
Wed.	30-Jan	at Springfield	2	3 (ot)		21-15-4
Fri.	1-Feb	at Boston	4	4		21-15-5
Sat.	2-Feb	Boston	1	2	3,289	21-16-5
Sun.	3-Feb	Boston	4	1	2,438	22-16-5
Fri.	8-Feb	at Atlantic City	1	4		22-17-5
Sat.	9-Feb	New York	5	3	3,409	23-17-5
Tues.	12-Feb	Boston	3	0	1,579	24-17-5
Wed.	13-Feb	Boston	4	2	2,257	25-17-5
Sat.	16-Feb	at Atlantic City	4	2		26-17-5
Sun.	17-Feb	Atlantic City	3	0	2,227	27-17-5
Thur.	21-Feb	at Springfield	3	0		28-17-5
Sat.	23-Feb	at Atlantic City	2	1		29-17-5
Sun.	24-Feb	Atlantic City	8	5	2,303	30-17-5
Tues.	26-Feb	New York	6	1	1,797	31-17-5
Wed.	27-Feb	at Springfield	2	5		31-18-5
Fri.	29-Feb	at Boston	3	2		32-18-5
Sat.	1-Mar	Springfield	1	0	3,429	33-18-5
Sun.	2-Mar	Springfield	2	1	2,748	34-18-5
Wed.	5-Mar	Boston	3	0	4,139	35-18-5
Fri.	7-Mar	at Boston	4	2		36-18-5
Sun.	9-Mar	at New York	3	2 (ot)		37-18-5
Fri.	14-Mar	New Haven	8	1	3,719	38-18-5
Sat.	15-Mar	New Haven	6	8	4,143	38-19-5
Sun.	16-Mar	at New Haven	1	4		38-20-5
Thur.	20-Mar	Springfield	3	5	1,551	38-21-5
Sat.	22-Mar	Springfield	4	1	2,302	39-21-5

* Game was to be played in Troy, N.Y.

JETS IN THE FIFTIES

Playoff Results

Day	Date	Opponent	Johnstown	Opponent	Attendance	Record
Tues.	25-Mar	Springfield	6	1	2,205	1-0
Thur.	27-Mar	Springfield	7	2	2,468	2-0
Sat.	29-Mar	at Springfield	6	2		3-0
Sat.	5-Apr	New Haven	4	3	3,278	1-0
Sun.	6-Apr	New Haven	2	1	2,468	2-0
Tues.	8-Apr	at New Haven	1	2		2-1
Thur.	10-Apr	at New Haven	4	1		3-1
Sun.	13-Apr	at New Haven	5	3		4-1
Tues.	15-Apr	Toledo (IHL)	3	2	3,416	1-0
Sat.	19-Apr	at Toledo (IHL)	6	4		2-0
Sun.	20-Apr	at Toledo (IHL)	0	4		2-1
Tues.	22-Apr	Toledo (IHL)	6	1	3,347	3-1
Thur.	24-Apr	Toledo (IHL)	7	1	3,568	4-1

Attendance Figures

	Dates	Totals	Average
Regular Season Attendance Totals	34	87,856	2,584
Playoff Attendance Totals	7	20,750	2,964
Exhibition Attendance Totals	2	3,564	1,782
TOTAL ATTENDANCE	43	112,170	2,609

1951-52 Player Statistics

	Regular Season Scoring					Playoff Scoring				
	Games	G	A	Pts	PIM	Games	G	A	Pts	PIM
16 Fred Burchell	57	37	56	93	73	13	5	18	23	18
12 John Horvath	65	17	68	85	64	13	6	9	15	10
9 Don Hall	61	36	45	81	19	13	9	9	18	7
11 Reg Grigg	58	39	37	76	20	13	13	8	21	12
7 John Bobenic	58	38	21	59	51	13	9	4	13	12
14 Wilf Gorman	61	23	25	48	8	6	0	0	0	0
15 George Harrison	61	16	20	36	6	12	1	1	2	2
6 Norm Grinke	57	7	20	27	51	13	2	6	8	17
3 Orville Kelly	52	7	15	22	146	9	2	4	6	26
17 Joe Krahulec	57	7	15	22	61	12	0	3	3	8
8 Ed Barber	43	8	11	19	88					
4 Ed Montigny	34	5	14	19	93	13	3	5	8	41
18 Edgar Blondin	21	5	11	16	54	13	3	5	8	44
2 Ken McNally	51	5	11	16	45	12	1	4	5	18
19 Larry Archambeault	29	3	12	15	16	13	3	2	5	4
10 Edgar Brenchley	17	3	7	10	4					
5 Wayne Stephenson	20	6	3	9	46					
5 Bud Platt	11	1	3	4	8					
17 Vic DeMarco	6	1	1	2	6					
4 Hal Cowan	16	0	2	2	10					
4 Clement Doyon	2	0	1	1	4					
3 Bill Russell	4	0	1	1	2					
1 Doug Coxon (g)	1	0	0	0	0					
1 Ivan Walmsley (g)	64	0	0	0	25	13	0	0	0	2
Bench					2					
TOTALS	65	264	399	663	902	13	57	78	135	221

Regular Season Goaltending

	G	Min	GA	ENG	SO	GAA	W	L	T
1 Doug Coxon	1	60	1	0	0	1.00	1	0	0
1 Ivan Walmsley	64	3,906	184	1	6	2.83	38	21	5
TOTALS	65	3,966	185	1	6	2.81	39	21	5

Playoff Goaltending

	G	Min	GA	ENG	SO	GAA	W	L
1 Ivan Walmsley	13	800	27	0	0	2.07	1	2
TOTALS	13	800	27	0	0	2.07	1	2

Krahulec wore No. 10 for a game.
Blondin wore No. 10 for a game.

1952-53 Johnstown Jets

(From left) Head coach Wally Kilrea, Roy Colligan, John Horvath, trainer/spare goalie Dan Canney, Joe Krahulec, Ken McNally, Desmond Kelly, Ed Montigny, Ivan Walmsley, Norm Grinke, John Sherban, George Hayes, Don Hall, Milt Pridham.

1952-53 FINAL EASTERN AMATEUR HOCKEY LEAGUE STANDINGS

	Games played	Won	Lost	Tied	Points	Goals for	Goals against
Springfield Indians	60	39	19	2	80	296	234
Johnstown Jets	60	28	29	3	59	226	244
New Haven Nutmegs	60	28	31	1	57	251	223
Washington Lions	60	26	31	3	55	201	215
Troy Uncle Sam Trojans	60	23	34	3	49	220	278

Johnstown won Hershey Challenge Trophy as regular-season runner-up.
Johnstown won Atlantic City Boardwalk Trophy as playoff champion.

Johnstown Jets
General Manager - Wally Kilrea
Manager - Charles Kunkle Jr.
Coach - Wally Kilrea
Trainer/Spare Goalie - Dan Canney
Colors - Red and White

JETS IN THE FIFTIES

1952-53 Game Results

Preseason Results
No Preseason Games

Regular Season Results

Day	Date	Opponent	Johnstown	Opponent	Attendance	Record
Sat.	25-Oct	at Washington	4	2		1-0-0
Sun.	26-Oct	New Haven	4	3	2,969	2-0-0
Tues.	28-Oct	Washington	3	8	1,851	2-1-0
Wed.	29-Oct	at New Haven	5	4		3-1-0
Fri.	31-Oct	at Springfield	3	7		3-2-0
Sun.	2-Nov	Troy	4	1	2,007	4-2-0
Thur.	6-Nov	Springfield	3	3(ot)	2,101	4-2-1
Sun.	9-Nov	at New Haven	5	3		5-2-1
Wed.	12-Nov	at Springfield	2	9		5-3-1
Fri.	14-Nov	at Washington	4	2		6-3-1
Sat.	15-Nov	New Haven	5	3	2,575	7-3-1
Sun.	16-Nov	New Haven	8	2	1,840	8-3-1
Wed.	19-Nov	at Troy	3	4		8-4-1
Thur.	20-Nov	Washington	4	1	1,939	9-4-1
Sun.	23-Nov	Troy	9	4	1,933	10-4-1
Tues.	25-Nov	Troy	10	5	1,528	11-4-1
Thur.	27-Nov	Springfield	2	6	2,940	11-5-1
Sat.	29-Nov	Springfield	3	4 (ot)	3,006	11-6-1
Tues.	2-Dec	Washington	4	5 (ot)	1,131	11-7-1
Wed.	3-Dec	at Troy	3	2		12-7-1
Sat.	6-Dec	New Haven	3	5	1,945	12-8-1
Wed.	10-Dec	Troy	5	1	1,236	13-8-1
Sat.	13-Dec	at Washington	6	4		14-8-1
Sun.	14-Dec	Washington	2	2 (ot)	1,356	14-8-2
Thur.	18-Dec	Troy	5	2	1,350	15-8-2
Sat.	27-Dec	at Springfield	2	7		15-9-2
Sun.	28-Dec	at Troy	2	3		15-10-2
Sat.	3-Jan	at Washington	1	6		15-11-2
Sun.	4-Jan	Washington	5	2	1,642	16-11-2
Wed.	7-Jan	at New Haven	3	3 (ot)		16-11-3
Thur.	8-Jan	Troy	Postponed – weather – rescheduled for Jan. 9			
Fri.	9-Jan	Troy	7	2	1,124	17-11-3
Sat.	10-Jan	New Haven	5	4 (ot)	2,177	18-11-3
Sun.	11-Jan	at New Haven	2	6		18-12-3
Wed.	14-Jan	Washington	4	6	2,072	18-13-3
Fri.	16-Jan	at Washington	4	1		19-13-3
Sat.	17-Jan	New Haven	0	7	1,804	19-14-3
Wed.	21-Jan	Springfield	3	5	1,958	19-15-3
Sat.	24-Jan	at Washington	4	6		19-16-3
Sun.	25-Jan	Washington	5	2	1,517	20-16-3
Thur.	29-Jan	Troy	7	2	1,297	21-16-3
Sat.	31-Jan	at Springfield	5	4		22-16-3
Sun.	1-Feb	at Troy	4	5 (ot)		22-17-3
Wed.	4-Feb	at New Haven	4	7		22-18-3
Sat.	7-Feb	New Haven	1	6	3,225	22-19-3
Thur.	12-Feb	Washington	3	1	1,110	23-19-3
Sat.	14-Feb	Washington	0	3	2,351	23-20-3
Thur.	19-Feb	Springfield	3	2	1,757	24-20-3
Fri.	20-Feb	at Troy	3	2		25-20-3
Sat.	21-Feb	at Springfield	3	6		25-21-3
Sun.	22-Feb	at Troy	2	3		25-22-3
Wed.	25-Feb	at Washington	2	3 (ot)		25-23-3
Sat.	28-Feb	at Springfield	5	10		25-24-3
Sun.	1-Mar	at Troy	2	4		25-25-3
Fri.	6-Mar	at Washington	6	3		26-25-3
Sat.	7-Mar	at Washington	1	4		26-26-3
Sun.	8-Mar	at New Haven	3	6		26-27-3
Wed.	11-Mar	at Springfield	2	5		26-28-3
Sat.	14-Mar	Springfield	5	4 (ot)	2,536	27-28-3
Sun.	15-Mar	Springfield	6	5	2,054	28-28-3
Sun.	22-Mar	at New Haven	3	7		28-29-3

79

Playoff Results

Day	Date	Opponent	Score Johnstown	Opponent	Attendance	Record
Wed.	25-Mar	at Washington	3	2		1-0
Fri.	27-Mar	Washington	4	3	1,503	2-0
Sat.	28-Mar	at Washington	1	6		2-1
Sun.	29-Mar	Washington	4	3	1,792	3-1
Wed.	1-Apr	at Washington	1	3		3-2
Mon.	2-Apr	Washington	6	3	1,535	4-2
Sat.	4-Apr	at Springfield	3	2		1-0
Sun.	5-Apr	at Springfield	5	4		2-0
Tues.	7-Apr	Springfield	2	1	3,521	3-0
Thur.	9-Apr	Springfield	0	2	3,190	3-1
Sat.	11-Apr	at Springfield	2	7		3-2
Sun.	12-Apr	Springfield	2	0	2,273	4-2
Mon.	13-Apr	Cincinnati (IHL)	1	4	2,268	0-1
Wed.	15-Apr	Cincinnati (IHL)	1	4	1,371	0-2
Fri.	17-Apr	Cincinnati (IHL)	3	5	1,706	0-3

Attendance Figures

	Dates	Totals	Average
Regular Season Attendance Totals	30	58,331	1,944
Playoff Attendance Totals	9	19,159	2,129
TOTAL ATTENDANCE	39	77,490	1,987

1952-53 Player Statistics

	Regular Season Scoring					Playoff Scoring				
	Games	G	A	Pts	PIM	Games	G	A	Pts	PIM
11 George Hayes	56	29	58	87	21	15	7	5	12	0
9 Don Hall	57	40	46	86	38	8	4	6	10	6
7 John Bobenic	53	37	30	67	37	15	4	6	10	14
1 Milt Pridham	58	22	27	49	8	11	1	2	3	0
14 Art Dorrington	57	25	22	47	21	15	4	1	5	0
12 John Horvath	35	8	37	45	32	15	2	9	11	13
2 Ken McNally	56	7	27	34	108	15	5	6	11	16
8 John Sherban	44	17	16	33	24					
6 Norm Grinke	58	4	26	30	52	13	0	3	3	14
10 Bob Fero	34	12	16	28	32					
4 Ed Montigny	38	3	22	25	134					
17 Joe Krahulec	52	2	16	18	63	13	1	3	4	26
3 Orville Kelly	25	6	9	15	79					
10 Fern Lapointe	7	4	2	6	2	13	2	2	4	6
8 Gord Hudson	14	4	2	6	22	11	1	2	3	10
4 Ted Hodgson	7	2	2	4	20	14	0	7	7	57
10 Bob Daniels	9	1	2	3	6					
3 Larry Regan	1	1	0	1	0	15	7	5	12	24
10 Desmond Kelly	7	1	0	1	4					
8 Jim Turner	9	1	0	1	11					
1 Dan Canney (g)	1	0	0	0	0					
1 Dennis Mooney (g)	1	0	0	0	0					
1 Ivan Walmsley (g)	59	0	0	0	14	15	0	0	0	0
15 George Harrison						1	0	1	1	0
5 Joe Medynski						2	0	0	0	4
6 Bill Mitchell				1	0	0	0	0		
TOTALS	60	226	360	586	728	15	38	58	86	190

Regular Season Goaltending

	G	Min	GA	ENG	SO	GAA	W	L	T
1 Dan Canney	1	10	0	0	0	0.00	0	0	0
1 Ivan Walmsley	59	3,594	237	0	1	3.96	28	28	3
1 Dennis Mooney	1	50	7	0	0	8.40	0	1	0
TOTALS	60	3,654	244	0	1	4.01	28	29	3

Playoff Goaltending

	G	Min	GA	ENG	SO	GAA	W	L
1 Ivan Walmsley	15	900	49	0	1	3.26	8	7
TOTALS	15	900	49	0	1	3.26	8	7

JETS IN THE FIFTIES

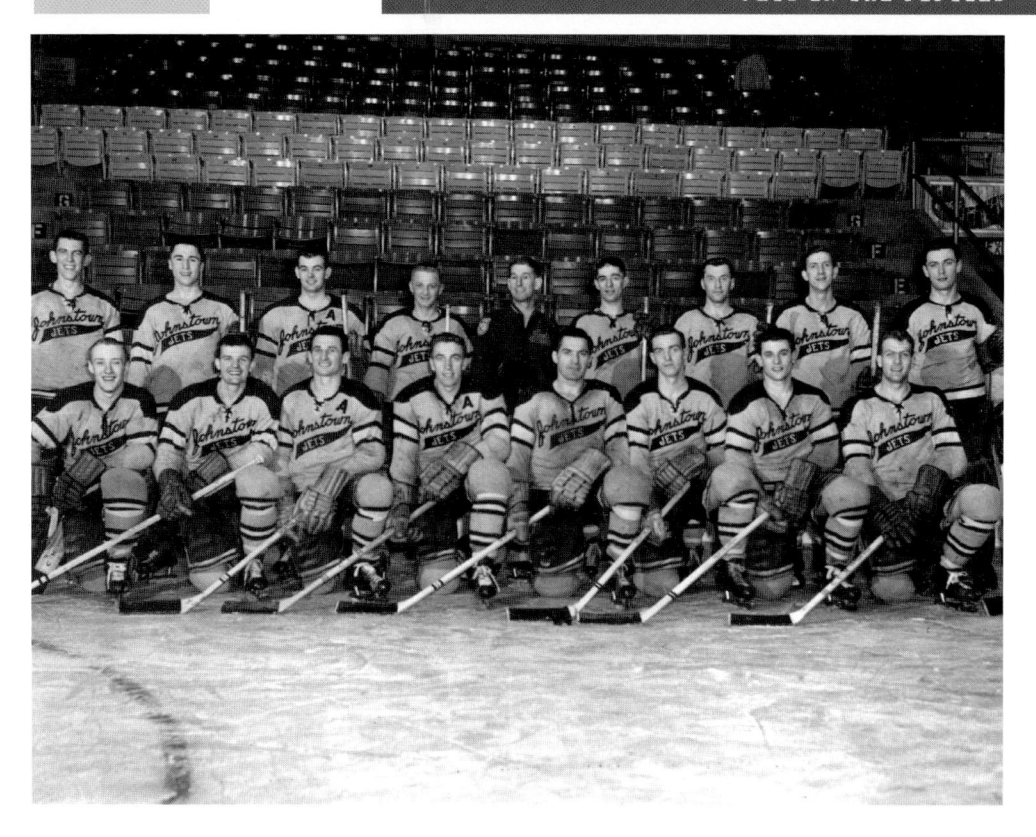

1953-54 Johnstown Jets

(Front, from left) Larry Winder, Ron Castalane, John Horvath, Bill Gallagher, Joe Medynski, Ross Kelly, Alex Zubatiuk, Dan Nixon. (Back) Don Simmons, Al Bruce, Don Hall, Fraser Kilpatrick, head coach Edgar Brenchley, Arnie Schmautz, Ed Ruml, Cliff McArthur, trainer/spare goalie Dan Canney. Missing from photo: Art Dorrington

1953-54 FINAL INTERNATIONAL HOCKEY LEAGUE STANDINGS

	Games played	Won	Lost	Tied	Points	Goals for	Goals against
Cincinnati Mohawks	64	47	15	2	96	325	153
Marion Barons	64	40	24	0	80	279	207
Johnstown Jets	64	35	26	3	73	254	222
Toledo Mercurys	64	33	26	5	71	221	157
Troy Bruins	64	31	32	1	63	241	258
Fort Wayne Komets	64	29	30	5	63	203	220
Grand Rapids Rockets	64	29	32	3	61	253	274
Louisville Shooting Stars	64	18	42	4	40	202	331
Milwaukee Chiefs	64	13	48	3	29	187	343

Johnstown Jets
General Manager - Edgar "Chirp" Brenchley
Manager - Charles Kramer
Coach - Edgar "Chirp" Brenchley
Trainer/Spare Goalie - Dan Canney
Colors - Gold, Brown and White

1953-54 Game Results

Preseason Results

Day	Date	Opponent	Score Johnstown	Opponent	Attendance	Record
Thur.	8-Oct	Grand Rapids *	4	8		

* Game played in Fort Erie, Ontario.

Regular Season Results

Day	Date	Opponent	Score Johnstown	Opponent	Attendance	Record
Thur.	15-Oct	Fort Wayne	7	7 (ot)	3,005	0-0-1
Sat.	17-Oct	at Fort Wayne	5	1		1-0-1
Sun.	18-Oct	at Toledo	0	6		1-1-1
Thur.	22-Oct	Louisville	12	3	2,349	2-1-1
Tues.	27-Oct	Cincinnati	3	7	2,357	2-2-1
Thur.	29-Oct	Troy	7	5	1,711	3-2-1
Sat.	31-Oct	at Grand Rapids	4	0		4-2-1
Sun.	1-Nov	at Milwaukee	6	1		5-2-1
Sat.	7-Nov	at Toledo	5	4		6-2-1
Sun.	8-Nov	at Troy	7	10		6-3-1
Wed.	11-Nov	at Louisville	3	1 (ot)		7-3-1
Thur.	12-Nov	Grand Rapids	8	3	2,250	8-3-1
Sun.	15-Nov	at Marion	3	4		8-4-1
Tues.	17-Nov	at Cincinnati	2	3		8-5-1
Thur.	19-Nov	Marion	2	5	2,271	8-6-1
Sat.	21-Nov	Milwaukee	8	3	2,072	9-6-1
Sat.	28-Nov	Cincinnati	3	1	3,820	10-6-1
Sun.	29-Nov	Toledo	3	1	2,352	11-6-1
Thur.	3-Dec	at Troy	5	7		11-7-1
Sat.	5-Dec	at Grand Rapids	7	6 (ot)		12-7-1
Sun.	6-Dec	Fort Wayne	5	1	2,047	13-7-1
Tues.	8-Dec	Louisville	2	2 (ot)	1,576	13-7-2
Sat.	12-Dec	Grand Rapids	5	4	2,140	14-7-2
Sun.	13-Dec	at Louisville	9	2		15-7-2
Tues.	15-Dec	Marion	6	3	1,695	16-7-2
Sat.	19-Dec	Milwaukee	5	4	2,520	17-7-2
Sun.	20-Dec	at Marion	1	8		17-8-2
Wed.	23-Dec	at Milwaukee	Postponed – prior booking at Milwaukee Arena			
Sat.	26-Dec	at Toledo	2	7		17-9-2
Sun.	27-Dec	at Cincinnati	3	8		17-10-2
Tues.	29-Dec	at Fort Wayne	2	3		17-11-2
Fri.	1-Jan	Fort Wayne	3	5	2,492	17-12-2
Sun.	3-Jan	at Troy	3	1		18-12-2
Tues.	5-Jan	Louisville	4	3	1,555	19-12-2
Sun.	10-Jan	Toledo	1	3	2,104	19-13-3
Tues.	12-Jan	at Cincinnati	0	5		19-14-3
Thur.	14-Jan	at Grand Rapids	6	3		20-14-3
Tues.	19-Jan	Troy	4	3	1,790	21-14-3
Sat.	23-Jan	Milwaukee	8	2	2,248	22-14-3
Sun.	24-Jan	Fort Wayne	8	6	1,932	23-14-3
Wed.	27-Jan	Cincinnati	4	4	3,060	23-14-4
Sat.	30-Jan	Troy	4	2	2,694	24-14-4
Tues.	2-Feb	at Milwaukee	3	5		24-15-4
Thur.	4-Feb	Louisville *	7	4	1,425	25-15-4
Sat.	6-Feb	Louisville *	5	3	3,027	26-15-4
Sun.	7-Feb	at Troy	3	1		27-15-4
Wed.	10-Feb	at Toledo	3	6		27-16-4
Thur.	11-Feb	Grand Rapids	8	0	1,842	28-16-4
Sun.	14-Feb	Toledo	3	0	2,220	29-16-4
Mon.	15-Feb	at Fort Wayne	0	3		29-17-4
Tues.	16-Feb	Troy	1	2	2,728	29-18-4
Sat.	20-Feb	at Cincinnati	2	5		29-19-4
Sun.	21-Feb	Milwaukee	5	4	2,132	30-19-4
Tues.	23-Feb	Milwaukee	3	2	1,470	31-19-4
Wed.	24-Feb	at Marion	1	3		31-20-4
Thur.	25-Feb	at Grand Rapids	0	5		31-21-4
Sat.	27-Feb	Marion	2	4	2,785	31-22-4
Sun.	28-Feb	Louisville *	7	4	1,202	32-22-4
Tues.	2-Mar	Grand Rapids	9	3	1,638	33-22-4

Day	Date	Opponent		Score	Attendance	Record
Thur.	4-Mar	Toledo	2	1	1,962	34-22-4
Fri.	5-Mar	at Fort Wayne	0	2		34-23-4
Sun.	7-Mar	Marion	1	2	2,362	34-24-4
Tues.	9-Mar	at Milwaukee	2	1		35-24-4
Sat.	13-Mar	Cincinnati	0	2	2,992	35-25-4
Sun.	14-Mar	at Marion	2	3		35-26-4

Playoff Results

			Score			
Day	Date	Opponent	Johnstown	Opponent	Attendance	Record
Tues.	16-Mar	Fort Wayne	5	4 (ot)	1,622	1-0
Wed.	17-Mar	at Fort Wayne	3	2		2-0
Sun.	21-Mar	Toledo	3	1	2,649	1-0
Tues.	23-Mar	at Toledo	3	0		2-0
Thurs.	25-Mar	at Cincinnati	0	3		0-1
Sat.	27-Mar	at Cincinnati	2	3		1-1
Sun.	28-Mar	Cincinnati	0	1	3,100	1-2
Tues.	30-Mar	Cincinnati	1	3	2,847	1-3
Thur.	1-Apr	Cincinnati	3	1	2,471	2-3
Sat.	3-Apr	Cincinnati	1	3	3,920	2-4

* Louisville played all games on road after Jan. 17

Attendance Figures

	Dates	Totals	Average
Regular Season Attendance Totals	35	77,825	2,224
Playoff Attendance Totals	6	16,609	2,768
TOTAL ATTENDANCE	41	94,434	2,303

1953-54 Player Statistics

	Regular Season Scoring					Playoff Scoring				
	Games	G	A	Pts	PIM	Games	G	A	Pts	PIM
9 Don Hall	63	43	67	110	46	10	7	2	9	4
11 Arnie Schmautz	63	38	52	90	61	10	2	2	4	2
10 Fraser Kilpatrick	62	37	45	82	40	10	0	3	3	6
7 John Horvath	42	18	34	52	26	10	0	4	4	6
12 Art Dorrington	61	30	18	48	32	9	1	2	3	0
14 Cliff McArthur	55	20	23	43	26	10	5	0	5	0
8 Larry Winder	58	20	18	38	31	10	1	3	4	5
2 Bill Gallagher	63	4	33	37	126	9	0	1	1	4
3 Ross Kelly	57	7	17	24	26	10	1	1	2	6
5 Joe Medynski	62	2	20	22	139	10	1	2	3	12
15 Al Bruce	55	14	7	21	21					
6 Ed Ruml	40	12	7	19	20	10	0	4	4	2
4 Alex Zubatiuk	61	1	15	16	141	10	0	2	2	18
16 Sid Puddicombe	15	2	6	8	13					
6 Del St. John	16	2	5	7	8					
16 Edgar Brenchley	25	0	7	7	48					
15 Ron Castalane	9	3	2	5	4	10	3	3	6	4
12 Frank Toyota	2	1	2	3	0					
16 Dan Nixon	8	0	1	1	6	10	1	0	1	4
14 Steve Chorney	3	0	0	0	2					
8 Jim Johnson	5	0	0	0	4					
1 Don Simmons (g)	24	0	0	0	7	10	0	0	0	14
1 Claude Roy (g)	40	0	0	0	10					
TOTALS	64	254	379	633	837	10	21	29	50	87

Regular Season Goaltending

	G	Min	GA	ENG	SO	GAA	W	L	T	Saves	Save %
1 Don Simmons	24	1,440	63	3	2	2.75	12	12	0	542	0.906
1 Claude Roy	40	2,440	152	3	1	3.88	23	14	3	789	0.865
TOTALS	64	3,880	215	7	3	3.43	35	26	3		

Note: Simmons and Roy totals for Saves and Save % incomplete – only calculated for available games.

Playoff Goaltending

	G	Min	GA	ENG	SO	GAA	W	L
1 Don Simmons	10	606	21	1	1	2.08	6	4
TOTALS	10	606	21	1	1	2.18	6	4

Dorrington and Toyota also wore No. 15.
Puddicombe also wore Nos. 6 and 8.
Johnson also wore No. 16.

1954-55 Johnstown Jets

(Front, from left) John Horvath, Mike Narduzzi, Al Bennett, Ed Ruml, Don Hall. (Middle) Dick Roberge, Duke MacDonald, Bill Gallagher, Joe Medynski, Art Stone, trainer/spare goalie Dan Canney, head coach Edgar "Chirp" Brenchley. (Back) Stickboy Francis Kabler, Alex Zubatiuk, Charles Marshall, Jim MacKenzie, Ernie Dick.

1954-55 FINAL INTERNATIONAL HOCKEY LEAGUE STANDINGS

	Games played	Won	Lost	Tied	Points	Goals for	Goals against
Cincinnati Mohawks	60	40	19	1	81	268	164
Troy Bruins	60	31	27	2	64	190	180
Toledo Mercurys	60	31	29	0	62	183	196
Grand Rapids Rockets	60	28	31	1	57	199	215
Johnstown Jets	60	25	34	1	51	188	219
Fort Wayne Komets	60	22	37	1	45	181	235

Johnstown Jets
General Manager - Edgar "Chirp" Brenchley
Manager - Charles Kramer
Coach - Edgar "Chirp" Brenchley
Trainer/Spare Goalie - Dan Canney
Stickboy - Francis Kabler
Colors - Gold, Brown and White

JETS IN THE FIFTIES

1954-55 Game Results

Preseason Results

Day	Date	Opponent	Johnstown	Opponent	Attendance	Record
Tues.	12-Oct	at Niagara Falls Cataractes	1	4		

Regular Season Results

Day	Date	Opponent	Johnstown	Opponent	Attendance	Record
Sun.	17-Oct	at Fort Wayne	0	7		0-1-0
Tues.	19-Oct	at Grand Rapids	3	1		1-1-0
Sat.	23-Oct	at Cincinnati	0	4		1-2-0
Sun.	24-Oct	Cincinnati	4	9	2,048	1-3-0
Sat.	30-Oct	at Toledo	2	3		1-4-0
Sun.	31-Oct	Toledo	0	3	1,436	1-5-0
Wed.	3-Nov	Troy	1	2	1,138	1-6-0
Sat.	6-Nov	Grand Rapids	1	3	1,734	1-7-0
Sun.	7-Nov	Grand Rapids	3	4	1,302	1-8-0
Sat.	13-Nov	at Fort Wayne	3	4		1-9-0
Sun.	14-Nov	Fort Wayne	3	1	1,384	2-9-0
Wed.	17-Nov	Troy	2	1	1,349	3-9-0
Sat.	20-Nov	at Toledo	4	2		4-9-0
Sun.	21-Nov	Cincinnati	0	7	1,853	4-10-0
Thur.	25-Nov	at Troy	2	2		4-10-1
Sun.	28-Nov	at Cincinnati	3	2		5-10-1
Tues.	30-Nov	at Grand Rapids	5	2		6-10-1
Wed.	1-Dec	Fort Wayne	4	2	1,560	7-10-1
Sat.	4-Dec	Toledo	4	1	1,909	8-10-1
Sun.	5-Dec	Toledo	3	4	2,140	8-11-1
Wed.	8-Dec	Cincinnati	4	5	1,767	8-12-1
Sat.	11-Dec	at Grand Rapids	3	4		8-13-1
Sun.	12-Dec	at Troy	1	4		8-14-1
Wed.	15-Dec	Grand Rapids	5	3	1,224	9-14-1
Sat.	18-Dec	at Fort Wayne	4	5		9-15-1
Sun.	19-Dec	Fort Wayne	3	2	1,750	10-15-1
Wed.	22-Dec	Troy	5	2	1,629	11-15-1
Sat.	25-Dec	at Toledo	3	2		12-15-1
Sun.	26-Dec	at Cincinnati	5	8		12-16-1
Sat.	1-Jan	at Fort Wayne	2	3		12-17-1
Wed.	5-Jan	Fort Wayne	8	5	1,924	13-17-1
Thur.	6-Jan	at Troy	3	6		13-18-1
Sat.	8-Jan	at Cincinnati	4	3		14-18-1
Wed.	12-Jan	Grand Rapids	9	2	2,291	15-18-1
Sat.	15-Jan	Troy	5	1	2,998	16-18-1
Sun.	16-Jan	at Troy	4	3		17-18-1
Tues.	18-Jan	at Grand Rapids	3	2		18-18-1
Thur.	20-Jan	at Cincinnati	1	5		18-19-1
Sat.	22-Jan	at Toledo	2	3		18-20-1
Wed.	26-Jan	Cincinnati	0	6	4,217	18-21-1
Sat.	29-Jan	at Fort Wayne	2	5		18-22-1
Wed.	2-Feb	Grand Rapids	2	3 (ot)	1,916	18-23-1
Sat.	5-Feb	at Toledo	1	5		18-24-1
Tues.	8-Feb	at Grand Rapids	2	5		18-25-1
Wed.	9-Feb	Toledo	6	2	1,796	19-25-1
Sun.	13-Feb	at Fort Wayne	5	7		19-26-1
Wed.	16-Feb	Fort Wayne	7	4	1,638	20-26-1
Thur.	17-Feb	at Cincinnati	2	3		20-27-1
Sat.	19-Feb	Troy	6	1	2,748	21-27-1
Sun.	20-Feb	Fort Wayne	8	5	2,194	22-27-1
Thur.	24-Feb	at Troy	2	5		22-28-1
Sat.	26-Feb	at Toledo	4	3		23-28-1
Sun.	27-Feb	Toledo	3	1	2,072	24-28-1
Tues.	1-Mar	at Grand Rapids	7	4		25-28-1
Thur.	3-Mar	Grand Rapids	1	3	2,428	25-29-1
Sat.	5-Mar	Cincinnati	3	4	2,816	25-30-1
Sun.	6-Mar	Cincinnati	2	7	1,893	25-31-1
Thur.	10-Mar	at Troy	2	3		25-32-1
Sat.	12-Mar	Troy	0	5	2,316	25-33-1
Sun.	13-Mar	Toledo	2	6	1,322	25-34-1

Attendance Figures

	Dates	Totals	Average
Regular Season Attendance Totals	30	58,792	1,960
TOTAL ATTENDANCE	30	58,792	1,960

1954-55 Player Statistics

Regular Season Scoring

	Games	G	A	Pts	PIM
7 John Horvath	60	33	53	86	54
9 Don Hall	55	26	47	73	15
15 Mike Narduzzi	29	23	19	42	18
11 Dick Roberge	60	17	23	40	20
12 Jim MacKenzie	41	15	17	32	19
6 Ed Ruml	59	6	21	27	20
17 Art Stone	33	9	15	24	21
15 George Harrison	30	9	13	22	4
16 Duke MacDonald	51	6	15	21	34
14 Charles Marshall	36	8	12	20	37
2 Bill Gallagher	46	4	16	20	87
3 Ross Kelly	37	4	12	16	47
10 Maurice Chevrefils	41	8	6	14	20
10 Ernie Dick	19	8	5	13	12
8 Pete Koval	32	2	11	13	51
5 Joe Medynski	60	1	12	13	90
12 Bob Taylor	18	7	4	11	7
4 Alex Zubatiuk	60	2	5	7	132
1 Steve Pataran (g)	4	0	0	0	0
16 Frank Holliday	9	0	0	0	9
1 Al Bennett (g)	19	0	0	0	2
1 Norm Defelice (g)	37	0	0	0	16
TOTALS	60	188	306	494	715

Regular Season Goaltending

	G	Min	GA	ENG	SO	GAA	W	L	T	Saves	Save %
1 Norm Defelice	37	2,226	122	0	0	3.23	17	19	1	1,062	0.900
1 Al Bennett	19	1,148	75	1	0	3.92	7	12	0	617	0.892
1 Steve Pataran	4	240	21	0	0	5.25	1	3	0	130	0.861
TOTALS	60	3,614	218	1	0	3.64	25	34	1	1,809	0.892

JETS IN THE FIFTIES

1955-56 Johnstown Jets

(Front, from left) Don Hall, Jim Mattson, head coach Lloyd Ailsby, Bill Anderson, Ken Coombes. (Middle) Norm "Skip" MacKay, Bill Gallagher, Ron Lee, Pentti Hiironen, Alex Zubatiuk, Alex McDonald, general manager Dave Faunce. (Back) Stickboy Francis Kabler, George Harrison, Ed Ferenz, Dick Roberge, Don Rizzo, Paul Olafson, Ed Ruml, trainer Harry Andrews.

1955-56 FINAL EASTERN HOCKEY LEAGUE STANDINGS

	Games played	Won	Lost	Tied	Points	Goals for	Goals against
New Haven Blades	64	43	18	3	89	318	206
Clinton Comets	64	33	28	3	69	298	269
Washington Lions	64	33	28	3	69	258	267
Johnstown Jets	64	32	32	0	64	312	298
Baltimore/Charlotte Clippers	64	23	40	1	47	236	327
Philadelphia Ramblers	64	23	41	0	46	246	301

Baltimore franchise moved to Charlotte after arena fire on Jan. 23, 1956

Johnstown Jets
General Manager - Dave Faunce
Coach - Lloyd Ailsby
Trainer - Harry Andrews
Stickboy - Francis Kabler, Bob Cameron
Colors - Gold, Brown and White

1955-56 Game Results

Preseason Results
No Preseason Games.
Regular Season

Day	Date	Opponent	Johnstown Score	Opponent Score	Attendance	Record
Wed.	2-Nov	Clinton	6	8	2,573	0-1-0
Fri.	4-Nov	at Baltimore	4	1		1-1-0
Sat.	5-Nov	Baltimore	2	4	2,291	1-2-0
Wed.	9-Nov	Philadelphia	4	2	1,734	2-2-0
Sat.	12-Nov	New Haven	7	6	2,337	3-2-0
Sun.	13-Nov	Washington	6	8	1,626	3-3-0
Tues.	15-Nov	at Philadelphia	6	7 (ot)		3-4-0
Wed.	16-Nov	Clinton	11	5	1,707	4-4-0
Thur.	17-Nov	at New Haven	2	6		4-5-0
Fri.	18-Nov	Philadelphia	8	2	2,746	5-5-0
Sun.	20-Nov	at Baltimore	2	5		5-6-0
Wed.	23-Nov	New Haven	7	3	2,592	6-6-0
Sat.	26-Nov	at Washington	2	3		6-7-0
Wed.	30-Nov	at New Haven	2	10		6-8-0
Fri.	2-Dec	at Philadelphia	5	6		6-9-0
Sat.	3-Dec	Philadelphia	5	2	2,702	7-9-0
Sun.	4-Dec	Washington	11	1	1,747	8-9-0
Tues.	6-Dec	at Clinton	1	14		8-10-0
Wed.	7-Dec	Baltimore	8	5	1,775	9-10-0
Sat.	10-Dec	at Washington	5	6 (ot)		9-11-0
Wed.	14-Dec	Philadelphia	6	5	1,838	10-11-0
Sat.	17-Dec	Baltimore	3	1	2,375	11-11-0
Wed.	21-Dec	at New Haven	6	14		11-12-0
Mon.	26-Dec	at Baltimore	3	6		11-13-0
Tues.	27-Dec	at Washington	5	7		11-14-0
Sat.	31-Dec	at Philadelphia **	7	2		12-14-0
Sun.	1-Jan	at New Haven	3	4 (ot)		12-15-0
Wed.	4-Jan	Clinton	6	3	1,871	13-15-0
Sat.	7-Jan	Philadelphia	5	1	2,733	14-15-0
Sun.	8-Jan	at Baltimore	5	2		15-15-0
Tues.	10-Jan	at Clinton	4	8		15-16-0
Wed.	11-Jan	Clinton	4	6	2,246	15-17-0
Sat.	14-Jan	Baltimore	7	4	2,954	16-17-0
Sun.	15-Jan	Washington	3	4(ot)	2,037	16-18-0
Wed.	18-Jan	at Washington	9	8		17-18-0
Fri.	20-Jan	at Philadelphia	6	8		17-19-0
Sat.	21-Jan	Philadelphia	5	4	3,117	18-19-0
Sun.	22-Jan	at New Haven	4	6		18-20-0
Tues.	24-Jan	at Clinton	3	5		18-21-0
Wed.	25-Jan	Philadelphia	7	4	2,303	19-21-0
Sat.	28-Jan	New Haven	1	3	3,610	19-22-0
Sun.	29-Jan	Washington	7	5	2,110	20-22-0
Wed.	1-Feb	New Haven	6	3	2,135	21-22-0
Thur.	2-Feb	at Charlotte	4	5 (ot)		21-23-0
Sat.	4-Feb	Washington	2	1 (ot)	3,076	22-23-0
Fri.	10-Feb	at Philadelphia	4	1		23-23-0
Sun.	12-Feb	at New Haven	7	6		24-23-0
Tues.	14-Feb	at Clinton	3	4		24-24-0
Wed.	15-Feb	Clinton	5	2	2,135	25-24-0
Fri.	17-Feb	at Philadelphia	3	9		25-25-0
Sat.	18-Feb	at Washington	3	4		25-26-0
Sun.	19-Feb	Washington	3	2	2,286	26-26-0
Tues.	21-Feb	at Washington	4	6		26-27-0
Wed.	22-Feb	New Haven	3	2 (ot)	1,835	27-27-0
Sat.	25-Feb	Charlotte	13	2	2,790	28-27-0
Sun.	26-Feb	Clinton	3	1	2,505	29-27-0
Tues.	28-Feb	at Clinton	5	3		30-27-0
Wed.	29-Feb	Charlotte	3	6	2,011	30-28-0
Thur.	1-Mar	Charlotte *	8	3	1,234	31-28-0
Fri.	2-Mar	at Philadelphia	5	6 (ot)		31-29-0
Sat.	3-Mar	at Washington	2	3		31-30-0
Sun.	4-Mar	Washington	9	5	2,604	32-30-0
Tues.	6-Mar	at Clinton	1	4		32-31-0
Sat.	10-Mar	New Haven	3	6	3,744	32-32-0

* Charlotte home game played in Johnstown on March 1, 1956.
** Game played in Atlantic City, N.J.

JETS IN THE FIFTIES

Playoff Results

Day	Date	Opponent	Johnstown	Opponent	Attendance	Record
Tues.	13-Mar	at New Haven	5	6 (ot)		0-1
Thur.	15-Mar	at New Haven	4	6		0-2
Sat.	17-Mar	New Haven	6	0	3,108	1-2
Sun.	18-Mar	New Haven	0	5	2,675	1-3

Attendance Figures

	Dates	Totals	Average
Regular Season Attendance Figures	33	77,379	2,345
Playoff Attendance Figures	2	5,783	2,892
TOTAL ATTENDANCE	35	83,162	2,376

1955-56 Player Statistics

	Regular Season Scoring					Playoff Scoring				
	Games	G	A	Pts	PIM	Games	G	A	Pts	PIM
11 Dick Roberge	64	64	54	118	30	4	2	4	6	0
9 Don Hall	55	43	71	114	56	4	2	3	5	0
10 Ken Coombes	64	33	68	101	34	4	1	2	3	0
7 Alex McDonald	64	39	50	89	44	4	2	3	5	4
6 Ed Ruml	63	34	49	83	16	4	2	2	4	0
8 Paul Olafson	63	31	43	74	10	4	2	1	3	0
2 Bill Gallagher	64	14	54	68	64	4	1	4	5	2
4 Alex Zubatiuk	64	6	18	24	82	4	2	0	2	2
17 Lloyd Ailsby	36	3	18	21	27	4	0	2	2	2
12 Ed Ferenz	57	6	13	19	19	1	0	0	0	0
15 George Harrison	33	5	11	16	10	4	0	1	1	0
14 Joe Cyr	23	4	11	15	28					
3 Orville Kelly	34	6	7	13	145	3	1	0	1	2
14 Al Jacques	16	4	9	13	9					
16 Pentti Hiironen	43	4	8	12	34					
14 Norm MacKay	19	5	4	9	10	4	0	1	1	0
5 Ron Lee	23	4	3	7	20	4	0	0	0	4
15 Emile Nadeau	21	4	2	6	6					
3 Ed Marcale	10	1	3	4	9					
15 Don Rizzo	8	2	1	3	2					
15 Martin Burton	3	0	0	0	0					
5 Len Brown	6	0	0	0	0					
1 Claude Labossiere (g)	7	0	0	0	10					
1 Jim Mattson (g)	18	0	0	0	6	4	0	0	0	0
1 George Anderson (g)	40	0	0	0	0					
Bench					4					
TOTALS	64	312	497	809	675 (-1)	4	15	23	38	16

Regular Season Goaltending

	G	Min	GA	ENG	SO	GAA	W	L	T
1 Jim Mattson	18	1,043	65	1	0	3.74	8	9	0
1 George Anderson	40	2,384	196	0	0	4.93	21	19	0
1 Claude Labossiere	7	426	36	0	0	5.07	3	4	0
TOTALS	64	3,853	297	1	0	4.64	32	32	0

Playoff Goaltending

	G	Min	GA	ENG	SO	GAA	W	L	Shots	Save %
1 Jim Mattson	4	247	16	1	0	3.89	1	3	105	0.868
TOTALS	4	247	16	1	0	4.13	1	3	105	0.861

Ferenz also wore No. 16.
Harrison also wore No. 5.
Kelly also wore No. 16.
Hiironen also wore No. 17.
MacKay also wore No. 3.
Nadeau also wore No. 16.
Rizzo also wore Nos. 12 and 5.

1956-57 Johnstown Jets

(Front, from left) Chuck Stuart, Ron Lee, Jim Mattson, Don Hall, Paul Olafson. (Middle) General manager Jack Riley, Dave Lucas, Roy Hammond, Glen McKenney, Marlow McDonald, Dan Morgan, trainer Harry Andrews. (Back) Bill Binnie, head coach Lloyd Ailsby, Joe Nolan, Ken Coombes, Ed Ruml.

1956-57 FINAL EASTERN HOCKEY LEAGUE STANDINGS

	Games played	Won	Lost	Tie	Points	Goals for	Goals against
Charlotte Clippers	64	50	13	1	101	364	239
Philadelphia Ramblers	64	34	27	3	71	277	233
New Haven Blades	64	31	30	3	65	276	263
Johnstown Jets	64	31	33	0	62	320	290
Clinton Comets	64	23	39	2	48	254	325
Washington Lions	64	18	45	1	37	256	397

Johnstown Jets
General Manager - Jack Riley
Coach - Lloyd Ailsby
Trainer - Harry Andrews
Colors - Carolina Blue, Black and White

Note: Jack Riley coached the team on Dec. 8, 1956 vs. Washington because Ailsby was ill.

1956-57 Game Results

Preseason Results
Score

Day	Date	Opponent	Johnstown	Opponent	Attendance	Record
Wed.	24-Oct	at Washington	3	3		
Sat.	27-Oct	at Charlotte	1	6		
Sun.	28-Oct	Charlotte *	3	6		

* Game played in Raleigh, N.C.

JETS IN THE FIFTIES

Regular Season Results

Day	Date	Opponent	Score Johnstown	Opponent	Attendance	Record
Wed.	31-Oct	Clinton	4	5	2,814	0-1-0
Fri.	2-Nov	at Washington	4	2		1-1-0
Sat.	3-Nov	Philadelphia	2	4	2,868	1-2-0
Wed.	7-Nov	Clinton	8	1	1,824	2-2-0
Fri.	9-Nov	at Philadelphia	2	3		2-3-0
Sat.	10-Nov	Washington	5	1	2,874	3-3-0
Sun.	11-Nov	New Haven	2	3	2,197	3-4-0
Tues.	13-Nov	at Charlotte	4	3		4-4-0
Thur.	15-Nov	at Charlotte	1	3		4-5-0
Sat.	17-Nov	Philadelphia	2	6	2,935	4-6-0
Tues.	20-Nov	at Philadelphia	3	5		4-7-0
Thur.	22-Nov	at New Haven	2	6		4-8-0
Sat.	24-Nov	at Charlotte	5	6		4-9-0
Tues.	27-Nov	at Clinton	7	5		5-9-0
Wed.	28-Nov	Charlotte	5	6	1,629	5-10-0
Sat.	1-Dec	at Washington	7	5		6-10-0
Sun.	2-Dec	Clinton	7	2	1,772	7-10-0
Tues.	4-Dec	at Philadelphia	1	2		7-11-0
Wed.	5-Dec	Philadelphia	6	7	2,127	7-12-0
Sat.	8-Dec	at Washington	4	8		7-13-0
Wed.	2-Dec	New Haven	0	6	1,612	7-14-0
Sat.	15-Dec	Philadelphia	1	4	2,128	7-15-0
Sun.	16-Dec	Washington	13	4	1,256	8-15-0
Wed.	19-Dec	at New Haven	2	3 (ot)		8-16-0
Sat.	22-Dec	at Washington	4	6		8-17-0
Tues.	25-Dec	at New Haven	3	4 (ot)		8-18-0
Wed.	26-Dec	at Clinton	4	3		9-18-0
Fri.	28-Dec	at Charlotte	3	5		9-19-0
Sat.	29-Dec	at Charlotte	3	10		9-20-0
Wed.	2-Jan	at Clinton	3	7		9-21-0
Thur.	3-Jan	New Haven	5	1	1,337	10-21-0
Sat.	5-Jan	Charlotte	9	6	2,685	11-21-0
Wed.	9-Jan	Clinton	6	8	1,871	11-22-0
Fri.	11-Jan	at Washington	3	6		11-23-0
Sat.	12-Jan	Washington	7	5	2,823	12-23-0
Tues.	15-Jan	at Philadelphia	4	7		12-24-0
Wed.	16-Jan	Charlotte	4	5	1,734	12-25-0
Sat.	19-Jan	New Haven	8	4	2,703	13-25-0
Sun.	20-Jan	at Charlotte	5	7		13-26-0
Tues.	22-Jan	at Philadelphia	4	2		14-26-0
Wed.	23-Jan	Clinton	5	2	1,720	15-26-0
Fri.	25-Jan	at Charlotte	3	4		15-27-0
Sat.	26-Jan	Philadelphia	1	0	3,510	16-27-0
Sun.	27-Jan	Charlotte	8	4	2,710	17-27-0
Wed.	30-Jan	Washington	7	5	2,085	18-27-0
Sat.	2-Feb	Philadelphia	3	5	4,172	18-28-0
Thur.	7-Feb	at New Haven	6	3		19-28-0
Fri.	8-Feb	at Philadelphia	4	2		20-28-0
Sat.	9-Feb	at Clinton	4	5 (ot)		20-29-0
Tues.	12-Feb	at New Haven	11	7		21-29-0
Wed.	13-Feb	Clinton	8	6	2,386	22-29-0
Sat.	16-Feb	Charlotte	8	5	3,736	23-29-0
Sun.	17-Feb	Washington	7	4	2,950	24-29-0
Tues.	19-Feb	at Philadelphia	4	7		24-30-0
Wed.	20-Feb	Charlotte	8	4	2,356	25-30-0
Sat.	23-Feb	New Haven	5	4 (ot)	3,853	26-30-0
Sun.	24-Feb	Washington	10	3	2,416	27-30-0
Wed.	27-Feb	at Charlotte	3	6		27-31-0
Sat.	2-Mar	at Washington	9	8		28-31-0
Sun.	3-Mar	Clinton	9	3	2,896	29-31-0
Tues.	5-Mar	at Clinton	2	4		29-32-0
Thur.	7-Mar	at New Haven	2	5		29-33-0
Sat.	9-Mar	New Haven	6	3	3,778	30-33-0
Sun.	10-Mar	Washington	15	5	2,471	31-33-0

** Note: Home games on Nov. 18 and Nov. 21 were postponed because of ice making problems at the War Memorial. The opponent for those two games could not be verified.

91

Playoff Results

Day	Date	Opponent	Score Johnstown	Opponent	Attendance	Record
Tues.	12-Mar	at Philadelphia	5	4		1-0
Fri.	15-Mar	at Philadelphia	1	8		1-1
Sat.	16-Mar	Philadelphia	4	1	4,042	2-1
Thur.	21-Mar	Philadelphia	0	6	4,162	2-2
Fri.	22-Mar	at Philadelphia	2	9		2-3
Sat.	23-Mar	Philadelphia	1	2	3,943	2-4

Attendance Figures

	Dates	Totals	Average
Regular Season Attendance Totals	32	80,228	2,507
Playoff Attendance Totals	3	12,147	4,049
TOTALS ATTENDANCE	35	92,375	2,639

1956-57 Player Statistics

	Regular Season Scoring					Playoff Scoring				
	Games	G	A	Pts	PIM	Games	G	A	Pts	PIM
7 Chuck Stuart	62	58	51	109	64	6	1	3	4	0
9 Don Hall	64	42	59	101	26	6	3	1	4	6
10 Ken Coombes	64	27	63	90	82	6	1	3	4	2
15 Bill Binnie	59	30	50	80	18	6	1	0	1	0
12 Glen McKenney	63	37	38	75	22	6	2	1	3	6
8 Paul Olafson	64	27	45	72	32	6	1	1	2	9
6 Ed Ruml	62	18	52	70	32	4	0	1	1	9
16 Marlow McDonald	53	23	25	48	20	6	1	0	1	6
3 Dave Lucas	63	12	28	40	96	6	1	2	3	4
2 Lloyd Ailsby	46	6	24	30	16	6	0	1	1	0
11 Joe Nolan	38	9	18	27	180	5	0	0	0	23
14 Dan Morgan	17	9	10	19	2	6	2	1	3	0
4 Roy Hammond	27	7	12	19	19	3	0	1	1	5
5 Ron Lee	61	4	13	17	81	6	0	0	0	10
4 Alex Zubatiuk	29	2	10	12	62					
14 Ron Johnson	18	3	5	8	6					
14 Bill Purcell	12	2	3	5	11					
14 Joe Howes	5	2	2	4	0					
11 Guy Periard	8	1	3	4	0					
11 Gerry Frenette	7	1	2	3	22					
15 George Harrison	4	0	2	2	0					
1 Don Oliver (g)	12	0	0	0	0					
1 Jim Mattson (g)	52	0	0	0	6	6	0	0	0	5
TOTALS	64	320	515	835	797	6	13	15	28	85

Regular Season Goaltending

	G	Min	GA	ENG	SO	GAA	W	L	T	Saves	Save %
1 Jim Mattson	52	3,131	222	1	1	4.25	26	26	0	1,416	0.875
1 Don Oliver	12	719	66	1	0	5.51	5	7	0	255	0.815
TOTALS	64	3,850	288	2	1	4.52	31	33	0		

Note: Mattson and Oliver totals for Saves and Save % incomplete – only calculated for available games.

Playoff Goaltending

	G	Min	GA	ENG	SO	GAA	W	L	Saves	Save %
1 Jim Mattson	6	360	30	0	0	5.00	2	4	168	0.848
TOTALS	6	360	30	0	0	5.00	2	4	168	0.848

Nolan also wore Nos. 4 and 15.
Harrison also wore No. 11.

JETS IN THE FIFTIES

1957-58 Johnstown Jets

(Front, from left) Paul Olafson, Don Hall, George Kemp, head coach Lloyd Ailsby, Ken Coombes. (Middle) General manager Jack Riley, Dick Roberge, Fern LaPointe, Doug Orvis, Dave Lucas, Jerry Frizzelle, trainer Fraser Gleason. (Back) Stickboy Steve Gergely, Howard Hornby, Ed Ruml, Alex McDonald, Jim Shropshire, Ron Lee, stickboy Barry Suskie.

1957-58 FINAL EASTERN HOCKEY LEAGUE STANDINGS

	Games played	Won	Lost	Tied	Points	Goals for	Goals against
Charlotte Clippers	64	38	25	1	77	275	243
Washington Presidents	64	36	24	4	76	221	195
New Haven Blades	64	33	26	5	71	204	180
Johnstown Jets	64	31	30	3	65	228	225
Philadelphia Ramblers	64	30	31	3	63	210	211
Clinton Comets	64	15	47	2	32	186	270

Johnstown Jets
General Manager - Jack Riley
Coach - Lloyd Ailsby
Trainer/Spare Goalie - Fraser Gleason
Stickboys - Steve Gergely, Barry Suskie
Colors - Powder Blue, Navy Blue and White

1957-58 Game Results

Preseason Results

Day	Date	Opponent	Score Johnstown	Opponent	Attendance	Record
Fri.	18-Oct	at Niagara Falls Cataractes	7	2		

Regular Season Results

Day	Date	Opponent	Score Johnstown	Opponent	Attendance	Record
Sat.	26-Oct	New Haven	10	3	4,072	1-0-0
Wed.	30-Oct	Clinton	5	3	2,034	2-0-0
Sat.	2-Nov	New Haven	7	1	3,878	3-0-0
Wed.	6-Nov	at New Haven	0	6		3-1-0
Fri.	8-Nov	at Philadelphia	2	4		3-2-0
Sat.	9-Nov	Philadelphia	3	1	4,123	4-2-0
Sun.	10-Nov	Washington	1	5	2,386	4-3-0
Tues.	12-Nov	at Clinton	9	7		5-3-0
Thur.	14-Nov	at Charlotte	4	2		6-3-0
Fri.	15-Nov	at Charlotte	1	5		6-4-0
Sat.	16-Nov	Charlotte	2	4	3,976	6-5-0
Wed.	20-Nov	at Washington	3	2		7-5-0
Sat.	23-Nov	Charlotte	3	5	3,965	7-6-0
Sun.	24-Nov	Washington	7	3	2,244	8-6-0
Wed.	27-Nov	New Haven	4	0	2,655	9-6-0
Fri.	29-Nov	at Charlotte	5	6		9-7-0
Sat.	30-Nov	at Charlotte	0	3		9-8-0
Wed.	4-Dec	Charlotte	7	4	1,960	10-8-0
Sat.	7-Dec	at Washington	2	2		10-8-1
Tues.	10-Dec	at Philadelphia	2	6		10-9-1
Wed.	11-Dec	Clinton	5	2	1,814	11-9-1
Sat.	14-Dec	Philadelphia	2	4	3,666	11-10-1
Sun.	15-Dec	Washington	5	2	2,006	12-10-1
Tues.	17-Dec	at Philadelphia	4	5		12-11-1
Wed.	18-Dec	at New Haven	2	7		12-12-1
Sat.	21-Dec	New Haven	2	3 (ot)	2,507	12-13-1
Wed.	25-Dec	Charlotte	7	4	2,082	13-13-1
Thur.	26-Dec	at Philadelphia *	3	4		Exhibition
Sat.	28-Dec	at Clinton	3	4		13-14-1
Sun.	29-Dec	at New Haven	2	7		13-15-1
Wed.	1-Jan	at Washington	2	3		13-16-1
Fri.	3-Jan	at Charlotte	7	6 (ot)		14-16-1
Sat.	4-Jan	Charlotte	3	7	3,106	14-17-1
Sun.	5-Jan	Washington	2	3	2,477	14-18-1
Fri.	10-Jan	at Charlotte	2	5		14-19-1
Sat.	11-Jan	Philadelphia	3	2	3,570	15-19-1
Sun.	12-Jan	at New Haven	2	3		15-20-1
Tues.	14-Jan	at Clinton	5	2		16-20-1
Wed.	15-Jan	Clinton	5	2	1,858	17-20-1
Fri.	17-Jan	at Philadelphia	4	8		17-21-1
Sat.	18-Jan	New Haven	3	2	3,021	18-21-1
Sun.	19-Jan	Washington	2	1	2,396	19-21-1
Wed.	22-Jan	Charlotte	4	3	2,525	20-21-1
Sat.	25-Jan	at Washington	2	2 (ot)		20-21-2
Sun.	26-Jan	Washington	9	0	2,935	21-21-2
Tues.	28-Jan	at Clinton	1	4		21-22-2
Sat.	1-Feb	New Haven	4	5 (ot)	4,052	21-23-2
Tues.	4-Feb	at Clinton	3	1		22-23-2
Wed.	5-Feb	Clinton	5	2	2,041	23-23-2
Fri.	7-Feb	at Philadelphia	3	3 (ot)		23-23-3
Sat.	8-Feb	Philadelphia	3	0	4,010	24-23-3
Tues.	11-Feb	at Charlotte	3	4		24-24-3
Sun.	16-Feb	at Washington	Postponed – no ice.			
Tues.	18-Feb	at New Haven	5	4 (ot)		25-24-3
Wed.	19-Feb	Clinton	3	1	1,937	26-24-3
Fri.	21-Feb	at Philadelphia	2	4		26-25-3
Sat.	22-Feb	Philadelphia	4	2	4,074	27-25-3
Tues.	25-Feb	at Clinton	3	2 (ot)		28-25-3
Wed.	26-Feb	Washington	4	2	2,734	29-25-3
Fri.	28-Feb	at Washington	3	5		29-26-3

JETS IN THE FIFTIES

Day	Date	Opponent			Attendance	Record
Sat.	1-Mar	Philadelphia	4	0	4,253	30-26-3
Sun.	2-Mar	Charlotte	3	5	4,053	30-27-3
Thur.	6-Mar	at New Haven	3	2		31-27-3
Fri.	7-Mar	Washington **	4	5 (ot)	3,536	31-28-3
Sat.	8-Mar	at Washington	2	8		31-29-3
Sun.	9-Mar	Clinton	2	7	3,409	31-30-3

* Game was played in Atlantic City, N.J.
** Rescheduled game on March 7 was played in Johnstown because no ice was available in Washington

Playoff Results

Day	Date	Opponent	Johnstown	Opponent	Attendance	Record
Tues.	11-Mar	Washington	6	3	2,715	1-0
Wed.	12-Mar	at Washington	1	3		1-1
Fri.	14-Mar	Washington	3	2 (2ot)	3,671	2-1
Sun.	16-Mar	at Washington	0	4		2-2
Fri.	21-Mar	at Washington	2	4		2-3
Sat.	22-Mar	Washington	1	4	4,050	2-4

Attendance Figures

	Dates	Totals	Average
Regular Season Attendance Totals	33	99,355	3,011
Playoff Attendance Totals	3	10,436	3,479
TOTAL ATTENDANCE	36	109,791	3,050

1957-58 Player Statistics

	Regular Season Scoring					Playoff Scoring				
	Games	G	A	Pts	PIM	Games	G	A	Pts	PIM
9 Don Hall	61	34	59	93	29	6	0	3	3	0
11 Dick Roberge	63	37	55	92	39	6	0	1	1	2
10 Ken Coombes	64	31	52	83	31	6	3	0	3	0
8 Paul Olafson	63	26	28	54	38	6	0	4	4	6
6 Ed Ruml	64	14	38	52	46	6	1	5	6	0
3 Dave Lucas	61	11	36	47	55	6	0	3	3	4
4 Gerry Frizzelle	63	14	20	34	27	6	2	0	2	6
15 Bill Binnie	34	13	13	26	8					
7 Ken Grabeldinger	35	6	16	22	6					
7 Fern LaPointe	21	9	11	20	10	6	5	2	7	4
12 Ray Lacroix	32	4	13	17	12					
2 Lloyd Ailsby	40	1	12	13	30	6	0	1	1	18
14 Howard Hornby	30	5	7	12	12	6	2	0	2	4
5 Ron Lee	46	4	5	9	54	6	0	1	1	0
16 Doug Orvis	44	3	6	9	15	3	0	0	0	0
15 Jim Shropshire	23	5	3	8	10	3	0	0	0	2
14 Barry McQueen	22	4	4	8	6					
12 Glen McKenney	16	4	3	7	4					
12 Alex McDonald	17	1	4	5	15	6	0	2	2	0
14 Dan Morgan	5	2	1	3	14					
16 Melvin Melanchuk	11	0	2	2	4					
7 Mike McGuire	1	0	1	1	0					
14 Bob Butler	8	0	1	1	6					
2 Ron McMillan	1	0	0	0	4					
14 Butch Neilson	1	0	0	0	0					
5 Harry Rutherford	1	0	0	0	0					
1 John Spencer (g)	2	0	0	0	0					
1 George Kemp (g)	62	0	0	0	5	6	0	0	0	0
Bench					2					
TOTALS	64	228	390	618	482	6	13	22	35	46

Regular Season Goaltending

	G	Min	GA	ENG	SO	GAA	W	L	T	Saves	Save %
1 George Kemp	62	3,772	213	3	4	3.39	30	29	3		
1 John Spencer	2	120	9	0	0	4.50	1	1	0	59	0.868
TOTALS	64	3,892	222	3	4	3.47	31	30	3		

Playoff Goaltending

	G	Min	GA	ENG	SO	GAA	W	L		Saves	Save %
1 George Kemp	6	381	20	0	0	3.15	2	4		156	0.886
TOTALS	6	381	20	0	0	3.15	2	4		156	0.886

Shropshire also wore No. 7.
McDonald also wore No. 14.
Butler also wore No. 16.

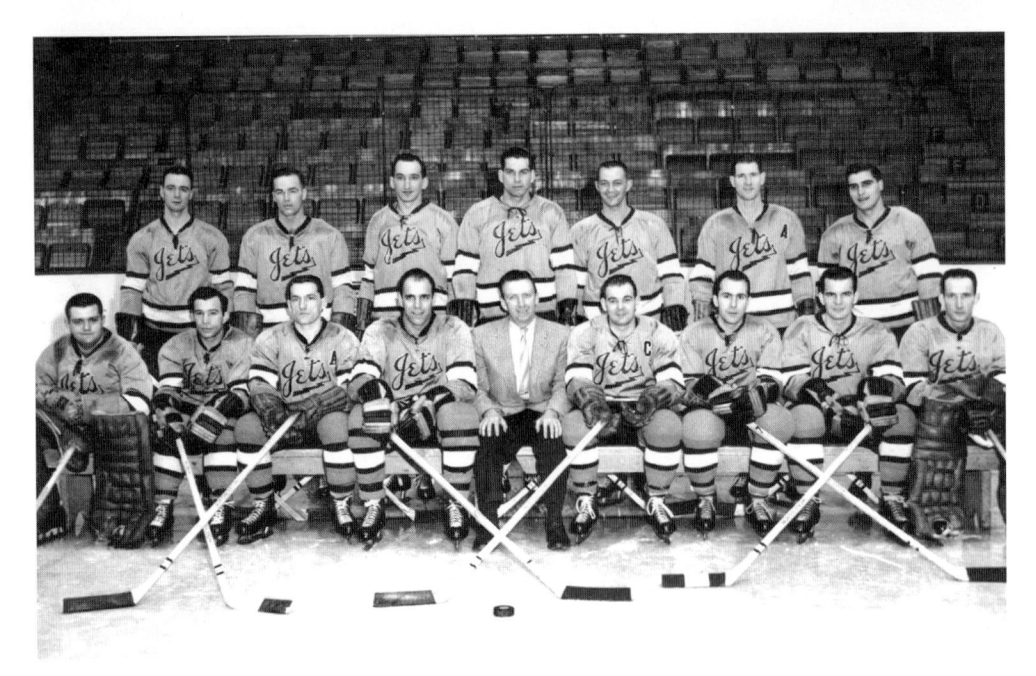

1958-59 Johnstown Jets

(Front, from left) Trainer/spare goalie Frasier Gleason, Ray Savard, Dick Roberge, head coach Steve Brklacich, general manager Jack Riley, Don Hall, Alf Cadman, Ken Coombes, Jim Shirley. (Back) Stan Parker, Dan O'Connor, Ron Rubic, Bobby Dawes, Frank Dorrington, Dave Lucas, Hank Therrien.

1958-59 FINAL EASTERN HOCKEY LEAGUE STANDINGS

	Games played	Won	Lost	Tied	Points	Goals for	Goals against
Clinton Comets	64	41	21	2	84	291	180
Johnstown Jets	64	33	28	3	69	252	223
New Haven Blades	64	29	31	4	62	201	216
Philadelphia Ramblers	64	30	33	1	61	215	237
Washington Presidents	64	29	35	0	58	242	271
Charlotte Clippers	64	24	38	2	50	209	283

Johnstown won Hershey Challenge Trophy as regular-season runner-up.

Johnstown Jets
General Manager - Jack Riley
Coach - Steve Brklacich
Trainer/Spare Goalie - Fraser Gleason
Colors - Powder Blue, Navy Blue and White

1958-59 Game Results

Preseason Results

Day	Date	Opponent	Johnstown	Opponent	Attendance	Record
Sun.	19-Oct	at Welland Seniors	7	11		
Tues.	21-Oct	Welland Seniors *	12	4		

* Game played in Niagara Falls, ONT

Regular Season Results

Day	Date	Opponent	Johnstown	Opponent	Attendance	Record
Sat.	5-Oct	Charlotte	2	4	3,958	0-1-0
Wed.	29-Oct	Washington	3	2	2,143	1-1-0

JETS IN THE FIFTIES

Day	Date	Opponent			Attendance	Record
Sat.	1-Nov	New Haven	7	1	3,596	2-1-0
Wed.	5-Nov	Clinton	4	3 (ot)	2,422	3-1-0
Fri.	7-Nov	at Philadelphia	1	2		3-2-0
Sat.	8-Nov	Philadelphia	7	3	4,027	4-2-0
Sun.	9-Nov	at New Haven	2	6		4-3-0
Wed.	12-Nov	at Clinton	3	2		5-3-0
Thur.	13-Nov	at New Haven	1	7		5-4-0
Sat.	15-Nov	Charlotte	7	1	3,695	6-4-0
Sun.	16-Nov	Washington	5	6 (ot)	2,702	6-5-0
Tues.	18-Nov	at Charlotte	2	4		6-6-0
Fri.	21-Nov	at Washington	4	3		7-6-0
Sun.	23-Nov	Philadelphia	5	2	3,645	8-6-0
Wed.	26-Nov	New Haven	0	4	2,723	8-7-0
Fri.	28-Nov	at Charlotte	4	3		9-7-0
Sat.	29-Nov	at Charlotte	4	5 (ot)		9-8-0
Wed.	3-Dec	Charlotte	5	2	2,616	10-8-0
Fri.	5-Dec	at Philadelphia	4	2		11-8-0
Sat.	6-Dec	Philadelphia	4	1	2,882	12-8-0
Sun.	7-Dec	Clinton	3	1	2,338	13-8-0
Wed.	10-Dec	at Clinton	2	5		13-9-0
Sat.	13-Dec	at Washington	1	3		13-10-0
Fri.	19-Dec	at Washington	1	5		13-11-0
Sat.	20-Dec	Charlotte	9	2	2,407	14-11-0
Sun.	21-Dec	Washington	9	3	1,681	15-11-0
Sat.	27-Dec	New Haven	3	4 (ot)	3,499	15-12-0
Sun.	28-Dec	at New Haven	5	1		16-12-0
Tues.	30-Dec	at Clinton	6	4		17-12-0
Thur.	1-Jan	at Charlotte	2	4		17-13-0
Fri.	2-Jan	at Charlotte	6	5 (ot)		18-13-0
Sun.	4-Jan	Clinton	5	2	2,548	19-13-0
Wed.	7-Jan	at Clinton	2	5		19-14-0
Sat.	10-Jan	Washington	8	1	3,433	20-14-0
Wed.	14-Jan	Clinton	1	3	2,238	20-15-0
Fri.	16-Jan	at Washington	5	4		21-15-0
Sat.	17-Jan	Washington	5	3	3,096	22-15-0
Sun.	18-Jan	at New Haven	4	4 (ot)		22-15-1
Tues.	20-Jan	at Philadelphia	4	3 (ot)		23-15-1
Thur.	22-Jan	at Charlotte	0	1		23-16-1
Fri.	23-Jan	New Haven	3	1	2,966	24-16-1
Sat.	24-Jan	at Clinton	1	3		24-17-1
Sun.	25-Jan	Clinton	4	5	3,516	24-18-1
Wed.	28-Jan	Washington	2	3 (ot)	2,115	24-19-1
Sat.	31-Jan	New Haven	2	0	3,778	25-19-1
Tues.	3-Feb	at Philadelphia	9	3		26-19-1
Wed.	4-Feb	Charlotte	2	1	2,150	27-19-1
Sat.	7-Feb	Philadelphia	7	1	4,082	28-19-1
Sun.	8-Feb	Clinton	2	5	3,280	28-20-1
Thur.	12-Feb	at Charlotte	6	6 (ot)		28-20-2
Sat.	14-Feb	at Clinton	1	8		28-21-2
Tues.	17-Feb	at Washington	5	1		29-21-2
Wed.	18-Feb	New Haven	3	4	2,259	29-22-2
Thur.	19-Feb	at New Haven	1	7		29-23-2
Sat.	21-Feb	Charlotte	4	0	3,507	30-23-2
Sun.	22-Feb	Washington	12	2	2,674	31-23-2
Wed.	25-Feb	at New Haven	3	3 (ot)		31-23-3
Fri.	27-Feb	at Philadelphia	0	3		31-24-3
Sat.	28-Feb	Philadelphia	6	5	3,917	32-24-3
Sun.	1-Mar	Philadelphia	5	6	3,603	32-25-3
Wed.	4-Mar	at Washington	3	11		32-26-3
Fri.	6-Mar	at Philadelphia	4	6		32-27-3
Sat.	7-Mar	at Washington	3	9		32-28-3
Sun.	8-Mar	Charlotte	9	4	2,890	33-28-3

Playoff Results

Day	Date	Opponent	Score Johnstown	Opponent	Attendance	Record
Wed.	11-Mar	Philadelphia	4	6	2315	0-1
Fri.	13-Mar	at Philadelphia	2	5		0-2

Day	Date	Opponent	GF	GA	Att	Record
Sat.	14-Mar	Philadelphia	3	2	3,735	1-2
Tues.	17-Mar	at Philadelphia	3	0		2-2
Wed.	18-Mar	Philadelphia	3	2	2,939	3-2
Fri.	20-Mar	at Philadelphia	4	2		4-2
Wed.	25-Mar	at Clinton	3	1		1-0
Thur.	26-Mar	Clinton	4	5	2,919	1-1
Sat.	28-Mar	Clinton	0	2	3,947	1-2
Sun.	29-Mar	at Clinton	2	0		2-2
Wed.	1-Apr	at Clinton	1	4		2-3
Thur.	2-Apr	Clinton	6	4	3,132	3-3
Sat.	4-Apr	at Clinton	1	5		3-4

Attendance Figures

	Dates	Totals	Average
Regular Season Attendance Totals	32	96,386	3,012
Playoff Attendance Totals	6	18,987	3,165
TOTAL ATTENDANCE	38	115,373	3,036

1958-59 Player Statistics

Player	Regular Season Games	G	A	Pts	PIM	Playoff Games	G	A	Pts	PIM
11 Dick Roberge	64	54	46	100	26	13	8	4	12	4
9 Don Hall	59	36	51	87	2	13	1	9	10	4
10 Ken Coombes	59	28	47	75	46	13	2	4	6	2
6 Stan Parker	64	27	36	63	25	13	4	3	7	0
14 Frank Dorrington	64	20	31	51	29	13	4	2	6	6
4 Steve Brklacich	64	8	38	46	143	13	1	9	10	12
5 Dan O'Connor	64	7	33	40	127	12	2	6	8	12
16 Bobby Dawes	37	14	23	37	24	12	4	4	8	8
3 Dave Lucas	61	10	24	34	96	12	0	4	4	6
15 Hank Therrien	62	12	18	30	57	13	0	1	1	0
7 Alf Cadman	40	11	15	26	20	13	3	3	6	6
2 Gerry Frizzell	30	7	12	19	6					
2 Ron Rubic	21	3	15	18	9	8	3	2	5	0
8 Paul Olafson	31	5	5	10	29					
12 Bob Fleming	24	4	6	10	12					
12 Ray Savard	12	3	5	8	2	13	4	3	7	2
7 Gil MacNeill	12	2	4	6	17					
12 Joe Formica	9	1	4	5	0					
1 Fraser Gleason (g)	1	0	0	0	0					
1 Dan Olesevich (g)	1	0	0	0	0					
1 Joe Shaffer (g)	1	0	0	0	0					
1 Ivan Walmsley (g)	1	0	0	0	0					
1 George Kemp	2	0	0	0	0					
7 Jim Shropshire	2	0	0	0	0					
1 Jim Shirley (g)	59	0	0	0	20	2	0	0	0	0
1 Lou Crowdis (g)						10	0	0	0	6
1 Bill Tibbs (g)						1	0	0	0	0
Bench					4					
TOTALS	64	252	413	665	694	13	36	54	90	68

Regular Season Goaltending

Player	G	Min	GA	ENG	SO	GAA	W	L	T	Saves	Save %
1 Ivan Walmsley	1	60	2	0	0	2.00	1	0	0	22	0.917
1 Dan Olesevich	1	70	3	0	0	2.57	0	0	1	24	0.889
1 Jim Shirley	59	3,550	192	2	2	3.24	31	25	2	1663	0.901
1 Fraser Gleason	1	33	2	0	0	3.65	0	1	0	28	0.933
1 George Kemp	2	120	11	0	0	5.50	1	1	0	63	0.851
1 Joe Shaffer	1	60	11	0	0	11.00	0	1	0	30	0.732
TOTALS	64	3,893	221	2	2	3.44	33	28	3		

* Note: Shirley totals for Saves and Save % incomplete – only calculated for available games.

Playoff Goaltending

Player	G	Min	GA	ENG	SO	GAA	W	L	Saves	Save %
1 Bill Tibbs	1	62	2	0	0	1.95	1	0	26	0.929
1 Lou Crowdis	10	604	25	0	2	2.49	6	4	276	0.917
1 Jim Shirley	2	120	10	1	0	5.50	0	2	44	0.800
TOTALS	13	786	37	1	0	2.90	7	6	346	0.899

MacNeil also wore No. 15.

JETS IN THE FIFTIES

1959-60 Johnstown Jets

(Front, from left) Ed Johnston, John Lumley, Ken Coombes, head coach Steve Brklacich, general manager John Mitchell, Don Hall, Sam Gregory, trainer Bill Higginson. (Back) Dick Roberge, Stan Parker, Dave Lucas, Bob Dawes, Jim Mikol, Frank Dorrington, Dan O'Connor, Remi Lesage.

1959-60 FINAL EASTERN HOCKEY LEAGUE STANDINGS

	Games played	Won	Lost	Tied	Points	Goals for	Goals against
North Division							
Clinton Comets	64	35	27	2	72	244	202
New Haven Blades	64	32	29	3	67	217	189
Philadelphia Ramblers	64	31	30	3	65	226	21
New York Rovers	64	19	44	1	39	205	294
South Division							
Johnstown Jets	64	45	18	1	91	255	176
Charlotte Clippers	64	31	29	4	66	243	244
Greensboro Generals	64	26	33	5	57	229	250
Washington Presidents	64	25	34	5	55	207	252

Johnstown won Mayor Walker Cup as regular-season champion
Johnstown won Atlantic City Boardwalk Trophy as playoff champion

Johnstown Jets
General Manager - John Mitchell
Coach - Steve Brklacich
Trainer/Spare Goalie - Bill Higginson
Colors - Powder Blue, Navy Blue and White

1959-60 Game Results

Preseason Results

Day	Date	Opponent	Score Johnstown	Opponent	Attendance	Record
Thur.	15-Oct	Greensboro *	3	4		
Fri.	16-Oct	Greensboro **	3	0		

* Game played in Stamford, Ontario.
* Game played in Niagara Falls, Ontario.

Regular Season Results

Day	Date	Opponent	Score Johnstown	Opponent	Attendance	Record
Sat.	24-Oct	New Haven	5	2	3,395	1-0-0
Sun.	25-Oct	Washington	5	4	1,978	2-0-0
Sat.	31-Oct	Charlotte	3	5	2,964	2-1-0
Sat.	7-Nov	New York	6	4	3,010	3-1-0
Sun.	8-Nov	at New York	3	1		4-1-0
Tues.	10-Nov	at Washington	3	4		4-2-0
Wed.	11-Nov	at Clinton	3	6		4-3-0
Sat.	14-Nov	New Haven	3	2 (ot)	3,072	5-3-0
Sun.	15-Nov	at New Haven	2	1		6-3-0
Tues.	17-Nov	at Charlotte	2	4		6-4-0
Wed.	18-Nov	Clinton	2	1	1,977	7-4-0
Fri.	20-Nov	at Philadelphia	3	2		8-4-0
Sat.	21-Nov	New York	9	1	3,225	9-4-0
Sun.	22-Nov	Clinton	4	2	2,218	10-4-0
Tues.	24-Nov	at Washington	1	2		10-5-0
Sat.	28-Nov	at Philadelphia	4	2		11-5-0
Sun.	29-Nov	at New Haven	2	1		12-5-0
Wed.	2-Dec	Philadelphia	5	2	2,214	13-5-0
Sat.	5-Dec	Greensboro	2	1	3,335	14-5-0
Sun.	6-Dec	Clinton	2	4	2,260	14-6-0
Wed.	9-Dec	at Clinton	5	2		15-6-0
Sat.	12-Dec	at Clinton	6	5		16-6-0
Sun.	13-Dec	at New York	4	3		17-6-0
Wed.	16-Dec	Greensboro	4	3	2,157	18-6-0
Sat.	19-Dec	Greensboro	6	1	3,058	19-6-0
Sun.	20-Dec	at Philadelphia	2	5		19-7-0
Sat.	26-Dec	at Clinton	1	2		19-8-0
Sun.	27-Dec	at New Haven	1	4		19-9-0
Tues.	29-Dec	at Charlotte	2	2 (ot)		19-9-1
Thur.	31-Dec	at Greensboro	3	1		20-9-1
Fri.	1-Jan	at Washington	7	6 (ot)		21-9-1
Sat.	2-Jan	Philadelphia	0	5	3,749	21-10-1
Sun.	3-Jan	at New York	9	0		22-10-1
Sat.	9-Jan	Charlotte	7	3	3,582	23-10-1
Sun.	10-Jan	Charlotte	10	3	2,441	24-10-1
Thur.	14-Jan	at Charlotte	1	4		24-11-1
Fri.	15-Jan	at Greensboro	4	2		25-11-1
Sat.	16-Jan	New Haven	4	2	3,280	26-11-1
Sun.	17-Jan	Philadelphia	5	2	2,507	27-11-1
Wed.	20-Jan	Charlotte	7	2	1,851	28-11-1
Sat.	23-Jan	Greensboro	3	0	3,399	29-11-1
Sun.	24-Jan	Washington	9	6	2,566	30-11-1
Tues.	26-Jan	at Washington	3	2		31-11-1
Wed.	27-Jan	Philadelphia	3	0	2,285	32-11-1
Sat.	30-Jan	New York	3	5	3,769	32-12-1
Sun.	31-Jan	at New Haven	1	5		32-13-1
Wed.	3-Feb	Washington	7	1	2,179	33-13-1
Sat.	6-Feb	New Haven	4	1	3,737	34-13-1
Sun.	7-Feb	at New York	3	4		34-14-1
Wed.	10-Feb	at Clinton	0	3		34-15-1
Sat.	13-Feb	at Greensboro	7	2		35-15-1
Sun.	14-Feb	at Greensboro	2	4		35-16-1
Tues.	16-Feb	at Charlotte	2	1 (ot)		36-16-1
Wed.	17-Feb	Clinton	4	3	2,323	37-16-1
Sat.	20-Feb	Greensboro	4	2	3,178	38-16-1
Sun.	21-Feb	at Greensboro	6	5 (ot)		39-16-1
Mon.	22-Feb	at Charlotte	2	4		39-17-1

100

JETS IN THE FIFTIES

Day	Date	Opponent		Score	Attendance	Record
Wed.	24-Feb	Washington	6	4	2,286	40-17-1
Sat.	27-Feb	New York	6	1	3,491	41-17-1
Sun.	28-Feb	Washington	2	1 (ot)	2,470	42-17-1
Tues.	1-Mar	at Washington	5	6		42-18-1
Wed.	2-Mar	Charlotte	9	6	1,960	43-18-1
Fri.	4-Mar	at Philadelphia	3	1		44-18-1
Sun.	6-Mar	Clinton	4	1	3,116	45-18-1

Playoff Results

Day	Date	Opponent	Johnstown	Opponent	Attendance	Record
Wed.	9-Mar	at Clinton	1	3		0-1
Sat.	12-Mar	at Clinton	4	2		1-1
Sun.	13-Mar	Clinton	5	1	3,203	2-1
Tues.	15-Mar	Clinton	1	0	2,418	3-1
Thur.	17-Mar	Clinton	2	3	2,942	3-2
Sat.	19-Mar	Clinton	5	0	4,247	4-2
Sun.	20-Mar	at Clinton	0	3		4-3
Sun.	27-Mar	at Clinton	5	1		5-3
Wed.	30-Mar	at New Haven	4	2		1-0
Fri.	1-Apr	at New Haven	2	6		1-1
Sat.	2-Apr	New Haven	2	1	3,904	2-1
Sun.	3-Apr	New Haven	4	1	3,125	3-1
Tues.	5-Apr	New Haven	4	2	2,974	4-1

Attendance Figures

	Dates	Totals	Average
Regular Season Attendance Totals	32	89,032	2,782
Playoff Attendance Totals	7	22,813	3,259
TOTAL ATTENDANCE	39	111,845	2,868

1959-60 Player Statistics

	Regular Season Scoring					Playoff Scoring				
	Games	G	A	Pts	PIM	Games	G	A	Pts	PIM
11 Dick Roberge	64	46	53	99	31	13	7	7	14	10
10 Ken Coombes	62	20	63	83	28	13	3	5	8	22
9 Don Hall	64	33	49	82	17	13	3	9	12	4
8 John Lumley	64	40	35	75	124	13	5	6	11	44
16 Bob Dawes	50	19	40	59	8	13	0	11	11	9
6 Stan Parker	63	21	24	45	13	13	3	4	7	2
14 Frank Dorrington	64	11	30	41	38	13	5	3	8	10
4 Steve Brklacich	62	6	34	40	37	13	1	4	5	16
7 Sam Gregory	49	11	26	37	96					
3 Dave Lucas	63	13	19	32	91	13	3	5	8	17
15 Remi Lesage	63	11	15	26	23	13	6	3	9	4
5 Dan O'Connor	40	6	20	26	112					
2 Jim Mikol	64	11	14	25	101	13	2	5	7	16
7 Clare Wakshinski	15	3	10	13	4	13	1	5	6	5
5 Ted Lanyon	14	4	3	7	25	13	0	0	0	10
16 Rod Gaudreault	4	0	2	2	0					
1 Bill Higginson (g)	1	0	0	0	0					
1 Jim Shirley (g)	2	0	0	0	0					
5 Tony Poeta	3	0	0	0	0					
1 Ed Johnston (g)	62	0	0	0	31	13	0	0	0	0
TOTALS	64	255	437	692	779	13	39	67	106	169

Regular Season Goaltending

	G	Min	GA	ENG	SO	GAA	W	L	T	Saves	Save%
1 Bill Higginson	1	22	0	0	0	0.00	0	0	0	5	1.000
1 Ed Johnston	62	3,717	166	4	4	2.68	43	18	1	1,567	0.904
1 Jim Shirley	2	120	6	0	0	3.00	2	0	0	42	0.875
TOTALS	64	3,859	172	4	4	2.74	45	18	1	1,614	0.902

Playoff Goaltending

	G	Min	GA	ENG	SO	GAA	W	L		Saves	Save %
1 Ed Johnston	13	779	24	1	2	1.84	9	4		315	0.929
TOTALS	13	780	24	1	2	1.92	9	4		315	0.926

Wakshinski also wore No. 12.

Jets captain Don Hall drinks from the Walker Cup after the Jets won the 1960 Eastern Hockey League regular-season title.

1960s Overview:
Golden Age for Hockey and the City

By Mike Mastovich

No decade had more talented Johnstown Jets players than the 1960s. Three players who eventually had their uniform numbers retired skated during the decade.

Don Hall was in the final seasons of a brilliant career that included nine all-star selections and 978 points scored. Dick Roberge, in his prime, had begun playing in the '50s and finished as the minor leagues' all-time leading scorer in the '70s, and many of his best years came in the '60s. Mainstays such as Ken Laufman, John Lumley, Ken Coombes and Dave Lucas played then. Youngsters named Galen Head and Reg Kent had their pro starts late in the '60s, and goaltenders Ed Johnston, Joe Daley, Andy Brown and Marv Edwards were rock solid. Two of the most prominent general managers in Johnstown hockey history served during 1960s, as John Mitchell's two tenures were sandwiched around a four-year term by John Daley.

"We had some characters, like John Lumley, Danny O'Connor," said Johnston, the goalie on the 1959-60 Jets team that won the Boardwalk Trophy as the EHL playoff champion — starting a string of three consecutive title runs.

"Dick Roberge was the comedian on our club," added Johnston, a Boston Bruins goalie and Pittsburgh Penguins coach-GM during his lengthy hockey career. "Guys like Jimmy Mikol, Kenny Coombes — we had some characters. I don't know how (player-coach) Steve Brklacich was able to keep those guys under control. They were great team players, but they enjoyed being with each other."

Team, town rolling

The Detroit Red Wings sent Mitchell to Johnstown in 1959-60, and the Jets won three straight playoff titles until "Big Daddy" was summoned back to the NHL in 1962.

The '59-60 Jets handily won the regular-season Walker Cup. Southern Division winner Johnstown finished with 45 wins and 91 points. That was 10 wins and 19 more points than North Division champ Clinton.

Goaltender Johnston played in 62 of 64 games and helped the Jets win 10 of the final 12 regular-season games. "It was a great year. I played with some great people, and we ended up winning the championship," Johnston said. "I really enjoyed Johnstown. The people were great up there. Our captain was Donnie Hall. Steve Brklacich was our coach and he ended up in the National League with the New York Rangers. That year was good not only for me but for the city of Johnstown. Our attendance was good. It was a special year up there for us."

In fact, the early 1960s might be considered a "golden age" not only for Johnstown hockey but also for the city itself. "Back then, the mills would be going 24 hours a day. Everybody was working then. The city was alive at night time," Johnston said. "I remember a few times I'd go to the bars and the bars would be lined up with beers and shots. The (mill) guys would come in before their shifts and have one shot and a beer before they went into the mills. They'd have a shot and beer before they went home. The bartender never took any money. At the end of the week, they'd pay up on pay day. That was the honor system. That tells you a lot about the city of Johnstown."

The 1960-61 Jets continued to pace the EHL. Johnstown and Greensboro finished with identical 40-22-2 records in the Southern Division, but Greensboro won the tiebreaker. Roberge and Laufman each had 116 points, and Edwards won 40 regular-season games.

Once in the playoffs, the Jets swept both Philadelphia and New Jersey before beating New Haven 4-2 in a best-of-7 championship series. The Jets clinched the title with a 4-2 win at New Haven Arena behind Marv Edwards' 31 saves.

"We had better players. That's why we won," said former Jets defenseman-coach Dave Lucas, a career 100-goal scorer. "Donnie Hall was a good player. Dick Roberge was a good player. The rest of us filled in. I was an all-star. We had good backing. When we needed a player, management seemed to go out and find one. We won three years in a row. We had the best team in the league for three years in a row, and that's why we won."

Lucas' assessment was to the point. It also rang true again in 1961-62. The Jets were runner-up to North Division champ Clinton during the regular season, but Johnstown stormed through the playoffs with series wins over New Haven, Knoxville and Greensboro.

Goalies galore

Edwards played 55 regular-season games in net and won 33. But Edwards created uncertainty and turmoil by abruptly departing the team on Jan. 29, 1962. He headed back home to St. Catherines, Ontario. "I pulled out because I feel I'm hurting the team and that I can't carry my share of the load with my hand in its present condition," Edwards told The Tribune-Democrat when reached soon after he left. Edwards had bruised his right hand. Playing in pain, he allowed 35 goals in a five-game stretch, four of those losses.

Because Eastern League teams typically only carried one goaltender, the league permitted clubs to borrow netminders during emergencies. The Jets used Long Island's Gilles Villemure, Philadelphia's Ross Brooks, AHL Hershey's Dennis Jordan, IHL Muskegon's Jim McLeod, Winnipeg native Gordon Dibley and Windsor's Monty Reynolds over the course of a few weeks. Jim Helkie, who played 11 games for Charlotte in the EHL, joined the Jets for the regular-season finale and beat Clinton, the team that earlier had eliminated Johnstown in the chase for the regular-season title. The Jets used nine goaltenders during the season. Edwards briefly returned but once again quit after he and Mitchell disagreed on whether the goalie should be paid for the two weeks he initially had left the team.

In the playoffs, the 21-year-old Helkie posted 10 wins, a 2.20 goals-against average and

.923 save percentage. The Jets clinched their third consecutive Boardwalk Trophy with a 3-1 victory at Greensboro, N.C., on March 31, 1962. Johnstown won three straight on the Generals' ice after splitting a pair at the War Memorial. Helkie made 26 saves, and Johnstown had goals by Lumley, Laufman and Butch Martin in the clincher.

With Mitchell back in the Detroit system, Johnstown's John Daley took over as GM. The Jets won 155 regular-season games during Daley's four-year tenure, including 41 in 1963-64 when Johnstown claimed the regular-season crown under coach Butch Martin and advanced to the second round of the playoffs before falling to Clinton.

In 1964-65, with Dave Lucas as player-coach, Johnstown again won 41 games but lost to Clinton in the first round of the postseason. Roberge scored 139 regular-season points and Neil Forth, 104. Goalie Joe Daley had 41 wins.

The following year under Lucas, Johnstown won 39 games, with goalie Andy Brown winning 37 of those. Once again, nemesis Clinton eliminated the Jets in the first round.

Mitchell returned as general manager in 1966-67.

The next generation of Jets prolific scorers arrived as well.

New wave of talent

The old guard led the way in 1966-67 as Roberge had 93 points, and Forth, 78. But a youngster named Reg (Taschuk) Kent also collected 68 points. The following season, Kent led the way with a whopping 144 points, followed by Johnny Gofton (122), Galen Head (105) and Roberge (100) as Johnstown produced four 100-point men.

In 1968-69, Kent tallied 139 points, and Head had 121 points, including a then single-season record 67 goals. Jack Dale also had 100 points.

The line of Kent at center, Head at right wing and Gene Peacosh at left wing was formidable. So was the later line of Kent, Head and Gofton.

"That was probably one of the best lines that ever played here," Kent said of playing with Head and Peacosh. "Galen could really shoot the puck and score. I had a sixth sense of where they would be and where they should be. I could get them the puck. If you got in the open, I could get you the puck. I had 105 assists one season.

"Galen didn't have the nifty moves, but if you gave him the puck he'd put it into the corner of the net. Galen and Dick Roberge were probably two of the best right-wing snipers I ever saw in this league." The Kent-Head-Gofton line played into the 1970s.

"We were together the longest. That was a good line," Kent said. "Johnny Gofton was a good skater. He could get up that ice. If he was getting into the open, he'd give you a yell. He'd put it in the net. He knew how to find the open spot."

Tragic loss

The most devastating 1960s moment for the Jets involved the tragic death of popular player Mike Crupi in a Jan. 10, 1969 automobile accident. The University of Minnesota standout played 60 games as a Jets rookie in 1967-68 and 42 the following year. Crupi left quite a legacy, as the Golden Gophers named their annual Most Determined Player Award after Crupi. "One of the toughest things John Mitchell had to endure was when Mike Crupi was killed here," said long-time Tribune-Democrat sports writer John James, who also did media relations work for the Jets. "John Mitchell brought Mike here. He was his project. Mike was everything John thought he would be. He was like a son to (Mitchell). He was tough and he didn't back away from anybody.

"I said very little for two or three weeks to John after the accident," James added. "I knew how badly he was hurting. I don't think he ever got over Mike Crupi."

Jets captain Dick Roberge has scored more points than any other minor-league player in history.

Dick Roberge

'Above the rest'
Roberge Starred as a Player and Coach

By Mike Mastovich

Dick Roberge accumulated numbers and statistics that never will be surpassed in Johnstown. In fact, the right wing from Saskatoon, Sask., scored more points than any other minor-league player in history. Had he skated during a different era, Roberge probably would have advanced to the National Hockey League. But he starred at a time when the NHL only included the Original Six teams.

Roberge played an astounding 17 seasons for the Johnstown Jets. He spent two seasons as a player-coach and two more as a head coach in Johnstown, a role in which he won a playoff championship with the 1974-75 Jets squad that inspired the movie "Slap Shot."

"The people of Johnstown had a lot to do with my staying so long," said Roberge, now a retired golf professional residing in Myrtle Beach, S.C. "I thought the fans knew hockey real well and they supported the team when they could. There were a couple years when the mines were down and the mills were down but you still had your core of people who came every year, 2,000 or so.

"The reason I played so long is I enjoyed playing. I played and coached. I bench-coached. That was really the highlight of my whole life."

'Talented winger'

Highlight. That's an appropriate word to describe Roberge's tenure in Johnstown. He first wore a Jets uniform in 1954-55, when Johnstown played in the International League and Dwight D. Eisenhower was President of the United States. Roberge played until 1972,

> "The people of Johnstown had a lot to do with my staying so long."
>
> — Dick Roberge, who played 17 seasons for the Johnstown Jets.

when the Jets were in the EHL and Ike's former VP Richard Nixon occupied the White House. Roberge played 1,158 regular-season games with Johnstown. He scored 737 goals, 962 assists and 1,699 points. Factor in his Jets' postseason games, and Roberge's numbers increase to 790 goals, 1,044 assists and 1,834 points.

"Dick Roberge was a talented winger. He could put the puck in the net," said seven-time all-star Jets defenseman Dave Lucas, who played in Johnstown from 1956-67 and spent two seasons as a player-coach. "Dick was a little above the rest. Some guys were good players but they just couldn't finish like Dick could finish. Dick was a good scorer and an honest up-and-down right winger.

"Dick was probably the best scorer that I played with in Johnstown," Lucas added. "He had a knack at putting the puck in the net but he could play both ways, forward and back-checking."

Roberge was surrounded by talent. Don Hall played on his line early in Roberge's Johnstown career. Ken Coombes, John Lumley and Ken Laufman also played key roles in Roberge and the Jets' success.

"Kenny Coombes was our centerman and he was the rock," Roberge said. "He was the tough guy who handled all the rough stuff. He was really good. Don Hall was at left wing. That was the line that I remember most. We played really well together."

Those Jets won three straight playoff championships from 1960 to 1962.

"We always had a high-scoring team," said Hall (No. 9), who like Roberge (No. 11) had his uniform number retired in Johnstown. "That was appealing to the fans. Unlike today, we had teams where players stayed. We didn't have huge turnover. Fans got to know some of the players. They took them into their homes, entertained them and became friendly with them."

'We won it all'

The 1960 team won both the Walker Cup as regular-season champion and the Atlantic City Boardwalk Trophy as the playoff winner. Roberge (99 regular-season points), Coombes (83) and Hall (82) were prolific scorers.

"The one year we had Steve Brklacich as coach, John Lumley and Danny O'Connor, and Ed Johnston was in the nets," Roberge said of the 1959-60 champs. "Of course Don Hall was the standout all the years he played. Kenny Coombes, too. We won it all. That was a great year. We were tough. We had good coaching. Brklacich kept the guys on their toes."

A 10-time Eastern League all-star selection, Roberge became only the second professional player to score 700 career goals — joining Detroit Red Wings great Gordie Howe — when he hit the net 6:51 into the first period of a Feb. 4, 1970 game in Clinton, N.Y. Roberge tallied 100-plus regular-season points 10 times. His personal best was a 63-goal, 139-point campaign in 1964-65. Ironically, his most impressive statistic isn't universally recognized in the pro hockey world. Including a season with New Westminster in the Western Hockey League, Roberge scored 756 goals, 985 assists and 1,741 regular-season points in the minors. That point total is more than any minor league player in hockey history.

But hockey historians don't recognize Roberge's record because the Eastern Hockey League inexplicably wasn't considered a pro league by statisticians early on, despite the fact that players earned salaries. "I'm not too much on records," Roberge said. "If it's that way, it's that way. It doesn't bother me."

As his career wound down, Roberge was coach-GM of the 1974-75 Jets in the North

American Hockey League. John Mitchell was executive director of the club, which had a strong affiliation with the Minnesota Fighting Saints.

Coaching and movies

The Jets were mired in seventh place on Jan. 19, 1975 but Johnstown won 23 of the final 31 games to earn a playoff spot.

Once in the postseason, the Jets were unstoppable while beating Cape Cod (3-1) in the first round, edging arch rival Syracuse (4-3) in the semifinals and sweeping Binghamton (4-0) in the championship final. "I got a real charge out of the kids the year we won," Roberge said. "The first half of the year we were pretty bad. I don't know what happened. We came to life and played well down the stretch. It was enjoyable watching those kids play. They were tough.

"The fans were right there," added Roberge, who also is a member of the Cambria County Sports Hall of Fame. "They were wild about that team. It was fun for me."

Roberge's final year in Johnstown was 1978-79. He coached a last-place Johnstown Wings team in the Northeast Hockey League.

He also had a role in the movie "Slap Shot" during filming in Johnstown in 1976. The "actor" Roberge was a referee in several of the Paul Newman movie's memorable scenes. "I only worked a couple days on the movie because on March 1, I had to open up the pro shop in Windber," said Roberge, who took over as Windber Country Club's golf professional in 1967. "I worked two days on the movie. The one scene I faced off at the beginning of the game. The other one I threw Paul Newman out of the game.

"Paul Newman was a very nice man. The kids enjoyed playing in the movie. I think they made more money playing in that movie than they did playing hockey."

Roberge might not have become a movie star, but his spot in Johnstown hockey lore is secure.

Goaltender Ed Johnston led the 1959-60 Jets to the Eastern League playoff title.

JETS IN THE SIXTIES

REPRINT

Eddie Johnston appeared in 63 of 64 regular-season games and was an Eastern League all-star for the 1959-60 Johnstown Jets. Johnston helped his team capture the EHL playoff championship in his only season in Johnstown. The following article appeared on Oct. 17, 2004, as Johnston, in his administrative role with the Pittsburgh Penguins, watched a Johnstown Chiefs exhibition game played in a Pittsburgh suburb:

Eddie and the Jets
Johnston reflects on Johnstown

By Mike Mastovich

Eddie Johnston stood behind the boards and watched through the glass as the Johnstown Chiefs and Wheeling Nailers played an ECHL exhibition game at Blade Runners Ice Complex on Thursday. By his own admission, Johnston became a bit nostalgic while passing the time during the NHL lockout.

After all, the Pittsburgh Penguins assistant general manager in some ways caught a glimpse of his past that night in Harmarville, Allegheny County.

Longtime Johnstown hockey fans certainly remember Johnston as a first-team Eastern Hockey League all-star netminder on the 1959-60 Johnstown Jets' regular-season and playoff championship squad. Johnston appeared in 63 of 64 regular season games for player-coach Steve Brklacich's 45-18-1 Jets.

"I have great memories up there," Johnston said of Johnstown and the then-relatively new Cambria County War Memorial Arena. "I just had a wonderful time and met a lot of nice people. We had a championship club. I have a good friend who still resides there, Donnie Hall. He was one of the premier players in the history of that league. I was very fortunate to play up there that one year and gain the experience."

A successful local businessman who resides in Southmont, Hall said Johnston combined hockey skills and a sharp wit to make a long, successful season even more enjoyable. "Montreal sent him down to get him some experience," said Hall, who scored

> "We had some great goaltenders over the years that I played, but he was by far the guy that could keep you in the game if things were going bad."
> — Don Hall

111

393 goals and 979 points in 11 seasons with the Jets. "He was the only guy that I remember, when guys would cut across in front of the net to deke him or stick-handle by him, he would just reach down and take the puck off their stick.

"We had some great goaltenders over the years that I played, but he was by far the guy that could keep you in the game if things were going bad."

Johnston established Jets regular season (2.67) and playoff (1.85) records for goals against average. The 1959-60 Jets went 28-4 at home during the regular season and 6-1 in the playoffs at the War Memorial. Official EHL attendance records state that 111,832 Johnstown fans watched the championship season that started a string of three consecutive Jets playoff title runs.

"First of all, the support of the fans, they were terrific," said Johnston, one of six Jets all-stars in '59-60. "We had a great team. We had John Lumley (40 goals, 35 assists, 75 points). Steve Brklacich (6-34-40) was our coach. We had Dick Roberge (46-53-99), Danny O'Connor (6-20-26) and Donnie Hall (33-49-82). We had a hell of a hockey club. I had pretty good support."

Johnston won two Stanley Cup rings with the Boston Bruins and spent 16 seasons in the NHL, winning 234 games with Boston, Toronto, St. Louis and Chicago. He was the last goaltender to play every minute of a season — 70 games for the 1963-64 Bruins.

Penguins fans know Johnston better as the general manager who selected Hall of Fame center and franchise savior/owner Mario Lemieux with the first pick of the 1984 NHL Draft. In his 19 years with the Penguins, Johnston served as the head coach from 1980-83 and 1993-97, going 232-224-60 to make him the winningest coach in franchise history. He served as Pittsburgh's general manager for five seasons in the mid-1980s and is in his sixth year as assistant GM to Craig Patrick.

But the NHL lockout has vastly altered the workload. "The NHL was supposed to open up (Wednesday) night," Johnston said. "I'm optimistic, hopefully, that both sides will get together and be able to resolve the situation. It's not good for anybody."

Johnston didn't say whether he might catch another Chiefs game during the down time, perhaps at his former home rink.

"I was back there last year and they're starting to do some nice things with the rink," Johnston said of the War Memorial.

JETS IN THE SIXTIES

Top left: Jets prolific scorer Dick Roberge.

Top right: Captain Don Hall tapes his stick.

Left: The trio of Galen Head, Reg Kent and Gene Peacosh began their careers in the 1960s.

Don Hall accepts the Boardwalk Trophy from EHL President Tom Lockhart.

JETS IN THE SIXTIES

REPRINT

The 1960-61 Johnstown Jets won the Boardwalk Trophy as the Eastern Hockey League team claimed the second of three straight playoff titles and established Johnstown as one of the league's elite. A March 30, 2001 Tribune-Democrat article commemorating the 40th anniversary of the 1961 championship follows:

'We could beat anybody'

By Mike Mastovich

Forty years ago, the Johnstown Jets ruled the Eastern Hockey League and practically had a stranglehold on the Boardwalk Cup Trophy. The Jets were the class of the EHL in 1960-61, winning the second of three consecutive league playoff championships in the days when teams carried only four defensemen, eight forwards and goaltenders, such as Johnstown's Marvin Edwards, played 64 regular season games.

"That team, in my opinion, could have played in the World Hockey Association as a group," said former Jets captain Don Hall, a Johnstown hockey legend whose No. 9 jersey is retired. "Marvin Edwards went on to become a National League goaltender. Bobby Dawes already had been in the National League. Leon Bouchard was a perennial all-star. Dave Lucas was a perennial all-star and one of the best defensemen that ever played in that league. We could walk into anybody's building and beat them. It was one of those years where we figured we could beat anybody on any given night."

In fact, the Jets won the title on March 29, 1961, via their first win of the season at New Haven, Conn., in Game 6 of the Boardwalk Cup championship series. Johnstown had breezed through the first two rounds of the playoffs with three-game sweeps of Philadelphia and Jersey, but New Haven offered a bit more resistance against player-coach Steve Brklacich's Jets.

The Blades won Game 1 at New Haven, 2-1, before Johnstown bounced back with three straight victories at the then 10-year-old Cambria County War Memorial Arena (4-2, 2-0 and 3-1). In Game 5 at New Haven, the Blades jumped back into the series with a 5-3 win. "We're not dead yet," New Haven coach Wally Kullman declared in a newspaper article after the fifth game. But former Tribune-Democrat sportswriter Jesse Isenberg had the last word in the March 30, 1961 edition after Johnstown's 4-2 win in front of 2,800 diehard fans at New Haven Arena.

"They're dead now, and Bobby Dawes, Dick Roberge, Leon (Butch) Bouchard and

115

captain Don Hall performed the embalming job as each netted a goal," Isenberg wrote.

"We had a good hockey club," said Roberge, a former right wing who tied his linemate Ken Laufman for the EHL scoring lead with 116 regular-season points in 1960-61. "When you can go in a place like New Haven and win, that's pretty strong," Roberge, a golf professional who will turn 68 next month, said during a telephone interview from Myrtle Beach, S.C. "That was a real den of iniquity there."

Twist and shout

The 1960-61 Johnstown Jets were tough and talented. They were a close bunch.

"The littlest guy contributed as much as the biggest guy," former forward John Lumley, 69, said from Owen Sound, Canada. "That's why we won. ... We were close. We did a lot of things together. That's when the dance 'The Twist' was big. Our club, we used to take over places (nightclubs) when we went in and twisted."

The Jets were even more graceful on the ice while posting a 40-22-2 regular-season record and 82 points, which tied Greensboro (N.C.) for the Southern Division lead. Roberge and Laufman played on a line with the tough-as-nails Lumley. Roberge had 56 goals and 116 points in 64 regular-season games. Laufman had 41 goals and 116 points. Lumley pitched in with 40 goals, 97 points and 86 penalty minutes.

"When I played there, I took on anyone they wanted me to take on, whether he was big or small," Lumley said. "I've had my (health) problems from all the wars, but it was a wonderful time and I wouldn't trade it for nothing. Johnstown will always be very near and dear to my heart. We had a dynasty there. We had chemistry."

The veteran Hall had 32 goals and 76 points in his next-to-last season of an 11-year career with the Jets. Forward Kenny Coombes had 68 points, defenseman Dave Lucas, 43, defenseman Danny O'Connor, 42, and forward Bobby Dawes, 38.

"That was the year they split Kenny Coombes, Dick and myself up (on the lines)," Hall said. "They put Lumley on that line (with Roberge and Laufman). They needed somebody on that line with toughness. We had three scoring lines. That was something nobody else in the league had."

Marvin Edwards was an ironman in net. The 5-foot-8, 155-pound goalie played 64 games and led the league with a 3.35 goals against average and four shutouts.

Sniper and plugger

Roberge was almost midway through a 17-year career in Johnstown in which he scored a minor-league record 737 goals, 961 assists and 1,698 points in 1,159 games.

His No. 11 is retired. Roberge joined Hall, Laufman and defenseman-coach Brklacich as EHL All-Stars that season. "Hall was always an intelligent player," Lumley said. "Dicky Roberge was what I called a sniper. He could thread the needle with the puck. Coombes was a plugger."

The Jets were diverse on the ice, but the players also showed versatility away from the arena. Forty years ago, hockey wasn't a full-time job. A Johnstown utility company employed Brklacich during the offseason. Hall became a stockbroker and still resides in Southmont. Lumley lived in Johnstown during the summer and worked as an appliance salesman, and Laufman was a paint salesman.

"We had good camaraderie on the team, too," Hall, 70, said. "The guys were all good friends. Those teams were really the class of the league."

"I don't think that hockey club would look too much out of place playing in a lot of these leagues now," Lumley said.

JETS IN THE SIXTIES

Jets defenseman John Nickerson battles for the puck with the Syracuse Blazers goaltender during 1967-68.

Jets captain Dave Lucas.

JETS IN THE SIXTIES

Dave Lucas

'Old Reliable'

Lucas First Jets Defenseman to Score 100 Goals

By Mike Mastovich

Already in his 11th season with the Johnstown Jets, Dave Lucas still was the first player on the ice prior to a practice at Cambria County War Memorial Arena that fall morning in 1966. Lucas didn't have to show up early for a routine workout. After all, he already had established himself as the first Jets defenseman to net 100 career goals.

The native of Downeyville, Ontario, had been recognized as a league all-star seven times. Yet, there was Lucas, moving up and down the rink even before coach Jack McIntyre arrived. "Alone on the ice, Dave set up the nets for practice. He shot pucks into the empty nets and awaited his teammates. Soon his mates joined him and practice was under way," Tribune-Democrat sports writer John P. James wrote.

James' account didn't document a game-winning goal, spectacular save or rowdy fight. But the anecdote revealed plenty about Lucas. His approach never was flashy. The defenseman simply performed his job and did so with consistency. Years earlier, The Tribune-Democrat labeled Lucas as "old reliable of the Blueshirts' backline."

'Do what you had to do'

Lucas joined the Jets in 1956-57 and played in Johnstown through the 1966-67 season. He had 142 goals and 506 points in 730 regular-season games with the Jets.

The EHL recognized Lucas as an all-star in 1958, 1960 and five consecutive seasons from 1962

> "You had confidence in your own ability. You knew the other players. You'd go out and you'd do what you had to do."
>
> — *Dave Lucas*

119

through '66. "You had confidence in your own ability," said Lucas, who spent 30 years as a scout for the NHL's Chicago Blackhawks until his 1999 retirement. "You knew the other players. You'd go out and you'd do what you had to do. We had probably the best team in the league for three years running."

Lucas was part of the Jets' three-year run of EHL playoff championships from 1960 to 1962. He complemented teammates such as high-scoring forwards Don Hall, Ken Coombes and Dick Roberge, goaltenders Ed Johnston and Marv Edwards, and player-coach Steve Brklacich.

"We also had a good team the year when Butch Martin coached (in 1963-64)," Lucas said of a group that led the nine-team EHL in regular-season wins (41) and points (87). "We finished first overall but got knocked off in the playoffs. We were a bit inexperienced. Then, I had a shot at coaching for two years."

Lucas was the Jets' player-coach in 1964-65 and 1965-66. Both teams finished third in the standings, though Lucas led the Jets to a combined 80 regular-season wins. Johnstown fell to the Clinton Comets in the first round of the playoffs both years.

"I wasn't a bad coach, but I wasn't a great coach either," Lucas said.

'30 years scouting'

Lucas' status as a seven-time all-star was a testament to his durability.

"At that time we were only allowed to carry 13 players," Lucas said, referring to an Eastern League rule that would be unimaginable in the current ECHL, where teams carry 20 players and dress 18 on game nights. "You had three lines and three defensemen, or you had four defenseman and two lines and two-thirds of another line. You had a goaltender of course. The trainer usually practiced just in case you had an emergency and he needed to go into goal.

"Steve Brklacich coached for all championships, and he was a defenseman. Danny O'Connor and Jimmy Mikol were defensemen for one year, and Danny Blair for a year and a half. You had to pace yourself. If you were playing three defensemen, you would play the left side one shift and be on the right side the next shift."

The heavy workload apparently didn't bother Lucas. He actually played a hockey doubleheader and appeared in his only NHL game on Feb. 24, 1963.

Lucas skated with the Jets in a 6-4 loss at Long Island, N.Y., that Sunday afternoon. Following the EHL contest, Lucas hopped in a taxi cab and traveled to New York's Madison Square Garden for the Detroit Red Wings game against the Rangers.

Johnstown and Detroit had a working agreement. Lucas played for the Red Wings, who were shorthanded because of Howie Young's suspension and Pete Goegen's injury. After coaching the EHL's Salem Rebels for two seasons, Lucas retired in 1969.

He returned to the game a few years later.

"I started as a scout with Pittsburgh, but they (Penguins) went bankrupt in 1975," Lucas said. "We were all out of a job. That was the very first year of Central Scouting Bureau in the National Hockey League. I was one of nine original Central scouts.

"Three years later the Blackhawks called and needed a guy to take over in eastern Canada. I spent 30 years scouting with them until I retired in 1999."

JETS IN THE SIXTIES

Top: Hockey legend Gordie Howe (second from left) speaks to Johnstown General Manager John Daley (far left), Jack Riley, then-former Jets GM John Mitchell and inductee Don Hall during the 1965 Cambria County Sports Hall of Fame ceremony at the War Memorial.

Right: Jets all-star defenseman Dave Lucas is honored at the War Memorial.

Bottom: Jets and New York Rovers fight for positioning.

121

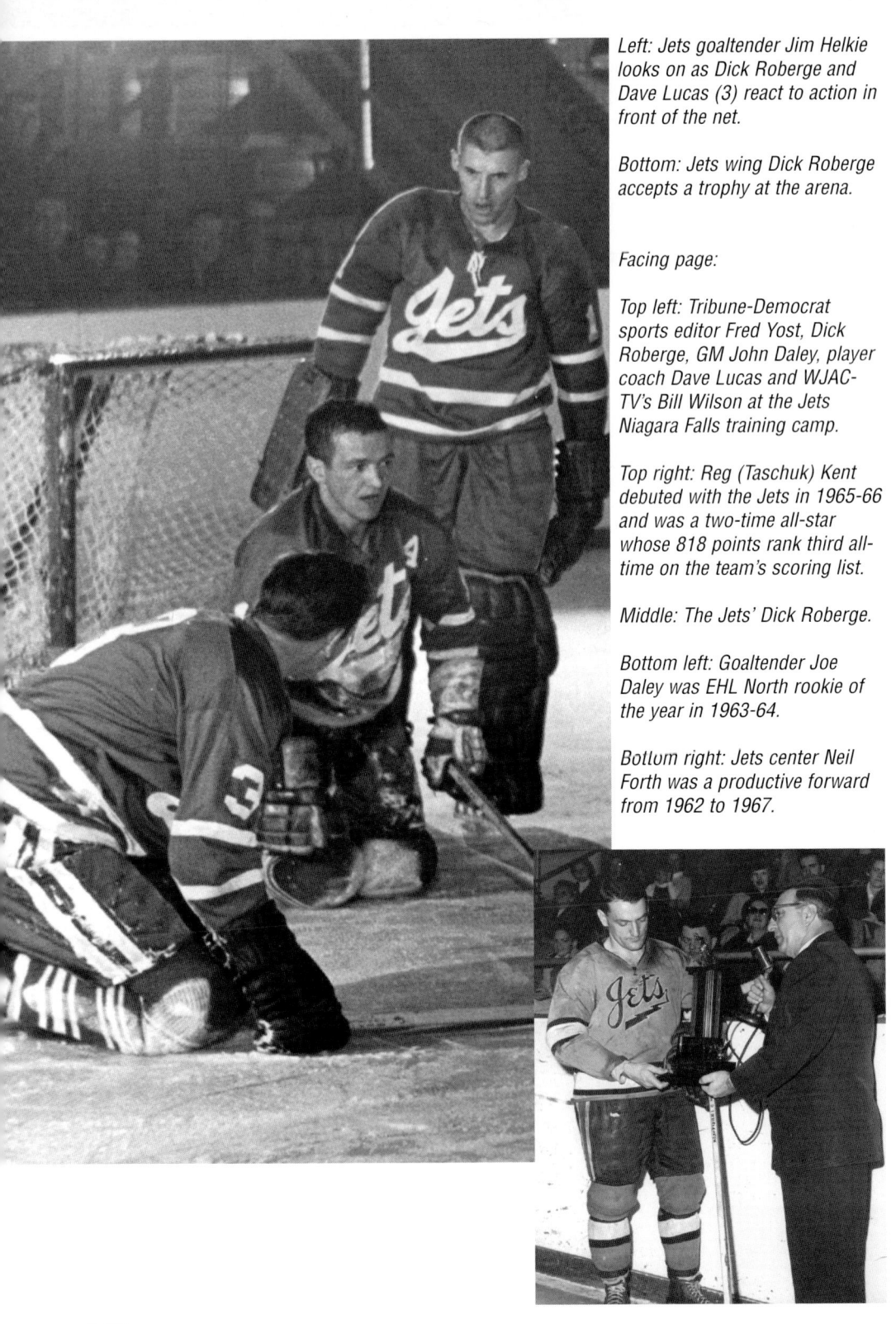

Left: Jets goaltender Jim Helkie looks on as Dick Roberge and Dave Lucas (3) react to action in front of the net.

Bottom: Jets wing Dick Roberge accepts a trophy at the arena.

Facing page:

Top left: Tribune-Democrat sports editor Fred Yost, Dick Roberge, GM John Daley, player coach Dave Lucas and WJAC-TV's Bill Wilson at the Jets Niagara Falls training camp.

Top right: Reg (Taschuk) Kent debuted with the Jets in 1965-66 and was a two-time all-star whose 818 points rank third all-time on the team's scoring list.

Middle: The Jets' Dick Roberge.

Bottom left: Goaltender Joe Daley was EHL North rookie of the year in 1963-64.

Bottom right: Jets center Neil Forth was a productive forward from 1962 to 1967.

122

JETS IN THE SIXTIES

123

Top left: Jet Claude Bernard.

Top right: High-scoring center Billy Ives.

Above: Player-coach Steve Brklacich led the Jets to three straight playoff crowns.

Right: All-star center Ken Coombes.

124

JETS IN THE SIXTIES

1960-61 Johnstown Jets

(Front, from left) Dick Roberge, Don Hall, Marv Edwards, Ken Coombes, head coach Steve Brklacich. (Middle) General manager John Mitchell, John Lumley, Bud Bodman, Remi Lesage, Ken Laufman, Bruno Talbot, trainer Bill Higginson. (Back) Leon Bouchard, Dave Lucas, Bob Dawes, Danny O'Connor, Danny Blair.

1960-61 FINAL EASTERN HOCKEY LEAGUE STANDINGS

	Games played	Won	Lost	Tied	Points	Goals for	Goals against
North Division							
New Haven Blades	64	38	25	1	77	278	221
Clinton Comets	64	30	32	2	62	267	228
Jersey Larks	64	24	39	1	49	215	254
New York Rovers	64	18	45	1	37	196	293
South Division							
Greensboro Generals	64	40	22	2	82	339	257
Johnstown Jets	64	40	22	2	82	273	215
Philadelphia Ramblers	64	32	28	4	68	227	278
Charlotte Checkers	64	25	34	5	55	221	265

Johnstown won Hershey Challenge Trophy as regular-season runner-up.
Johnstown won Atlantic City Boardwalk Trophy as playoff champion.

Johnstown Jets
General Manager - John Mitchell
Coach - Steve Brklacich
Trainer/Spare Goalie - Bill Higginson
Colors - Royal Blue and White

JETS IN THE SIXTIES

1960-61 Game Results

Preseason Results

Day	Date	Opponent	Johnstown	Opponent	Attendance	Record
Fri.	14-Oct	at Welland Warriors	6	3		
Tues.	18-Oct	Woodstock Athletics	Postponed – not rescheduled			

Regular Season Results

Day	Date	Opponent	Johnstown	Opponent	Attendance	Record
Sat.	22-Oct	New Haven	5	4 (ot)	3,433	1-0-0
Sun.	23-Oct	Jersey	7	2	1,916	2-0-0
Sat.	29-Oct	Philadelphia	15	0	2,823	3-0-0
Wed.	2-Nov	at Clinton	1	5		3-1-0
Sat.	5-Nov	Jersey	6	3	2,934	4-1-0
Wed.	9-Nov	at Charlotte	3	0		5-1-0
Thur.	10-Nov	at Greensboro	1	5		5-2-0
Sat.	12-Nov	Philadelphia	3	4	2,960	5-3-0
Sun.	13-Nov	Philadelphia	6	2	1,830	6-3-0
Tues.	15-Nov	at Philadelphia	7	2		7-3-0
Wed.	16-Nov	at Clinton	2	1		8-3-0
Fri.	18-Nov	at New York	7	2		9-3-0
Sat.	19-Nov	New Haven	8	1	2,970	10-3-0
Sun.	20-Nov	Clinton	2	4	1,982	10-4-0
Wed.	23-Nov	Jersey	9	3	2,255	11-4-0
Sat.	26-Nov	at New Haven	1	5		11-5-0
Sun.	27-Nov	at Clinton	1	6		11-6-0
Tues.	29-Nov	at Charlotte	0	2		11-7-0
Thur.	1-Dec	at Greensboro	4	2		12-7-0
Sat.	3-Dec	Greensboro	4	5	2,861	12-8-0
Sun.	4-Dec	Clinton	8	2	1,789	13-8-0
Fri.	9-Dec	at Greensboro	7	5		14-8-0
Sat.	10-Dec	at Greensboro	4	5		14-9-0
Wed.	14-Dec	at Philadelphia	3	1		15-9-0
Sat.	17-Dec	New Haven	4	3	2,275	16-9-0
Sun.	18-Dec	Clinton	3	2	1,458	17-9-0
Mon.	26-Dec	at New York	4	2		18-9-0
Wed.	28-Dec	at New Haven	1	9		18-10-0
Thur.	29-Dec	at New York	3	7		18-11-0
Fri.	30-Dec	at Jersey	3	5		18-12-0
Sat.	31-Dec	Charlotte	2	6	2,173	18-13-0
Sun.	1-Jan	Charlotte	5	4 (ot)	1,408	19-13-0
Wed.	4-Jan	at New Haven	3	7		19-14-0
Fri.	6-Jan	at Charlotte	3	6		19-15-0
Sat.	7-Jan	Greensboro	5	4	2,414	20-15-0
Sun.	8-Jan	Greensboro	4	3	1,745	21-15-0
Wed.	11-Jan	at Clinton	3	0		22-15-0
Fri.	13-Jan	at New York	2	5		22-16-0
Sat.	14-Jan	Jersey	3	3 (ot)	2,789	22-16-1
Sun.	15-Jan	Greensboro	8	6	1,941	23-16-1
Wed.	18-Jan	Charlotte	3	7	1,668	23-17-1
Fri.	20-Jan	at Jersey	4	2		24-17-1
Sat.	21-Jan	New York	6	3	2,629	25-17-1
Sun.	22-Jan	Philadelphia	5	1	2,013	26-17-1
Sat.	28-Jan	Charlotte	5	3	2,835	27-17-1
Sun.	29-Jan	Clinton	3	2 (ot)	2,146	28-17-1
Wed.	1-Feb	at Philadelphia	1	3		28-18-1
Fri.	3-Feb	at Charlotte	4	2		29-18-1
Fri.	10-Feb	at Greensboro	4	5 (ot)		29-19-1
Sat.	11-Feb	at Charlotte	7	2		30-19-1
Sun.	12-Feb	at Jersey	4	5 (ot)		30-20-1
Tues.	14-Feb	New York	4	1	1,631	31-20-1
Wed.	15-Feb	at Philadelphia	4	4 (ot)		31-20-2
Thur.	16-Feb	Philadelphia	5	1	1,685	32-20-2
Sat.	18-Feb	New York	7	4	2,706	33-20-2
Sun.	19-Feb	Greensboro	7	5	2,980	34-20-2
Tues.	21-Feb	at Jersey	0	3		34-21-2
Wed.	22-Feb	at Philadelphia	4	3		35-21-2
Sat.	25-Feb	New Haven	8	2	3,301	36-21-2

Day	Date	Opponent			Attendance	Record
Sun.	26-Feb	Charlotte	1	0	2,329	37-21-2
Mon.	27-Feb	at New Haven	2	5		37-22-2
Wed.	1-Mar	at Philadelphia	5	3		38-22-2
Sat.	4-Mar	New York	4	2	3,301	39-22-2
Sun.	5-Mar	Philadelphia	6	4	2,595	40-22-2

Playoff Results

Day	Date	Opponent	Score Johnstown	Opponent	Attendance	Record
Wed.	8-Mar	Philadelphia	8	0	1,571	1-0
Fri.	10-Mar	at Philadelphia	4	2		2-0
Sat.	11-Mar	at Philadelphia	1	0		3-0
Tues.	14-Mar	Jersey	10	2	1,730	1-0
Wed.	15-Mar	at Jersey	3	0		2-0
Fri.	17-Mar	at Jersey	4	2		3-0
Tues.	21-Mar	at New Haven	1	2		0-1
Thur.	23-Mar	New Haven	4	2	1,994	1-1
Sat.	25-Mar	New Haven	2	0	3,364	2-1
Sun.	26-Mar	New Haven	3	1	2,277	3-1
Tues.	28-Mar	at New Haven	3	5		3-2
Wed.	29-Mar	at New Haven	4	2		4-2

Attendance Figures

	Dates	Totals	Average
Regular Season Attendance Figures	32	75,775	2,368
Playoff Attendance Totals	5	10,936	2,187
TOTAL ATTENDANCE	37	86,711	2,344

1960-61 Player Statistics

	Regular Season Scoring					Playoff Scoring				
	Games	G	A	Pts	PIM	Games	G	A	Pts	PIM
11 Dick Roberge	64	56	60	116	19	12	8	13	21	4
7 Ken Laufman	64	41	75	116	26	7	6	8	14	0
8 John Lumley	64	40	57	97	86	12	7	6	13	6
9 Don Hall	64	31	45	76	14	12	4	9	13	14
10 Ken Coombes	64	20	48	68	51	12	2	5	7	12
3 Dave Lucas	61	9	34	43	68	12	1	3	4	6
5 Danny O'Connor	64	8	33	42	127	12	0	5	5	25
16 Bob Dawes	56	12	26	38	10	11	4	6	10	2
14 Bud Bodman	56	13	17	30	143	12	7	3	10	18
6 Bruno Talbot	64	10	16	26	92	12	1	2	3	7
2 Danny Blair	26	6	13	19	8	12	2	6	8	15
15 Remi Lesage	26	6	12	18	10					
4 Steve Brklacich	63	2	16	18	45	12	0	5	5	12
12 Clare Wakshinski	26	8	7	15	10					
12 Gary Luyben	14	7	4	11	2					
12 Leon Bouchard	14	3	5	8	2	12	5	3	8	0
14 Frank Dorrington	5	1	1	2	2					
1 Marv Edwards (g)	64	0	2	2	32	12	0	0	0	21
2 Ted Lebioda	6	0	1	1	8					
Bench										
TOTALS	64	273	472	746	755	12	47	74	121	152
					(-2)					(+2)

Regular Season Goaltending

	G	Min	GA	ENG	SO	GAA	W	L	T	Saves	Save %
1 Marv Edwards	64	3,895	214	1	4	3.30	40	22	2	1,724	0.890
TOTALS	64	3,895	214	1	4	3.31	0	22	2	1,724	0.890

Playoff Goaltending

	G	Min	GA	ENG	SO	GAA	W	L	Saves	Save %
1 Marv Edwards	12	720	18	0	4	1.50	10	2	343	0.950
TOTALS	12	720	18	0	4	1.50	10	2	343	0.950

JETS IN THE SIXTIES

1961-62 Johnstown Jets

1961-62 FINAL EASTERN HOCKEY LEAGUE STANDINGS

	Games played	Won	Lost	Tied	Points	Goals for	Goals against
North Division							
Clinton Comets	68	45	22	1	91	314	204
Johnstown Jets	68	41	26	1	83	296	255
New Haven Blades	68	34	34	0	68	239	224
Long Island Ducks	68	26	41	1	53	234	266
South Division							
Greensboro Generals	68	36	30	2	74	284	258
Knoxville Knights	68	30	35	3	63	216	256
Philadelphia Ramblers	68	28	38	2	58	265	341
Charlotte Checkers	68	26	40	2	54	226	270

Johnstown won Hershey Challenge Trophy as regular-season runner-up.
Johnstown won Atlantic City Boardwalk Trophy as playoff champion.

Johnstown Jets
General Manager - John Mitchell
Coach - Steve Brklacich
Trainer/Spare Goalie - Carl Buschert (training camp); Ken "Gunnar" Garrett - from Oct. 17.
Colors - Royal Blue and White

1961-62 Game Results
Preseason Results
No Preseason Games
Note: Johnstown was to play Galt, Ontario – the Canadian entry in the World Championship Tournament – on Mon., Oct. 15 in Hespeler, Ontario. The game was cancelled due to ice refrigeration problems.

129

Regular Season Results

Day	Date	Opponent	Johnstown	Opponent	Attendance	Record
Fri.	20-Oct	Long Island	8	2	2,283	1-0-0
Sat.	21-Oct	New Haven	4	2	2,643	2-0-0
Sun.	22-Oct	at Long Island	3	4		2-1-0
Wed.	25-Oct	Knoxville	9	3	1,664	3-1-0
Sat.	28-Oct	Philadelphia	3	2	2,717	4-1-0
Tues.	31-Oct	Charlotte	6	4	1,554	5-1-0
Wed.	1-Nov	Greensboro	4	2	1,644	6-1-0
Sat.	4-Nov	New Haven	1	2	3,254	6-2-0
Sun.	5-Nov	at New Haven	6	1		7-2-0
Tues.	7-Nov	at Philadelphia	6	5 (ot)		8-2-0
Wed.	8-Nov	at Clinton	0	5		8-3-0
Sat.	11-Nov	Long Island	8	3	2,612	9-3-0
Sun.	12-Nov	Philadelphia	7	1	1,890	10-3-0
Wed.	15-Nov	Knoxville	6	1	1,671	11-3-0
Sat.	18-Nov	Long Island	6	4	2,300	12-3-0
Sun.	19-Nov	at Long Island	3	1		13-3-0
Wed.	22-Nov	Greensboro	3	5	1,802	13-4-0
Thur.	23-Nov	Greensboro	10	4	2,430	14-4-0
Fri.	24-Nov	at Knoxville	0	0 (ot)		14-4-1
Sat.	25-Nov	at Greensboro	3	8		14-5-1
Sun.	26-Nov	at Greensboro	2	4		14-6-1
Wed.	29-Nov	at New Haven	4	3		15-6-1
Fri.	1-Dec	Clinton	5	1	2,278	16-6-1
Sat.	2-Dec	New Haven	6	4	2,535	17-6-1
Sun.	3-Dec	at Long Island	4	3		18-6-1
Sat.	9-Dec	at Charlotte	3	0		19-6-1
Sun.	10-Dec	at Greensboro	1	4		19-7-1
Tues.	12-Dec	Long Island	7	1	1,424	20-7-1
Sat.	16-Dec	at Clinton	6	5		21-7-1
Sun.	17-Dec	at Long Island	1	3		21-8-1
Fri.	22-Dec	at Philadelphia	1	6		21-9-1
Sat.	23-Dec	New Haven	6	2	2,030	22-9-1
Wed.	27-Dec	at Clinton	3	4 (ot)		22-10-1
Fri.	29-Dec	at Charlotte	2	3		22-11-1
Mon.	1-Jan	at Charlotte	1	3		22-12-1
Tues.	2-Jan	at Knoxville	3	4		22-13-1
Fri.	5-Jan	at Knoxville	4	5 (ot)		22-14-1
Sat.	6-Jan	Philadelphia	13	5	2,329	23-14-1
Sun.	7-Jan	Clinton	4	1	2,103	24-14-1
Wed.	10-Jan	at New Haven	5	3		25-14-1
Sat.	13-Jan	Charlotte	2	8	2,484	25-15-1
Sun.	14-Jan	Clinton	5	2	1,853	26-15-1
Wed.	17-Jan	Knoxville	6	4	1,443	27-15-1
Sat.	20-Jan	Long Island	8	1	2,139	28-15-1
Sun.	21-Jan	Greensboro	8	3	3,602	29-15-1
Wed.	24-Jan	at Clinton	3	11		29-16-1
Thur.	25-Jan	at Long Island	4	2		30-16-1
Fri.	26-Jan	at Philadelphia	3	8		30-17-1
Sat.	27-Jan	New Haven	0	5	2,511	30-18-1
Sun.	28-Jan	at New Haven	5	9		30-19-1
Wed.	31-Jan	at New Haven	4	2		31-19-1
Fri.	2-Feb	at Philadelphia	2	7		31-20-1
Sat.	3-Feb	Charlotte	6	2	2,303	32-20-1
Sun.	4-Feb	Clinton	4	3	2,653	33-20-1
Wed.	7-Feb	at Clinton	6	10		33-21-1
Sat.	10-Feb	Philadelphia	9	3	2,593	34-21-1
Sun.	11-Feb	Clinton	6	1	3,451	35-21-1
Tues.	13-Feb	at Charlotte	7	4		36-21-1
Wed.	14-Feb	at Knoxville	0	7		36-22-1
Fri.	16-Feb	at Greensboro	1	3		36-23-1
Sat.	17-Feb	Knoxville	2	0	2,262	37-23-1
Sun.	18-Feb	Charlotte	5	4 (ot)	2,393	38-23-1
Wed.	21-Feb	at Clinton	0	8		38-24-1
Thur.	22-Feb	at New Haven	3	5		38-25-1
Sat.	24-Feb	Long Island	8	2	2,074	39-25-1
Sun.	25-Feb	at Long Island	3	11		39-26-1
Sat.	3-Mar	New Haven	5	4	2,009	40-26-1
Sun.	4-Mar	Clinton	4	3	2,320	41-26-1

JETS IN THE SIXTIES

Playoff Results

Day	Date	Opponent	Score Johnstown	Opponent	Attendance	Record
Wed.	7-Mar	at New Haven	4	7		0-1
Fri.	9-Mar	New Haven	3	1	2,035	1-1
Sat.	10-Mar	New Haven	5	0	2,535	2-1
Sun.	11-Mar	at New Haven	3	4		2-2
Tues.	13-Mar	New Haven	7	1	2,035	3-2
Thur.	15-Mar	at Knoxville	1	6		0-1
Sat.	17-Mar	Knoxville	2	0	2,713	1-1
Sun.	18-Mar	Knoxville	3	0	2,356	2-1
Tues.	20-Mar	at Knoxville	0	2		2-2
Thur.	22-Mar	Knoxville	6	1	2,234	3-2
Sat.	24-Mar	Greensboro	6	1	2,726	1-0
Sun.	25-Mar	Greensboro	4	5	2,174	1-1
Wed.	28-Mar	at Greensboro	4	3		2-1
Fri.	30-Mar	at Greensboro	4	2		3-1
Sat.	31-Mar	at Greensboro	3	1		4-1

Attendance Figures

	Dates	Totals	Average
Regular Season Attendance Figures	34	77,253	2,272
Playoff Attendance Figures	8	18,808	2,351
TOTAL ATTENDANCE	42	96,061	2,287

1961-62 Player Statistics

	Regular Season Scoring					Playoff Scoring				
	Games	G	A	Pts	PIM	Games	G	A	Pts	PIM
7 Ken Laufman	68	38	90	128	25	15	6	15	21	8
8 John Lumley	68	58	59	117	105	15	9	8	17	8
11 Dick Roberge	65	51	66	117	21	7	5	4	9	2
15 Butch Martin	65	37	41	78	37	7	4	8	12	0
9 Don Hall	66	28	44	72	23	7	4	5	9	2
6 Danny Patrick	68	21	41	62	102	14	5	4	9	13
16 Bob Dawes	68	16	30	46	24	15	6	8	14	2
3 Dave Lucas	68	14	30	44	70	15	2	5	7	8
4 Steve Brklacich	68	2	35	37	47	15	2	4	6	14
12 Leon Bouchard	68	11	22	33	14	15	2	3	5	4
2 Danny Blair	61	7	25	32	30	15	0	7	7	2
14 Don Curry	43	5	9	14	67					
10 Ken Coombes	11	3	5	8	11					
5 Jim Maxwell	1	3	2	5	0	8	4	6	10	0
14 Bud Bodman	14	2	3	5	31	14	1	1	2	10
10 Moe Savard	1	0	1	1	0	8	3	8	11	0
1 Marv Edwards (g)	55	0	1	1	12					
1 Ken Garrett (g)	1	0	0	0	0					
1 Jim Helkie (g)	1	0	0	0	0	15	0	0	0	0
1 Jim McLeod (g)	1	0	0	0	0					
1 Gilles Villemure (g)	1	0	0	0	0					
1 Ross Brooks (g)	2	0	0	0	0					
1 Gord Dibley (g)	2	0	0	0	0					
1 Monty Reynolds (g)	2	0	0	0	0					
1 Dennis Jordan (g)	3	0	0	0	0					
15 Ken Murphy						8	2	0	2	9
TOTALS	68	296	504	800	619	15	55	86	141	82

Regular Season Goaltending

	G	Min	GA	ENG	SO	GAA	W	L	T	Saves	Save %
1 Gord Dibley	2	120	4	0	0	2.00	2	0	0	58	0.935
1 Gilles Villemure	1	60	2	0	0	2.00	1	0	0	25	0.926
1 Jim Helkie	1	60	3	0	0	3.00	1	0	0	24	0.889
1 Jim McLeod	1	60	3	0	0	3.00	1	0	0	20	0.870
1 Marv Edwards	55	3,321	193	1	3	3.50	33	21	1	1,440	0.882
1 Ken Garrett	1	60	4	0	0	4.00	1	0	0	28	0.875
1 Ross Brooks	2	120	12	0	0	6.00	1	1	0	1	0.855
1 Monty Reynolds	2	120	13	0	0	6.50	1	1	0	60	0.822
1 Dennis Jordan	3	180	20	0	0	6.67	0	3	0	125	0.862
TOTALS	68	4,101	254	1	3	3.73	41	26	1	851	0.879

Playoff Goaltending

	G	Min	GA	ENG	SO	GAA	W	L	Saves	Save %
1 Jim Helkie	15	899	33	1	3	2.20	10	5	393	0.923
TOTALS	15	900	33	1	3	2.27	10	5	393	0.923

1962-63 Johnstown Jets

(Front, from left) Jim Helkie, Danny Patrick, Dave Lucas, general manager John Daley, head coach Floyd "Butch" Martin, Neil Forth, Don Duke, trainer/spare goalie Ken "Gunner" Garrett. (Back) Dick Roberge, Buddy Bodman, Danny Blair, Billy Ives, Tony Bukovich, Dave Garner, Gary Collins, Don Atamanchuk.

1962-63 FINAL EASTERN HOCKEY LEAGUE STANDINGS

	Games played	Won	Lost	Tied	Points	Goals for	Goals against
North Division							
Clinton Comets	68	38	24	6	82	289	186
Long Island Ducks	68	36	28	4	76	287	261
Johnstown Jets	68	34	31	3	71	254	309
Philadelphia Ramblers	68	29	36	3	61	287	304
New Haven Blades	68	27	40	1	55	249	293
South Division							
Greensboro Generals	68	40	26	2	82	305	263
Knoxville Knights	68	37	28	3	77	295	245
Charlotte Checkers	68	35	31	2	72	242	264
Nashville Dixie Flyers	68	16	48	4	36	181	264

Johnstown Jets
General Manager - John Daley
Coach - Floyd "Butch" Martin
Trainer/Spare Goalie - Ken "Gunner" Garrett
Colors - Royal Blue and White

1962-63 Game Results

Preseason Results
Score

Day	Date	Opponent	Johnstown	Opponent	Attendance	Record
Thur.	11-Oct	Nashville *	4	3		
Sun.	14-Oct	Nashville **	5	3		

* Played in Niagara Falls, Ontario.
** Played in Port Colborne, Ontario.

Regular Season Results

Day	Date	Opponent	Johnstown	Opponent	Attendance	Record
Fri.	19-Oct	Clinton	1	6	2,071	0-1-0
Sat.	20-Oct	New Haven	7	4	1,649	1-1-0
Sun.	21-Oct	at Philadelphia	7	3		2-1-0
Wed.	24-Oct	Nashville	4	2	1,512	3-1-0
Sat.	27-Oct	Philadelphia	6	4	1,940	4-1-0
Sun.	28-Oct	at Long Island	5	8		4-2-0
Tues.	30-Oct	at Philadelphia	1	8		4-3-0
Sat.	3-Nov	New Haven	5	1	2,112	5-3-0
Sun.	4-Nov	at New Haven	2	6		5-4-0
Fri.	9-Nov	at Clinton	3	5		5-5-0
Sat.	10-Nov	Long Island	4	1	1,969	6-5-0
Sun.	11-Nov	Clinton	3	1	1,800	7-5-0
Wed.	14-Nov	New Haven	4	3 (ot)	1,316	8-5-0
Sat.	17-Nov	Charlotte	3	1	2,382	9-5-0
Sun.	18-Nov	Knoxville	6	3	1,971	10-5-0
Wed.	21-Nov	Philadelphia	5	4 (ot)	1,921	11-5-0
Thur.	22-Nov	Clinton	6	3	2,579	12-5-0
Fri.	23-Nov	at Greensboro	2	5		12-6-0
Sat.	24-Nov	at Charlotte	1	6		12-7-0
Sun.	25-Nov	at Nashville	3	8		12-8-0
Wed.	28-Nov	at Knoxville	6	6 (ot)		12-8-1
Thur.	29-Nov	at Nashville	3	2 (ot)		13-8-1
Sat.	1-Dec	Philadelphia	8	5	2,502	14-8-1
Wed.	5-Dec	at Greensboro	3	5		14-9-1
Fri.	7-Dec	at Charlotte	1	5		14-10-1
Sat.	8-Dec	at Knoxville	5	7		14-11-1
Sun.	9-Dec	at Nashville	3	2 (ot)		15-11-1
Sat.	15-Dec	Charlotte	3	7	1,946	15-12-1
Sun.	16-Dec	at Philadelphia	2	7		15-13-1
Fri.	21-Dec	at Philadelphia	2	4		15-14-1
Sat.	22-Dec	New Haven	4	3	1,558	16-14-1
Sun.	23-Dec	Clinton	7	1	1,431	17-14-1
Wed.	26-Dec	at New Haven	6	13		17-15-1
Thur.	27-Dec	at Long Island	2	10		17-16-1
Sat.	29-Dec	at Clinton	2	2 (ot)		17-16-2
Sun.	30-Dec	at Long Island	5	4		18-16-2
Mon.	31-Dec	Clinton	3	3 (ot)	1,545	18-16-3
Wed.	2-Jan	at Clinton	4	3		19-16-3
Thur.	3-Jan	at New Haven	1	3		19-17-3
Sat.	5-Jan	Long Island	6	5	2,519	20-17-3
Sun.	6-Jan	at New Haven	5	3		21-17-3
Sat.	12-Jan	New Haven	8	2	2,910	22-17-3
Wed.	16-Jan	at New Haven	2	4		22-18-3
Sat.	19-Jan	Greensboro	1	6	2,950	22-19-3
Sun.	20-Jan	Clinton	3	7	3,027	22-20-3
Wed.	23-Jan	at Clinton	0	5		22-21-3
Thur.	24-Jan	at Long Island	3	10		22-22-3
Sat.	26-Jan	Philadelphia	6	3	1,852	23-22-3
Sun.	27-Jan	Charlotte	4	1	1,510	24-22-3
Tues.	29-Jan	at Philadelphia	3	14		24-23-3
Wed.	30-Jan	at Long Island		Postponed – rescheduled for Feb. 12		
Sat.	2-Feb	Long Island	5	2	2,050	25-23-3
Sun.	3-Feb	Nashville	5	2	1,551	26-23-3
Tues.	5-Feb	at Charlotte	5	3		27-23-3
Wed.	6-Feb	at Knoxville	3	6		27-24-3
Fri.	8-Feb	at Greensboro	1	5		27-25-3
Sat.	9-Feb	Philadelphia	7	5	1,852	28-25-3
Sun.	10-Feb	Knoxville	4	3	2,210	29-25-3
Tues.	12-Feb	Long Island	2	3	1,302	29-26-3
Wed.	13-Feb	Greensboro	4	2	1,625	30-26-3
Sat.	16-Feb	Greensboro	3	5	2,332	30-27-3
Sun.	17-Feb	Knoxville	3	2	2,010	31-27-3
Wed.	20-Feb	Nashville	2	1	1,269	32-27-3
Fri.	22-Feb	at Clinton	1	10		32-28-3
Sat.	23-Feb	Philadelphia	7	4	2,125	33-28-3

Day	Date	Opponent				Attendance	Record
Sun.	24-Feb	at Long Island	4	6			33-29-3
Wed.	27-Feb	at Clinton	5	4 (ot)			34-29-3
Fri.	1-Mar	at Philadelphia	2	7			34-30-3
Sat.	2-Mar	Long Island	2	5		3101	34-31-3

Playoff Results

Day	Date	Opponent	Johnstown	Opponent	Attendance	Record
Tues.	5-Mar	at Long Island	2	4		0-1
Sat.	9-Mar	Long Island	0	1	2,702	0-2
Sun.	10-Mar	at Long Island	3	5		0-3

Attendance Figures

	Dates	Totals	Average
Regular Season Attendance Totals	34	68,399	2,012
Playoff Attendance Totals	1	2,702	2,702
TOTAL ATTENDANCE	35	71,101	2,031

1962-63 Player Statistics

	Regular Season Scoring					Playoff Scoring				
	Games	G	A	Pts	PIM	Games	G	A	Pts	PIM
15 Floyd "Butch" Martin	68	44	65	109	67	3	2	1	3	0
11 Dick Roberge	68	40	59	99	35	3	0	2	2	4
6 Danny Patrick	63	25	41	66	93	3	0	0	0	0
5 Don Atamanchuk	59	27	28	55	23	3	1	0	1	4
14 Buddy Bodman	68	18	32	50	143	3	0	1	1	4
12 Billy Ives	57	22	27	49	6	3	0	0	0	0
7 Tony Bukovich	64	23	25	48	80	3	1	0	1	2
3 Dave Lucas	68	15	33	48	54	3	0	1	1	6
10 Carlo Rossi	38	9	16	25	15					
4 Neil Forth	21	10	14	24	25	3	0	1	1	0
2 Danny Blair	68	4	16	20	14	3	0	0	0	0
4 Larry Ziliotto	45	3	13	16	96					
12 Ken Saunders	9	3	10	13	10					
10 Don Duke	11	5	6	11	4	3	1	0	1	0
8 Larry McLaren	20	0	11	11	2					
8 Gary Collins	17	2	4	6	11	3	0	2	2	0
5 Don Curry	7	2	2	4	6					
6 Jacques Larchevesque	7	0	4	4	9					
8 Dave Garner	16	2	0	2	25					
10 Junior Brash	6	0	2	2	0					
10 Dave Megill	3	0	0	0	5					
1 Bob Wardle (g)	4	0	0	0	0					
1 Jim Helkie (g)	64	0	0	0	8	3	0	0	0	0
Bench					4					
TOTALS	68	254	408 (+1)	662	735	3	5	8	13	20

Regular Season Goaltending

	G	Min	GA	ENG	SO	GAA	W	L	T	Saves	Save %
1 Jim Helkie	64	3,897	279	3	0	4.35	32	29	2	1,925	0.876
1 Bob Wardle	4	240	27	0	0	6.75	2	2	0	97	0.782
TOTALS	68	4,137	306	3	0	4.48	34	31	2		

Note: Helkie's totals for Saves and Save % not complete – only calculated for available games.

Playoff Goaltending

	G	Min	GA	ENG	SO	GAA	W	L	Saves	Save %
1 Jim Helkie	3	179	9	1	0	3.02	0	3	83	0.902
TOTALS	3	180	9	1	0	3.33	0	3	83	0.892

JETS IN THE SIXTIES

1963-64 Johnstown Jets

(Front, from left) Joe Daley, Dave Lucas, general manager John Daley, head coach Floyd "Butch" Martin, trainer/spare goaltender Ken "Gunner" Garrett. (Middle) Danny Patrick, Dick Roberge, Tony Bukovich, Billy Ives, Larry Johnston, Arlie Parker. (Back) Jean-Claude Lepage, Jack Faulkner, Ernie Dyda, Neil Forth.

1963-64 FINAL EASTERN HOCKEY LEAGUE STANDINGS

	Games played	Won	Lost	Tied	Points	Goals for	Goals against
North Division							
Johnstown Jets	72	41	26	5	87	297	245
Clinton Comets	72	37	28	7	81	289	215
Long Island Ducks	72	32	34	6	70	245	263
New Haven Blades	72	27	42	3	57	252	296
Philadelphia Ramblers	72	21	44	7	49	261	374
South Division							
Greensboro Generals	72	41	29	2	84	294	257
Knoxville Knights	72	40	31	1	81	340	289
Nashville Dixie Flyers	72	37	31	4	78	231	242
Charlotte Checkers	72	30	41	1	61	276	304

Johnstown Jets
General Manager - John Daley
Coach - Floyd "Butch" Martin
Trainer/Spare Goalie - Ken "Gunner" Garrett
Colors - Royal Blue and White

1963-64 Game Results

Preseason Results

Day	Date	Opponent	Score Johnstown	Opponent	Attendance	Record
Sat.	12-Oct	at Philadelphia	4	2		
Tues.	15-Oct	Philadelphia *	6	1		

* Played in Norristown, Pa.

135

Regular Season Results

Day	Date	Opponent	Johnstown	Opponent	Attendance	Record
Thur.	17-Oct	Philadelphia	3	2	1,250	1-0-0
Fri.	18-Oct	at Long Island	6	3		2-0-0
Sat.	19-Oct	New Haven	4	2	1,750	3-0-0
Wed.	23-Oct	Greensboro	2	4	1,338	3-1-0
Fri.	25-Oct	at Clinton	3	2		4-1-0
Sat.	26-Oct	Long Island	7	5	1,867	5-1-0
Sun.	27-Oct	at Long Island	2	4		5-2-0
Wed.	30-Oct	Clinton	6	4	1,250	6-2-0
Fri.	1-Nov	at Philadelphia	8	0		7-2-0
Sat.	2-Nov	Philadelphia	1	2	2,087	7-3-0
Sat.	9-Nov	New Haven	7	3	2,401	8-3-0
Sun.	10-Nov	Clinton	6	3	1,777	9-3-0
Wed.	13-Nov	at Nashville	4	3		10-3-0
Fri.	15-Nov	at Knoxville	5	4		11-3-0
Sat.	16-Nov	Long Island	6	1	2,553	12-3-0
Sun.	17-Nov	at Long Island	3	4		12-4-0
Wed.	20-Nov	Clinton	5	3	1,459	13-4-0
Sat.	23-Nov	New Haven	6	5	2,500	14-4-0
Sun.	24-Nov	at New Haven	4	2		15-4-0
Wed.	27-Nov	Philadelphia	8	2	1,734	16-4-0
Thur.	28-Nov	New Haven	4	3 (ot)	3,024	17-4-0
Fri.	29-Nov	at Greensboro	3	7		17-5-0
Sat.	30-Nov	at Charlotte	2	10		17-6-0
Wed.	4-Dec	at Charlotte	4	3 (ot)		18-6-0
Thur.	5-Dec	at Nashville	0	3		18-7-0
Fri.	6-Dec	at Knoxville	2	4		18-8-0
Sat.	7-Dec	at Greensboro	4	5 (ot)		18-9-0
Sun.	8-Dec	at Philadelphia	3	1		19-9-0
Sat.	14-Dec	Philadelphia	7	3	1,756	20-9-0
Sun.	15-Dec	at Philadelphia	10	5		21-9-0
Wed.	18-Dec	Clinton	5	3	891	22-9-0
Sat.	21-Dec	Russian National	6	9	3,037	Exhibition
Sun.	22-Dec	Long Island	1	1 (ot)	2,155	22-9-1
Fri.	27-Dec	at Clinton	3	2		23-9-1
Sat.	28-Dec	at Clinton	1	3		23-10-1
Sun.	29-Dec	at New Haven	1	9		23-11-1
Tues.	31-Dec	USA Olympic Team	4	2	1,836	Exhibition
Fri.	3-Jan	at Greensboro	6	7		23-12-1
Sat.	4-Jan	Charlotte	2	3	2,156	23-13-1
Sun.	5-Jan	Philadelphia	7	4	1,250	24-13-1
Wed.	8-Jan	at Clinton	1	6		24-14-1
Sat.	11-Jan	Greensboro	3	4 (ot)	2,600	24-15-1
Sun.	12-Jan	Knoxville	5	8	1,266	24-16-1
Wed.	15-Jan	at New Haven	4	0		25-16-1
Thur.	16-Jan	at Long Island	2	5		25-17-1
Sat.	18-Jan	Charlotte	4	1	2,641	26-17-1
Sun.	19-Jan	Clinton	4	3 (ot)	1,680	27-17-1
Tues.	21-Jan	Charlotte	6	2	1,239	28-17-1
Sat.	25-Jan	New Haven	5	1	2,531	29-17-1
Sun.	26-Jan	Clinton	2	7	2,318	29-18-1
Wed.	29-Jan	Knoxville	3	2	2,155	30-18-1
Fri.	31-Jan	at Long Island	2	3		30-19-1
Sat.	1-Feb	Nashville	4	2	2,609	31-19-1
Sun.	2-Feb	Nashville	2	4	1,905	31-20-1
Wed.	5-Feb	at Clinton	0	0 (ot)		31-20-2
Sat.	8-Feb	Greensboro	3	3 (ot)	2,443	31-20-3
Sun.	9-Feb	Nashville	7	2	2,509	32-20-3
Tues.	11-Feb	at Charlotte	0	6		32-21-3
Wed.	12-Feb	at Knoxville	4	7		32-22-3
Thur.	13-Feb	at Nashville	0	6		32-23-3
Sat.	15-Feb	Long Island	5	0	3,104	33-23-3
Sun.	16-Feb	at New Haven	3	7		33-24-3
Wed.	19-Feb	Philadelphia	8	1	1,303	34-24-3
Fri.	21-Feb	at Philadelphia	4	6		34-25-3
Sat.	22-Feb	Long Island	8	1	4,115	35-25-3
Sun.	23-Feb	Knoxville	7	3	3,572	36-25-3

JETS IN THE SIXTIES

Day	Date	Opponent		Score	Attendance	Record
Wed.	26-Feb	at Clinton	3	3 (ot)		36-25-4
Thur.	27-Feb	at Philadelphia	6	6 (ot)		36-25-5
Fri.	28-Feb	at Long Island	2	3		36-26-5
Sat.	29-Feb	New Haven	8	0	3,124	37-26-5
Sun.	1-Mar	at New Haven	8	3		38-26-5
Fri.	6-Mar	at Philadelphia	5	4 (ot)		39-26-5
Sat.	7-Mar	Long Island	3	1	3,890	40-26-5
Sun.	8-Mar	at New Haven	5	1		41-26-5

Playoff Results

Day	Date	Opponent	Johnstown Score	Opponent	Attendance	Record
Tues.	10-Mar	New Haven	0	2	1,281	0-1
Wed.	11-Mar	at New Haven	1	4		0-2
Fri.	13-Mar	New Haven	4	2	2,165	1-2
Sun.	15-Mar	at New Haven	3	0		2-2
Wed.	18-Mar	New Haven	5	1	2,701	3-2
Sat.	21-Mar	Clinton	8	4	2,782	1-0
Sun.	22-Mar	at Clinton	2	3		1-1
Thur.	26-Mar	Clinton	8	1	2,012	2-1
Fri.	27-Mar	at Clinton	4	6		2-2
Sat.	28-Mar	Clinton	3	5	2,969	2-3

Attendance Figures

	Dates	Totals	Average
Regular Season Attendance Totals	36	78,202	2,172
Playoff Attendance Totals	6	13,910	2,318
Exhibition Attendance Totals	2	4,873	2,437
TOTAL ATTENDANCE	44	96,985	2,204

1963-64 Player Statistics

	Regular Season Scoring					Playoff Scoring				
	Games	G	A	Pts	PIM	Games	G	A	Pts	PIM
11 Dick Roberge	72	41	67	108	15	10	4	11	15	4
8 Neil Forth	72	36	71	107	82	10	3	9	12	4
15 Floyd "Butch" Martin	72	30	65	95	36	10	6	5	11	17
10 Jack Faulkner	68	31	39	70	16	9	6	4	10	0
14 Ernie Dyda	72	38	31	69	19	10	2	5	7	2
12 Billy Ives	72	24	44	68	14	10	6	2	8	11
6 Jean-Claude Lepage	69	32	30	62	34	10	4	4	8	6
3 Dave Lucas	69	17	36	53	86	10	0	6	6	34
2 Larry Johnston	71	7	39	46	356	10	3	5	8	50
7 Tony Bukovich	53	22	21	43	75	10	1	7	8	37
4 Arlie Parker	68	6	26	32	94	8	1	1	2	12
16 Danny Patrick	28	9	11	20	54	10	2	3	5	31
5 Rick McClocklin	33	2	1	3	101					
5 Don McGowan	10	1	1	2	17					
6 Mike Denihan	3	0	2	2	0					
7 Yvon Lacoste	8	1	0	1	4					
7 Marcel Mongrain	6	0	1	1	0					
1 Ken Garrett (g)	1	0	0	0	0					
1 Claude Hardy (g)	1	0	0	0	0					
1 Ross Brooks (g)	5	0	0	0	0					
1 Joe Daley (g)	66	0	0	0	27	10	0	0	0	12
Bench					2					2
TOTALS	72	297	485	782	1032	10	38	62	100	222

Regular Season Goaltending

	G	Min	GA	ENG	SO	GAA	W	L	T	Saves	Save %
1 Ross Brooks	5	300	11	0	0	2.20	4	1	0	113	0.911
1 Joe Daley	66	4,013	221	2	4	3.30	37	23	5	2,115	0.905
1 Ken Garrett	1	31	3	0	0	5.80	0	1	0	15	0.833
1 Claude Hardy	1	60	8	0	0	8.00	0	1	0	23	0.742
TOTALS	72	4,404	243	2	4	3.34	41	26	5	2,266	0.902

Playoff Goaltending

	G	Min	GA	ENG	SO	GAA	W	L	Saves	Save %
1 Joe Daley	10	606	27	1	1	2.68	5	5	302	0.918
TOTALS	10	606	27	1	1	2.77	5	5	302	0.915

Note: Don Hall – No. 9 – came out of retirement to play both exhibition games during the season. He had no goals, assists, points or penalty minutes.

McGowan also wore No. 7.

1964-65 Johnstown Jets

(Front, from left) Joe Daley, Dave Lucas, general manager John Daley, Dick Roberge, trainer/spare goalie Ken "Gunner" Garrett. (Middle) Billy Ives, Harry Shaw, Billy Reid, Danny Patrick, Bobby Brown, Neil Forth. (Back) Jean-Claude Lepage, Ralph MacSweyn, Jim Lorette, Billy Ostwald, John Gofton.

1964-65 FINAL EASTERN HOCKEY LEAGUE STANDINGS

	Games played	Won	Lost	Tied	Points	Goals for	Goals against
North Division							
Long Island Ducks	72	50	20	2	102	336	182
Clinton Comets	72	42	29	1	85	279	233
Johnstown Jets	72	41	31	0	82	330	294
Jersey Devils	72	34	34	4	72	297	312
New York Rovers	72	25	39	8	58	206	270
New Haven Blades	72	19	52	1	39	238	379
South Division							
Nashville Dixie Flyers	72	54	18	0	108	349	196
Greensboro Generals	72	37	33	2	76	333	301
Charlotte Checkers	72	35	35	2	72	262	286
Knoxville Knights	72	34	36	2	70	281	284
Jacksonville Rockets	72	13	57	2	28	211	385

Johnstown Jets
General Manager - John Daley
Coach - Dave Lucas
Trainer/Spare Goalie - Ken "Gunner" Garrett
Colors - Royal Blue and White

1964-65 Game Results

Preseason Results

Day	Date	Opponent	Score Johnstown	Opponent	Attendance	Record
Thur.	8-Oct	Nashville *	1	2		
Sun.	11-Oct	Jersey	7	3	981	

* Played in Port Colborne, Ontario.

Regular Season Results

Day	Date	Opponent	Score Johnstown	Opponent	Attendance	Record
Wed.	14-Oct	New York	5	1	2,200	1-0-0
Fri.	16-Oct	at Jersey	5	6		1-1-0
Sat.	17-Oct	New Haven	6	4	1,839	2-1-0
Wed.	21-Oct	at Clinton	0	7		2-2-0
Fri.	23-Oct	Clinton	0	2	1,594	2-3-0
Sat.	24-Oct	New York	4	2	2,098	3-3-0
Sun.	25-Oct	at Long Island	4	6		3-4-0
Wed.	28-Oct	Long Island	4	1	1,249	4-4-0
Fri.	30-Oct	at Clinton	1	8		4-5-0
Sat.	31-Oct	New Haven	3	2	2,105	5-5-0
Sun.	1-Nov	at New York	0	2		5-6-0
Wed.	4-Nov	Clinton	6	1	1,425	6-6-0
Fri.	6-Nov	at Jersey	5	4		7-6-0
Sat.	7-Nov	Long Island	4	2	2,725	8-6-0
Sat.	14-Nov	New Haven	8	4	2,112	9-6-0
Sun.	15-Nov	at New Haven	0	6		9-7-0
Wed.	18-Nov	Clinton	4	2	2,476	10-7-0
Fri.	20-Nov	at Clinton	0	4		10-8-0
Sat.	21-Nov	Jersey	2	4	2,211	10-9-0
Sun.	22-Nov	at Long Island	2	5		10-10-0
Wed.	25-Nov	Long Island	7	5	2,045	11-10-0
Thur.	26-Nov	Jersey	8	4	2,769	12-10-0
Fri.	27-Nov	at Jersey	7	5		13-10-0
Sat.	28-Nov	at New Haven	4	3		14-10-0
Sun.	29-Nov	at Long Island	3	9		14-11-0
Wed.	2-Dec	Clinton	3	4	1,506	14-12-0
Fri.	4-Dec	at Jersey *	Postponed - Power failure			
Sat.	5-Dec	Nashville	2	4	2,109	14-13-0
Sun.	6-Dec	Clinton	3	4 (ot)	1,471	14-14-0
Wed.	9-Dec	at Jacksonville	7	3		15-14-0
Fri.	11-Dec	at Charlotte	6	2		16-14-0
Sat.	12-Dec	at Knoxville	2	4		16-15-0
Sun.	13-Dec	at Nashville	2	7		16-16-0
Fri.	18-Dec	at Jersey	4	9		16-17-0
Sat.	19-Dec	Charlotte	2	4	1,908	16-18-0
Sun.	20-Dec	at New Haven	10	1		17-18-0
Sat.	26-Dec	at Long Island	3	10		17-19-0
Sun.	27-Dec	Long Island	2	3 (ot)	1,916	17-20-0
Wed.	30-Dec	at Clinton	2	5		17-21-0
Thur.	31-Dec	New Haven	6	4	1,689	18-21-0
Sat.	2-Jan	Jersey	6	1	2,030	19-21-0
Sun.	3-Jan	at New York	5	3		20-21-0
Fri.	8-Jan	Long Island	8	3	2,098	21-21-0
Sat.	9-Jan	New York	5	1	2,189	22-21-0
Sun.	10-Jan	at New Haven	6	2		23-21-0
Tues.	12-Jan	at Jersey	4	5		23-22-0
Fri.	15-Jan	at Clinton	0	7		23-23-0
Sat.	16-Jan	Long Island	8	3	2,045	24-23-0
Sun.	17-Jan	Jacksonville	8	3	2,208	25-23-0
Wed.	20-Jan	New York	5	3	1,200	26-23-0
Thur.	21-Jan	New York **	3	4	782	26-24-0
Sat.	23-Jan	Jersey	7	5	2,796	27-24-0
Wed.	27-Jan	at New York *	0	2		27-25-0
Fri.	29-Jan	at Jersey	5	7		27-26-0
Sat.	30-Jan	Jersey	4	3 (ot)	3,002	28-26-0
Sun.	31-Jan	at Long Island	4	8		28-27-0
Wed.	3-Feb	at New York *	4	5		28-28-0
Fri.	5-Feb	Jersey	8	2	1,595	29-28-0

Day	Date	Opponent	Score		Attendance	Record
Sat.	6-Feb	New Haven	10	5	3,202	30-28-0
Sun.	7-Feb	at New Haven	5	2		31-28-0
Fri.	12-Feb	New Haven	7	0	3,336	32-28-0
Sat.	13-Feb	Greensboro	6	4	3,305	33-28-0
Sun.	14-Feb	at Long Island	5	2		34-28-0
Wed.	17-Feb	at Greensboro	9	7		35-28-0
Sat.	20-Feb	New York	6	4	3,148	36-28-0
Sun.	21-Feb	Jersey	8	3	2,440	37-28-0
Wed.	24-Feb	Clinton	2	4	2,314	37-29-0
Fri.	26-Feb	at Clinton	4	9		37-30-0
Sat.	27-Feb	at Jersey	3	12		37-31-0
Sun.	28-Feb	at New Haven	10	3		38-31-0
Wed.	3-Mar	Knoxville	6	5	2,404	39-31-0
Sat.	6-Mar	New York	8	4	3,702	40-31-0
Sun.	7-Mar	at New York	5	0		41-31-0

* Games were played in Philadelphia, Pa.
** New York home game – rescheduled in Johnstown

Playoff Results

Day	Date	Opponent	Johnstown	Opponent	Attendance	Record
Wed	10-Mar	at Clinton	3	4 (ot)		0-1
Fri.	12-Mar	Clinton	6	3	2,330	1-1
Sat.	13-Mar	at Clinton	2	5		1-2
Sun.	14-Mar	Clinton	2	0	2,482	2-2
Wed	17-Mar	at Clinton	6	7		2-3

Attendance Figures

	Dates	Totals	Average
Preseason Attendance Total	1	981	981
Regular Season Attendance Totals	37	81,243	2,196
Playoff Attendance Totals	2	4,812	2,406
TOTAL ATTENDANCE FIGURES	40	87,036	2,176

1964-65 Player Statistics

	Regular Season Scoring					Playoff Scoring				
	Games	G	A	Pts	PIM	Games	G	A	Pts	PIM
11 Dick Roberge	72	63	76	139	44	5	2	6	8	0
8 Neil Forth	71	33	71	104	41	5	1	5	6	6
12 Billy Ives	72	47	48	95	66	4	3	1	4	4
6 Jean-Claude Lepage	70	40	49	89	55	5	3	1	4	6
14 Dan Patrick	71	27	54	81	108	5	4	5	9	6
10 Bobby Brown	59	29	47	76	20					
3 Dave Lucas	72	12	48	60	126	5	2	4	6	16
16 John Gofton	58	30	23	53	51	5	1	2	3	2
2 Dennis Rathwell	19	12	16	28	22	5	1	1	2	0
7 Billy Reid	32	11	15	26	29	5	2	2	4	16
7 Tony Bukovich	37	6	13	19	54					
4 Ralph MacSweyn	52	2	17	19	19	5	0	1	1	6
15 Bill Ostwald	28	6	12	18	35	5	0	2	2	2
2 Jim Lorette	40	3	15	18	91					
5 Harry Shaw	52	3	10	13	135					
15 Jim McCloskey	21	4	7	11	36					
15 Jim O'Brien	11	1	6	7	5					
4 Ron Mason	5	1	4	5	2					
5 Gord Matheson	9	0	2	2	14	5	0	0	0	6
1 Joe Daley (g)	72	0	2	2	26	5	0	0	0	0
1 Ken Garrett (g)	1	0	0	0	0					
15 Terry Moore	1	0	0	0	0					
Bench					12					
TOTALS	72	330	535	865	991	5	19	30	49	70

Regular Season Goaltending

	G	Min	GA	ENG	SO	GAA	W	L	T	Saves	Save %
1 Joe Daley	72	4,297	288	2	2	4.02	41	31	0	219	0.885
1 Ken Garrett	1	35	4	0	0	6.86	0	0	0	21	0.840
TOTALS	72	4,332	292	2	2	4.07	41	31	0	2,240	0.884

Playoff Goaltending

	G	Min	GA	ENG	SO	GAA	W	L		Saves	Save %
1 Joe Daley	5	300	19	0	1	3.80	2	3		183	0.906
TOTALS	5	300	19	0	1	3.80	2	3		183	0.906

Reid also wore No. 10.

1965-66 Johnstown Jets

(Front, from left) Dave Lucas, general manager John Daley, Andy Brown, Dick Roberge. (Middle) Neil Forth, Danny Patrick, Billy Reid, Pete Loveless, John Gofton, Denny Rathwell. (Back) Bob Howard, Ralph MacSweyn, Reggie Taschuk, Billy Ives, Gordie Carruthers.

1965-66 FINAL EASTERN HOCKEY LEAGUE STANDINGS

	Games played	Won	Lost	Tied	Points	Goals for	Goals against
North Division							
Long Island Ducks	72	46	23	3	95	292	208
Clinton Comets	72	41	28	3	85	276	212
Johnstown Jets	72	39	31	2	80	303	267
New Haven Blades	72	27	43	2	56	283	353
Jersey Devils	72	25	43	4	54	239	311
South Division							
Nashville Dixie Flyers	72	42	23	7	91	277	179
Charlotte Checkers	72	42	30	0	84	300	251
Greensboro Generals	72	37	31	4	78	291	263
Knoxville Knights	72	34	36	2	70	278	261
Jacksonville Rockets	72	12	57	3	27	207	441

Johnstown Jets
General Manager - John Daley
Coach - Dave Lucas
Trainer/Spare Goalie - Danny Woods until Dec. 9; Joe Sylvestry replaced Woods from Dec. 10 to Jan. 12; Jack Kline from Jan. 12
Stickboys - Kevin Grady, Mike Hudec, Mike McNamara
Colors - Royal Blue and White

1965-66 Game Results

Preseason Results

Day	Date	Opponent	Score Johnstown	Opponent	Attendance	Record
Wed.	13-Oct	* Team Roberge 4, Team Lucas 4				
Sat.	16-Oct	Jacksonville	7	5	1200	
Sun.	17-Oct	Jacksonville	7	0	1000	

* 90 minute inter-squad scrimmage took place of cancelled game against Charlotte.

141

Regular Season Results

Day	Date	Opponent	Score Johnstown	Opponent	Attendance	Record
Wed.	20-Oct	Knoxville	7	5	2,232	1-0-0
Sat.	23-Oct	Jacksonville	9	5	2,104	2-0-0
Wed.	27-Oct	Clinton	1	2	1,850	2-1-0
Fri.	29-Oct	at Clinton	3	5		2-2-0
Sat.	30-Oct	New Haven	7	5	1,845	3-2-0
Sun.	31-Oct	at New Haven	8	2		4-2-0
Wed.	3-Nov	at Jersey	4	2		5-2-0
Fri.	5-Nov	at Clinton	1	7		5-3-0
Sat.	6-Nov	Long Island	3	2	2,412	6-3-0
Sun.	7-Nov	at Long Island	0	1		6-4-0
Fri.	12-Nov	Clinton	1	3	2,175	6-5-0
Sat.	13-Nov	New Haven	3	4 (ot)	3,231	6-6-0
Sun.	14-Nov	at New Haven	4	5 (ot)		6-7-0
Tues.	16-Nov	Jersey	6	1	1,111	7-7-0
Fri.	19-Nov	at Jersey	2	4		7-8-0
Sat.	20-Nov	at Jersey	5	6 (ot)		7-9-0
Sun.	21-Nov	at Long Island	2	9		7-10-0
Wed.	24-Nov	Charlotte	9	2	2,440	8-10-0
Thur.	25-Nov	Clinton	4	3	2,354	9-10-0
Fri.	26-Nov	at Greensboro	3	2		10-10-0
Sat.	27-Nov	at Charlotte	5	2		11-10-0
Tues.	30-Nov	Jersey	7	3	1,467	12-10-0
Fri.	3-Dec	at Clinton	0	6		12-11-0
Sat.	4-Dec	New Haven	7	2	2,072	13-11-0
Sun.	5-Dec	at New Haven	8	10		13-12-0
Wed.	8-Dec	at Jacksonville	8	2		14-12-0
Thur.	9-Dec	at Knoxville	4	6		14-13-0
Sat.	11-Dec	at Knoxville	3	5		14-14-0
Wed.	15-Dec	at Jersey	6	3		15-14-0
Fri.	17-Dec	Greensboro	7	3	1,821	16-14-0
Sat.	18-Dec	Long Island	4	2	2,301	17-14-0
Sat.	25-Dec	at Nashville	1	3		17-15-0
Sun.	26-Dec	at Nashville	1	6		17-16-0
Tues.	28-Dec	at Jersey	3	4		17-17-0
Wed.	29-Dec	at Clinton	1	4		17-18-0
Fri.	31-Dec	Clinton	8	1	1,986	18-18-0
Sat.	1-Jan	New Haven	10	3	1,970	19-18-0
Sun.	2-Jan	at Long Island	3	7		19-19-0
Wed.	5-Jan	at New Haven	2	7		19-20-0
Sat.	8-Jan	Long Island	4	2	2,337	20-20-0
Sun.	9-Jan	at Greensboro	3	5		20-21-0
Wed.	12-Jan	at Clinton	3	9		20-22-0
Fri.	14-Jan	Clinton	6	3	2,005	21-22-0
Sat.	15-Jan	Jersey	9	5	2,578	22-22-0
Sun.	16-Jan	at New Haven	9	4		23-22-0
Fri.	21-Jan	Clinton	4	2	1,752	24-22-0
Sat.	22-Jan	New Haven	7	4	1,210	25-22-0
Wed.	26-Jan	at Jersey	2	2 (ot)		25-22-1
Fri.	28-Jan	Jersey	5	4	1,515	26-22-1
Sat.	29-Jan	Long Island	2	4	2,783	26-23-1
Sun.	30-Jan	at New Haven	3	4		26-24-1
Fri.	4-Feb	New Haven	8	5	3,420	27-24-1
Sat.	5-Feb	Long Island	7	1	2,410	28-24-1
Sun.	6-Feb	at Long Island	0	6		28-25-1
Sat.	12-Feb	Jersey	4	1	2,358	29-25-1
Sun.	13-Feb	Greensboro	5	3	1,964	30-25-1
Thur.	17-Feb	New Haven	4	3	1,005	31-25-1
Sat.	19-Feb	Long Island	1	3	2,260	31-26-1
Sun.	20-Feb	at Long Island	2	3		31-27-1
Tues.	22-Feb	at Jersey	3	2		32-27-1
Wed	23-Feb	at Clinton	2	5		32-28-1
Thur.	24-Feb	at Long Island	3	2		33-28-1
Fri.	25-Feb	Clinton	6	2	1,658	34-28-1
Sat.	26-Feb	Jersey	5	3	2,447	35-28-1
Sun.	27-Feb	at Greensboro	4	2		36-28-1

Day	Date	Opponent			Attendance	Record
Tues.	1-Mar	Nashville	3	3 (ot)	1583	36-28-2
Thur.	3-Mar	at Clinton	2	5		36-29-2
Fri.	4-Mar	Greensboro	7	3	2107	37-29-2
Sat.	5-Mar	Long Island	4	1	3117	38-29-2
Sun.	6-Mar	at Long Island	1	6		38-30-2
Sat.	12-Mar	Nashville	1	3	2820	38-31-2
Sun.	13-Mar	Nashville	4	3	2034	39-31-2

Playoff Results

Day	Date	Opponent	Johnstown	Score Opponent	Attendance	Record
Wed.	16-Mar	at Clinton	1	6		0-1
Fri.	18-Mar	Clinton	4	5 (ot)	1591	0-2
Sat.	19-Mar	at Clinton	2	3 (2ot)		0-3

Attendance Figures

	Dates	Totals	Average
Preseason Attendance Totals	2	2,200	1,100
Regular Season Attendance Totals	36	76,734	2,132
Playoff Attendance Totals	1	1,591	1,591
TOTAL ATTENDANCE	39	80,525	2,065

1965-66 Player Statistics

	Regular Season Scoring					Playoff Scoring				
	Games	G	A	Pts	PIM	Games	G	A	Pts	PIM
11 Dick Roberge	65	51	64	115	24	3	1	3	4	0
8 Neil Forth	70	30	67	97	72	3	2	1	3	0
14 Danny Patrick	72	39	47	86	69	3	0	1	1	4
12 Bill Ives	59	37	46	83	45	3	2	1	3	0
7 Reggie Taschuk	70	27	43	70	28	3	0	0	0	0
6 Pete Loveless	72	22	36	58	55	3	0	0	0	0
5 Denny Rathwell	54	27	28	55	64	3	2	0	2	0
3 Dave Lucas	72	13	35	48	84	2	0	0	0	2
10 Bill Reid	55	17	26	43	39	3	0	1	1	0
16 John Gofton	48	17	19	36	52	3	0	0	0	0
4 Ralph MacSweyn	71	6	26	32	40	3	0	0	0	0
2 Gordie Carruthers	69	7	23	30	120	3	0	2	2	6
15 Bob Howard	30	4	8	12	26					
10 Claude Bernard	15	5	3	8	29					
15 Ken Thompson	16	1	2	3	0					
5 Terry Grindle	14	0	1	1	8					
4 Rick Bradford	1	0	0	0	0					
1 Jim Letcher (g)	2	0	0	0	0					
5 Jack Kline	7	0	0	0	8					
1 Andy Brown (g)	70	0	0	0	53	3	0	0	0	0
Bench					4					
TOTALS	72	303	474	777	820	3	7	9	16	12

Regular Season Goaltending

	G	Min	GA	ENG	SO	GAA	W	L	T	Saves	Save %
1 Andy Brown	70	4,228	252	5	0	3.58	37	31	3	2,035	0.890
1 Jim Letcher	2	120	10	0	0	5.00	2	0	0	51	0.836
TOTALS	72	4,348	262	5	0	3.68	39	31	2	2,086	0.887

Playoff Goaltending

	G	Min	GA	ENG	SO	GA	W	L	Saves	Save %
1 Andy Brown	3	214	14	0	0	3.93	0	3	117	0.893
TOTALS	3	214	14	0	0	3.93	0	3	117	0.893

Taschuk also wore No. 12.
Reid also wore No. 7.
Grindle also wore No. 16.

1966-67 Johnstown Jets

(Front, from left) Ralph MacSweyn, Dick Roberge, general manager/coach Jack MacIntyre, Roger Lalancette, Dave Lucas, trainer/spare goalie Jim Barton. (Middle) Tom Schiller, Claire Alexander, Billy Ives, Jim Mair, Reggie Taschuk. (Back) Dan Patrick, Claude Bernard, Dennis Rathwell, John Gofton, Mel Wakabayashi, Neil Forth.

1966-67 FINAL EASTERN HOCKEY LEAGUE STANDINGS

	Games played	Won	Lost	Tied	Points	Goals for	Goals against
North Division							
Clinton Comets	72	44	26	2	90	285	202
Jersey Devils	72	39	30	3	81	292	210
Johnstown Jets	72	34	36	2	70	267	290
Long Island Ducks	72	29	39	4	62	198	233
New Haven Blades	72	27	44	1	55	241	346
South Division							
Nashville Dixie Flyers	72	51	19	2	104	287	169
Charlotte Checkers	72	36	33	3	75	259	235
Greensboro Generals	72	35	37	0	70	265	279
Knoxville Knights	72	27	42	3	57	232	268
Florida Rockets	72	27	43	2	56	221	315

Johnstown Jets
General Manager - Jack MacIntyre
Coach - Jack MacIntyre
Trainer/Spare Goalie - Jim Barton
Stickboys - Kevin Grady, Mike Hudec, Mike McNamara, Larry Labarko
Colors - Royal Blue and White

1966-67 Game Results

Preseason Results

Day	Date	Opponent	Score Johnstown	Opponent	Attendance	Record
Sat.	15-Oct	at Clinton	1	8		
Tues.	18-Oct	Clinton *	0	3		
Wed.	19-Oct	Clinton **	2	1		

* Game played in Utica, N.Y.
** Game played in Troy, N.Y.

JETS IN THE SIXTIES

Regular Season Results

Day	Date	Opponent	Johnstown	Opponent	Attendance	Record
Thur.	20-Oct	at Long Island	2	3		0-1-0
Fri.	21-Oct	New Haven	4	5	2,365	0-2-0
Sat.	22-Oct	Florida	5	3	3,209	1-2-0
Sun.	23-Oct	at New Haven	3	4 (ot)		1-3-0
Wed.	26-Oct	at Clinton	2	1		2-3-0
Fri.	28-Oct	Clinton	4	2	1,397	3-3-0
Sat.	29-Oct	Long Island	4	1	2,974	4-3-0
Sun.	30-Oct	at New Haven	4	7		4-4-0
Wed.	2-Nov	at Clinton	4	5 (ot)		4-5-0
Fri.	4-Nov	at Greensboro	1	3		4-6-0
Sat.	5-Nov	New Haven	10	3	3,141	5-6-0
Sun.	6-Nov	Charlotte	8	2	1,855	6-6-0
Fri.	11-Nov	New Haven	4	3	1,955	7-6-0
Sat.	12-Nov	Jersey	2	4	3,293	7-7-0
Sun.	13-Nov	at Long Island	4	1		8-7-0
Fri.	18-Nov	at Clinton	1	5		8-8-0
Sat.	19-Nov	Long Island	3	1	3,602	9-8-0
Sun.	20-Nov	Jersey	4	3 (ot)	1,982	10-8-0
Wed.	23-Nov	Charlotte	3	4	2,241	10-9-0
Thur.	24-Nov	Jersey	4	3	3,308	11-9-0
Fri.	25-Nov	at Charlotte	2	4		11-10-0
Sat.	26-Nov	at Greensboro	1	5		11-11-0
Wed.	30-Nov	at Clinton	0	10		11-12-0
Fri.	2-Dec	Greensboro	4	2	1,961	12-12-0
Sat.	3-Dec	Jersey	8	3	2,262	13-12-0
Sun.	4-Dec	at Long Island	2	5		13-13-0
Wed.	7-Dec	at Knoxville	5	3		14-13-0
Fri.	9-Dec	at Florida	3	2 (ot)		15-13-0
Sat.	10-Dec	at Nashville	1	6		15-14-0
Tues.	13-Dec	at Jersey	2	6		15-15-0
Fri.	16-Dec	Clinton	5	6 (ot)	1,835	15-16-0
Sat.	17-Dec	New Haven	7	1	2,301	16-16-0
Sun.	25-Dec	at New Haven	3	5		16-17-0
Tues.	27-Dec	at Jersey	3	5		16-18-0
Wed.	28-Dec	at Clinton	1	8		16-19-0
Fri.	30-Dec	Greensboro	5	3	2,702	17-19-0
Sat.	31-Dec	Long Island	6	5	2,518	18-19-0
Sun.	1-Jan	at New Haven	6	4		19-19-0
Fri.	6-Jan	at Greensboro	1	11		19-20-0
Sat.	7-Jan	Long Island	3	3 (ot)	2,925	19-20-1
Sun.	8-Jan	Charlotte	4	3 (ot)	1,784	20-20-1
Wed.	11-Jan	at New Haven	4	9		20-21-1
Fri.	13-Jan	Clinton	4	1	2,124	21-21-1
Sat.	14-Jan	Greensboro	0	1	3,193	21-22-1
Sun.	15-Jan	at Long Island	0	4		21-23-1
Tues.	17-Jan	at Florida	4	5 (ot)		21-24-1
Wed.	18-Jan	at Florida	6	8		21-25-1
Fri.	20-Jan	at Clinton	3	1		22-25-1
Sat.	21-Jan	Florida	6	5	3,018	23-25-1
Sun.	22-Jan	Clinton	1	3	4,069	23-26-1
Wed.	25-Jan	at New Haven	2	6		23-27-1
Fri.	27-Jan	Clinton	6	3	2,237	24-27-1
Sat.	28-Jan	Long Island	3	3 (ot)	2,960	24-27-2
Sun.	29-Jan	at Long Island	5	4		25-27-2
Tues.	31-Jan	at Jersey	2	1		26-27-2
Fri.	3-Feb	at Clinton	5	1		27-27-2
Sat.	4-Feb	Jersey	4	5	4,016	27-28-2
Fri.	10-Feb	at Jersey	3	8		27-29-2
Sat.	11-Feb	Nashville	2	3	3,551	27-30-2
Sun.	12-Feb	Florida	1	3	2,562	27-31-2
Sat.	18-Feb	Long Island	2	6	3,553	27-32-2
Wed.	22-Feb	at Clinton	5	8		27-33-2
Fri.	24-Feb	Clinton	8	4	2,123	28-33-2
Sat.	25-Feb	Jersey	4	2	2,621	29-33-2
Sun.	26-Feb	at New Haven	4	3		30-33-2

145

Day	Date	Opponent			Attendance	Record
Wed.	1-Mar	at New Haven	4	8		30-34-2
Fri.	3-Mar	at Jersey	2	9		30-35-2
Sat.	4-Mar	Knoxville	4	2	3,088	31-35-2
Sun.	5-Mar	Knoxville	4	2	2,114	32-35-2
Fri.	10-Mar	at Jersey	2	5		32-36-2
Sat.	11-Mar	New Haven	16	3	3,509	33-36-2
Sun.	12-Mar	Jersey	3	1	2,827	34-36-2

Playoff Results
Score

Day	Date	Opponent	Johnstown	Opponent	Attendance	Record
Tues.	14-Mar	at Jersey	1	4		0-1
Wed.	15-Mar	Jersey	4	3	1,732	1-1
Fri.	17-Mar	at Jersey	4	2		2-1
Sat.	18-Mar	Jersey	3	4	3,768	2-2
Tues.	21-Mar	at Jersey	3	4		2-3

Attendance Figures

	Dates	Totals	Average
Regular Season Attendance Totals	36	97,175	2,699
Playoff Attendance Totals	2	5,500	2,750
TOTAL ATTENDANCE	38	102,675	2,702

1966-67 Player Statistics

	Regular Season Scoring					Playoff Scoring				
	Games	G	A	Pts	PIM	Games	G	A	Pts	PIM
11 Dick Roberge	71	41	52	93	22	5	3	2	5	4
8 Neil Forth	68	25	53	78	33	5	2	4	6	2
7 Reggie Taschuk	72	32	36	68	18	5	0	2	2	2
14 Danny Patrick	72	28	40	68	53	5	2	2	4	8
3 Dave Lucas	72	16	41	57	72	5	0	2	2	2
12 Billy Ives	52	26	28	54	32	5	2	3	5	4
5 Dennis Rathwell	68	26	27	53	123	5	0	0	0	4
10 Claude Bernard	71	12	34	46	132	5	1	0	1	9
2 Jim Mair	62	10	25	35	245	5	2	3	5	11
4 Ralph MacSweyn	72	6	28	34	82	5	0	3	3	6
6 Tom Schiller	42	11	19	30	67	5	0	0	0	10
15 Mel Wakabayashi	21	8	18	26	2	5	3	4	7	0
15 John Gofton	17	10	14	24	15	5	0	1	1	4
15 Dick Sarrazin	18	4	8	12	2					
10 Claire Alexander	18	5	3	8	0					
6 Pete Loveless	12	4	3	7	7					
15 Hank Brand	13	2	4	6	25					
2 Len Bazay	15	1	2	3	6					
12 Dave Lee	5	0	3	3	0					
16 Jack McIntyre	5	0	1	1	4					
1 Roger Lalancette (g)	67	0	1	1	6	5	0	0	0	10
16 Jack Nairn	2	0	0	0	2					
1 Ross Childs (g)	2	0	0	0	0					
1 Jim Barton (g)	3	0	0	0	0					
15 Bob Howard	7	0	0	0	2					
1 Andy Brown (g)	1	0	0	0	17					
Bench					2					
TOTALS	72	267	440	707	969 (+8)	5	15	26	41	76

Regular Season Goaltending

	G	Min	GA	ENG	SO	GAA	W	L	T	Saves	Save %
1 Ross Childs	2	129	7	0	0	3.26	1	0	1	86	0.925
1 Roger Lalancette	67	4,020	262	0	0	3.97	32	33	1	1,758	0.872
1 Jim Barton	3	157	15	0	0	5.73	1	2	0	52	0.776
1 Andy Brown	1	60	6	0	0	6.00	0	1	0	19	0.760
TOTALS	72	4,366	290	0	0	3.99	34	36	2		

Note: Lalancette's totals for Saves and Save % incomplete – only calculated for available games.

Playoff Goaltending

	G	Min	GA	ENG	SO	GAA	W	L	Saves	Save %
1 Roger Lalancette	5	297	17	0	0	3.43	2	3	113	0.869
TOTALS	5	300	17	0	0	3.40	2	3	113	0.869

JETS IN THE SIXTIES

1967-68 Johnstown Jets

(Front, from left) Head coach Dick Roberge, John Nickerson, Andy Brown, Billy Ives, general manager John Mitchell. (Middle) Trainer Lou Klashinsky, Carlo Longarini, Jim Randle, John Gofton, Reggie Kent, Billy Reid. (Back) Galen Head, Mike Crupi, Bill Armour, Jim Mair, Danny Patrick, Pierre Roy, Jack Dale.

1967-68 FINAL EASTERN HOCKEY LEAGUE STANDINGS

	Games played	Won	Lost	Tied	Points	Goals for	Goals against
North Division							
Clinton Comets	72	57	5	10	124	436	185
New Haven Blades	72	43	22	7	93	387	242
Johnstown Jets	72	38	25	9	85	386	273
Long Island Ducks	72	29	36	7	65	333	329
Jersey Devils	72	17	51	4	38	251	458
Syracuse Blazers	72	12	57	3	27	277	583
South Division							
Greensboro Generals	72	46	20	6	98	364	248
Charlotte Checkers	72	42	21	9	93	333	243
Nashville Dixie Flyers	72	42	23	7	91	341	256
Jacksonville Rockets	72	30	34	8	68	262	288
Knoxville Knights	72	23	43	6	52	250	294
Salem Rebels	72	11	53	8	30	211	432

Johnstown Jets
General Manager - John Mitchell
Coach - Dick Roberge
Trainer - Lou Klashinsky
Stickboys - Kevin Grady, Mike Hudec, Mike McNamara
Colors - Royal Blue and White

1967-68 Games Results

Preseason Results

Day	Date	Opponent	Johnstown	Opponent	Attendance	Record
Sat.	14-Oct	Salem *	4	4		
Mon.	16-Oct	Wade Red Wings **	5	2		

* Game played in Erie, Pa.
** Game played in St. Catharines, Ontario.

147

Regular Season Results

Day	Date	Opponent	Score Johnstown	Opponent	Attendance	Record
Fri.	20-Oct	Syracuse	4	4	2,170	0-0-1
Sat.	21-Oct	New Haven	6	1	2,604	1-0-1
Sun.	22-Oct	at New Haven	4	5		1-1-1
Fri.	27-Oct	Jersey	10	3	1,622	2-1-1
Sat.	28-Oct	Long Island	3	1	2,522	3-1-1
Fri.	3-Nov	New Haven	5	1	1,855	4-1-1
Sat.	4-Nov	Syracuse	8	0	3,189	5-1-1
Sun.	5-Nov	at Long Island	4	7		5-2-1
Tues.	7-Nov	at Syracuse	4	1		6-2-1
Thur.	9-Nov	at Syracuse	14	4		7-2-1
Fri.	10-Nov	Clinton	5	5	2,838	7-2-2
Sat.	11-Nov	Long Island	9	4	3,113	8-2-2
Sun.	12-Nov	at Long Island	1	5		8-3-2
Tues.	14-Nov	at Jersey	5	0		9-3-2
Wed.	15-Nov	at New Haven	4	4		9-3-3
Fri.	17-Nov	at Clinton	2	8		9-4-3
Sat.	18-Nov	New Haven	7	4	3,212	10-4-3
Sun.	19-Nov	Clinton	3	3	2,545	10-4-4
Wed.	22-Nov	Long Island	7	3	2,302	11-4-4
Thur.	23-Nov	Clinton	0	8	4,217	11-5-4
Fri.	24-Nov	at Long Island	5	9		11-6-4
Sat.	25-Nov	at Clinton	4	4		11-6-5
Sun.	26-Nov	at New Haven	2	9		11-7-5
Fri.	1-Dec	Long Island	6	4	1,834	12-7-5
Sat.	2-Dec	Long Island	2	2	2,986	12-7-6
Tues.	5-Dec	at Syracuse	3	5		12-8-6
Wed.	6-Dec	at New Haven	2	2		12-8-7
Thur.	7-Dec	at Syracuse	9	5		13-8-7
Sat.	9-Dec	at Clinton	2	7		13-9-7
Sun.	10-Dec	at Long Island	2	3		13-10-7
Sat.	16-Dec	New Haven	9	3	2,384	14-10-7
Sun.	17-Dec	Clinton	3	5	2,073	14-11-7
Sat.	23-Dec	Clinton	0	3	2,556	14-12-7
Mon.	25-Dec	at Long Island	3	4		14-13-7
Tues.	26-Dec	at Jersey	0	4		14-14-7
Sat.	30-Dec	Long Island	8	4	2,709	15-14-7
Sun.	31-Dec	Jersey	11	2	2,000	16-14-7
Fri.	5-Jan	at Clinton	4	3		17-14-7
Sat.	6-Jan	Syracuse	14	5	2,718	18-14-7
Sun.	7-Jan	at Syracuse	8	2		19-14-7
Fri.	12-Jan	Jersey	9	0	2,741	20-14-7
Sat.	13-Jan	New Haven	8	3	3,236	21-14-7
Fri.	19-Jan	at Jersey	9	3		22-14-7
Sat.	20-Jan	Syracuse	13	1	3,147	23-14-7
Sun.	21-Jan	Clinton	7	5	4,280	24-14-7
Wed.	24-Jan	at New Haven	3	7		24-15-7
Thur.	25-Jan	at Syracuse	4	1		25-15-7
Fri.	26-Jan	at Clinton	2	5		25-16-7
Sat.	27-Jan	Jersey	6	2	3,749	26-16-7
Sun.	28-Jan	Jersey	11	1	2,375	27-16-7
Fri.	2-Feb	at Long Island	1	5		27-17-7
Sat.	3-Feb	New Haven	4	6	3,905	27-18-7
Sun.	4-Feb	at New Haven	1	3		27-19-7
Tues.	6-Feb	at Jersey	4	6		27-20-7
Fri.	9-Feb	Jersey	7	4	2,702	28-20-7
Sat.	10-Feb	Long Island	8	1	3,087	29-20-7
Sun.	11-Feb	at Syracuse	9	5		30-20-7
Tues.	13-Feb	at Jersey	2	8		30-21-7
Wed.	14-Feb	at New Haven	2	5		30-22-7
Fri.	16-Feb	at Clinton	4	8		30-23-7
Sat.	17-Feb	Syracuse	10	4	2,409	31-23-7
Sun.	18-Feb	Clinton	2	3	3,130	31-24-7
Fri.	23-Feb	at Jersey	5	5		31-24-8
Sat.	24-Feb	New Haven	2	2	3,153	31-24-9
Sun.	25-Feb	Syracuse	11	4	2,079	32-24-9

JETS IN THE SIXTIES

Day	Date	Opponent		Score	Attendance	Record
Wed.	28-Feb	at Clinton	2	6		32-25-9
Fri.	1-Mar	at Jersey	7	3		33-25-9
Sat.	2-Mar	Syracuse	7	4	2,596	34-25-9
Sun.	3-Mar	at Long Island	5	2		35-25-9
Fri.	8-Mar	at Jersey	4	3		36-25-9
Sat.	9-Mar	Jersey	8	0	3,322	37-25-9
Sun.	10-Mar	Jersey	7	2	2,662	38-25-9

Playoff Results

Day	Date	Opponent	Johnstown	Opponent	Attendance	Record
Wed.	13-Mar	at New Haven	0	10		0-1
Fri.	15-Mar	New Haven	5	6	2,354	0-2
Sun.	17-Mar	at New Haven	1	7		0-3

Attendance Figures

	Dates	Totals	Average
Regular Season Attendance Totals	36	100,022	2,778
Playoff Attendance Totals	1	2,354	2,354
TOTAL ATTENDANCE	37	102,376	2,767

1967-68 Player Statistics

	Regular Season Scoring					Playoff Scoring				
	Games	G	A	Pts	PIM	Games	G	A	Pts	PIM
7 Reggie Kent	63	38	106	144	6					
10 John Gofton	61	63	59	122	40					
16 Galen Head	70	53	52	105	31	3	2	0	2	0
11 Dick Roberge	72	41	59	100	32	3	0	1	1	4
8 Billy Reid	67	42	48	90	31					
12 Billy Ives	47	33	34	67	28	3	3	0	3	10
2 Jim Mair	71	20	45	65	247	3	0	0	0	6
15 Danny Patrick	32	20	33	53	25	3	0	3	3	0
14 Wayne Wilson	45	15	23	38	7					
4 Mike Crupi	60	6	32	38	227	3	0	2	2	8
3 Billy Armour	30	7	28	35	48	3	1	0	1	0
5 John Nickerson	70	11	22	33	130	3	0	0	0	0
6 Pierre Roy	42	5	26	31	148	3	0	0	0	4
15 Bob Mullins	25	7	10	17	18					
17 Carlo Longarini	10	5	9	14	4	3	0	2	2	0
17 Gerry Beggs	30	5	5	10	5					
15 Pete Inkster	18	2	8	10	41					
6 Bob Delcourt	26	5	4	9	23					
15 Ron Barkwell	21	1	7	8	21					
17 Meehan Bonnar	10	3	4	7	10					
14 Bob Young	9	1	5	6	6					
14 Jack Dale	7	3	2	5	5					
1 Andy Brown (g)	72	0	5	5	108	2	0	0	0	0
3 Jim Randle	2	0	1	1	2					
6 Gordie Rice	7	0	1	1	4					
1 Chuck Rutledge (g)						1	0	0	0	0
Bench					4					2
TOTALS	72	386	628	1,014	1,251 (+15)	3	6	8	14	34

Regular Season Goaltending

	G	Min	GA	ENG	SO	GAA	W	L	T	Saves	Save %
1 Andy Brown	72	4,320	273	0	4	3.79	38	25	9	2,179	0.889
TOTALS	72	4,320	273	0	4	3.79	38	25	9	2,179	0.889

Playoff Goaltending

	G	Min	GA	ENG	SO	GAA	W	L	Saves	Save %
1 Andy Brown	2	120	13	0	0	6.50	0	2	67	0.838
1 Chuck Rutledge	1	60	10	0	0	10.00	0	1	44	0.815
TOTALS	3	180	23	0	0	7.67	0	3	111	0.828

Inkster also wore No. 3.

1968-69 Johnstown Jets

(Front, from left) Jim Coombs, Reggie Kent, general manager John Mitchell, Galen Head, Lynn Zimmerman. (Middle) Trainer Lou Klashinsky, Gene Peacosh, Dick Paradise, Norm Ryder, Wally Chase, Gary Sharp, head coach Dick Roberge. (Back) Jack Dale, Bob Lindberg, Dick Mortenson, Jim Mair, Joe Zanussi.

1968-69 FINAL EASTERN HOCKEY LEAGUE STANDINGS

	Games played	Won	Lost	Tied	Points	Goals for	Goals against
North Division							
Clinton Comets	72	44	18	10	98	284	181
Johnstown Jets	72	42	23	7	91	358	230
New Haven Blades	72	39	23	10	88	343	271
Long Island Ducks	72	27	37	8	62	256	318
Jersey Devils	72	26	39	7	59	245	301
Syracuse Blazers	72	9	59	4	22	178	401
South Division							
Greensboro Generals	72	41	22	9	91	350	279
Nashville Dixie Flyers	72	41	25	6	88	336	253
Charlotte Checkers	72	37	29	6	83	274	281
Jacksonville Rockets	72	27	37	8	62	267	295
Salem Rebels	72	24	45	3	51	240	321

Johnstown Jets
General Manager - John Mitchell
Coach - Dick Roberge
Trainer - Lou Klashinsky
Stickboy - Dave Zeigler
Colors - Royal Blue and White

1968-69 Game Results

Preseason Results
Score

Day	Date	Opponent	Johnstown	Opponent	Attendance	Record
Thur.	10-Oct	Charlotte *	5	1		
Sat.	12-Oct	Toledo **	6	4		
Mon.	14-Oct	Wade Red Wings ***	17	3		

* Game played as 90-minute scrimmage.
** Game played at Toronto, Ontario.
*** Game played at St. Catharines, Ontario.

JETS IN THE SIXTIES

Regular Seaon Results

Day	Date	Opponent	Johnstown	Opponent	Attendance	Record
Thur.	17-Oct	at Syracuse	6	1		1-0-0
Fri.	18-Oct	Clinton	5	4	2,886	2-0-0
Sat.	19-Oct	Syracuse	4	0	3,301	3-0-0
Sun.	20-Oct	at Long Island	1	5		3-1-0
Fri.	25-Oct	at Jersey	5	8		3-2-0
Sat.	26-Oct	New Haven	8	6	3,418	4-2-0
Sun.	27-Oct	at New Haven	2	4		4-3-0
Fri.	1-Nov	at Clinton	2	6		4-4-0
Sat.	2-Nov	Jersey	4	1	3,801	5-4-0
Sun.	3-Nov	at New Haven	4	3		6-4-0
Fri.	8-Nov	at Jersey	1	2		6-5-0
Sat.	9-Nov	Long Island	3	6	4,004	6-6-0
Sun.	10-Nov	Clinton	2	4	2,415	6-7-0
Tues.	12-Nov	at Syracuse	Postponed snow – rescheduled for March 7 in Johnstown			
Wed.	13-Nov	at New Haven	8	8		6-7-1
Fri.	15-Nov	New Haven	4	9	2,095	6-8-1
Sat.	16-Nov	Syracuse	8	2	2,704	7-8-1
Fri.	22-Nov	at Long Island	4	3		8-8-1
Sat.	23-Nov	Long Island	7	1	3,401	9-8-1
Sun.	24-Nov	at Syracuse	5	2		10-8-1
Wed.	27-Nov	Syracuse	8	1	1,965	11-8-1
Thur.	28-Nov	Clinton	0	7	3,344	11-9-1
Fri.	29-Nov	at Jersey	3	2		12-9-1
Sat.	30-Nov	Long Island	5	3	4,119	13-9-1
Fri.	6-Dec	Salem	5	0	2,001	14-9-1
Sat.	7-Dec	at New Haven	6	1		15-9-1
Sun.	8-Dec	at New Haven	1	3		15-10-1
Tues.	10-Dec	at Jacksonville	9	3		16-10-1
Fri.	13-Dec	at Charlotte	6	1		17-10-1
Sat.	14-Dec	at Greensboro	3	8		17-11-1
Sun.	15-Dec	at Nashville	1	4		17-12-1
Sat.	21-Dec	New Haven	3	3	2,177	17-12-2
Sun.	22-Dec	Czech National Team	4	8	2,069	Exhibition
Wed.	25-Dec	at Syracuse	4	5		17-13-2
Thur.	26-Dec	at Syracuse	5	1		18-13-2
Fri.	27-Dec	at Clinton	2	2		18-13-3
Sat.	28-Dec	at Long Island	4	8		18-14-3
Sun.	29-Dec	Jersey	3	3	1,951	18-14-4
Tues.	31-Dec	Long Island	2	5	2,539	18-15-4
Wed.	1-Jan	at New Haven	8	5		19-15-4
Fri.	3-Jan	at Clinton	0	4		19-16-4
Sat.	4-Jan	Jersey	6	0	2,652	20-16-4
Sun.	5-Jan	Jersey	9	1	1,527	21-16-4
Wed.	8-Jan	at Long Island	2	4		21-17-4
Sat.	11-Jan	Syracuse	14	1	2,702	22-17-4
Sun.	12-Jan	Clinton	4	0	2,067	23-17-4
Wed.	15-Jan	at Salem	5	3		24-17-4
Fri.	17-Jan	at Jersey	2	2		24-17-5
Sat.	18-Jan	Jersey	9	2	3,058	25-17-5
Sun.	19-Jan	Clinton	4	4	3,045	25-17-6
Sat.	25-Jan	Long Island	9	3	4,001	26-17-6
Sun.	26-Jan	Jersey	6	3	2,647	27-17-6
Tues.	28-Jan	at Jersey	6	3		28-17-6
Wed.	29-Jan	at Clinton	2	4		28-18-6
Sat.	1-Feb	Syracuse	12	1	1,753	29-18-6
Sun.	2-Feb	at New Haven	4	7		29-19-6
Wed.	5-Feb	at Long Island	1	6		29-20-6
Fri.	7-Feb	at Clinton	2	4		29-21-6
Sat.	8-Feb	Jersey	5	2	2,950	30-21-6
Sun.	9-Feb	Charlotte	1	3	2,281	31-21-6
Sat.	15-Feb	Nashville	7	5	3,130	32-21-6
Sun.	16-Feb	Greensboro	4	2	2,445	33-21-6
Wed.	19-Feb	at Long Island	7	7		33-21-7
Fri.	21-Feb	at Syracuse	8	2		34-21-7
Sat.	22-Feb	New Haven	6	1	4,052	35-21-7

151

Day	Date	Opponent		Score	Attendance	Record
Sun.	23-Feb	Jacksonville	5	2	2,332	36-21-7
Tues.	25-Feb	at Jersey	5	2		37-21-7
Fri.	28-Feb	Long Island	9	0	2,700	38-21-7
Sat.	1-Mar	Syracuse	11	0	2,809	39-21-7
Tues.	4-Mar	at Jersey	4	3		40-21-7
Wed.	5-Mar	at Clinton	0	2		40-22-7
Fri.	7-Mar	Syracuse	9	1	3,220	41-22-7
Sat.	8-Mar	New Haven	6	3	4,181	42-22-7
Sun.	9-Mar	Clinton	13	3	3,718	43-22-7

Playoff Results

Day	Date	Opponent	Johnstown Score	Opponent	Attendance	Record
Wed.	12-Mar	New Haven	4	5	2,062	0-1
Thur.	13-Mar	at New Haven	2	6		0-2
Sat.	15-Mar	New Haven	4	5	4,116	0-3

Attendance Figures

	Dates	Totals	Average
Regular Season Attendance Figures	37	103,391	2,794
Playoff Attendance Totals	2	6,178	3,089
Exhibition Attendance Totals	1	2,069	2,069
TOTAL ATTENDANCE	40	111,638	2,791

1968-69 Player Statistics

	Regular Season Scoring					Playoff Scoring				
	Games	G	A	Pts	PIM	Games	G	A	Pts	PIM
7 Reggie Kent	72	42	97	139	4	3	0	0	0	0
8 Galen Head	72	67	54	121	76	3	2	0	2	2
10 Jack Dale	71	37	63	100	72	3	1	1	2	0
15 Gene Peacosh	71	44	43	87	38	3	0	1	1	0
17 Gary Sharp	51	35	36	71	0	3	2	1	3	5
11 Dick Roberge	72	26	42	68	44	3	1	3	4	0
16 Jim Mair	60	27	31	58	158	3	0	1	1	0
2 Joe Zanussi	72	20	36	56	107	3	2	1	3	12
3 Dick Paradise	72	8	31	39	246	3	0	1	1	41
14 Danny Patrick	42	7	24	31	26					
6 Ken Gustafson	27	10	18	28	4					
6 Bob Lindberg	33	13	14	27	4	3	1	0	1	0
5 Terry Sexsmith	42	1	22	23	146					
14 Dick Mortenson	14	4	18	22	14	3	0	2	2	5
5 Norm Ryder	12	4	10	14	31	3	1	2	3	10
4 Mike Crupi	42	4	7	11	195					
12 Billy Ives	17	3	8	11	4					
12 Wally Chase	10	5	5	10	2	3	0	2	2	0
6 Ted Staeheli	28	0	4	4	57					
12 George Forgie	14	1	2	3	48					
1 Lynn Zimmerman (g)	35	0	3	3	41	3	0	0	0	0
17 Fred Bassi	7	0	2	2	11					
6 Bob Shupe	2	0	1	1	2					
5 Rene Lavigueuer	1	0	0	0	0					
1 Jim Coombs (g) *	51	0	0	0	113					
Bench					6					
TOTALS	72	358	571	929	1,449 (-12)	3	10	15	25	75

Regular Season Goaltending

	G	Min	GA	ENG	SO	GAA	W	L	T	Saves	Save %
1 Lynn Zimmerman	35	2,046	91	1	4	2.67	23	8	3	1,026	0.919
1 Jim Coombs	38	2,258	137	0	2	3.64	19	15	3	1,191	0.897
16 Jim Mair	1	15	1	0	0	3.94	0	0	1	11	0.917
TOTALS	72	4,320	229	1	6	3.19	42	23	7		

Note: Zimmerman totals for Saves and Save % are incomplete – only calculated for available games.

Playoff Goaltending

	G	Min	GA	ENG	SO	GAA	W	L	Saves	Save %
1 Lynn Zimmerman	3	180	16	0	0	5.33	0	3	110	.873
TOTALS	3	180	16	0	0	5.33	0	3	110	.873

Chase also wore No. 14.

* Coombs, a goaltender, also dressed 13 games as a position player and wore Nos. 5,12,14 and 16.

1969-70 Johnstown Jets

(Front, from left) Trainer Lou Klashinsky, Reggie Kent, Jim Coombs, head coach Dick Roberge, general manager John Mitchell. (Middle) Guy Delparte, Bob Taylor, Archie MacDonald, Jack Brewer, Dom DiBerardino, public relations director Terry Schiffhauer. (Back) Ron LaPointe, Scott Buchan, Aurel Beaudin, Gene Peacosh, Rick Loe, Wayne Hoganson

1969-70 FINAL EASTERN HOCKEY LEAGUE STANDINGS

	Games played	Won	Lost	Tied	Points	Goals for	Goals against
North Division							
Clinton Comets	74	50	16	8	108	394	222
New Haven Blades	74	39	20	15	93	377	244
Johnstown Jets	74	27	33	14	68	318	344
Syracuse Blazers	74	23	37	14	60	292	350
Long Island Ducks	74	24	44	6	54	281	364
Jersey Devils	74	20	48	6	46	278	440
South Division							
Greensboro Generals	74	45	22	7	97	333	241
Salem Rebels	74	37	27	10	84	279	266
Charlotte Checkers	74	34	31	9	77	284	266
Jacksonville Rockets	74	27	37	10	64	282	355
Nashville Dixie Flyers	74	27	38	9	63	279	305

Johnstown Jets
General Manager - John Mitchell
Coach - Dick Roberge
Trainer - Lou Klashinsky
Stickboy - Dave Zeigler
Colors - Royal Blue and White

1969-70 Game Results

			Preseason Results Score			
Day	Date	Opponent	Johnstown	Opponent	Attendance	Record
Thur.	9-Oct	Charlotte *	1	8		
Fri.	10-Oct	Clinton **	2	4		
Sat.	11-Oct	at Clinton	5	15		

* 60-minute scrimmage.
** Game played in Utica, N.Y.

Regular Season Results

Day	Date	Opponent	Johnstown	Opponent	Attendance	Record
Wed.	15-Oct	at Syracuse	1	6		0-1-0
Fri.	17-Oct	at Jersey	2	9		0-2-0
Sat.	18-Oct	at Long Island	3	6		0-3-0
Sun	19-Oct	at New Haven	3	8		0-4-0
Fri.	24-Oct	Long Island	6	5	1,991	1-4-0
Sat.	25-Oct	Jersey	6	4	1,930	2-4-0
Fri.	31-Oct	Syracuse	10	5	1,465	3-4-0
Sat.	1-Nov	Charlotte	3	3	2,479	3-4-1
Sun.	2-Nov	at Jersey	4	3		4-4-1
Fri.	7-Nov	Long Island	5	0	1,879	5-4-1
Sat.	8-Nov	Syracuse	7	2	2,861	6-4-1
Sun.	9-Nov	at New Haven	1	10		6-5-1
Tues.	11-Nov	at Charlotte	2	4		6-6-1
Fri.	14-Nov	Clinton	0	4	1,836	6-7-1
Sat.	15-Nov	New Haven	5	5	2,861	6-7-2
Wed.	19-Nov	at New Haven	2	6		6-8-2
Thur.	20-Nov	at Long Island	5	5		6-8-3
Fri.	21-Nov	at Syracuse	5	5		6-8-4
Sat.	22-Nov	New Haven	5	3	3,071	7-8-4
Sun.	23-Nov	Jersey	7	6	1,602	8-8-4
Wed.	26-Nov	Clinton	3	2	2,062	9-8-4
Thur.	27-Nov	Syracuse	3	5	2,820	9-9-4
Fri.	28-Nov	at Clinton	0	6		9-10-4
Sat.	29-Nov	at Jersey	3	5		9-11-4
Sun.	30-Nov	at New Haven	3	7		9-12-4
Fri.	5-Dec	Long Island	2	5	1,877	9-13-4
Sat.	6-Dec	Syracuse	3	3	2,073	9-13-5
Sun.	7-Dec	at New Haven	4	9		9-14-5
Tues.	9-Dec	at Jacksonville	5	5		9-14-6
Thur.	11-Dec	at Nashville	4	4		10-14-6
Fri.	12-Dec	at Greensboro	7	2		11-14-6
Sat.	13-Dec	at Salem	2	7		11-15-6
Sun.	14-Dec	at Jersey	2	8		11-16-6
Fri.	19-Dec	Salem	5	1	1,527	12-16-6
Sat.	20-Dec	Syracuse	5	2	1,857	13-16-6
Sun.	21-Dec	at Syracuse	6	6		13-16-7
Fri.	26-Dec	at Clinton	Postponed – rescheduled for Jan. 28			
Sat.	27-Dec	New Haven	4	4	1,930	13-16-8
Sun.	28-Dec	at Jersey	Postponed – rescheduled for Jan. 21			
Wed.	31-Dec	Clinton	3	5	2,186	13-17-8
Fri.	2-Jan	at Clinton	3	9		13-18-8
Sat.	3-Jan	New Haven	5	6	2,802	13-19-8
Thur.	8-Jan	at Syracuse	3	6		13-20-8
Sat.	10-Jan	Long Island	7	5	2,486	14-20-8
Sun.	11-Jan	Clinton	4	0	1,869	15-20-8
Wed.	14-Jan	at Clinton	5	7		15-21-8
Fri.	16-Jan	Clinton	3	5	1,865	15-22-8
Sat.	17-Jan	Jersey	8	1	2,991	16-22-8
Sun.	18-Jan	at Long Island	2	6		16-23-8
Wed.	21-Jan	Jersey	12	3	1,046	17-23-8
Fri.	23-Jan	at Jersey	8	4		18-23-8
Sat.	24-Jan	New Haven	3	3	3,062	18-23-9
Sun.	25-Jan	at New Haven	2	7		18-24-9
Tues.	27-Jan	at Syracuse	4	4		18-24-10
Wed.	28-Jan	at Clinton	1	3		18-25-10
Fri.	30-Jan	Long Island	7	4	1,907	19-25-10
Sat.	31-Jan	Jersey	10	2	2,600	20-25-10
Sun.	1-Feb	at Long Island	8	4		21-25-10
Wed.	4-Feb	at Clinton	4	10		21-26-10
Sat	7-Feb	Nashville	6	6	2,989	21-26-11
Sun.	8-Feb	Jacksonville	4	5	2,673	21-27-11
Wed.	11-Feb	Long Island	3	1	987	22-27-11
Fri.	13-Feb	at Long Island	5	4		23-27-11
Sat.	14-Feb	Greensboro	2	4	2,329	23-28-11
Sun.	15-Feb	at Jersey	2	4		23-29-11

JETS IN THE SIXTIES

Day	Date	Opponent			Score		Attendance	Record
Tues.	17-Feb	at Syracuse	5	5				23-29-12
Fri.	20-Feb	at Clinton	3	8				23-30-12
Sat.	21-Feb	Jersey	8	5			2,589	24-30-12
Sun.	22-Feb	Jersey	5	2			3,677	25-30-12
Sat.	28-Feb	New Haven	3	3			3,357	25-30-13
Sun.	1-Mar	Clinton	4	6			1,873	25-31-13
Mon.	2-Mar	at Jersey	4	0				26-31-13
Wed.	4-Mar	at New Haven	1	5				26-32-13
Fri.	6-Mar	Syracuse	9	1			1,512	27-32-13
Sat.	7-Mar	New Haven	5	5			3,309	27-32-14
Sun.	8-Mar	at Long Island	4	8				27-33-14

Playoff Results

Day	Date	Opponent	Score Johnstown	Opponent	Attendance	Record
Tues.	10-Mar	at New Haven	4	5		0-1
Wed.	11-Mar	at New Haven	4	7		0-2
Thur.	12-Mar	New Haven	3	5	1,406	0-3
Fri.	13-Mar	New Haven	2	4	2,179	0-4

Attendance Figures

	Dates	Totals	Average
Regular Season Attendance Totals	37	84,230	2,276
Playoff Attendance Totals	2	3,585	1,793
TOTAL ATTENDANCE	39	87,815	2,252

1969-70 Player Statistics

	Regular Season Scoring					Playoff Scoring				
	Games	G	A	Pts	PIM	Games	G	A	Pts	PIM
7 Reggie Kent	65	46	79	125	10	4	3	2	5	2
11 Dick Roberge	74	42	75	117	41	4	3	5	8	0
8 Gene Peacosh	74	49	66	115	42	4	1	0	1	2
15 Rick Loe	70	42	35	77	78	4	0	0	0	0
16 Guy Delparte	68	31	39	70	28	4	1	5	6	0
6 Archie MacDonald	70	25	33	58	32	4	1	1	2	2
17 Wayne Hoganson	74	13	25	38	64	4	0	0	0	0
2 Ron LaPointe	74	6	29	35	159	4	0	1	1	0
10 Pete Christian	33	8	21	29	18					
10 Dom DiBerardino	27	10	17	27	16	4	4	1	5	0
14 Aurel Beaudin	49	11	13	24	64	4	0	2	2	2
4 Larry Young	43	7	16	23	17					
5 Bob Taylor	35	2	18	20	66	4	0	1	1	2
14 Gary Gresdal	19	4	9	13	45					
12 Jack Brewer	21	4	8	12	16	4	0	2	2	0
3 Scott Buchan	48	4	7	11	111	4	0	0	0	21
12 Jean Bouchard	27	4	5	9	83					
3 Jim Pinnegar	25	3	4	7	30					
12 Pete Fichuk	9	2	3	5	2					
5 Mike Embro	21	1	3	4	36					
10 Tom Burgess	12	0	3	3	4					
1 Jim Coombs (g)	74	0	3	3	148	3	0	0	0	17
14 Joe Beggs	3	1	1	2	0					
16 Dave Hunt	3	1	1	2	2					
15 Pierre Belanger	3	0	1	1	0					
6 Bill Kitson	4	1	0	1	0					
17 Keith McKinnon	4	1	0	1	0					
3 Jim McCaffery	4	0	0	0	0					
1 Al Cecile (g)	2	0	0	0	0					
Bench					2					2
TOTALS	74	318	514 (+4)	832	1,114 (-6)	4	13	20	33	50

Regular Season Goaltending

	G	Min	GA	ENG	SO	GAA	W	L	T	Saves	Save %
1 Jim Coombs	74	4,440	340	4	4	4.59	27	33	14	2,591	0.884
TOTALS	74	4,440	340	4	4	4.65	27	33	14	2,591	0.883

Playoff Goaltending

	G	Min	GA	ENG	SO	GAA	W	L		Saves	Save %
1 Al Cecile	2	89	7	0	0	4.72	0	1		49	.875
1 Jim Coombs	3	150	14	0	0	5.60	0	3		108	.885
TOTALS	4	240	21	0	0	5.25	0	4		157	.882

The Tribune-Democrat
Weekender

SATURDAY, OCTOBER 19, 1974

156

The Brothers Carlson— See Page

1970s Overview:
'Tough Hockey,' Tough Town

By Mike Mastovich

So much happened in Johnstown professional hockey during the 1970s that the decade probably would fit nicely into a movie script. Of course, thanks to the classic "Slap Shot" screenplay written by Nancy Dowd, that's exactly what happened.

Johnstown and its hockey team made its way into theaters, a la the Charlestown Chiefs. Aggressive hockey, as the saying went, was back in town during the '70s.

"Back then, the town was blue-collar workers. They wanted to see a team that was tough and played the game tough," said Vern Campigotto, a forward who played for the Jets and Wings from 1971 through 1979.

"It wasn't whether you won or lost," Campigotto said. "The fans appreciated the tough hockey and they appreciated the players who played it tough."

"Slap Shot" aside, Johnstown hockey in the 1970s had much to offer.

An NAHL Rookie of the Year, Henry "Hank" Taylor, shined. The Carlson brothers rocked. Louie Levasseur "saved." Dave Hanson was a "killer." After nearly a decade, Galen Head held a championship trophy. During one magical season in 1974-75, the Johnstown Jets soared from seventh place in January to an NAHL playoff championship in April. That was the team that inspired Dowd's "Slap Shot." Her brother, Ned Dowd, played for Johnstown, and Nancy followed the Jets — observing many of the moments that made it into the Paul Newman film.

"I tore my knee up and missed six weeks that season," said Galen Head, the veteran captain of the 1974-75 Jets. "We started off the season and were struggling a bit. We were working with the WHA Minnesota Fighting Saints at that time.

"We kept adding players ... Mike Chernoff came into the team. Reg Bechtold came in. (General Manager) Johnny Mitchell did a pretty good job of putting the team together. I was fortunate to be able to come back and play with Campy (Vern Campigotto) and Mike Chernoff in the playoffs. Everything started to click. It was one

157

of those things, once you start winning, the guys made up their minds to start playing."

'It all came together'

There was more to the '70s than "Slap Shot" and the team that inspired the movie.

Earlier in the decade, coach Tom McVie simply left the Jets in December 1972, creating uncertainty and a hectic search. Head temporarily ran practices and a few games as Mitchell used his connections to find a new coach. Defenseman Ted Lanyon, a 33-year-old veteran purchased from Greensboro, was named coach.

The Eastern League folded after the 1972-73 season. The North American Hockey League was born a few months later. Head was named coach of the Jets for 1973-74.

A year later, Mitchell called on a familiar name to coach his Jets. Dick Roberge assembled the colorful cast that gradually formed a champion. Players such as Ron Docken, Steve, Jeff and Jack Carlson, Dave Hanson, Campigotto, Jean Tetreault, Guido Tenesi, Reg Bechtold, John Gofton and Mike Chernoff were contributors.

"It all came together when a group of guys came together," said Campigotto, who still resides in Johnstown, where he coached the Greater Johnstown Trojans to a pair of high school state runner-up finishes in the early 1990s.

"The lines were formed. The WHA was folding," Campigotto said. "Players were floating around here and there. All of a sudden, the team came together. I played on a line with Johnny Gofton and Galen Head. We were considered the old-timers, but we contributed. Mike Chernoff was one of the guys who really brought everybody together. We had experience. We had young players. We had chemistry. Plus we were tough. We played a real physical part of the game."

Taylor's time

The following season, coach Jim Cardiff's Jets won their division and appeared poised to make a run at another title. Among the top players on that talented team was a rookie from Oakland, Calif., named Henry "Hank" Taylor. By his own admission in a 1976 Tribune-Democrat feature article, Taylor sometimes felt out of place as a black hockey player from California. But Taylor's play made a statement. He scored 50 goals and 93 points to lead a team that won the NAHL's Western Division. Taylor was an NAHL Rookie of the Year at age 20.

Ironically, the Jets almost lost him. Taylor began the season in the Minnesota Fighting Saints rookie camp, then was sent to Johnstown's training camp in Niagara Falls. He returned to Pennsylvania with the team, but after one game Minnesota sent multiple players to the Jets, and Taylor subsequently was released.

Before he had a chance to sign on with another team, Jets Executive Director John Mitchell called Taylor and invited him back.

"I was going to Green Bay in the United States League," Taylor said in an Oct. 16, 1976 Tribune-Democrat article. "I talked to the people in Green Bay less than an hour before Mitchell asked me to come back. I was going to Green Bay the next day."

Legendary brawl

That 1975-76 team had a strong cast that included the likes of future NHL standout Paul Holmgren, enforcer Dave Birch, championship-winning goalies Ron Docken and Levasseur, Head, Hanson, Gofton, Tenesi, Tetreault, Bruce Boudreau, Francois Ouimet and Jim Adair.

During the 1976 playoffs, Campigotto was a key figure in a bizarre scene that unfolded much like something in "Slap Shot." The decisive fifth game of a Lockhart Cup playoff series ended without a shot being fired on goal at the War Memorial. The opposition refused to take the ice after a pregame brawl and forfeited.

Buffalo Norsemen defenseman Greg Neeld had agitated the Jets and their fans throughout the NAHL quarterfinal playoff series. Neeld had already served a two-game suspension for firing a stick into a crowd of Johnstown fans during Game 2 at the War Memorial. Neeld and Jets tough guy Hanson previously had mixed it up as well. Campigotto and Neeld had tangled off the ice after the Norsemen's 3-2 win in Game 4 at Buffalo. The suspended Neeld was in street clothes for that one.

"That incident ... I remember Davey Hanson going after Gregg Neeld a number of times. It all started up in Buffalo," Campigotto said. "Greg Neeld, I admired the kid. He was a good hockey player. But nobody could ever figure out how to fight him because he wore a mask. We were tied in the best-of-5 at 2-2, and we're coming back on the bus. I said to Davey Hanson, 'I'm going to get him.' I figured it out. He didn't wear his mask during warm ups."

Campigotto and Neeld exchanged words as the teams skated past each other during warm ups prior to Game 5. After the brief verbal encounter, Campigotto skated in front of Neeld. The Buffalo player threw off his gloves and charged Campigotto. Mayhem followed as players on both teams paired up before the officials even were on the ice. Neeld, bleeding from a cut above his eye, eventually was carried away on a stretcher. "We were in the dressing room. Davey asked, 'Are you going after him?' I said, 'Yeah, I'm going to get him,'" Campigotto recalled.

No repeat

NAHL Commissioner Jack Timmins was in attendance and witnessed the melee. Buffalo General Manager Willie Marshall refused to put his team back on the ice "to possibly subject them to injury," according to Timmins in newspaper reports.

When Buffalo's players ignored orders to take the ice, referee Steve Dowling entered the visitors dressing room and gave them a five-minute ultimatum. Coach Guy Trottier chose to remain in the room, accepting a forfeit and handing the series to Johnstown.

A standing-room-only crowd had to leave the War Memorial without seeing a game, though there was plenty of entertainment. The Jets reported that the gate that night was $19,000, and the team requested compensation from the Norsemen through the league office.

The Norsemen left the arena with an escort from two police officers and their canine dogs.

Coach Jim Cardiff's Jets lost to Philadelphia in the semifinals, ending hopes of a repeat. That Jets team was considered as good as, if not more accomplished than, the NAHL champions. Some felt the team was distracted by the filming of "Slap Shot" that spring involving many of the Jets players.

"We had the team that should have won it two years in a row," Campigotto said. "Maybe the movie (distracted the Jets), maybe this, or maybe that."

The 1976-77 Jets slipped to seventh place. There was no opportunity to rebound. The devastating 1977 Johnstown Flood wiped out hockey for a season. When the Johnstown Wings returned in 1978-79 in the Northeast League and the Red Wings followed in 1979-80 in a new Eastern League, the financial hurdles and the instability of their respective leagues led to an eight-year hockey hiatus.

Galen Head played in 561 games over eight seasons in Johnstown.

REPRINT

On Oct. 18, 2003, the Johnstown Chiefs retired the No. 8 uniform worn for eight seasons and 561 games by Johnstown Jets forward Galen Head, one of the most prolific scorers in Johnstown hockey history. Head, who later coached Bishop McCort High School to three state championships, is a member of both the Johnstown Hockey Hall of Fame and Cambria County Sports Hall of Fame. The following story appeared on Oct. 12, 2003:

No. 8 joining Johnstown's elite

By Mike Mastovich

For eight seasons and 561 games, No. 8 was the Johnstown Jets' No. 1 ambassador on the ice. Galen Head, the prolific scorer, team leader, gentleman and all-around good guy, represented the Jets as a star player, team captain and player-coach.

The Grand Prairie, Alberta, native who eventually made Johnstown his home captained the city's last professional hockey championship team, the renown 1974-75 Jets squad that inspired the motion picture "Slap Shot."

All of those facts certainly justify the ECHL Johnstown Chiefs' decision to retire Head's No. 8 uniform, making Head, 56, only the third former Johnstown hockey player honored in such a manner and the first since both Don Hall and Dick Roberge had their No. 9 and No. 11 jerseys retired in the 1990-91 season.

But there are so many more reasons Head merits this recognition.

He's been a volunteer assistant coach of the Chiefs since 1997-98, offering expertise, experience and game-night scouting reports to three different head coaches, Nick Fotiu, Scott Allen and Toby O'Brien. Head's impact as a coach and role model has been even more significant at the high school level, where he helped start the Bishop McCort program in 1985-86 and spent 11 seasons with the Crimson Crushers, leading his team to three straight Class A state championships before retiring in 1996.

"I think it's an honor that is both worthy and overdue," O'Brien said prior to the Chiefs exhibition tournament with Roanoke and Wheeling yesterday at Cambria County War Memorial Arena. "The Jets, Bishop McCort, the Chiefs, the student hockey league. We just felt it was right to retire the No. 8 because of all of those associations and what Galen has meant to the Greater Johnstown hockey community.

"Unlike the other two numbers, who are great players and great people and represented the Jets and the city of Johnstown in a great manner, Galen crossed several generations of hockey in our community. It's an honor and a pleasure to have him involved in our organization now."

Head's impact as a player with the Jets was remarkable. The 5-foot-9, 160-pound right wing broke into the organization in 1967-68 in the former Eastern Hockey League. As a rookie, Head scored 53 goals and 105 points in 70 games.

That same season, he earned a brief call up to the National Hockey League Detroit Red Wings. Officially, Head appeared in one NHL game. His best season in Johnstown was in 1968-69, when Head scored 67 goals and 121 points. His 67 regular-season goals and 69 goals including the playoffs were Johnstown franchise records that stood until the Chiefs' Mark Green scored 68 and 70 in 1991-92.

Head played 43 games for the Salt Lake Golden Eagles in the former Western Hockey League in 1969-70. A shattered cheekbone injury cut short his season and, many believe, prevented Head from making a return to the NHL.

He rejoined the Jets in 1970-71 and played the next six seasons with Johnstown.

Head's 308 goals rank third all-time in Johnstown history, and his 601 points rank fourth. He also had 293 assists, sixth all-time.

That background made Head a natural to coach the Crushers high school team. His program was 134-98-9 and won Pennsylvania Cups in 1994, 1995 and 1996.

"No question, Galen has got hockey to the level that it's at in the Johnstown area, not only as a player but certainly as a coach. Everything he has done in his involvement in hockey has been tremendous," said current McCort coach John Bradley, an assistant under Head before taking the top job. "I've never seen him play, but from what I've heard around town, he probably was one of the best to play here. As far as coaching, there's probably no one else in town with his knowledge of hockey. Nobody.

"He was the type of guy kids wanted to play for. He was a real good guy as a coach. He is special. He is one of a kind. Gordie Howe may be Mr. Hockey. But Galen Head is Johnstown's version of Mr. Hockey."

Head joins an elite club. Hall, known as Jet 9, had 393 goals, 585 assists and 978 points in 667 games with Johnstown in the 1950s and early 1960s. Roberge is minor-league hockey's all-time leading scorer with 1,699 points, 737 goals and 962 assists in 1,158 games during 17 seasons. Hall, Roberge and Head are among the six inductees to the Johnstown Hockey Hall of Fame. Hall and Roberge are also members of the Cambria County Sports Hall of Fame.

"Even though he was not a Johnstown Chiefs player, we would like to recognize him by retiring that number for everything he has done for and brought to our organization," Chiefs General Manager Jim Brazill said.

The Galen Head Jr. Memorial Scholarship Fund honors Galen and Gracie Head's first son, who died tragically in an automobile accident in 1996.

Galen Jr. was the Chiefs' first trainer and was working for the International Hockey League's Fort Wayne Komets and headed to the Milwaukee Admirals at the time of his death.

The scholarship has financially assisted local hockey players pursue their college aspirations.

Head might not be a Johnstown native, but his bond to the community is evident.

"In this area not only is Galen recognized as a great hockey player and a great coach, but he's also recognized as one heck of a guy," Bradley said.

"He's special. He's a great guy and that's probably the most important thing.

"My own kids call him Pop Pop. My kids look at him as if he was their grandfather. He's a father figure to me. That's the type of guy he is."

JETS IN THE SEVENTIES

Top: Jets captain Galen Head (8) challenges Mohawk Valley goaltender Michel Dion.

Middle: Mohawk Valley and Johnstown players square off.

Bottom: Galen Head in action against Philadelphia Firebirds goalie Reggie Lemelin.

163

John Mitchell was a scout for the NHL's Detroit Red Wings before coming to Johnstown.

A Good Hockey Man
'Big Daddy' Mitchell Helped Keep Hockey in Johnstown

By Mike Mastovich

John Mitchell might not have been responsible for bringing professional hockey to Johnstown. But the no-nonsense general manager/executive director ensured the sport's survival throughout difficult economic conditions and more than one crisis that seemed to doom the club's long-term future.

He stood only about 5-feet, 4-inches tall, but Mitchell still was known as "Big Daddy" to anyone familiar with the Johnstown Jets. Among his other nicknames were "Mr. Hockey," "Mr. Johnstown Jet," "Mitch" and the "Lord of the Rink."

Mitchell achieved almost legendary status in Johnstown during two tenures with the Jets and a season with the Johnstown Wings. Players, coaches and even reporters were called "son" by Mitch: "Son, I'm going to tell you a story," or "Pull up a chair, son."

"Mitch was a character. He was a short man, but we should have been looking up at him," said former Jets all-star defenseman Dave Lucas, who played on Mitchell's playoff championship squads in 1960, '61 and '62. "He was a good hockey man. He knew what he wanted and wasn't afraid to go out and get it."

A native of Kirkintillock, Scotland, Mitchell became a naturalized American citizen. He was a hockey clubhouse boy at age 15 and spent the next six decades devoted to the sport. "Mitch reminded me of an Art Rooney type. It was always about the team, not the players," said former Tribune-Democrat sports writer John P. James. "He would do whatever it took to keep the team in Johnstown. He was so bright. He was not educated, not a college graduate. But he could wheel and deal with the best of them. John knew hockey."

Mitchell was a National Hockey League official for five years. He served as general manager of the American Hockey League Pittsburgh Hornets for nine seasons and worked for AHL clubs in Springfield, Mass., Buffalo, N.Y., and Providence, R.I.

His coaching career included stays with New Haven, St. Louis and Los Angeles in the minors. He spent a year as a scout with the Chicago Blackhawks.

Mitchell's big break came in 1952, when the Detroit Red Wings named him as chief scout and farm director. In 1959, he accepted the general manager position with Johnstown in the Eastern League.

"At that time, John probably was one of the best scouts in the National Hockey League," James said. "At about the same time, Johnstown's team was struggling. (Johnstown Hockey Co. President) Charlie Kunkle called the Detroit Red Wings and asked if the Jets could have John Mitchell to clean things up here in Johnstown. "The original plan was that John would come here one or two years just to get things squared away."

Mission accomplished. Mitchell's Jets reeled off three consecutive Boardwalk Trophy EHL championships. Those teams, coached by Steve Brklacich, featured stars such as Don Hall, Dick Roberge, Ken Coombes, Ed Johnston, Lucas and Ken Laufman.

"He was 5-foot-4, a tough old guy," Roberge said of Mitchell. "He had a lot of determination. He had the greatest dressing room talks ever to get guys going. He lived hockey 24 hours a day. There was no other sport. Nothing. Hockey was his life."

After that third title in 1961-62, Mitchell returned to the Red Wings as an assistant to Detroit GM-coach Sid Abel. The Johnstown Hockey Co. released Mitchell from the final two years of his contract with the Jets, allowing him to move back into the NHL.

"John Mitchell was really a character. John Mitchell had no conversation and nothing in life except hockey," Johnstown's Kunkle said during a 2006 interview. "He never talked about anything else, and he gave all of his efforts to whomever he was working for. Tom Lockhart talked the Detroit Red Wings into sending John Mitchell here. He was very controversial. He was extremely frugal and he handled the club money magnificently."

'Smartest hockey man'

Minus Mitchell, the Jets had mixed success on the ice the next four seasons and struggled financially. The NHL expanded from six to 12 teams in 1967, a move that increased competition for players and made the EHL's developmental role more significant. The Red Wings and Johnstown Hockey Co. brought Mitchell back to the Jets for the 1967-68 season. "This is a great day for hockey in Johnstown," Kunkle said in the June 29, 1967 Tribune-Democrat. The Jets didn't have the immediate championship success Mitchell's teams enjoyed earlier in the decade. But Johnstown operated on more solid ground and began to assemble talented players, a few of whom would bring the city a championship less than a decade later.

"John was without a doubt the smartest hockey man that I've been around," said James, who also performed media relations duties for the Jets under Mitchell. "Mitch could pick up the phone and call Clarence Campbell, the commissioner at the National Hockey League, and he would get straight through. There was no, 'Mr. Campbell will return your call.'"

James recounted some of Mitchell's best front-office anecdotes. "One year, Detroit told John they couldn't get him any goalies," James said. "They told him to start looking around. He knew every player who put on skates in Canada, it seemed. He came back and said we got a couple goalies. One was Eddie Johnston and the other was Eddie Giacomin. They were both here, and John had to cut one of those goalies."

Johnston made the club and led the Jets to a title, showing the skills that later made him an NHL star with the Boston Bruins. Giacomin landed with the EHL's Clinton Comets on the way to a Hall of Fame career with the New York Rangers.

Mitchell also could be a psychologist if the situation called for such an approach.

"One of the players had been nursing a thumb injury and hadn't been rehabbing as well as he should have been," James said. "There was a knock on John's door and the player walked in and asked if John wanted to talk to him. John said to the player, 'I know that thumb is bothering you. But you've got us in a bad position. Detroit wants to send us down a young winger. I don't know how long I can put them off. When can you get back on skates?' "

James said the player had a worrisome expression on his face.

"He said he actually was coming to tell John that he'd be ready the next night," James said. "That player went out and had a bunch of goals the next night and went on to a great career. Later, John said he didn't have any young winger coming down. He knew the player just needed motivated."

Mitchell also knew the old-school tricks of the trade.

"The Jets had a goalie that had a problem with coming out of the net too far," James said. "During practice John put a rope around the goaltender and tied it to the net. The guy would go so far and the rope would stop him."

'When the kids won ...'

The Eastern League broke up after the 1972-73 season, and the Jets joined the new North American Hockey League. Mitch's boys were mired in seventh place on Jan. 19, 1975 but won 23 of the final 31 games to secure a playoff spot. Once in the postseason, the Jets won series against Cape Cod, Syracuse and Binghamton to win the championship. Mitchell found a young French-Canadian goalie named Louie Levasseur, who blossomed into a playoff star en route to a Lockhart Cup.

Other characters on that Jets squad were the Carlson brothers — Steve, Jeff and Jack — Dave Hanson, Ron Docken, Galen Head and Johnny Gofton. "I think that really did it for him," said Roberge, who coached the 1974-75 Jets and played on Mitchell's three other playoff champs. "Big Daddy was getting older and older. When the kids won that, he was a happy man. I think he could go to his death after that and say everything was perfect."

The 1975-76 Jets were supposed to be even better. Johnstown won its division but lost to Philadelphia in the playoffs. Filming of the movie "Slap Shot" was underway, and many players were extras. Some felt the distractions contributed to the upset loss.

Mitchell was rehired by new ownership in June 1976, but two weeks later the executive director and his Jets parted ways. Some accounts said he resigned. Mitchell said in published reports he was fired. "Hockey will be history in two years," center Steve Carlson said in a newspaper account on May 29, 1976. "Who's going to bring in players? I can't believe it. I don't know who let him go but it's the biggest mistake they'll ever make."

In fact, hockey was gone by 1977-78, but that had as much to do with the 1977 Johnstown Flood destroying much of the War Memorial as it did the team's typical financial woes. Still, Mitchell was back in the winter of 1977-78 attempting to revive hockey in Johnstown. He was instrumental in assembling the Johnstown Wings and the Northeast Hockey League.

"John Mitchell made a great impression on me," said former Jets forward Vern Campigotto, who played under Mitchell's watch from 1971-79. "My feeling was you either liked him or didn't like him. I liked him. He was very opinionated. He was hockey-oriented. That was his whole life. He was great for Johnstown.

"We had our tussles. Every time I tried to walk away from him, he always told me, 'Son, you don't walk away from me. We settle this right now.'"

Mitchell died in December 1986 at age 85. But his legacy in Johnstown endures.

Galen Head hoists the Lockhart Cup during a May 1975 championship parade through the streets of downtown Johnstown.

JETS IN THE SEVENTIES

REPRINT

The Johnstown Jets were near the bottom of the North American Hockey League standings at Christmas, but soared to a Lockhart Cup playoff title a few months later. To commemorate the 25th anniversary of the Jets' 1974-75 championship, The Tribune-Democrat published the following article on April 30, 2000:

The year the Jets soared

By Mike Mastovich

Galen Head clutched the Lockhart Cup Trophy with two hands, held it above his head and smiled at the thousands of Johnstown Jets fans gathered along the downtown streets for a hastily organized parade. The image of Head, wearing sunglasses, a leisure suit and bell-bottom pants, is unforgettable for longtime Johnstown fans.

Twenty-five years have passed since the Jets swept the Binghamton, N.Y., Broome Dusters in the best-of-7 North American Hockey League championship series. At 10:42 p.m. on Thursday, May 1, 1975, the Jets clinched the playoff title. The milestone remains Johnstown's most recent professional hockey championship. It was another era for Johnstown and an important chapter in the city's storied hockey legacy.

In 1975, steel and coal mining still were major employers in the region. Johnstown had withstood only two of its three devastating floods. On the ice, the Jets rallied behind the slogan, "Aggressive Hockey is Back in Johnstown" and captured the NAHL's Lockhart Cup. The championship team inspired Nancy Dowd's screenplay to the Paul Newman movie "Slap Shot," filmed here a year after the title run.

"It was a great time. It was a wonderful time for Johnstown hockey," said Ron Docken, a goaltender on the championship team. "I don't know if any other community at that particular time supported their hockey team like Johnstown."

Docken, 51, sells tools and plumbing supplies in Apple Valley, Minn., a suburb of Minneapolis. He was the Jets' No. 1 goalie for most of 1974-75, playing 2,302 minutes during the regular season. But Docken watched a young, often unorthodox French-Canadian goalie named Louie Levasseur catch fire in the post-season.

"He came to Johnstown really as a nobody," said Head, the '75 Jets veteran captain, who eventually made Johnstown his home and now is the East Coast Hockey League Johnstown Chiefs assistant coach. "Louie was a typical goaltender. He had his quirks. He was a little bit different. But when it came down to money time and winning, this guy was unbelievable." So were the Jets.

169

As late as Jan. 19, Johnstown was mired in seventh place. There was no talk of the postseason. But something magical happened. The Jets won, and won, and won. Twenty-three victories in their last 31 regular-season games. "It was an interesting season. We were only a couple points out of last place at a point and time in the year," Docken said. "All of a sudden we kind of caught fire. We went through the second half of the season with one of the best records ever put out."

Tough guys Jeff Carlson and Dave "Killer" Hanson combined for 1,594 penalty minutes and clearly intimidated opponents. Players such as Jim Adair, Mike Chernoff and Reg Bechtold provided offense. Steve Carlson, a future NHL player and coach of the Johnstown Chiefs for five seasons, collected a team-best 87 points. Defensemen Guido Tenesi, Bob Boyd, Francois Ouimet and Pat Westrum were among the best in the league. Head, Johnny Gofton, Jean Tetreault, Ned Dowd (whose sister Nancy wrote "Slap Shot") and Jerry Welsh scored points, while gritty players such as Vern Campigotto filled multiple roles in the absence of tough standout Jack Carlson, who was on recall to the Minnesota Fighting Saints of the World Hockey Association.

"We had the Carlsons (brothers Steve, Jeff and Jack) and they kept everybody loose," said Gofton, 56, a left wing on the championship team and now a rental equipment manager in Tillsonburg, Ontario. "They were a good bunch of guys and everything just worked out. We had three good lines. Everybody scored goals. We were pretty loose. We had a lot of fun while we played hockey."

Jets coach Dick Roberge already was a hockey legend after playing 17 seasons in Johnstown. Winning a championship as a coach enhanced a resume that led to Roberge's No. 11 uniform being retired with ex-Jets great Don Hall's No. 9. "The team itself, they all came together real well and they all had a lot of fun playing that year. They were tough kids," said Roberge, 66, a retired golf professional from Myrtle Beach, S.C. "They had a lot of talent and a lot of strengths. It was fun coaching them."

The Binghamton Brawl

Roberge remembered a turning point during the regular season.

"We battled all year," Roberge said. "We got into Binghamton about two or three weeks before the playoffs. In the team warm up, we're out there and all the Binghamton players came out with the plastic glasses and big noses, every one of them, poking fun at the Carlson brothers. We went back in the dressing room and the boys said, 'Coach, as soon as that puck is dropped, we're pairing up.' We had one heckuva fight. They went about 30 minutes until everyone got tired. We met them again in the finals and beat them four straight."

Getting to the finals was another story. The Jets finished the regular season in fourth place and met the Cape Cod, Mass., Codders in the first round of the playoffs. Docken had a 39-save shutout in a 3-0 victory in Game 1 at the Cape Cod Coliseum. Cape Cod won Game 2 at the Cambria County War Memorial Arena, but Johnstown bounced back to win the next two games and the series. The Jets next met Syracuse in a best-of-7 semifinal series that many called the unofficial championship round.

The Jets had five regular-season wins over the Blazers at the Cambria County War Memorial. The Blazers beat the Jets five times at the Onondaga County War Memorial.

Syracuse was 32-5 at home. Worse yet, Johnstown hadn't won at Syracuse since 1971. The home-ice advantage continued in the semifinals. The Jets won games 2, 3 and 6 at home, and the Blazers took games 1, 4 and 5. That set up the decisive seventh game at Onondaga County.

"We never won in Syracuse for five years," said Steve Carlson, now a television color commentator for the International League Milwaukee Admirals. "We were going into that seventh game thinking, 'Let's play, let's not get embarrassed.' Going into the third period, we're going out there saying, 'Hey, we can win this game.' "

Carlson, then 19 years old, scored twice in Game 7, including a 15-foot wrist shot at 16:51 of the final period. Johnstown beat the Blazers 5-4 and ended a 41-game winless streak at Syracuse.

The championship series was delayed 10 days. The War Memorial was booked with a home show for four days and an arts festival for three days. Binghamton's arena was unavailable because a circus was in town. The Jets practiced at Alpine Arena in the Wilkinsburg section of Pittsburgh. Binghamton traveled to Elmira, N.Y., to work out.

The Jets didn't waste any time disposing of Binghamton, winning 5-1 behind Levasseur's 34 saves in Game 1, with 3,483 fans watching at the War Memorial. Johnstown won Game 2, 7-4, before a sellout crowd of 4,700 at Broome County Veterans Memorial Arena. Levasseur had 36 saves in a 2-1 victory at Binghamton in Game 3, and Chernoff netted the game-winner.

Anticipating a sweep, fans lined up early for Game 4 at Johnstown. The attendance officially was listed as 4,088. "It was unbelievable," Head said. "People were hanging off the rafters watching us play that game. I think there was like 4,300 people in a building that holds only 4,040."

A right wing, Head skated through the Dusters crease from the right corner then backhanded a shot past Binghamton goalie Rick Lemay in the second period. He used an almost identical move to tally again 30 seconds later in the Jets' 6-2 victory.

The postgame party

Head and Campigotto attempted a victory skate while holding the Lockhart Trophy presented by Tom Lockhart, the former Eastern Hockey League president. But they only made it halfway around the arena before dozens of fans mobbed them. More than 100 fans were on the ice, ignoring pleas from the public address announcer asking them to leave. Several Jets basked in the moment with team executive director John Mitchell, the venerable front office leader known as "Mr. Hockey" in Johnstown.

The arena concourse was packed with people waiting for the players, who were inside the locker room, where champagne flowed and shaving cream was squirted on players, bystanders and the walls. When told the players' wives were waiting outside, the team sent a bottle of champagne to the concourse and continued the locker room celebration. "There was something special about that team," Steve Carlson said. "We had a lot of talent. We hung out together as a team. We'd go to Brownies for lunch. We'd go to the Professor's Inn and the Hendler Lounge, the Golden Key, the Forest Park Club. All the team members and their wives and girlfriends would show up. We enjoyed each other a lot. It was a special team."

The team got together, red-eyed and hung over, for an impromptu parade on May 2. Spaced between high school bands from Greater Johnstown, Richland and Johnstown Vo-Tech, the players were cheered by several thousand fans. Then-Johnstown Mayor Herb Pfuhl made the Jets honorary citizens.

"The parade was quite frankly shocking," Docken said. "We just won the championship. Fine. That's great. To show up the next day, and they have this parade ... You see the people turn out like they did, it was absolutely unbelievable. It was like a New York type of thing. It was overwhelming. It was wonderful."

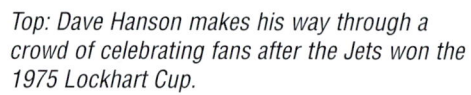

Top: Dave Hanson makes his way through a crowd of celebrating fans after the Jets won the 1975 Lockhart Cup.

Middle left: Veterans Vern Campigotto (left) and Galen Head (right) skate a victory lap with the Lockhart Cup at Cambria County War Memorial Arena.

Middle right: The post-game party.

Bottom right: Coach Dick Roberge with the Lockhart Cup.

172

JETS IN THE SEVENTIES

Top left: Henry "Hank" Taylor won NAHL Rookie of the Year honors in 1975-76.

Top right: Galen Head (8) carries the puck toward Binghamton goaltender Rick Lemay.

Above: Jets right wing Jeff Carlson (18) locks up with Syracuse defenseman Reg Krezanski.

Left: Jets forward Remi Lesage.

173

Top left: Jim Wilcox (4), Jerry Welsh (15) and Moe St. Jacques (7) in pregame warmups.

Top right: Philadelphia Firebirds tough guy Ray Schultz.

Left: Jets goaltender Don Atchison defends the net.

Bottom: Red Bull Inn trading cards of Reg Kent, Tom McCarthy and Brian Coughlin from 1972-73.

174

JETS IN THE SEVENTIES

Top left: Coach Dick Roberge and his defensemen — Jim Trewin, Blake Ball and Len Cunning.

Top right: Paul Holmgren at practice.

Middle right: Jets center Steve Carlson (17) shoots on Mohawk Valley goalie Michel Dion.

Bottom: Henry "Hank" Taylor (7) works the puck in front of Binghamton goalie Rick Lemay as Paul Stewart (2) defends.

Top: Jets and Charlotte Checkers brawl in 1970-71.

Left: The Jets and Cape Codders brawled during Game 2 of a first-round playoff series on March 27, 1975 at the War Memorial.

Below left: Fans stream through the War Memorial concourse after the Buffalo Norsemen forfeited a 1976 playoff game.

Below: Johnstown's Brian Vescio (10) skates toward the Clinton Comets net. Teammate Kevin Collins watches the play.

JETS IN THE SEVENTIES

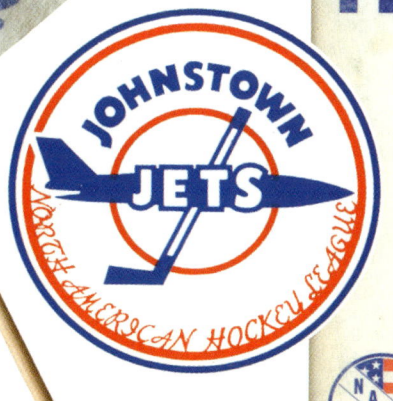

1970-71 Johnstown Jets

(Front, from left) Bob Vroman, head coach Dick Roberge, general manager John Mitchell, Gene Peacosh, Jim Coombs. (Middle) Len Cunning, Jim Trewin, trainer Lou Klashinsky, Blake Ball, Gary Wood, Dave Birch. (Back) Reg Kent, Bob Warner, Aurel Beaudin, Gary Brown, Galen Head, Alan Cameron, Guy Delparte

1970-71 FINAL EASTERN HOCKEY LEAGUE STANDINGS

	Games played	Won	Lost	Tied	Points	Goals for	Goals against
North Division							
New Haven Blades	74	38	21	15	91	339	244
Syracuse Blazers	74	36	30	8	80	303	286
Johnstown Jets	74	30	29	15	75	275	298
Clinton Comets	74	31	32	11	73	257	236
Long Island Ducks	74	29	35	10	68	286	296
Jersey Devils	74	22	39	13	57	282	353
South Division							
Charlotte Checkers	74	55	12	7	117	383	153
Greensboro Generals	74	44	21	8	96	337	234
Salem Rebels	74	31	34	9	71	252	297
Nashville Dixie Flyers	74	26	42	5	57	264	337
Jacksonville Rockets	74	11	58	5	27	206	450

Johnstown Jets
General Manager - John Mitchell
Coach - Dick Roberge
Trainer - Lou Klashinsky
Stickboy - Dave Zeigler, Pete Bach
Colors - Royal Blue and White

1970-71 Game Results

Preseason Results

Day	Date	Opponent	Johnstown	Opponent	Attendance	Record
Fri.	9-Oct	Dundas	9	1		
Sun.	11-Oct	at Brantford	9	0		

JETS IN THE SEVENTIES

Regular Season Results

Day	Date	Opponent	Score Johnstown	Opponent	Attendance	Record
Fri.	16-Oct	at Jersey	3	3		0-0-1
Sat.	17-Oct	at Long Island	4	1		1-0-1
Fri.	23-Oct	Clinton	3	1	3,141	2-0-1
Sat.	24-Oct	New Haven	3	2	3,731	3-0-1
Wed.	28-Oct	at New Haven	1	6		3-1-1
Fri.	30-Oct	Long Island	6	6	2,366	3-1-2
Sat.	31-Oct	Syracuse	4	4	3,451	3-1-3
Fri.	6-Nov	at Clinton	5	3		4-1-3
Sat.	7-Nov	Jersey	3	3	3,708	4-1-4
Sun.	8-Nov	Clinton	0	3	2,231	4-2-4
Wed.	11-Nov	at New Haven	Postponed – rescheduled for Dec. 3			
Fri.	13-Nov	Long Island	7	1	2,261	5-2-4
Sat.	14-Nov	Jersey	7	3	3,325	6-2-4
Fri.	20-Nov	at Clinton	1	1		6-2-5
Sat.	21-Nov	New Haven	5	5	3,876	6-2-6
Sun.	22-Nov	Long Island	3	3	1,968	6-2-7
Wed.	25-Nov	Clinton	3	3	2,121	6-2-8
Thur.	26-Nov	Jersey	4	3	3,569	7-2-8
Fri.	27-Nov	at Jersey	4	6		7-3-8
Sat.	28-Nov	at Clinton	2	6		7-4-8
Sun.	29-Nov	Long Island	6	3	2,256	8-4-8
Thur.	3-Dec	at New Haven	3	10		8-5-8
Fri.	4-Dec	at Long Island	1	4		8-6-8
Sat.	5-Dec	Syracuse	4	5	2,936	8-7-8
Sun.	6-Dec	Clinton	4	4	1,509	8-7-9
Tues.	8-Dec	at Charlotte	1	5		8-8-9
Wed.	9-Dec	at Greensboro	0	9		8-9-9
Fri.	11-Dec	at Jacksonville	2	1		9-9-9
Sat.	12-Dec	at Nashville	3	8		9-10-9
Wed.	16-Dec	at New Haven	4	10		9-11-9
Fri.	18-Dec	at Jersey	2	3		9-12-9
Sat.	19-Dec	New Haven	6	2	2,485	10-12-9
Sun.	20-Dec	at Syracuse	2	9		10-13-9
Wed.	23-Dec	at Syracuse	3	5		10-14-9
Sat.	26-Dec	at Clinton	2	7		10-15-9
Sun.	27-Dec	Jersey	7	1	2,434	11-15-9
Wed.	30-Dec	at New Haven	4	7		11-16-9
Thur.	31-Dec	New Haven	5	1	1,951	12-16-9
Fri.	1-Jan	at Clinton	4	5		12-17-9
Sat.	2-Jan	Jersey	2	1	2,802	13-17-9
Wed.	6-Jan	Syracuse	4	4	1,702	13-17-10
Fri.	8-Jan	at Jersey	5	5		13-17-11
Sat.	9-Jan	Jacksonville	6	1	3,118	14-17-11
Wed.	13-Jan	at Jersey	3	2		15-17-11
Fri.	15-Jan	New Haven	4	5	2,281	15-18-11
Sat.	16-Jan	Salem	6	1	2,850	16-18-11
Sun.	17-Jan	at Salem	5	5		16-18-12
Wed.	20-Jan	at Clinton	4	1		17-18-12
Thur.	21-Jan	at Syracuse	3	8		17-19-12
Fri.	22-Jan	Clinton	3	1	2,275	18-19-12
Sat.	23-Jan	Long Island	7	3	3,350	19-19-12
Sun.	24-Jan	at New Haven	3	10		19-20-12
Wed.	27-Jan	Long Island	6	4	1,207	20-20-12
Fri.	29-Jan	at Jersey	5	5		20-20-13
Sat.	30-Jan	Jersey	7	2	2,379	21-20-13
Sun.	31-Jan	at Long Island	4	0		22-20-13
Thur.	4-Feb	at Long Island	1	3		22-21-13
Sat.	6-Feb	Syracuse	6	4	4,152	23-21-13
Sun.	7-Feb	Charlotte	7	5	2,807	24-21-13
Wed.	10-Feb	Jersey	3	4	1,645	24-22-13
Fri.	12-Feb	at Long Island	2	2		24-22-14
Sat.	13-Feb	New Haven	4	2	2,807	25-22-14
Wed.	17-Feb	at Long Island	4	6		25-23-14
Fri.	19-Feb	at Syracuse	Forfeit*			25-24-14
Sat.	20-Feb	Syracuse	4	3	4,001	26-24-14

179

Day	Date	Opponent			Attendance	Record
Sun.	21-Feb	Nashville	3	4	4,002	26-25-14
Tues.	23-Feb	at Syracuse	3	3		26-25-15
Wed.	24-Feb	at New Haven	2	10		26-26-15
Fri.	26-Feb	at Long Island	4	2		27-26-15
Sat.	27-Feb	Greensboro	8	5	3,395	28-26-15
Sun.	28-Feb	Clinton	3	2	2,352	29-26-15
Wed.	3-Mar	at Syracuse	1	7		29-27-15
Fri.	5-Mar	Long Island	4	6	1,943	29-28-15
Sat.	6-Mar	Syracuse	5	2	4,004	30-28-15
Sun.	7-Mar	at Jersey	3	8		30-29-15

* Johnstown forfeited game to Syracuse when they refused to take ice after brawl – Feb. 19

Playoff Results

Day	Date	Opponent	Score Johnstown	Opponent	Attendance	Record
Thur.	11-Mar	at Syracuse	8	4		1-0
Sat.	13-Mar	Syracuse	7	2	3861	2-0
Sun.	14-Mar	at Syracuse	2	10		2-1
Tues.	16-Mar	at Syracuse	4	7		2-2
Thur.	18-Mar	Syracuse	10	2	2723	3-2
Sat.	20-Mar	Syracuse	4	1	4023	4-2
Tues.	23-Mar	at New Haven	1	5		0-1
Thur.	25-Mar	at New Haven	3	10		0-2
Fri.	26-Mar	New Haven	2	6	2613	0-3
Sat.	27-Mar	New Haven	2	8	3727	0-4

Attendance Figures

	Dates	Totals	Average
Regular Season Attendance Totals	37	102,391	2,767
Playoff Attendance Totals	5	16,947	3,389
TOTAL ATTENDANCE	42	119,338	2,841

1970-71 Player Statistics

	Regular Season Scoring					Playoff Scoring				
	Games	G	A	Pts	PIM	Games	G	A	Pts	PIM
8 Gene Peacosh	74	50	66	116	28	10	9	4	13	20
11 Dick Roberge	74	38	65	103	36	10	4	13	17	8
7 Reggie Kent	74	34	42	76	12	10	2	8	10	2
10 Galen Head	67	35	27	62	40	10	7	2	9	2
14 Aurel Beaudin	73	18	31	49	88	10	1	5	6	4
16 Alan Cameron	66	17	28	45	24	10	3	4	7	2
12 Bob Warner	71	20	24	44	141	10	5	5	10	16
15 Rick Loe	40	20	22	42	47					
3 Blake Ball	71	4	37	41	312	10	2	7	9	50
6 Guy Delparte	67	11	27	38	68	10	5	4	9	30
4 Jim Trewin	74	7	23	30	121	10	2	2	4	13
2 Len Cunning	69	3	20	23	82	6	0	0	0	14
5 Gary Wood	45	6	13	19	143	10	0	1	1	38
15 Gary Brown	22	4	7	11	4					
15 Dave Birch	19	4	6	10	54	10	3	3	6	44
5 Dennis Henderson	23	2	5	7	128					
5 Brian Vescio	6	1	1	2	0					
10 Armand Pipom	5	1	0	1	2					
6 Brian Kozak	4	0	0	0	0					
17 Paul McKibben	7	0	0	0	2					
1 Jim Coombs (g)	38	0	0	0	104	2	0	0	0	2
17 Bob Vroman (g)	40	0	0	0	2	10	0	0	0	0
Bench					4					2
TOTAL	74	275	444	719	1,442	10	43	58	101	247

Regular Season Goaltending

	G	Min	GA	ENG	SO	GAA	W	L	T	Saves	Save%
17 Bob Vroman	40	2,259	144	2	1	3.82	18	14	7	1,258	0.897
1 Jim Coombs	38	2,119	151	1	0	4.28	12	14	8	1,154	0.884
TOTALS	73	4,380	295	3	1	4.08	30	28	15	2,412	0.891

Playoff Goaltending

	G	Min	GA	ENG	SO	GAA	W	L	Saves	Save%
1 Jim Coombs	2	60	5	0	0	5.00	0	1	62	0.925
17 Bob Vroman	10	540	50	0	0	5.56	4	5	333	0.869
TOTALS	10	600	55	0	0	5.50	4	6	395	0.877

1971-72 Johnstown Jets

(Front, from left) Dave Birch, Bob Vroman, Gene Peacosh, Ron Docken, Reg Kent. (Middle) General manager John Mitchell, Guy Delparte, Dick Roberge, Wynne Dempster, Galen Head, head coach Ed Kachur. (Back) Trainer Gary Kazmierczyk, Vern Campigotto, Gary Wood, Len Cunning, Jim Trewin, Jerry MacDonald, Brian Vescio.

1971-72 FINAL EASTERN HOCKEY LEAGUE STANDINGS

	Games played	Won	Lost	Tied	Points	Goals for	Goals against
North Division							
Syracuse Blazers	75	38	27	10	86	340	276
Johnstown Jets	75	33	28	14	80	290	269
Clinton Comets	75	30	32	13	73	272	278
New Haven Blades	75	30	35	10	70	307	333
Long Island Ducks	75	29	35	11	69	279	310
Jersey Devils	75	25	40	10	60	237	294
South Division							
Charlotte Checkers	73	47	18	8	102	330	180
Greensboro Generals	73	34	27	12	80	284	252
Roanoke Valley Rebels	73	30	33	10	70	241	266
St. Petersburg Suns	73	27	34	12	66	248	291
Jacksonville Rockets *	28	6	20	2	14	81	160

* Jacksonville Rockets ceased operations – Dec. 13, 1971

Johnstown Jets
General Manager - John Mitchell
Coach - Ed Kachur
Trainer - Gary Somerton from training camp to Dec. 1971; Gary Kazmierczyk beginning in Dec. 1971
Stickboy - Dave Zeigler, Pete Bach
Colors - Royal Blue and White

1971-72 Game Results

Preseason Results

Day	Date	Opponent	Score Johnstown	Opponent	Attendance	Record
Fri.	8-Oct	Clinton*	4	12		
Sat.	9-Oct	at Clinton	3	4		

* Game played at Utica, N.Y.

Regular Season Results

Day	Date	Opponent	Johnstown	Opponent	Attendance	Record
Wed.	13-Oct	at Syracuse	3	8		0-1-0
Fri.	15-Oct	at Clinton	3	5		0-2-0
Sat.	16-Oct	at Long Island	4	2		1-2-0
Wed.	20-Oct	Clinton	4	1	2,127	2-2-0
Fri.	22-Oct	Charlotte	4	6	2,132	2-3-0
Sat.	23-Oct	Jersey	4	2	3,030	3-3-0
Fri.	29-Oct	at Clinton	6	4		4-3-0
Sat.	30-Oct	Syracuse	6	4	3,021	5-3-0
Sun.	31-Oct	at Jersey	3	3		5-3-1
Fri.	5-Nov	at Syracuse	3	3		5-3-2
Sat.	6-Nov	New Haven	7	3	3,392	6-3-2
Sun.	7-Nov	at New Haven	2	4		6-4-2
Wed.	10-Nov	Jersey	1	3	1,435	6-5-2
Fri.	12-Nov	Long Island	4	4	2,198	6-5-3
Sat.	13-Nov	Syracuse	10	4	3,056	7-5-3
Sun.	14-Nov	at Jersey	2	2		7-5-4
Thur.	18-Nov	New Haven	4	3	1,568	8-5-4
Fri.	19-Nov	at Clinton	3	3		8-5-5
Sat.	20-Nov	Long Island	3	2	3,003	9-5-5
Thur.	25-Nov	Long Island	3	3	2,605	9-5-6
Sun.	28-Nov	at New Haven	3	5		9-6-6
Tues.	30-Nov	at Long Island	3	7		9-7-6
Thur.	2-Dec	Jersey	5	1	1,249	10-7-6
Fri.	3-Dec	at Jersey	2	4		10-8-6
Sat.	4-Dec	New Haven	5	3	2,983	11-8-6
Thur.	9-Dec	Jersey	6	2	1,328	12-8-6
Fri.	10-Dec	at Syracuse	1	3		12-9-6
Sat.	11-Dec	at Clinton	1	1		12-9-7
Sun.	12-Dec	at Jersey	1	9		12-10-7
Thur.	16-Dec	Syracuse	3	1	1,401	13-10-7
Sat.	18-Dec	Greensboro	4	3	2,445	14-10-7
Sun.	19-Dec	at New Haven	2	3		14-11-7
Thur.	23-Dec	at St. Petersburg	3	5		14-12-7
Sat.	25-Dec	at Greensboro	3	6		14-13-7
Sun.	26-Dec	at Roanoke Valley	1	7		14-14-7
Tues.	28-Dec	at Charlotte	1	5		14-15-7
Wed.	29-Dec	at Jersey	3	2		15-15-7
Fri.	31-Dec	Clinton	9	1	2,445	16-15-7
Sat.	1-Jan	Syracuse	3	6	2,716	16-16-7
Sun.	2-Jan	at New Haven	1	3		16-17-7
Wed.	5-Jan	at Syracuse	5	5		16-17-8
Fri.	7-Jan	St. Petersburg	8	4	1,927	17-17-8
Sat.	8-Jan	Jersey	10	1	3,191	18-17-8
Wed.	12-Jan	Long Island	5	2	1,600	19-17-8
Fri.	14-Jan	at Long Island	5	5		19-17-9
Sat.	15-Jan	Long Island	2	4	2,990	19-18-9
Sun.	16-Jan	Clinton	10	2	1,599	20-18-9
Fri.	21-Jan	Syracuse	5	5	2,212	20-18-10
Sat.	22-Jan	Jersey	2	0	3,182	21-18-10
Sun.	23-Jan	at New Haven	0	4		21-19-10
Thur.	27-Jan	at Long Island	1	4		21-20-10
Fri.	28-Jan	at Syracuse	3	3		21-20-11
Sat.	29-Jan	Roanoke Valley	4	4	3,163	21-20-12
Sun.	30-Jan	Clinton	5	0	2,055	22-20-12
Wed.	2-Feb	at Jersey	2	3		22-21-12
Thur.	3-Feb	Clinton	5	3	757	23-21-12
Fri.	4-Feb	Clinton	3	3	1,405	23-21-13
Sat.	5-Feb	Long Island	7	2	2,675	24-21-13
Sun.	6-Feb	at Long Island	4	3		25-21-13
Wed.	9-Feb	at Jersey	1	9		25-22-13
Fri.	11-Feb	at Jersey	2	6		25-23-13
Sat.	12-Feb	Syracuse	4	4	3,664	25-23-14
Sun.	13-Feb	Clinton	3	0	1,598	26-23-14
Wed.	16-Feb	at Clinton	1	4		26-24-14
Fri.	18-Feb	New Haven	12	3	1,756	27-24-14

Day	Date	Opponent	Johnstown	Opponent	Attendance	Record
Sun.	20-Feb	at Long Island	5	1		28-24-14
Wed.	23-Feb	at New Haven	3	10		28-25-14
Fri.	25-Feb	at Long Island	2	6		28-26-14
Sat.	26-Feb	Long Island	5	3	3,201	29-26-14
Sun.	27-Feb	Jersey	4	1	4,035	30-26-14
Tues.	29-Feb	Long Island	7	2	1,902	31-26-14
Wed.	1-Mar	at Clinton	5	7		31-27-14
Thur.	2-Mar	New Haven	2	1	1,674	32-27-14
Sat.	4-Mar	New Haven	6	3	4,133	33-27-14
Sun.	5-Mar	at Syracuse	3	6		33-28-14

Playoff Results

Day	Date	Opponent	Johnstown	Opponent	Attendance	Record
Wed.	8-Mar	Clinton	8	0	1,761	1-0
Sat.	11-Mar	Clinton	4	3	3,677	2-0
Sun.	12-Mar	at Clinton	2	6		2-1
Tues.	14-Mar	at Clinton	3	0		3-1
Thur.	16-Mar	Clinton	2	1	2,299	4-1
Thur.	23-Mar	at Syracuse	1	7		0-1
Fri.	24-Mar	at Syracuse	2	8		0-2
Sat.	25-Mar	Syracuse	9	2	3,211	1-2
Tues.	28-Mar	Syracuse	7	5	2,613	2-2
Thur.	30-Mar	at Syracuse	0	4		2-3
Fri.	1-Apr	Syracuse	2	5	3,614	2-4

Attendance Figures

	Dates	Totals	Average
Regular Season Attendance Figures	38	90,853	2,391
Playoff Attendance Figures	6	17,175	2,863
TOTAL ATTENDANCE	44	108,028	2,455

1971-72 Player Statistics

	Regular Season Scoring					Playoff Scoring				
	Games	G	A	Pts	PIM	Games	G	A	Pts	PIM
8 Gene Peacosh	75	43	64	107	30	11	11	5	16	9
11 Dick Roberge	75	28	47	75	12	11	5	2	7	0
10 Galen Head	75	37	34	71	43	11	2	4	6	2
7 Reg Kent	70	17	52	69	10					
16 Guy Delparte	75	25	41	66	66	11	5	8	13	8
6 Vern Campigotto	75	22	43	65	68	11	5	6	11	4
3 Brian Vescio	75	29	28	57	37	11	5	3	8	4
14 Wynne Dempster	57	26	29	55	94	11	0	5	5	30
15 Dave Birch	64	24	24	48	150	11	3	3	6	21
5 Gary Wood	75	6	30	36	131	11	1	6	7	20
4 Jim Trewin	75	8	25	33	80	11	2	1	3	10
12 Ed Kachur	24	16	13	29	6					
2 Len Cunning	71	6	21	27	72	11	1	5	6	8
17 Jerry MacDonald	71	2	25	27	22	11	0	4	4	2
17 Doug Stumpf	6	1	1	2	6					
15 Mel Gushattey	3	0	0	0	4					
18 Ron Docken (g)	10	0	1	1	0					
1 Bob Vroman (g)	67	0	0	0	17	11	0	0	0	2
Bench					8					2
TOTALS	75	290	478	768	856	11	40	52	92	122

Regular Season Goaltending

	G	Min	GA	ENG	SO	GAA	W	L	T	Saves	Save %
1 Bob Vroman	67	3,959	223	1	3	3.38	30	23	14	2,032	0.907
18 Ron Docken	10	540	45	0	0	5.00	3	5	0	307	0.872
TOTALS	75	4,500	268	1	3	3.59	33	28	14		

Note: Vroman totals for Saves and Save % are incomplete – only calculated for available games.

Playoff Goaltending

	G	Min	GA	ENG	SO	GAA	W	L	Saves	Save %
1 Bob Vroman	11	660	41	0	2	3.73	6	5	307	.882
TOTALS	11	660	41	0	2	3.73	6	5	307	.882

1972-73 Johnstown Jets

(Front, from left) Dennis Erickson, Galen Head, head coach Ted Lanyon, general manager John Mitchell, Reg Kent, Ron Docken. (Middle) Dave Birch, Kevin Collins, Gary Wood, Brian Coughlin, Jerry MacDonald, Doug Anderson, Bill McEwan. (Back) Trainer Gary Kazmierczyk, Tom Steeves, Tony McCarthy, Brian Vescio, Vern Campigotto, Wynne Dempster, trainer Eddie Neisner.

1972-73 FINAL EASTERN HOCKEY LEAGUE STANDINGS

	Games played	Won	Lost	Tied	Points	Goals for	Goals against
North Division							
Syracuse Blazers	76	63	9	4	130	453	190
Johnstown Jets	76	36	28	12	84	283	255
Clinton Comets	76	18	51	7	43	256	415
New England Blades *	24	9	13	2	20	91	109
Central Division							
Cape Cod Cubs	76	36	29	11	83	338	314
Rhode Island Eagles	76	32	35	9	73	320	307
Long Island Ducks	76	26	43	7	59	287	386
Jersey Devils	76	23	41	12	58	239	300
South Division							
Roanoke Valley Rebels	76	40	25	11	91	345	27
Greensboro Generals	76	40	28	8	88	391	315
Suncoast Suns	76	30	37	9	69	301	365
Charlotte Checkers	76	26	40	10	62	241	313

* New England Blades ceased operations Dec. 6, 1972

Johnstown Jets
General Manager - John Mitchell
Coach - Tom McVie (12-12-6); Galen Head (2-0-0); Ted Lanyon (22-16-6)
Trainer - Gary Kazmierczyk
Stickboy - Pete Bach, Eddie Neisner
Colors - Blue, White and Gold

1972-73 Game Results

Preseason Results
No Preseason games

JETS IN THE SEVENTIES

Regular Season Results

Day	Date	Opponent	Johnstown	Opponent	Attendance	Record
Fri.	13-Oct	at Clinton	4	4		0-0-1
Sat.	14-Oct	at Long Island	2	2		0-0-2
Sun.	15-Oct	at Rhode Island	4	6		0-1-2
Fri.	20-Oct	Syracuse	7	4	2,691	1-1-2
Sat.	21-Oct	Long Island	1	4	3,119	1-2-2
Sun.	22-Oct	at New England	5	7		1-3-2
Fri.	27-Oct	at Clinton	3	1		2-3-2
Sat.	28-Oct	New England	3	5	2,602	2-4-2
Sun.	29-Oct	Suncoast	10	5	1,770	3-4-2
Wed.	1-Nov	Clinton	7	1	1,270	4-4-2
Fri.	3-Nov	at Syracuse	2	7		4-5-2
Sat.	4-Nov	Syracuse	4	2	3,263	5-5-2
Sun.	5-Nov	Jersey	4	4	1,450	5-5-3
Tues.	7-Nov	at Suncoast	10	3		6-5-3
Wed.	8-Nov	at Greensboro	2	10		6-6-3
Thur.	9-Nov	at Roanoke Valley	3	3		6-6-4
Fri.	10-Nov	at Charlotte	0	3		6-7-4
Wed.	15-Nov	at Syracuse	2	3		6-8-4
Sat.	18-Nov	New England	6	1	2,711	7-8-4
Sun.	19-Nov	at New England	5	3		8-8-4
Wed.	22-Nov	Clinton	3	1	1,808	9-8-4
Thur.	23-Nov	Syracuse	3	4	3,083	9-9-4
Sat.	25-Nov	at Long Island	6	3		10-9-4
Thur.	30-Nov	Syracuse	3	3	1,350	10-9-5
Fri.	1-Dec	at Jersey	4	2		11-9-5
Sun.	3-Dec	Clinton	0	4	1,504	11-10-5
Wed.	6-Dec	Syracuse	4	2	1,517	12-10-5
Fri.	8-Dec	at Jersey	2	3		12-11-5
Sat.	9-Dec	at Clinton	3	3		12-11-6
Sun.	10-Dec	at Rhode Island	0	4		12-12-6
Sat.	16-Dec	Roanoke Valley	8	3	1,829	13-12-6
Sun.	17-Dec	Greensboro	3	0	1,413	14-12-6
Wed.	20-Dec	at Syracuse	0	4		14-13-6
Sat.	23-Dec	Jersey	5	5	2,016	14-13-7
Wed.	27-Dec	at Syracuse	4	9		14-14-7
Fri.	29-Dec	at Cape Cod	1	1		14-14-8
Sat.	30-Dec	at Clinton	3	2		15-14-8
Sun.	31-Dec	Rhode Island	4	2	1,910	16-14-8
Thur.	4-Jan	Clinton	10	4	1,197	17-14-8
Fri.	5-Jan	at Clinton	7	2		18-14-8
Sat.	6-Jan	Jersey	3	2	2,534	19-14-8
Sun	7-Jan	Jersey	4	1	1,864	20-14-8
Tues.	9-Jan	at Syracuse	2	4		20-15-8
Fri.	12-Jan	at Clinton	3	4		20-16-8
Sat.	13-Jan	Syracuse	2	4	4,128	20-17-8
Sun.	14-Jan	Clinton	3	0	1,309	21-17-8
Wed.	17-Jan	at Cape Cod	4	6		21-18-8
Sat.	20-Jan	Long Island	6	3	2,438	22-18-8
Sun.	21-Jan	Clinton	10	1	1,378	23-18-8
Wed.	24-Jan	at Syracuse	3	3		23-18-9
Fri.	26-Jan	at Clinton	7	4		24-18-9
Sat.	27-Jan	Rhode Island	4	2	2,428	25-18-9
Sun.	28-Jan	Clinton	4	7	1,378	25-19-9
Wed.	31-Jan	at Syracuse	1	6		25-20-9
Fri.	2-Feb	at Jersey	4	1		26-20-9
Sat.	3-Feb	Syracuse	3	3	3,482	26-20-10
Sun.	4-Feb	Charlotte	4	0	1,582	27-20-10
Wed.	7-Feb	at Jersey	4	2		28-20-10
Thur.	8-Feb	Clinton	5	3	958	29-20-10
Fri.	9-Feb	at Syracuse	3	3		29-20-11
Sat.	10-Feb	Rhode Island	3	6	2,352	29-21-11
Sun.	11-Feb	Syracuse	1	4	2,013	29-22-11
Wed.	14-Feb	at Clinton	4	3		30-22-11
Thur.	15-Feb	Syracuse	3	1	1,307	31-22-11
Sat.	17-Feb	Roanoke Valley	1	0	1,631	32-22-11
Sun.	18-Feb	at Long Island	4	3		33-22-11
Mon.	19-Feb	at Roanoke Valley	3	6		33-23-11
Thur.	22-Feb	Cape Cod	1	4	1,438	33-24-11
Sat.	24-Feb	Jersey	4	1	2,423	34-24-11

Day	Date	Opponent			Attendance	Record
Sun.	25-Feb	Clinton	6	2	2,963	35-24-11
Tues.	27-Feb	at Rhode Island	2	5		35-25-11
Wed.	28-Feb	at Syracuse	0	7		35-26-11
Thur.	1-Mar	at Jersey	3	3		35-26-12
Fri.	2-Mar	Clinton	8	3	2,126	36-26-12
Sat.	3-Mar	Syracuse	3	5	3,562	36-27-12
Sun.	4-Mar	at Syracuse	1	4		36-28-12

Playoff Results

			Score			
Day	Date	Opponent	Johnstown	Opponent	Attendance	Record
Tues.	6-Mar	at Greensboro	3	6		0-1
Sat.	10-Mar	Greensboro	1	4	2,310	0-2
Sun.	11-Mar	Greensboro	5	4	1,262	1-2
Tues.	13-Mar	at Greensboro	4	2		2-2
Wed.	14-Mar	at Greensboro	2	3		2-3
Sat.	17-Mar	Greensboro	7	0	2,463	3-3
Sun.	18-Mar	at Greensboro	9	3		4-3
Tues.	20-Mar	at Roanoke Valley	0	4		0-1
Thur.	22-Mar	at Roanoke Valley	3	7		0-2
Sat.	24-Mar	Roanoke Valley	6	2	2,738	1-2
Tues.	27-Mar	Roanoke Valley	3	4 (3ot)	2,125	1-3
Fri.	30-Mar	at Roanoke Valley	2	5		1-4

Attendance Figures

	Dates	Totals	Average
Regular Season Attendance Figures	38	79,797	2,100
Playoff Attendance Figures	5	10,898	2,180
TOTAL ATTENDANCE	43	90,695	2,109

1972-73 Player Statistics

	Regular Season Scoring					Playoff Scoring				
	Games	G	A	Pts	PIM	Games	G	A	Pts	PIM
8 Galen Head	73	44	33	77	35	12	4	6	10	10
14 Wynne Dempster	72	32	38	70	233	12	6	6	12	26
6 Tony McCarthy	71	17	52	69	62	12	2	9	11	6
16 Vern Campigotto	75	28	40	68	111	12	6	9	15	0
15 Dave Birch	67	29	27	56	168	12	6	4	10	12
5 Gary Wood	69	11	32	43	168	12	1	6	7	21
7 Reggie Kent	41	11	28	39	7	12	2	5	7	2
17 Bill McEwan	53	20	18	38	110	12	1	2	3	4
10 Kevin Collins	48	16	22	38	42	12	3	4	7	8
3 Jerry MacDonald	73	5	32	37	72	12	1	4	5	2
2 Brian Coughlin	76	9	27	36	183	12	2	3	5	8
4 Doug Anderson	57	12	17	29	34					
4 Ted Lanyon	41	6	23	29	43	12	3	6	9	0
10 Brian Vescio	46	12	16	28	69	12	3	5	8	2
11 Archie MacDonald	34	12	15	27	22					
12 Tom McVie	30	13	12	25	64					
12 Tom Steeves	22	6	16	22	15	12	5	6	11	6
18 Dennis Erickson (g)	29	0	1	1	23	2	0	0	0	0
1 Ron Docken (g)	54	0	0	0	8	11	0	1	1	2
Bench					8					
TOTALS	76	283	449	732	1,477	12	45	76	121	109

Regular Season Goaltending

	G	Min	GA	ENG	SO	GAA	W	L	T	Saves	Save%
18 Dennis Erickson	29	1,522	82	0	1	3.23	15	7	3	669	0.891
1 Ron Docken	54	3,035	169	4	3	3.34	21	21	9	1,425	0.896
TOTALS	76	4,560	251	4	4	3.36	36	28	12		

Note: Docken totals for Saves and Save % are incomplete – only calculated for available games.

Playoff Goaltending

	G	Min	GA	ENG	SO	GAA	W	L	Saves	Save %
1 Ron Docken	11	688	35	1	1	3.05	4	6	379	.915
18 Dennis Erickson	2	92	8	0	0	5.22	1	1	48	.857
TOTALS	12	780	43	1	1	3.31	5	7	427	.909

Collins also wore No. 12.
Anderson also wore Nos. 7 and 17.
MacDonald also wore No. 4.

1973-74 Johnstown Jets

(Front, from left) Ted Lenssen, Vern Campigotto, general manager John Mitchell, head coach Galen Head, Reggie Kent, Ron Docken. (Middle) Brian Vescio, Jim Wilcox, Guy Ross, Brian Coughlin, Ned Dowd, Jerry MacDonald, Michel Latreille. (Back) Tom Young, Dave Johnson, Tony McCarthy, Norm Descoteaux, Bobby Thompson, trainer Gary Kazmierczyk.

1973-74 NORTH AMERICAN HOCKEY LEAGUE STANDINGS

	Games played	Won	Lost	Tied	Points	Goals For	Goals Against
Syracuse Blazers	74	54	16	4	112	359	219
Maine Nordiques	74	45	26	3	93	398	307
Long Island Cougars	74	35	36	3	73	310	277
Cape Cod Cubs	74	34	39	1	69	338	345
Johnstown Jets	74	32	38	4	68	265	303
Binghamton Dusters	74	28	41	5	61	277	352
Mohawk Valley Comets	74	20	52	2	42	240	384

Johnstown Jets
General Manager - John Mitchell
Coach - Galen Head
Trainer - Gary Kazmierczyk
Stickboy - Pete Bach, Eddie Neisner, Woody Espey
Colors - Blue, White and Gold

1973-74 Game Results

Preseason Results
No preseason games
Regular Season Results
Score

Day	Date	Opponent	Johnstown	Opponent	Attendance	Record
Fri.	12-Oct	Syracuse	3	7	2,650	0-1-0
Sat.	13-Oct	Binghamton	5	4 (ot)	2,009	1-1-0
Wed.	17-Oct	at Long Island	4	7		1-2-0
Fri.	19-Oct	Mohawk Valley	6	3	1,344	2-2-0
Sat.	20-Oct	Long Island	5	3	2,173	3-2-0
Sun.	21-Oct	at Cape Cod	0	4		3-3-0
Tues.	23-Oct	at Cape Cod	5	10		3-4-0
Sat.	27-Oct	at Mohawk Valley	4	3		4-4-0
Wed.	31-Oct	Syracuse	4	1	1,367	5-4-0
Sat.	3-Nov	Long Island	4	3	2,192	6-4-0
Wed.	7-Nov	at Mohawk Valley	3	2		7-4-0

187

Day	Date	Opponent		Score	Attendance	Record
Fri.	9-Nov	Mohawk Valley	5	3	1,242	8-4-0
Sat.	10-Nov	Cape Cod	6	4	2,213	9-4-0
Sun.	11-Oct	Cape Cod	12	6	1,472	10-4-0
Tues.	13-Nov	at Cape Cod	3	5		10-5-0
Wed.	14-Nov	at Long Island	1	6		10-6-0
Sat.	17-Nov	Syracuse	2	2	2,668	10-6-1
Mon.	19-Nov	at Binghamton	6	2		11-6-1
Thur.	22-Nov	Long Island	2	1	1,944	12-6-1
Sat.	24-Nov	Maine	1	4	2,699	12-7-1
Sun.	25-Nov	Maine	2	5	2,010	12-8-1
Tues.	27-Nov	at Maine	1	4		12-9-1
Wed.	28-Nov	at Binghamton	3	5		12-10-1
Sat.	1-Dec	Long Island	4	5 (ot)	1,972	12-11-1
Sun.	2-Dec	Mohawk Valley	6	2	1,107	13-11-1
Wed.	5-Dec	Maine	7	6 (ot)	1,107	14-11-1
Fri.	7-Dec	at Syracuse	1	2 (ot)		14-12-1
Sat.	8-Dec	at Maine	0	3		14-13-1
Sun.	9-Dec	at Maine	2	6		14-14-1
Wed.	12-Dec	at Binghamton	3	5		14-15-1
Fri.	14-Dec	at Syracuse	3	6		14-16-1
Sat.	15-Dec	Syracuse	3	2	1,936	15-16-1
Sun.	16-Dec	Cape Cod	6	2	1,073	16-16-1
Wed.	19-Dec	Cape Cod	3	4	957	16-17-1
Thur.	20-Dec	at Long Island	4	8		16-18-1
Fri.	21-Dec	at Binghamton	3	3		16-18-2
Sun.	23-Dec	at Syracuse	2	8		16-19-2
Thur.	27-Dec	at Cape Cod	2	5		16-20-2
Fri.	28-Dec	at Mohawk Valley	5	0		17-20-2
Sun.	30-Dec	at Syracuse	4	5		17-21-2
Mon.	31-Dec	Binghamton	6	0	1,328	18-21-2
Wed.	2-Jan	Syracuse	0	7	1,280	18-22-2
Fri.	4-Jan	at Long Island	3	4		18-23-2
Sat.	5-Jan	Cape Cod	2	6	2,005	18-24-2
Sun.	6-Jan	Cape Cod	4	3	1,052	19-24-2
Tues.	8-Jan	at Maine	5	9		19-25-2
Wed.	9-Jan	at Binghamton	2	5		19-26-2
Fri.	11-Jan	at Syracuse	2	5		19-27-2
Sat.	12-Jan	Maine	4	1	1,850	20-27-2
Sun.	13-Jan	Maine	3	3	1,145	20-27-3
Wed.	16-Jan	Mohawk Valley	4	1	969	21-27-3
Sat.	19-Jan	Binghamton	6	3	2,250	22-27-3
Wed.	23-Jan	Syracuse	3	5	2,042	22-28-3
Fri	25-Jan	at Long Island	0	3		22-29-3
Sat.	26-Jan	Long Island	4	1	2,098	23-29-3
Sun.	27-Jan	at Syracuse	2	9		23-30-3
Tues.	29-Jan	at Cape Cod	2	7		23-31-3
Wed.	30-Jan	at Maine	3	5		23-32-3
Sat.	2-Feb	Binghamton	4	1	1,928	24-32-3
Wed.	6-Feb	Mohawk Valley	1	3	858	24-33-3
Sat.	9-Feb	Binghamton	4	4	1,651	24-33-4
Tues.	12-Feb	at Mohawk Valley	2	4		24-34-4
Wed.	13-Feb	Maine	5	2	1,035	25-34-4
Fri.	15-Feb	at Long Island	5	4		26-34-4
Sat.	16-Feb	Syracuse	6	1	2,592	27-34-4
Wed.	20-Feb	Mohawk Valley	7	4	2,418	28-34-4
Fri.	22-Feb	at Mohawk Valley	3	4		28-35-4
Sat.	23-Feb	Binghamton	5	3	2,435	29-35-4
Sun.	24-Feb	at Binghamton	2	5		29-36-4
Tues.	26-Feb	at Cape Cod	4	6		29-37-4
Wed.	27-Feb	at Maine	3	1		30-37-4
Fri.	1-Mar	at Mohawk Valley	5	3		31-37-4
Sat.	2-Mar	Long Island	8	5	3,096	32-37-4
Sun.	3-Mar	at Syracuse	1	10		32-38-4

Playoff Results

Day	Date	Opponent	Score Johnstown	Opponent	Attendance	Record
Wed.	6-Mar	at Syracuse	1	5		0-1
Sat.	9-Mar	Syracuse	3	4	3,144	0-2
Sun.	10-Mar	Cape Cod	2	5	1,507	0-3
Tues.	12-Mar	at Cape Cod	2	3		0-4
Thur.	14-Mar	Maine	5	4	1,300	1-4

JETS IN THE SEVENTIES

Sat.	16-Mar	at Maine	6	5		2-4	
Tues.	19-Mar	at Long Island	0	4		2-5	
Wed.	20-Mar	Long Island	8	2	1,491	3-5	
Fri.	22-Mar	at Syracuse	3	5		0-1	
Sun.	24-Mar	at Syracuse	0	3		0-2	
Wed.	27-Mar	Syracuse	2	3	1,585	0-3	
Sat.	30-Mar	Syracuse *	1	0	2,189	1-3	
Sun.	31-Mar	at Syracuse **	0	1		1-4	

* Game stopped in second period because of brawl – Syracuse refused to take ice and Johnstown awarded 1-0 forfeit on March 30.
** Johnstown refused to go to Syracuse to play March 31 because of brawl. Syracuse was awarded a 1-0 forfeit, ending the series.

Attendance Figures

	Dates	Totals	Average
Regular Season Attendance Totals	37	66,167	1,788
Playoff Attendance Totals	5	9,027	1,805
TOTAL ATTENDANCE	42	75,194	1,790

1973-74 Player Statistics

	Regular Season Scoring					Playoff Scoring				
	Games	G	A	Pts	PIM	Games	G	A	Pts	PIM
7 Reggie Kent	74	26	58	84	10	12	1	5	6	0
14 Dave Johnson	73	41	29	70	66	12	8	1	9	14
8 Galen Head	74	31	40	71	22	12	5	3	8	2
19 Ned Dowd	74	32	31	63	69	12	3	4	7	4
16 Vern Campigotto	73	20	42	62	166	12	2	5	7	9
6 Tony McCarthy	74	17	32	49	69	12	2	4	6	6
15 Brian Vescio	74	17	31	48	52	11	5	6	11	15
4 Jim Wilcox	71	5	36	41	27	12	0	3	3	7
3 Jerry MacDonald	71	1	34	35	32	12	0	3	3	9
18 Brian Macklin	53	19	15	34	19					
10 Norm Descoteaux	71	14	13	27	146	12	0	1	1	14
2 Brian Coughlin	58	3	24	27	105	12	1	2	3	17
5 Rick Loe	48	10	15	25	31					
12 Bob Thompson	14	11	5	16	35	10	3	2	5	2
17 Cam Fryer	31	6	7	13	16					
17 Tom Young	20	5	5	10	5	12	3	2	6	0
2 Gary Davidson	32	3	4	7	20					
5 Michel Latrielle	13	1	6	7	2	11	0	1	1	2
18 Guy Ross	19	0	5	5	39	12	0	1	1	32
5 Phil Branston	16	0	4	4	10					
1 Ron Docken (g)	59	0	4	4	29	11	0	0	0	2
12 Kevin Collins	10	2	1	3	10					
17 Clem Morrison	16	0	2	2	12					
5 Francois Ouimet	5	1	0	1	2					
4 Serge Lefebvre	2	0	1	1	2					
5 Richie Bayes	3	0	1	1	0					
1 Don Wallis (g)	5	0	1	1	0					
2 Pete Bartkiewicz	8	0	1	1	2					
20 Ted Lenssen (g)	15	0	1	1	4	1	0	0	0	0
18 Hank Graham	1	0	0	0	0					
18 Rich Polutnik	1	0	0	0	0					
18 Pierre Viau	3	0	0	0	0					
20 Tony Tatangelo (g)	5	0	0	0	0					
Bench										2
TOTALS	74	265	448	713	1,002	12	33	43	76	137

Regular Season Goaltending

	G	Min	GA	ENG	SO	GAA	W	L	T	Saves	Save%
1 Don Wallis	5	310	14	0	0	2.71	2	2	1	158	0.919
20 Ted Lenssen	15	704	46	0	0	3.88	3	5	1	306	0.874
1 Ron Docken	59	3,351	225	2	2	4.09	26	29	2		
20 Tony Tatangelo	5	141	16	0	0	6.16	1	2	0	86	0.843
TOTALS	74	4,506	301	2	2	4.03	32	38	4		

Playoff Goaltending

	G	Min	GA	ENG	SO	GAA	W	L	Saves	Save%
1 Ron Docken	10	613	38	1	0	3.72	4	6	370	.907
20 Ted Lenssen	1	60	4	0	0	4.00	0	1	27	.871
TOTALS	12	712	42	1	0	3.88	4	8	397	.902

Note: All player stats for March 30 game vs. Syracuse that was stopped in second period are not included.

Loe also wore No. 12; Davidson also wore No. 5; Branston also wore No. 2; Bartkiewicz also wore No. 12; Docken also wore No. 17

1974-75 Johnstown Jets

(Front, from left) Louie Levasseur, Jerry Welsh, John Gofton, Mike Chernoff, executive director John Mitchell, Ron Docken, Jean Tetreault, Galen Head, Reg Bechtold, Don Atchison. (Back) General manager/coach Dick Roberge, trainer Gary Kazmierczyk, Francois Ouimet, Dave Hanson, Steve Carlson, Jack Carlson, Jeff Carlson, Ned Dowd, Bob Boyd, John Perpich, Guido Tenesi, Vern Campigotto, Jim Adair.

1974-75 FINAL NORTH AMERICAN HOCKEY LEAGUE STANDINGS

	Games played	Won	Lost	Tied	Points	Goals for	Goals against
Syracuse Blazers	74	46	25	3	95	345	232
Philadelphia Firebirds	74	40	31	3	83	310	289
Binghamton Dusters	74	39	32	3	81	293	285
Johnstown Jets	74	38	32	4	80	274	255
Cape Codders	74	32	38	4	68	319	310
Mohawk Valley Comets	74	31	38	5	67	312	345
Long Island Cougars	74	29	46	5	63	271	280
Maine Nordiques	74	27	46	1	55	266	394

Johnstown won Lockhart Cup as playoff champions.

Johnstown Jets
Executive Director - John Mitchell
General Manager/Coach - Dick Roberge
Trainer - Gary Kazmierczyk
Stickboy - Eddie Neisner, Woody Espey, Jeff Mastervich
Colors - Blue, White and Gold

1974-75 Game Results

Preseason Results

Day	Date	Opponent	Johnstown	Opponent	Attendance	Record
Thur.	10-Oct	at Binghamton	4	1		

Games against Binghamton scheduled for Oct. 8 and 9 were cancelled.

Regular Season Results

Day	Date	Opponent	Johnstown	Opponent	Attendance	Record
Fri.	18-Oct	at Maine	4	3 (ot)		1-0-0
Sat.	19-Oct	Philadelphia	3	4 (ot)	4,115	1-1-0
Mon.	20-Oct	at Binghamton	2	5		1-2-0
Wed.	23-Oct	at Philadelphia	1	2		1-3-0
Fri.	25-Oct	Syracuse	7	1	3,200	2-3-0
Sat.	26-Oct	Mohawk Valley	4	3	3,150	3-3-0
Sun.	27-Oct	at Binghamton	1	4		3-4-0
Wed.	30-Oct	at Cape Codders	3	3		3-4-1
Fri.	1-Nov	Long Island	1	5	1,820	3-5-1
Sat.	2-Nov	Long Island	0	5	3,599	3-6-1
Tues.	5-Nov	at Philadelphia	1	2		3-7-1
Wed.	6-Nov	at Long Island	0	6		3-8-1

JETS IN THE SEVENTIES

Day	Date	Opponent	Johnstown	Opponent	Attendance	Record
Fri.	8-Nov	Syracuse	4	1	1,739	4-8-1
Sat.	9-Nov	Binghamton	1	1	3,099	4-8-2
Wed.	13-Nov	at Syracuse	0	6		4-9-2
Sat.	16-Nov	Maine	4	3	2,658	5-9-2
Sun.	17-Nov	Maine	7	3	2,229	6-9-2
Wed.	20-Nov	Binghamton	1	2 (ot)	3,342	6-10-2
Fri.	22-Nov	Cape Codders	2	5	2,218	6-11-2
Sat.	23-Nov	Cape Codders	4	1	2,741	7-11-2
Thur.	28-Nov	Long Island	2	2	2,190	7-11-3
Fri.	29-Nov	at Philadelphia	3	5		7-12-3
Sat.	30-Nov	Philadelphia	4	3 (ot)	2,042	8-12-3
Sun.	1-Dec	Mohawk Valley	6	2	1,659	9-12-3
Wed.	4-Dec	at Binghamton	2	5		9-13-3
Sat.	7-Dec	at Mohawk Valley	6	8		9-14-3
Sun.	8-Dec	at Binghamton	5	4		10-14-3
Fri.	13-Dec	at Syracuse	3	7		10-15-3
Sat.	14-Dec	Maine	3	4 (ot)	2,473	10-16-3
Sun.	15-Dec	Maine	3	4	2,206	10-17-3
Wed.	18-Dec	at Philadelphia	5	6		10-18-3
Sat.	21-Dec	Binghamton	4	2	2,327	11-18-3
Sat.	28-Dec	at Mohawk Valley	6	2		12-18-3
Sun.	29-Dec	Philadelphia	3	3	2,918	12-18-4
Tues.	31-Dec	Mohawk Valley	3	1	1,518	13-18-4
Wed.	1-Jan	at Binghamton	1	2		13-19-4
Fri.	3-Jan	at Syracuse	1	4		13-20-4
Sat.	4-Jan	Syracuse	7	6 (ot)	2,453	14-20-4
Sun.	5-Jan	Philadelphia	0	3	2,850	14-21-4
Fri.	10-Jan	at Binghamton	4	6		14-22-4
Wed.	15-Jan	at Long Island	2	1		15-22-4
Thur.	16-Jan	at Mohawk Valley	1	7		15-23-4
Sat.	18-Jan	Cape Codders	0	2	2,385	15-24-4
Sun.	19-Jan	Cape Codders	8	5	1,848	16-24-4
Wed.	22-Jan	at Mohawk Valley	4	2		17-24-4
Fri.	24-Jan	Long Island	5	2	1,989	18-24-4
Sat.	25-Jan	Binghamton	7	2	2,746	19-24-4
Tues.	28-Jan	at Maine	5	4 (ot)		20-24-4
Wed.	29-Jan	at Cape Codders	4	3		21-24-4
Sat.	1-Feb	Binghamton	8	4	3,864	22-24-4
Sun.	2-Feb	at Binghamton	3	6		22-25-4
Wed.	5-Feb	at Syracuse	4	7		22-26-4
Fri.	7-Feb	at Long Island	2	1 (ot)		23-26-4
Sat.	8-Feb	at Maine	6	4		24-26-4
Sun.	9-Feb	at Cape Codders	3	5		24-27-4
Fri.	14-Feb	at Philadelphia	6	5 (ot)		25-27-4
Sat.	15-Feb	Mohawk Valley	7	1	3,739	26-27-4
Fri.	21-Feb	Syracuse	8	1	3,026	27-27-4
Sat.	22-Feb	Long Island	3	1	3,098	28-27-4
Sun.	23-Feb	at Long Island	2	4		28-28-4
Wed.	26-Feb	Philadelphia	9	3	2,749	29-28-4
Fri.	28-Feb	Cape Codders	7	1	2,447	30-28-4
Sat.	1-Mar	Maine	2	4	3,143	30-29-4
Tues.	4-Mar	at Maine	5	4		31-29-4
Wed.	5-Mar	at Cape Codders	3	2		32-29-4
Fri.	7-Mar	Binghamton	5	2	3,387	33-29-4
Sat.	8-Mar	Binghamton	3	5	3,586	33-30-4
Wed.	12-Mar	Mohawk Valley	6	1	2,225	34-30-4
Fri.	14-Mar	at Long Island	4	3 (ot)		35-30-4
Sat.	15-Mar	Syracuse	5	3	4,049	36-30-4
Sun.	16-Mar	at Syracuse	1	6		36-31-4
Wed.	19-Mar	at Cape Codders	2	0		37-31-4
Thur.	20-Mar	at Maine	3	5		37-32-4
Sun.	23-Mar	at Mohawk Valley	10	5		38-32-4

Playoff Results

Day	Date	Opponent	Johnstown	Opponent	Attendance	Record
Tues.	25-Mar	at Cape Codders	3	0		1-0
Thur.	27-Mar	Cape Codders	4	6	2,300	1-1
Sat.	29-Mar	Cape Codders	6	3	3,483	2-1
Mon.	31-Mar	at Cape Codders	4	2		3-1
Wed.	2-Apr	at Syracuse	3	4		0-1
Thur.	3-Apr	Syracuse	3	2	2,144	1-1

191

Day	Date	Opponent			Attendance	Score
Sat.	5-Apr	Syracuse	5	3	4,022	2-1
Wed.	9-Apr	at Syracuse	0	4		2-2
Fri.	11-Apr	at Syracuse	4	6		2-3
Sat.	12-Apr	Syracuse	6	3	3,661	3-3
Mon.	14-Apr	at Syracuse	5	4		4-3
Wed.	23-Apr	Binghamton	5	1	3,483	1-0
Thur.	24-Apr	at Binghamton	7	4		2-0
Sun.	27-Apr	at Binghamton	2	1		3-0
Thur.	1-May	Binghamton	6	2	4,088	4-0

Attendance Figures

	Dates	Totals	Average
Regular Season Attendance Totals	37	100,827	2,725
Playoff Attendance Totals	7	23,181	3,312
TOTAL ATTENDANCE	44	124,008	2,818

1974-75 Player Statistics

	Regular Season Scoring					Playoff Scoring				
	Games	G	A	Pts	PIM	Games	G	A	Pts	PIM
17 Steve Carlson	70	30	58	88	84	12	6	4	10	39
15 Jerry Welsh	70	30	34	64	56	15	9	8	17	2
10 Jean Tetreault	57	22	32	54	62	15	6	10	16	4
16 Jack Carlson	50	27	22	49	246					
18 Jeff Carlson	64	15	32	47	250	14	5	4	9	46
2 Guido Tenesi	69	12	30	42	112	14	1	5	6	44
8 Galen Head	58	18	23	41	30	15	8	10	18	2
4 John Gofton	47	20	15	35	17	15	4	5	9	8
14 Vern Campigotto	68	11	24	35	41	15	5	8	13	16
20 Dave Hanson	72	10	24	34	249	14	1	0	1	44
19 Francois Ouimet	55	12	21	33	60	15	1	4	5	8
7 Mike Chernoff	41	9	19	28	32	14	8	6	14	9
5 Reg Bechtold	25	11	16	27	4	15	6	12	18	4
3 Bob Boyd	43	6	21	27	77	15	1	13	14	2
12 Ned Dowd	43	10	16	26	26	5	1	2	3	0
16 Pat Westrum	34	2	11	13	53	15	1	4	5	25
5 Jim Adair	14	7	4	11	9					
7 Moe St. Jacques	24	4	7	11	9					
6 John Perpich	40	3	8	11	40					
4 Jim Wilcox	27	0	11	11	13					
5 Wayne Bianchin	7	8	2	10	4					
5 Gary Gambucci	7	1	7	8	2					
7 Joe Robertson	5	4	2	6	7					
6 Morris Stefaniw	17	1	5	6	6					
5 Doug Falls	13	0	3	3	21					
10 Norm Descoteaux	15	1	0	1	34					
4 Jim Murray	5	0	2	2	2					
7 Mike Cayer	1	0	0	0	0					
14 Don McLeod	2	0	0	0	0					
12 Renaud Duguay	7	0	0	0	4					
5 Derrick Emerson	8	0	0	0	9					
19 Don Atchison (g)	14	0	0	0	0					
21 Louie Levasseur (g)	26	0	0	0	12	12	0	0	0	0
1 Ron Docken (g)	40	0	0	0	12	5	0	0	0	5
Bench					18					2
TOTALS	74	274	449	723	1,601	15	63	95	158	260
					(+7)					(-10)					(+11)

Regular Season Goaltending

	G	Min	GA	ENG	SO	GAA	W	L	T	Saves	Save%
21 Louie Levasseur	26	1,525	79	0	1	3.15	12	10	2	864	0.916
1 Ron Docken	40	2,309	132	3	0	3.42	22	16	1	1,230	0.902
19 Don Atchison	14	683	41	0	0	3.60	4	6	1	365	0.899
TOTALS	74	4,517	252	3	1	3.39	38	32	4	2,459	0.907

Note: Docken totals for Saves and Save % are incomplete – only calculated for available games.

Playoff Goaltending

	G	Min	GA	ENG	SO	GAA	W	L	Saves	Save %
21 Louie Levasseur	12	654	29	0	0	2.66	10	1	353	.924
1 Ron Docken	5	246	15	1	1	3.70	1	3	112	.882
TOTALS	15	900	44	1	1	3.00	11	4	465	.912

Gofton also wore No. 12; Westrum also wore No. 3; Emerson also wore Nos. 6 and 19; Falls also wore No. 10; Murray also wore No. 6; Duguay also wore No. 2; Atchison also wore No. 21.

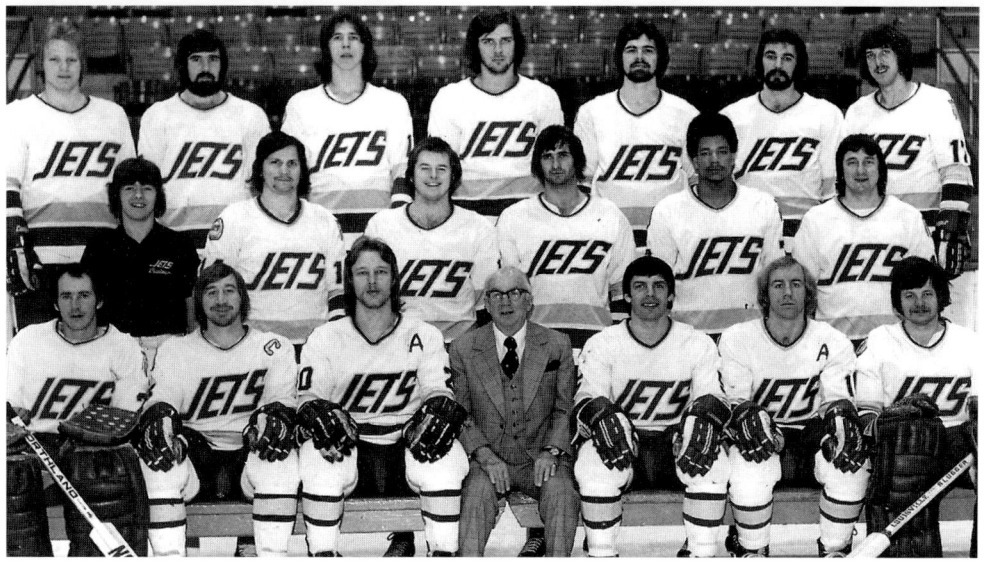

1975-76 Johnstown Jets

(Front, from left) Louie Levasseur, Galen Head, Dave Hanson, general manager John Mitchell, head coach Jim Cardiff, John Gofton, Ron Docken. (Middle) Trainer Eddie Neisner, Vern Campigotto, Bruce Boudreau, Reg Bechtold, Henry Taylor, Wynne Dempster. (Back) Guido Tenesi, Dave Birch, Steve Carlson, Jeff Carlson, Francois Ouimet, Bill Reed, Jean Tetreault.

1975-76 FINAL NORTH AMERICAN HOCKEY LEAGUE STANDINGS

	Games played	Won	Lost	Tied	Points	Goals for	Goals against
Division							
Beauce Jaros	74	54	18	2	110	462	306
Syracuse Blazers	74	38	33	3	79	284	278
Mohawk Valley Comets	74	30	40	4	64	306	354
Cape Codders *	52	24	25	3	51	244	227
Maine Nordiques	74	18	55	1	37	295	450
Division							
Johnstown Jets	74	47	25	2	96	346	257
Philadelphia Firebirds	74	45	29	0	90	373	319
Erie Blades	74	37	36	1	75	310	298
Buffalo Norsemen	74	30	44	0	60	323	375
Binghamton Dusters	74	27	45	2	56	258	337

* Cape Codders ceased operation – Feb. 13, 1976.

Johnstown Jets
General Manager - John Mitchell
Coach - Jim Cardiff
Trainer - Eddie Neisner
Stickboy - Woody Espey, Jeff Mastervich
Colors - Blue, White and Gold

1975-76 Game Results

Preseason Results
No preseason games.
Regular Season Results
Score

Day	Date	Opponent	Johnstown	Opponent	Attendance	Record
Fri.	17-Oct	Erie	4	3	3,239	1-0-0
Sat.	18-Oct	Binghamton	5	1	2,763	2-0-0

Day	Date	Opponent	GF	GA	Att.	Record
Tues.	21-Oct	at Binghamton	3	4		2-1-0
Wed.	22-Oct	at Philadelphia	4	3		3-1-0
Fri.	24-Oct	Philadelphia	6	4	2,500	4-1-0
Sat.	25-Oct	Buffalo	8	2	3,216	5-1-0
Fri.	31-Oct	at Buffalo	4	7		5-2-0
Sat.	1-Nov	Philadelphia	5	1	3,654	6-2-0
Sun.	2-Nov	at Maine	3	4		6-3-0
Tues.	4-Nov	at Cape Codders	2	2		6-3-1
Wed.	5-Nov	at Beauce	5	3		7-3-1
Sat.	8-Nov	Syracuse	3	5	4,016	7-4-1
Wed.	12-Nov	at Binghamton	4	2		8-4-1
Thur.	13-Nov	at Mohawk Valley	1	4		8-5-1
Fri.	14-Nov	Cape Codders	6	4	2,846	9-5-1
Wed.	19-Nov	at Philadelphia	6	5		10-5-1
Fri.	21-Nov	at Buffalo	4	3		11-5-1
Sat.	22-Nov	Buffalo	8	1	3,361	12-5-1
Sun.	23-Nov	Syracuse	6	2	2,555	13-5-1
Wed.	26-Nov	at Mohawk Valley	5	0		14-5-1
Thur.	27-Nov	Mohawk Valley	3	1	3,279	15-5-1
Sat.	29-Nov	Erie	6	4	3,695	16-5-1
Wed.	3-Dec	at Syracuse	7	2		17-5-1
Fri.	5-Dec	at Philadelphia	6	10		17-6-1
Sat.	6-Dec	at Erie	3	5		17-7-1
Mon.	8-Dec	at Beauce	1	8		17-8-1
Tues.	9-Dec	at Maine	9	5		18-8-1
Wed.	10-Dec	at Cape Codders	2	3		18-9-1
Thur.	11-Dec	at Beauce	2	3		18-10-1
Sat.	13-Dec	Cape Codders	5	4	3,065	19-10-1
Sun.	14-Dec	Cape Codders	5	3	2,114	20-10-1
Wed.	17-Dec	at Erie	0	4		20-11-1
Fri.	19-Dec	Erie	3	1	2,052	21-11-1
Fri.	26-Dec	at Mohawk Valley	12	2		22-11-1
Sat.	27-Dec	Mohawk Valley	6	1	2,690	23-11-1
Sun.	28-Dec	Syracuse	3	4 (ot)	2,470	23-12-1
Tues.	30-Dec	at Syracuse	2	2		23-13-1
Wed.	31-Dec	Erie	5	1	2,502	24-13-1
Fri.	2-Jan	at Buffalo	6	3		25-13-1
Sat.	3-Jan	Philadelphia	5	1	3,043	26-13-1
Sun.	4-Jan	Philadelphia	7	2	2,475	27-13-1
Fri.	9-Jan	at Binghamton	5	2		28-13-1
Sat.	10-Jan	at Erie	3	2		29-13-1
Tues.	13-Jan	at Buffalo	3	2		30-13-1
Fri.	16-Jan	Binghamton	2	3	2,177	30-14-1
Sat.	17-Jan	Mohawk Valley	6	1	3,142	31-14-1
Mon.	19-Jan	at Binghamton	3	5		31-15-1
Fri.	23-Jan	Beauce	5	7	2,824	31-16-1
Sat.	24-Jan	Beauce	4	3	4,028	32-16-1
Fri.	30-Jan	Maine	10	1	2,134	33-16-1
Sat.	31-Jan	Maine	5	4	2,947	34-16-1
Wed.	4-Feb	Binghamton	3	0	1,948	35-16-1
Sat.	7-Feb	Erie	8	4	3,083	36-16-1
Sun.	8-Feb	at Erie	7	5		37-16-1
Wed.	11-Feb	at Philadelphia	3	4		37-17-1
Fri.	13-Feb	Maine	5	3	2,110	38-17-1
Sat.	14-Feb	Buffalo	6	4	2,859	39-17-1
Wed.	18-Feb	at Buffalo	2	4		39-18-1
Fri.	20-Feb	Philadelphia	12	3	2,734	40-18-1
Sat.	21-Feb	Binghamton	8	2	2,934	41-18-1
Sun.	22-Feb	at Erie	4	2		42-18-1
Tues.	24-Feb	Beauce	4	5	4,018	42-19-1
Fri.	27-Feb	Binghamton	6	3	3,408	43-19-1
Sat.	28-Feb	Buffalo	7	4	2,796	44-19-1
Sun.	29-Feb	at Binghamton	5	8		44-20-1
Mon.	1-Mar	at Erie	1	9		44-21-1
Fri.	5-Mar	at Philadelphia	4	6		44-22-1
Sat.	6-Mar	Philadelphia	9	2	3,712	45-22-1
Sun.	7-Mar	at Syracuse	1	8		45-23-1
Wed.	10-Mar	at Maine	5	4		46-23-1
Fri.	12-Mar	at Philadelphia	0	5		46-24-1
Sat.	13-Mar	Philadelphia	2	5	3,833	46-25-1

JETS IN THE SEVENTIES

Day	Date	Opponent			Attendance	Record
Sun.	14-Mar	Buffalo	5	3	2,348	47-25-1
Wed.	17-Mar	at Philadelphia	3	5		47-26-1

Playoff Results

Day	Date	Opponent	Score Johnstown	Opponent	Attendance	Record
Sun.	21-Mar	at Buffalo	1	5		0-1
Mon.	22-Mar	Buffalo	6	4	2,379	1-1
Wed.	24-Mar	Buffalo	8	2	3,063	2-1
Thur.	25-Mar	at Buffalo	2	3		2-2
Sat.	27-Mar	Buffalo *	1	0	Forfeit	3-2
Sun.	28-Mar	at Philadelphia	4	5		0-1
Mon.	29-Mar	Philadelphia	6	3	3,344	1-1
Wed.	30-Mar	at Philadelphia	5	7		1-2
Thur.	1-Apr	Philadelphia	3	4 (ot)	3,122	1-3
Fri.	2-Apr	at Philadelphia	10	14		1-4

* Johnstown awarded 1-0 forfeit win on March 27 after Buffalo refused to take ice following a pre-game brawl. Attendance was more than 4300. Tickets were refunded.

Attendance Figures

	Dates	Totals	Average
Regular Season Attendance Totals	37	108,570	2,934
Playoff Attendance Totals	4	11,908	2,977
TOTAL ATTENDANCE	41	120,478	2,938

1975-76 Player Statistics

	Regular Season Scoring					Playoff Scoring				
	Games	G	A	Pts	PIM	Games	G	A	Pts	PIM
7 Henry Taylor	69	50	43	93	33	9	5	4	9	6
17 Jean Tetreault	72	25	49	74	73	9	4	9	13	23
3 Reg Bechtold	60	29	38	67	15	9	2	8	10	4
2 Guido Tenesi	67	13	50	63	134	7	1	5	6	18
16 Bruce Boudreau	34	25	35	60	14	9	6	5	11	7
12 John Gofton	74	32	27	59	26	9	6	3	9	8
14 Vern Campigotto	72	15	44	59	67	9	1	6	7	4
8 Galen Head	73	27	30	57	44	9	3	3	6	8
4 Francois Ouimet	58	7	50	57	73	4	3	1	4	7
5 Jim Cardiff	72	5	52	57	135	7	1	8	9	32
15 Dave Birch	54	27	23	50	93	9	3	9	12	5
18 Jeff Carlson	55	27	20	47	160	9	1	2	3	2
19 Steve Carlson	40	22	24	46	55	9	5	4	9	6
6 Jerry Zrymiak	42	5	30	35	53					
20 Dave Hanson	66	8	21	29	311	9	0	3	3	54
10 Wynne Dempster	29	11	14	25	47					
6 Bill Reed	28	3	19	22	47	9	1	6	7	12
10 Ray Delorenzi	26	7	12	19	16	9	3	0	3	2
18 Paul Holmgren	6	3	12	15	12					
5 Jim Adair	12	3	5	8	4					
4 Bob Young	16	2	1	3	8					
1 Ron Docken (g)	36	0	3	3	4	5	0	0	0	2
21 Louie Levasseur (g)	30	0	2	2	41	5	0	0	0	4
21 Rocky Farr (g)	1	0	0	0	0					
16 Dennis McLean	3	0	0	0	0					
21 Mike Curran (g)	9	0	0	0	0					
Bench					14		1	1		4
TOTALS	74	346	604	950	1479	10	46	76	122	208

Regular Season Goaltending

	G	Min	GA	ENG	SO	GAA	W	L	T	Saves	Save%
21 Louie Levasseur	30	1,757	89	0	1	3.04	22	7	1	806	0.901
1 Ron Docken	36	2,123	125	2	1	3.53	18	15	1	943	0.883
21 Mike Curran	9	547	33	0	0	3.62	7	2	0	302	0.901
21 Rocky Farr	1	60	8	0	0	8.00	0	1	0	37	0.822
TOTALS	74	4,487	255	2	2	3.44	47	25	2	2,088	0.890

Playoff Goaltending

	G	Min	GA	ENG	SO	GAA	W	L	Saves	Save%
21 Louie Levasseur	5	264	19	0	0	4.32	2	2	139	.880
1 Ron Docken	5	280	27	1	0	5.78	1	4	179	.869
TOTALS	10	544	46	1	0	5.18	4*	6	318	.871

* Totals include forfeit win over Buffalo – March 27.

Taylor also wore No. 15; Boudreau also wore No. 19; Ouimet also wore No. 3; Delorenzi also wore No. 16; Young also wore No. 3

1976-77 Johnstown Jets

(From left) Bob Sneddon, general manager/coach Jim Cardiff, Darryl Ferner, Wynne Dempster, Mike Fedorko, Jean Tetreault, Jean Trottier, Don Eastcott, Georges Gendron, Henry Taylor, Vern Campigotto, Guido Tenesi, Keith Jonathan, Dave Birch, Don McLean, Ron Docken.

1976-77 FINAL NORTH AMERICAN HOCKEY LEAGUE STANDINGS

	Games played	Won	Lost	Tied	Points	Goals for	Goals against
Syracuse Blazers	73	48	22	3	99	372	261
Maine Nordiques	74	40	29	5	85	311	284
Binghamton Dusters	74	41	31	2	84	363	324
Philadelphia Firebirds	74	38	33	3	79	319	294
Erie Blades	74	37	33	4	78	257	251
Mohawk Valley Comets	74	29	42	3	61	316	387
Johnstown Jets	73	22	49	2	46	253	334
Beauce Jaros *	30	6	22	2	14	109	165

*Beauce Jaros ceased operations - Dec. 22, 1976

Johnstown Jets
General Manager - Jim Cardiff
Coach - Jim Cardiff
Trainer - Eddie Neisner
Stickboy - Jeff Mastervich
Colors - Blue, White and Gold

1976-77 Game Results

Preseason Results

Day	Date	Opponent	Johnstown	Opponent	Attendance	Record
Wed.	13-Oct	at Erie	2	5		
Sun.	17-Oct	Erie	2	4	1,200	

Regular Season Results

Day	Date	Opponent	Johnstown	Opponent	Attendance	Record
Fri.	22-Oct	at Erie	6	3		1-0-0
Sat.	23-Oct	Erie	1	3	2,695	1-1-0
Fri.	29-Oct	Mohawk Valley	5	1	1,826	2-1-0
Sat.	30-Oct	at Mohawk Valley	1	7		2-2-0
Wed.	3-Nov	Maine	8	5	1,635	3-2-0
Fri.	5-Nov	Syracuse	4	5 (ot)	2,103	3-3-0
Sat.	6-Nov	at Erie	2	3		3-4-0
Wed.	10-Nov	at Binghamton	1	7		3-5-0
Fri.	12-Nov	Mohawk Valley	2	4	1,929	3-6-0

JETS IN THE SEVENTIES

Day	Date	Opponent	Johnstown	Opponent	Attendance	Record
Sat.	13-Nov	at Philadelphia	3	8		3-7-0
Sun.	14-Nov	at Erie	2	9		3-8-0
Wed.	17-Nov	Beauce	Cancelled			
Fri.	19-Nov	at Erie	3	5		3-9-0
Sat.	20-Nov	Binghamton	4	0	2,037	4-9-0
Sun.	21-Nov	at Syracuse	3	8		4-10-0
Thur.	25-Nov	Erie	4	2	1,899	5-10-0
Fri.	26-Nov	at Philadelphia	3	6		5-11-0
Sat.	27-Nov	Philadelphia	4	3	2,161	6-11-0
Sun.	28-Nov	at Syracuse	3	4		6-12-0
Wed.	1-Dec	Maine	6	1	1,172	7-12-0
Thur.	2-Dec	at Philadelphia	1	4		7-13-0
Fri.	3-Dec	Maine	2	6	1,449	7-14-0
Sat.	4-Dec	Syracuse	1	5	1,783	7-15-0
Fri.	10-Dec	at Beauce	6	3		8-15-0
Sat.	11-Dec	at Maine	3	6		8-16-0
Sun.	12-Dec	at Beauce	1	4		8-17-0
Tues.	14-Dec	at Maine	2	2		8-17-1
Fri.	17-Dec	Beauce	2	1 (ot)	1,558	9-17-1
Sat.	18-Dec	Mohawk Valley	5	0	1,591	10-17-1
Wed.	22-Dec	Erie	0	2	1,345	10-18-1
Thur.	23-Dec	at Syracuse	2	3		10-19-1
Sun.	26-Dec	at Mohawk Valley	4	8		10-20-1
Wed.	29-Dec	at Binghamton	3	5		10-21-1
Fri.	31-Dec	Erie	5	3	1,696	11-21-1
Sat.	1-Jan	Syracuse	5	6	1,792	11-22-1
Sun.	2-Jan	at Erie	4	2		12-22-1
Wed.	5-Jan	at Binghamton	2	7		12-23-1
Fri.	7-Jan	Erie	9	3	1,329	13-23-1
Sat.	8-Jan	Philadelphia	4	5	2,253	13-24-1
Fri.	14-Jan	Binghamton	4	4	1,826	13-24-2
Sat.	15-Jan	Syracuse	3	6	2,576	13-25-2
Sun.	16-Jan	at Binghamton	7	6 (ot)		14-25-2
Mon.	17-Jan	Philadelphia	1	3	1,209	14-26-2
Tues.	18-Jan	at Mohawk Valley	4	10		14-27-2
Wed.	19-Jan	at Binghamton	2	6		14-28-2
Sat.	22-Jan	Binghamton	6	3	3,121	15-28-2
Sun.	23-Jan	at Erie	3	1		16-28-2
Wed.	26-Jan	Maine	6	4	1,821	17-28-2
Fri.	28-Jan	Maine	3	5	1,628	17-29-2
Sun.	30-Jan	Philadelphia	1	3	2,732	17-30-2
Wed.	2-Feb	at Maine	1	6		17-31-2
Sat.	5-Feb	at Maine	2	7		17-32-2
Mon.	7-Feb	at Syracuse	4	8		17-33-2
Wed.	9-Feb	Erie	1	3	1,313	17-34-2
Fri.	11-Feb	Binghamton	3	7	1,625	17-35-2
Sat.	12-Feb	Syracuse	6	7	1,196	17-36-2
Sun.	13-Feb	at Mohawk Valley	5	9		17-37-2
Wed.	16-Feb	at Erie	2	5		17-38-2
Fri.	18-Feb	Maine	2	4	1,755	17-39-2
Sat.	19-Feb	Mohawk Valley	9	1	3,497	18-39-2
Sun.	20-Feb	at Philadelphia	4	7		18-40-2
Wed.	23-Feb	Philadelphia	3	4 (ot)	1,272	18-41-2
Fri.	25-Feb	at Syracuse	1	4		18-42-2
Sat.	26-Feb	at Maine	7	6		19-42-2
Wed.	2-Mar	at Binghamton	5	8		19-43-2
Thur.	3-Mar	at Mohawk Valley	3	4 (ot)		19-44-2
Sat.	5-Mar	Mohawk Valley	6	2	2,042	20-44-2
Sun.	6-Mar	Philadelphia	3	4	1,699	20-45-2
Tues.	8-Mar	at Philadelphia	3	9		20-46-2
Wed.	9-Mar	Mohawk Valley	5	3	1,298	21-46-2
Fri.	11-Mar	Binghamton	5	3	1,549	22-46-2
Sat.	12-Mar	at Maine	3	5		22-47-2
Sun.	13-Mar	at Mohawk Valley	2	4		22-48-2
Wed.	16-Mar	Erie	2	4	1,522	22-49-2

Playoff Results
Score

Day	Date	Opponent	Johnstown	Opponent	Attendance	Record
Fri.	18-Mar	at Maine	1	6		0-1
Sun.	20-Mar	at Maine	3	7		0-2
Tues.	22-Mar	Maine	3	6	1,379	0-3

197

Attendance Figures

	Dates	Totals	Average
Preseason Attendance Figures	1	1,200	1,200
Regular Season Attendance Figures	36	65,934	1,832
Playoff Attendance Figures	1	1,379	1,379
TOTAL ATTENDANCE	38	68,513	1,803

1976-77 Player Statistics

	Regular Season Scoring					Playoff Scoring				
	Games	G	A	Pts	PIM	Games	G	A	Pts	PIM
18 Jean Tetreault	68	29	56	85	81	3	0	2	2	12
7 Henry Taylor	73	43	26	69	12	3	1	1	2	0
14 Vern Campigotto	68	15	38	53	82	3	1	2	3	0
15 Dave Birch	64	21	27	48	50	3	0	1	1	0
4 Rob Walton	36	15	26	41	40					
2 Guido Tenesi	56	4	28	32	63					
8 Gerry Teeple	27	11	15	26	2	3	0	1	1	2
16 Wynne Dempster	39	7	16	23	80					
19 Remi Levesque	27	10	12	22	2	3	2	0	2	0
3 Georges Gendron	41	6	16	22	57					
5 Jim Cardiff	46	1	21	22	111	3	0	1	1	0
4 Ken Gassoff	16	8	11	19	44	3	1	2	3	0
12 Brian Marchinko	21	8	11	19	4	3	2	0	2	0
17 Jon Hammond	36	8	10	18	33					
8 Bob Whitlock	20	8	8	16	34					
10 Barry Scully	32	8	8	16	18					
20 Jim Pritchard	31	1	15	16	24	3	0	0	0	0
6 Jean Landry	33	10	5	15	30	3	0	0	0	0
10 Darrell Ferner	19	8	7	15	30					
16 Don Eastcott	33	6	9	15	22	2	0	0	0	0
17 Craig Reichmuth	33	5	8	13	52	3	0	0	0	2
2 Francois Ouimet	16	5	7	12	12	3	0	0	0	2
19 Les Burgess	19	4	7	11	6					
8 Jean Trottier	13	2	8	10	2					
20 Mike Fedorko	28	1	8	9	69					
8 Jim Minor	8	0	8	8	9					
3 Ralph MacSweyn	27	0	7	7	8	3	0	2	2	0
20 Rick Loe	17	3	3	6	8					
12 Rick Dorman	9	2	4	6	35					
12 Keith Jonathan	5	2	1	3	6					
20 Dave Hanson	6	0	3	3	27					
16 Claude Periard	11	1	1	2	4					
5 Jim Setters	4	0	2	2	2					
6 Don McLean	5	0	2	2	4					
21 Bob Sneddon (g)	18	0	0	0	2					
1 Ron Docken (g)	52	0	2	2	28	3	0	0	0	0
4 Bob Gryp	2	1	0	1	0					
6 Wayne Spooner	5	0	1	1	9					
3 Paul Peckham	2	0	0	0	0					
21 Jim Makey (g)	8	0	0	0	2					
Bench					14					
TOTALS	73	253	437	690	1118	3	7	12	19	18

Regular Season Goaltending

	G	Min	GA	ENG	SO	GAA	W	L	T	Saves	Save %
1 Ron Docken	52	3,130	211	1	2	4.04	19	31	2	1,450	0.873
21 Bob Sneddon	18	913	75	2	0	4.93	3	11	0	475	0.864
21 Jim Makey	8	429	45	0	0	6.29	0	7	0	248	0.846
TOTALS	73	4,472	331	3	2	4.48	22	49	2	2,173	0.867

Playoff Goaltending

	G	Min	GA	ENG	SO	GAA	W	L	Saves	Save %
1 Ron Docken	3	180	18	1	0	6.00	0	3	85	.825
TOTALS	3	180	18	1	0	6.33	0	3	85	.825

Eastcott also wore No. 19; MacSweyn also wore No. 12; Whitlock also wore No. 10; Ferner also wore No. 8; Burgess also wore No. 6 and No. 10; Setters also wore No. 19.

Players who were on roster and didn't play: 21 Dave Legree, Goal.

JETS IN THE SEVENTIES

Johnstown's Patty Watson believed Jets goalie Louie Levasseur had some help from a higher power in the Jets championship-clinching win over Binghamton at the War Memorial in 1975.

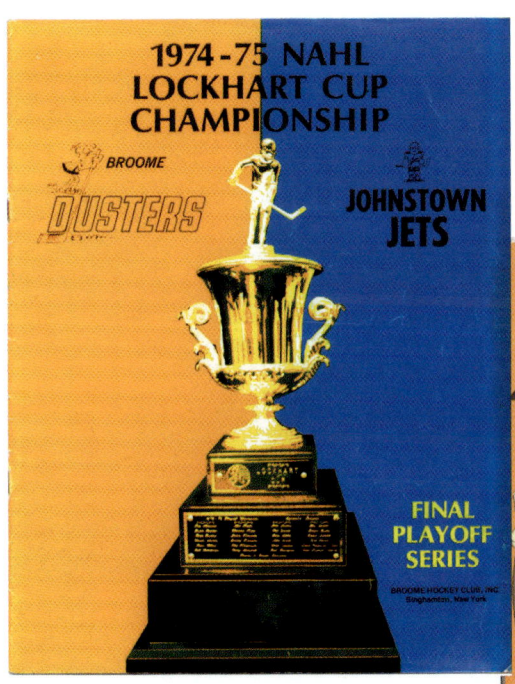

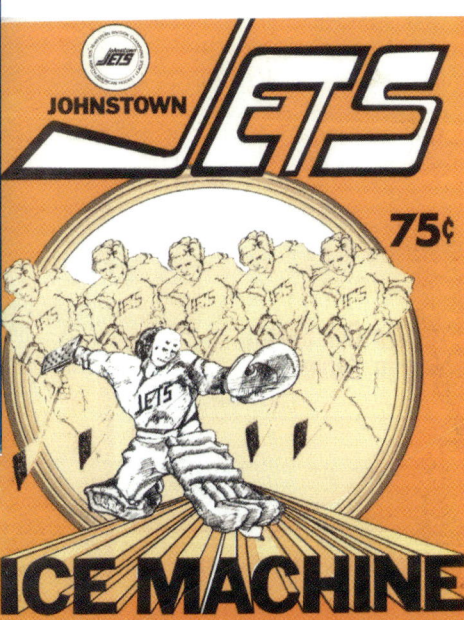

199

David Johns played 29 games in goal for the 1979-80 Johnstown Red Wings.

Wings and Red Wings Overview

By Mike Mastovich

After the Johnstown Flood of 1977, rebuilding a city, including parts of Cambria County War Memorial Arena, was the priority.

For obvious reasons, hockey games didn't seem quite so important in the immediate aftermath of a killer flood that claimed 85 lives and caused more than $200 million in damage. The muddy waters also dealt a devastating blow to an economy built largely around the steel and coal industries. People who traditionally purchased hockey tickets were rebuilding their homes and lives. Some were looking for work.

There was no professional hockey in Johnstown during the 1977-78 season. The NAHL Jets had been struggling financially even before the flood. Losing nearly all the team's equipment and uniforms, as well as the loss of the arena's ruined ice-making machinery, was just too much to overcome.

After one season away from the ice, former Jets General Manager John Mitchell did what he had done so often since 1960. He built a hockey operation, the Johnstown Wings Hockey Club, which played in the new Northeastern Hockey League that Mitchell helped assemble.

Mitchell once again turned to his long-standing ties to the NHL's Detroit Red Wings. Working with Lincoln Cavalieri, president of Olympia Stadium Corp., which owned the Detroit team, Mitchell secured an affiliation for the Johnstown Wings. Johnstown worked closely with Detroit General Manager Ted Lindsay and Assistant GM Jim Skinner to develop players.

"Mitch worked with Lincoln Cavalieri, Jim Skinner and Ted Lindsay. They helped him through that season," said James M. Edwards Sr., the former president and CEO of WJAC Inc. Edwards was among a group of individuals who assisted Mitchell during that 1978-79 season.

"At the end of that season," Edwards said, "Mitch ran out of money and the local business community came to the front and donated enough money to the Wings to fund the end of his operation and he was able to finish out the season without any debt."

In a letter to Edwards dated April 13, 1979, Mitchell thanked Edwards and the local television station for participating in the "Keep Hockey Alive" promotion. "You can be on my 'Team' anytime," Mitchell wrote.

The Wings struggled on the ice, too. Former Jets star Dick Roberge, who coached the 1974-75 NAHL championship team, couldn't recreate the magic. Johnstown finished last in the five-team league, posting only 25 wins while allowing 315 goals.

The Northeastern League itself was a model of inconsistency. Teams that began the season in New Hampshire and New Jersey moved to Cape Cod (Dec. 16, 1978) and Hampton (Jan. 4, 1979), respectively. Johnstown, Utica and Erie made it through the season.

"When the World Hockey Association folded, Mitch picked up players from the Minnesota camp, other than guys like Harry Shaw and Vern Campigotto, veterans who were in their 30s," said Steve Emmett, a rookie forward on the Wings. "Mitch built a young team. I was the youngest player on the team at 19."

The Wings leading scorers were Dave Lundeen (89 points), Mike Haerich (82) and Bruce Lind (67). Shaw, Campigotto, Wynne Dempster and goalie Ron Docken were veteran pros.

The Wings were Mitchell's final team in Johnstown. The financial challenges became too much for one individual to handle. It took a group effort to assemble the Johnstown Red Wings in a new version of the Eastern Hockey League in 1979-80.

"In order to keep it going, I put together a group of 10 people to take over ownership of the Johnstown Wings, and at the same time I was able to work with the Detroit Red Wings to strengthen the affiliation," said Edwards, who was president of the local ownership group. "The agreement we put together was that the Red Wings would hire the players, hire the general manager, and hire the coach. All we had to do was oversee the local operation and manage it from the local level. For all intents and purposes, for that season we were a farm team for the Detroit Red Wings. We didn't have to do any recruiting

Left: Fan favorite Harry Shaw.

Right: Red Wings 50-goal scorer Dave MacQueen.

or things of that nature. We just had to pay the bills."

Stockholders of the Johnstown Red Wings included Edwards, Edward Berkey, Carmen Crowe, James C. Dewar, Robert A. Gleason Jr., Crown American Corp., Constance Mayer, Dr. Bernard McQuillan, Alphonse A. Page, Howard M. Picking, Jeffrey Schwartz and John Whalley.

Al Blade was general manager, and Marty Read was the coach. The Red Wings won 24 games and placed fifth in a six-team league that also included Erie, Baltimore, Richmond (Va.), Utica and Hampton (Va.).

The Red Wings did produce a 50-goal scorer, Dave MacQueen, who tallied 53 goals and 110 points. Pierre Tremblay had 26 goals and 75 points.

The Red Wings' official statement of income and expense had the team losing $30,803 in 1979-80. That deficit might have been significantly higher had the team not had rights to concession money at the War Memorial. The report stated that concessions brought in $128,464 and that concession expenses were $93,426. That resulted in a net profit of $35,038.

"During that season, for the first and last time, the hockey team operated the concession stands," Edwards said. "The hockey operation lost $72,283, the concession stands earned $35,038, and promotions earned $6,493 for a net operating loss of $30,803."

The Red Wings and War Memorial met to discuss a new lease, but the Eastern League folded when several teams ceased operations.

"At the end of that 1979-80 season, we were negotiating for another season with the renewal of the lease with the arena, and the league folded, so we went out of business," Edwards said. "We went to the Pittsburgh Airport. All the team owners were there. I was there. We spent 24 hours developing a schedule for the 1980-81 season. We had the schedule in place. We hammered out who got this date and who got that date, and how many weekends we got. All of that was done.

"It became moot because the league folded. We just stopped operating. There were too many weak teams and too many teams that lost money. They just didn't want to go again."

Left: Wings rookie Steve Emmett.

Right: Conemaugh Valley graduate Jeff Mastervich, then 19, was the first Johnstown native to suit up in a regular-season game for a Johnstown pro team. He served as a backup in a 3-2 loss to the Hampton Aces on Feb. 28, 1980.

1978-79 Johnstown Wings

(Front, from left) Jerry Price, Doug Johnston, Tom Machowski, general manager John Mitchell, Dan Byers, Harry Shaw, Ron Docken. (Middle) Stickboy Jeff Mastervich, Vern Campigotto, Dean Willers, Mike Wong, Pete Mavroudis, Jim Cowell, Mike Haedrich, trainer Jeff Hall. (Back) Head coach Dick Roberge, Jim O'Neill, Earl Sergeant, Dave Lundeen, Bruce Lind, Ed Starkey.

1978-79 FINAL NORTHEAST HOCKEY LEAGUE STANDINGS

	Games played	Won	Lost	Tied	Points	Goals for	Goals against
Erie Blades	69	47	19	3	97	344	260
Jersey/Hampton Aces *	69	37	29	3	77	330	286
New Hampshire/Cape Cod Freedoms **	70	33	36	1	67	292	309
Utica Mohawks	70	27	43	0	54	308	355
Johnstown Wings	70	25	42	3	53	251	315

* New Hampshire moved to Cape Cod – Dec. 16, 1978
** Jersey moved to Hampton Jan. 4, 1979

Johnstown Wings
General Manager - John Mitchell
Coach - Dick Roberge
Trainer - Mike Bondy (until Dec. 15); Jeff Hall (from Dec. 15)
Stickboy - Jeff Mastervich
Colors - Blue, White and Gold

1978-79 Game Results

Preseason Results
No preseason games
Regular Season Results
Score

Day	Date	Opponent	Johnstown	Opponent	Attendance	Record
Wed.	1-Nov	at Erie	3	2		1-0-0

WINGS AND RED WINGS

Day	Date	Opponent	GF	GA	Att.	Record
Fri.	3-Nov	New Hampshire	2	7	2,866	1-1-0
Sat.	4-Nov	Jersey	3	5	2,474	1-2-0
Sun.	5-Nov	at Jersey	2	7		1-3-0
Tues.	7-Nov	at Erie	4	5		1-4-0
Wed.	8-Nov	at Utica	0	6		1-5-0
Fri.	10-Nov	Utica	7	2	1,637	2-5-0
Sat.	11-Nov	Utica	1	5	2,245	2-6-0
Wed.	15-Nov	at Jersey	0	7		2-7-0
Thur.	16-Nov	Erie	2	3 (ot)	1,172	2-8-0
Sat.	18-Nov	at Erie	3	4		2-9-0
Sun.	19-Nov	Erie	5	4	1,357	3-9-0
Thur.	23-Nov	Jersey	2	5	2,295	3-10-0
Fri.	24-Nov	at Utica	2	5		3-11-0
Sat.	25-Nov	at New Hampshire	5	4		4-11-0
Sun.	26-Nov	at New Hampshire	1	6		4-12-0
Wed.	29-Nov	Jersey	4	3	1,206	5-12-0
Sat.	2-Dec	Utica	10	5	2,007	6-12-0
Sun.	3-Dec	Utica	0	6	1,275	6-13-0
Tues.	5-Dec	at New Hampshire	2	5		6-14-0
Wed.	6-Dec	at New Hampshire	4	6		6-15-0
Fri.	8-Dec	at Utica	7	6 (ot)		7-15-0
Sat.	9-Dec	at Utica	5	9		7-16-0
Sun.	10-Dec	at New Hampshire	1	5		7-17-0
Wed.	13-Dec	at Jersey	1	8		7-18-0
Fri.	15-Dec	Jersey	3	4	1,247	7-19-0
Sat.	16-Dec	Utica	4	5	1,214	7-20-0
Sun.	17-Dec	Cape Cod	4	3 (ot)	1,118	8-20-0
Wed.	20-Dec	Erie	5	8	951	8-21-0
Sat.	23-Dec	at Erie	1	7		8-22-0
Wed.	27-Dec	Erie	7	5	1,569	9-22-0
Sat.	30-Dec	at Jersey	3	6		9-23-0
Tues.	2-Jan	at Utica	3	4 (ot)		9-24-0
Wed.	3-Jan	at Cape Cod	1	4		9-25-0
Fri.	5-Jan	Hampton	6	2	1,300	10-25-0
Sat.	6-Jan	Cape Cod	5	2	1,726	11-25-0
Sun.	7-Jan	at Hampton	Postponed – rescheduled for March 6			
Tues.	9-Jan	at Utica	2	8		11-26-0
Thur.	11-Jan	Hampton	7	2	1,394	12-26-0
Sat.	13-Jan	Hampton	7	5	2,464	13-26-0
Wed.	17-Jan	at Erie	1	2		13-27-0
Fri.	19-Jan	at Hampton *	6	6		13-27-1
Sat.	20-Jan	Erie	2	5	2,334	13-28-1
Tues.	23-Jan	at Erie	2	5		13-29-1
Fri.	26-Jan	Cape Cod	6	3	1,368	14-29-1
Sat.	27-Jan	Cape Cod	6	9	2,081	14-30-1
Wed.	31-Jan	at Erie	0	5		14-31-1
Fri.	2-Feb	at Erie	1	4		14-32-1
Sat.	3-Feb	at Utica	8	2		15-32-1
Sun.	4-Feb	at Hampton	2	7		15-33-1
Wed.	7-Feb	Erie	2	2	993	15-33-2
Fri.	9-Feb	at Utica	6	3		16-33-2
Sat.	10-Feb	Hampton	5	4	2,193	17-33-2
Sun.	11-Feb	Utica	7	2	1,514	18-33-2
Fri.	16-Feb	at Erie	6	3		19-33-2
Sun.	18-Feb	at Hampton	3	4 (ot)		19-34-2
Tues.	20-Feb	Hampton	5	4	1,415	20-34-2
Fri.	23-Feb	Utica	6	1	1,866	21-34-2
Sat.	24-Feb	Utica	3	2	2,990	22-34-2
Tues.	27-Feb	at Hampton	2	4		22-35-2
Wed.	28-Feb	Cape Cod	4	2	1,657	23-35-2
Thur.	1-Mar	at Hampton	4	6		23-36-2
Sat.	3-Mar	Hampton	7	5	2,728	24-36-2
Sun.	4-Mar	Hampton	2	3 (ot)	2,319	24-37-2
Tues.	6-Mar	at Hampton	3	5		24-38-2
Fri.	9-Mar	Cape Cod	5	3	2,594	25-38-2
Sat.	10-Mar	Erie	4	4	2,544	25-38-3
Wed.	14-Mar	at Cape Cod	3	5		25-39-3
Fri.	16-Mar	Erie	1	3	2,047	25-40-3

205

Sat.	17-Mar		Erie	2	3	2,771	25-41-3
Tues.	20-Mar		at Erie	3	4		25-42-3

* Note: No overtime was played in the Jan. 19, 1979 game due to poor ice conditions.

Attendance Figures

	Dates	Totals	Average
Regular Season Attendance Totals	35	64,931	1,855
TOTAL ATTENDANCE	35	64,931	1,855

1978-79 Player Statistics

Regular Season Scoring

	Games	G	A	Pts	PIM
8 Dave Lundeen	69	33	56	89	167
11 Mike Haedrich	69	37	45	82	54
7 Bruce Lind	59	32	35	67	76
10 Ed Starkey	67	20	30	50	143
12 Jim O'Neill	51	20	28	48	7
6 Mike Wong	53	18	26	44	81
15 Earl Sergeant	36	8	27	35	6
5 Harry Shaw	59	3	31	34	71
4 Doug Johnson	70	4	28	32	85
9 Dean Willers	30	16	15	31	62
14 Jim Cowell	23	14	17	31	18
16 Vern Campigotto	48	11	19	30	8
14 Wynne Dempster	49	10	17	27	44
17 Pete Mavroudis	53	10	12	22	139
2 Dan Byers	69	3	16	19	121
3 Tom Machowski	54	3	15	18	12
9 Mark Ciernia	34	7	10	17	31
6 Rex Lewis	17	1	2	3	7
15 Andre Boudreau	11	0	3	3	0
3 Tim Anderson	17	1	1	2	2
15 Steve Emmett	16	0	1	1	26
30 Jerry Price (g)	22	0	1	1	6
1 Ron Docken (g)	36	0	1	1	8
30 Jeff Tscherne (g)	20	0	0	0	6
Bench					6
TOTALS	70	251	436	687	1186

Regular Season Goaltending

	G	Min	GA	ENG	SO	GAA	W	L	T	Saves	Save%
30 Jerry Price	22	1,278	74	3	0	3.52	9	9	3	609	0.892
1 Ron Docken	36	1,982	154	4	0	4.51	10	23	0	943	0.860
30 Jeff Tscherne	20	976	80	0	0	5.44	6	10	0	447	0.860
TOTALS	70	4,236	308	7	0	4.46	25	42	3		

Note: Tscherne totals for Saves and Save % are incomplete – only calculated for available games.

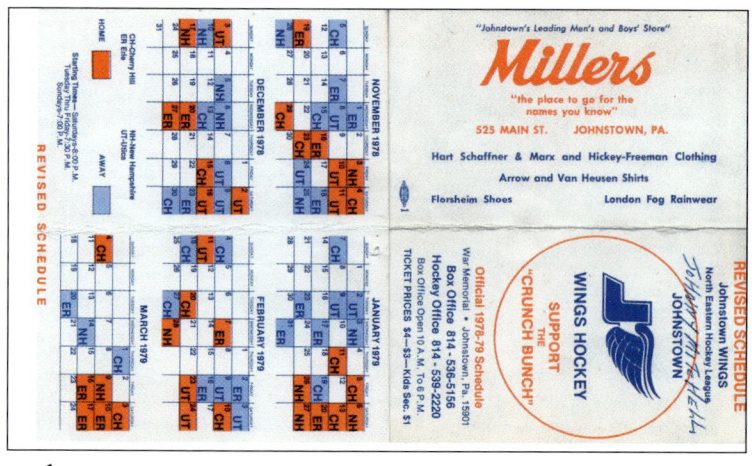

WINGS AND RED WINGS

1979-80 Johnstown Red Wings

(Front, from left) Bill Milner, Pierre Tremblay, Dave MacQueen, Wes George, Brian Shmyr, Colin Ahern, Jim Cardiff, David Johns. (Middle) Trainer Jeff Hall, general manager Al Blade, Lorry Gloeckner, Bob Phillips, Rick Carriere, director of public relations Tom Chavanec, assistant trainer Chuck Lamberson. (Back) Bruce Garber, Brian Paton, Don Stewart, Rob Clavette, Paul Mancini, Laurie Nordstrom, Harry Shaw, Ed Starkey.

1979-80 FINAL EASTERN HOCKEY LEAGUE STANDINGS

	Games played	Won	Lost	Tied	Points	Goals for	Goals against
Erie Blades	70	46	21	3	95	349	241
Baltimore Clippers	70	41	25	4	86	308	225
Richmond Rifles	70	40	24	6	86	315	240
Utica Mohawks	70	30	34	6	66	274	287
Johnstown Red Wings	70	24	45	1	49	281	384
Hampton Aces	70	17	49	4	38	214	364

Johnstown Red Wings
General Manager - Al Blade, Jim Cardiff
Coach - Marty Reed (until Feb. 4, 1980 – 18-26-0); Jim Cardiff (from Feb. 4, 1980, 6-19-1)
Trainer - Jeff Hall, Chuck Lamberson
Stickboy - Jeff Mastervich
Colors - Red and White

1979-80 Game Results

Preseason Results

			Score			
Day	Date	Opponent	Johnstown	Opponent	Attendance	Record
Fri.	19-Oct	Hampton	7	5	1,270	
Sat.	20-Oct	Baltimore	5	8	1,180	

Regular Season Results

Day	Date	Opponent	Score Johnstown	Opponent	Attendance	Record
Wed.	24-Oct	at Utica	5	7		0-1-0
Sat.	27-Oct	at Richmond	4	11		0-2-0
Fri.	2-Nov	Richmond	6	1	2,300	1-2-0
Sat.	3-Nov	Hampton	11	2	2,443	2-2-0
Fri.	9-Nov	Baltimore	5	4	3,196	3-2-0
Sat.	10-Nov	Utica	5	4	3,279	4-2-0
Wed.	14-Nov	at Richmond	3	8		4-3-0
Thur.	15-Nov	at Hampton	1	7		4-4-0
Sat.	17-Nov	Richmond	4	7	3,009	4-5-0
Sun.	18-Nov	Erie	3	5	3,239	4-6-0
Wed.	21-Nov	al Utica	3	5		4-7-0
Thur.	22-Nov	Utica	0	2	2,563	4-8-0
Fri.	23-Nov	at Baltimore	0	8		4-9-0
Sun.	25-Nov	at Erie	3	4		4-10-0
Wed.	28-Nov	Utica	11	3	1,500	5-10-0
Sat.	1-Dec	at Hampton	8	7		6-10-0
Sun.	2-Dec	Erie	5	8	2,232	6-11-0
Wed.	5-Dec	at Richmond	3	6		6-12-0
Fri.	7-Dec	at Erie	1	8		6-13-0
Sat.	8-Dec	Hampton	3	2	2,085	7-13-0
Sun.	9-Dec	Baltimore	3	6	2,311	7-14-0
Wed.	12-Dec	at Utica	6	10		7-15-0
Sat.	15-Dec	at Baltimore	3	7		7-16-0
Wed.	19-Dec	Hampton	5	2	1,913	8-16-0
Fri.	21-Dec	at Richmond	2	4		8-17-0
Sat.	22-Dec	Erie	3	1	2,015	9-17-0
Sun.	23-Dec	at Hampton	5	4		10-17-0
Fri.	28-Dec	at Utica	3	4		10-18-0
Sun.	30-Dec	Baltimore	5	1	2,563	11-18-0
Sat.	5-Jan	Utica	5	3	2,437	12-18-0
Sun.	6-Jan	Richmond	6	3	1,966	13-18-0
Fri.	11-Jan	at Hampton	2	3		13-19-0
Sat.	12-Jan	Baltimore	4	2	2,825	14-19-0
Sun.	13-Jan	Erie	8	7	2,600	15-19-0
Fri.	18-Jan	at Baltimore	2	10		15-20-0
Sat.	19-Jan	Erie	4	3	3,196	16-20-0
Wed.	23-Jan	at Baltimore	5	7		16-21-0
Thur.	24-Jan	at Richmond	0	3		16-22-0
Sat.	26-Jan	at Erie	3	10		16-23-0
Sun.	27-Jan	at Baltimore	1	8		16-24-0
Wed.	30-Jan	Richmond	2	5	2,309	16-25-0
Fri.	1-Feb	at Hampton	6	2		17-25-0
Sat.	2-Feb	Baltimore	2	5	2,498	17-26-0
Sun.	3-Feb	Richmond	7	4	1,961	18-26-0
Wed.	6-Feb	at Richmond	1	10		18-27-0
Fri.	8-Feb	Hampton	5	3	2,349	19-27-0
Sat.	9-Feb	Utica	5	6	2,996	19-28-0
Sun.	10-Feb	at Utica	4	9		19-29-0
Fri.	15-Feb	at Baltimore	3	8		19-30-0
Sat.	16-Feb	Richmond	7	2	2,030	20-30-0
Sun.	17-Feb	Erie	5	6	2,296	20-31-0
Wed.	20-Feb	at Hampton	5	9		20-32-0
Fri.	22-Feb	at Utica	0	4		20-33-0
Sat.	23-Feb	Utica	4	6	2,267	20-34-0
Sun.	24-Feb	at Erie	0	4		20-35-0
Fri.	29-Feb	Hampton	2	3	1,758	20-36-0
Sat.	1-Mar	at Baltimore	0	2		20-37-0
Sun.	2-Mar	Richmond	5	1	1,819	21-37-0
Fri.	7-Mar	at Utica	0	10		21-38-0
Sat.	8-Mar	Erie	1	10	2,510	21-39-0
Sun.	9-Mar	Baltimore	10	7	2,026	22-39-0
Wed.	12-Mar	Hampton	8	2	1,888	23-39-0
Fri.	14-Mar	at Erie	5	7		23-40-0
Sat.	15-Mar	Utica	4	5	2,532	23-41-0
Fri.	21-Mar	Hampton	13	6	1,911	24-41-0

WINGS AND RED WINGS

Sat.	22-Mar		Baltimore	4	5 (ot)	2,982	24-42-0
Sun.	23-Mar		at Hampton	5	9		24-43-0
Wed.	26-Mar		at Richmond	6	6		24-43-1
Fri.	28-Mar		at Erie	0	15		24-44-1
Sat.	29-Mar		at Erie	3	6		24-45-1

Attendance Figures

	Dates	Totals	Average
Preseason Attendance Totals	2	2450	1,225
Regular Season Attendance Figures	35	83,804	2,394
TOTAL ATTENDANCE	35	83,804	2,394

1979-80 Player Statistics

Regular Season Scoring

	Games	G	A	Pts	PIM
21 Dave MacQueen	64	53	57	110	39
18 Pierre Tremblay	52	26	49	75	133
7 Colin Ahern	66	24	50	74	14
12 Randy Betty	68	30	28	58	15
10 Ed Starkey	69	17	40	57	135
16 Brian Shmyr	68	27	27	54	74
15 Wes George	54	21	29	50	92
8 Brian Paton	31	19	23	42	26
3 Lorry Gloeckner	63	6	29	35	83
2 Bob Phillips	45	3	21	24	108
4 Don Stewart	64	5	16	21	79
14 Steve Salvucci	22	9	10	19	39
24 Paul Mancini	30	12	6	18	7
23 Jim Cardiff	41	0	15	15	77
17 Randy Wilson	14	7	6	13	7
19 Kip Churchill	24	6	7	13	12
20 Rob Clavette	28	7	3	10	31
22 Laurie Nordstrom	35	1	8	9	36
20 Dean Willers	10	4	4	8	12
17 Bruce Garber	36	2	6	8	8
5 Harry Shaw	21	0	8	8	54
2 John Hilworth	4	0	4	4	11
5 Peter Whiting	11	0	4	4	0
24 Jim Snodgrass	8	1	2	3	5
24 Mark Jackson	8	0	3	3	8
2 Guy Bohmer	2	1	1	2	24
23 Alan Stoneman	5	0	2	2	28
2 Paul Wilkins	6	0	2	2	6
14 Rick Carriere	24	0	2	2	24
2 Don Hawkes	7	0	1	1	22
31 Wayne Wood (g)	10	0	1	1	2
1 Bill Milner (g)	33	0	1	1	2
5 Rich Hutchinson	1	0	0	0	0
31 Claude Legris (g)	1	0	0	0	0
17 Jim Boyington	2	0	0	0	14
8 Bob Gordon	2	0	0	0	0
30 Jerry Price (g)	2	0	0	0	2
31 Rick Szabo (g)	4	0	0	0	0
19 Duke Johnson	7	0	0	0	7
25 David Johns (g)	29	0	0	0	21
Bench					14
TOTALS	70	281	465	746	1271

Regular Season Goaltending

	G	Min	GA	ENG	SO	GAA	W	L	T
31 Wayne Wood	10	581	27	1	0	2.79	6	3	0
25 David Johns	29	1,568	135	4	0	5.17	9	19	0
1 Bill Milner	33	1,742	174	2	0	5.99	8	19	1
30 Jerry Price	2	120	13	0	0	6.50	1	1	0
31 Claude Legris	33	4	0	0	0	7.27	0	1	0
31 Rick Szabo	4	166	23	1	0	8.31	0	2	0
TOTALS	70	4,210	376	8	0	5.47	24	45	1

Players who dressed but did not play: 31 Jeff Mastervich, Goal

The Chiefs of the 1980s developed a reputation for playing a tough brand of hockey.

1980s Overview:
Chiefs Bring a New Era to Johnstown

By Mike Mastovich

The hastily assembled group of Johnstown Chiefs sat in the home locker room at Cambria County War Memorial Arena, making "Slap Shot" references and anxiously exchanging pregame banter. Some of the players hardly had been together long enough to remember each other's names. No one knew what to expect as the Chiefs prepared for their first game in the All-American Hockey League on Jan. 13, 1988.

Johnstown had joined the AAHL in mid-season. Coach Joe Selenski and General Manager John Daley assembled a team and hockey operation in a matter of days. Selenski knew his boys probably wouldn't have the stamina to outskate the Carolina Thunderbirds, one of the AAHL's best teams. But the coach did promise that the Chiefs would play aggressive hockey.

A crowd of 3,620 fans nearly filled the 4,040-seat War Memorial for the first truly hometown professional hockey game in eight years. "The first time we went out, there was nobody out there," said Rick Boyd, one of the original Chiefs and a fan favorite because of his tough approach to the game. "There was a mix-up with the starting time. The Thunderbirds bus broke down. They brought us back in the locker room and we were sitting there disheartened. There were a handful of people there, and we were thinking it was going to be a big deal but no one showed up."

'It was time'

The next time the Chiefs took the ice that evening, the situation had changed dramatically. "Then, the visitors' bus arrived," Boyd said. "We were told they were going to introduce us as a team.

"The noise level started to pick up outside the dressing room. We were sitting in the room throwing out jokes about 'Slap Shot.' When they told us it was time, we went out and the lights were dimmed. You couldn't see what was going on."

"Gary Glitter, Rock 'n Roll was playing," Boyd added, referring to the 1970s-era song so frequently played at sports arenas throughout the country. "When they turned the lights up, people were hanging off the rafters. I still get goose bumps thinking about it. I think the fans had been through a lot and they had waited and were patient."

The Chiefs didn't disappoint. Fists flew early in that game. And, surprisingly, the home team won 5-3. A new era of Johnstown hockey began.

"Thirteen seconds in, I got my first fight in Johnstown," said Boyd, who twice came out of retirement to play for the ECHL Chiefs in the late 1990s. "What Joe Selenski told us in the dressing room before the game was that he didn't know much to tell us. He said the last things these fans remember about the game of hockey was the movie 'Slap Shot.' Thirteen seconds into it the gloves were off and we got going.

"That first game I ended up with three fights."

The official box score actually listed the first major fighting penalty 32 seconds into the game. But what are a few seconds? Fisticuffs aside, forward Rob Hrytsak became the first Chief to score a goal at 8:51 of the first period. Hrytsak stole a cross-ice pass and had a clear path to the net before he put the puck over goalie Bruce Billes' shoulder. Chiefs' goaltender Bob Deraney netted the first win, and future Chiefs GM/coach Toby O'Brien later recorded the first shutout as one of the inaugural team's goaltenders.

Scott Allen played for Carolina in that opening Chiefs' game. More than a decade later, Allen coached the Chiefs to some of the franchise's most memorable playoff success. "The Johnstown players looked up in the stands and saw the turnout," Allen recalled. "They also knew the type of hockey those people wanted to see and they were certainly prepared to deliver.

"Joe Selenski was the coach and he probably did as good a job as anybody as far as putting a team together at that time of the year. For him to be able to go out and find the type of players he found, it was outstanding."

The game set a foundation. The Chiefs went 13-13 and dropped three playoff games during that short season. But they won over fans and revived hockey in Johnstown. Attendance numbers were impressive. Crowds of 3,620; 4,332; 4,132; 3,537; and 4,072 watched the first five games at the War Memorial, respectively.

How did such an unthinkable scenario unfold in a hockey-starved town? Virginia oilman Henry Brabham's foresight and determination had plenty to do with hockey's return. Almost a year earlier, two Atlantic Coast Hockey League teams played an exhibition game at the War Memorial to gauge interest in the pro sport last played regularly in Johnstown in 1980.

"The reason I brought a team to Johnstown is because I was so enthused when we played the exhibition game here, with the people of this area and the way they liked hockey and how nice people were to me on the street," Brabham said.

Brabham owned the Virginia Lancers team that faced Erie in that exhibition game. When the ACHL crumbled and the AAHL had a mid-season franchise opening, Brabham remembered Johnstown. He traveled to Johnstown in December 1987 with Selenski, who had coached a Utica, N.Y., team to the ACHL finals a year earlier. Brabham met with War Memorial board member and marketing director Dennis Grenell, who suggested that the

> **The fans of Johnstown are hard-working people, blue-collar people. All they want out of their hockey team is 100 percent."**
>
> *- Rick Boyd, member of the first Johnstown Chiefs team in 1988*

team take the nickname, Chiefs, based on "Slap Shot's" Charlestown Chiefs. Grenell also steered Brabham to Daley, who had served as GM of the EHL's Johnstown Jets from 1962-66.

Selenski had player contacts from previous coaching experience and his earlier attempt to assemble a team that never materialized at the season's outset.

"I have had the good fortune in my life and career to be involved in many community projects, but no day will ever replace Dec. 27, 1987," Grenell said. "At 3:40 p.m. on that date, Henry Brabham and Joe Selenski walked into my office and introduced themselves. Henry said: 'I'm Henry Brabham and I understand you're the guy to talk to about putting a hockey team in Johnstown.' I said, 'When do you want to put this team in?' I was thinking it would be the next year. He said, 'Right now.' He said he wanted to start in two weeks.

"I told him I didn't know anything about running a hockey club, but I knew someone who did. I called John Daley and hooked those two up. Daley agreed to be the GM."

When the subject of a team nickname surfaced, it was believed the name Jets was owned by other parties, and a team being rushed into a league at midseason didn't have time to participate in legal maneuvering to secure a name.

"Henry said, 'What do you want to call this team?' The only thing that came to my mind was 'Slap Shot.' I said, 'How about the Chiefs?' He said, 'They're the Chiefs,' " Grenell said.

An emergency meeting of the War Memorial Board enabled all parties to quickly reach a lease agreement. Many fans thought the Chiefs wore black and gold uniforms to connect with the region's beloved Pittsburgh Steelers, Penguins and Pirates. That actually wasn't the case.

Team officials arranged for an equipment purchase in Niagara Falls, Ontario. The only available uniforms were those in the style of the Boston Bruins.

A van was dispatched from Johnstown that night to pick up the order in Canada.

The fans quickly took to their Chiefs. Players were treated like celebrities in downtown eateries and bars. Kids lined up for autographs of favorites such as Boyd, tough guy Brock Kelly, Hrytsak, Darren Servatius, Deraney, Scott Rettew and O'Brien. The turnstiles at the arena clicked with regularity.

"During the 1988 season, as short as it was, I went upstairs one time to talk to Mr. Daley. There was an elderly lady sitting outside his office waiting to see him," Boyd said. "She was a pleasant lady and she went in to talk to Mr. Daley. She was asking for time to pay for her hockey tickets because the rent was due. Here was a lady negotiating to keep her tickets and pay her rent. She was a person who represented what the fans in this city were about. The fans of Johnstown are hard-working people, blue-collar people. All they want out of their hockey team is 100 percent."

The rough-and-tumble AAHL gave way to the five-team East Coast Hockey League in 1988-89. Brabham had ownership interest in three of the teams — Johnstown, Virginia and Erie. Carolina (Winston-Salem,7 N.C.) and Knoxville (Tenn.) also were original members of the fledgling ECHL.

The Chiefs maintained their momentum during the 1988-89 season. Selenski was gone, but former Jets and "Slap Shot" star Steve Carlson took over as head coach. Carlson welcomed future NHL goaltender Scott Gordon (18-9-3) to camp.

Gordon joined ECHL Rookie of the Year Tom Sasso (101 points), Hrytsak (89), Joe Gurney (81), J.F. Nault (78), Mike Marcinkiewicz (73 points, 171 PIM), Kelly (365 penalty minutes) and Servatius (53 points, 177 PIM) on a successful and colorful unit.

Johnstown finished second to Erie in the regular season but swept past Knoxville in the first round of the playoffs, setting the stage for a wild Riley Cup Final against Carolina. Johnstown won the first two games of the best-of-7 series by a combined 14-2 score (8-1 in Game 1 and 6-1 in Game 2) at home.

But Carolina stormed back with three straight victories to put the Chiefs on the verge of elimination. In the middle of that run, the ice at Winston-Salem Coliseum melted prior to Game 4 because a compressor mysteriously shut down during the night. "This hasn't happened in five years," Carolina owner John Baker said at the time. The originally scheduled Game 5 in Johnstown was played in place of Game 4. Carolina won 5-3. After Carolina took a 3-2 series advantage with a 7-1 win, the Chiefs had a gut check, winning 7-4 in Winston-Salem to force a decisive Game 7 at Johnstown.

'It was a lot of fun'

"It was phenomenal," said Allen, recalling Game 7 from the opposing side's perspective. "We were down to 12 players because of suspensions and injuries. Johnstown had a full lineup. We were up 3-2 going into Game 6. We thought for sure we were going to win it at home but that wasn't the case. A couple guys in that game got a little goofy and got suspended for Game 7. It was right there for the taking for Johnstown. They had a full lineup. We had 12 guys."

ECHL Commissioner Pat Kelly made a statement and added credibility to the league by suspending those Carolina players despite the magnitude of Game 7.

"We pulled in the night before on the bus and there were people sleeping outside the War Memorial waiting for tickets," Allen recalled. "We came in for the morning skate and the line was out the door and along the sidewalk. People were greeting us with the one-finger salute. We actually were enjoying the atmosphere. Brandon Watson did a phenomenal job in coaching that night with what we had. As players we were just in the mindset that if we could keep it close for two periods, we could win the final period and win the whole thing.

"We made sure every time there was a whistle, whether 45 seconds of play or five seconds of play had gone by, we were going to change our personnel to slow down the pace of the game and get our players some rest. We got some timely goals from guys. It was a lot of fun."

Carolina won 7-4 in front of 4,146 fans who had their hockey dreams shattered that night. Still, the city threw a parade for the Chiefs and a Central Park pep rally that brought thousands of fans out for a final farewell to the 1988-89 team.

As the 1980s wound down, the Chiefs had established a foothold in the hearts of Johnstown hockey fans and the ECHL took its first strides toward becoming one of the elite developmental leagues.

Top: Chiefs center Rob Hrytsak (9) heads to the net in the inaugural ECHL game on Oct. 28, 1988 at Cambria County War Memorial Arena.

Bottom left: Chiefs 1989 ECHL Rookie of the Year Tom Sasso signs an autograph for a young fan.

Middle: Johnstown fan favorite Rick Boyd.

Bottom right: Henry Brabham was majority owner of the Chiefs from 1988 to 1993.

CHIEFS IN THE EIGHTIES

215

Chiefs General Manager John Daley and coach Steve Carlson during the 1988-89 season.

REPRINT

John Daley served two terms as general manager in Johnstown, including a four-season stint with the Jets that began in 1962. Daley was minority owner and GM of the first Johnstown Chiefs team in 1988. Daley died in October 1996. The ECHL eventually named its Rookie of the Year Award in his honor. The following article appeared on March 20, 1994 as Daley was about to retire:

Chiefs general manager ends 30-year hockey career

By Mike Mastovich

John Daley will watch his final regular-season game as general manager of the Chiefs today, ending his second front-office tenure in a hockey career that dates to 1962. The Chiefs' GM since the team began operations in January 1988, Daley, 70, will leave a legacy in the War Memorial Arena and the East Coast Hockey League.

"Without John Daley," said former Chiefs majority owner Henry Brabham, "there wouldn't be any hockey in Johnstown. He's the man who rammed it home. John did the work. I put up the money and took a gamble. John has done 99 percent of all the work up there. He's responsible for hockey staying there."

Brabham and Daley became partners almost by accident. Brabham, a Virginia businessman, and a group of local organizers met with the purpose of establishing a minor league hockey team in Johnstown, a city that had been without the sport on the pro level on a regular basis since 1980.

As a member of the War Memorial Arena Board of Directors, Daley was on hand to negotiate the fledgling team's lease with the arena.

"I went to the meeting because I was on the board," Daley said. "After the meeting, Henry said, 'I need someone to run the team.' Denny Grenell said, 'We have an ex-general manager right here.'"

Daley had spent four seasons as GM of the Eastern Hockey League Johnstown Jets from 1962 to 1966. He seemed like a logical choice to run a new team, especially on such short notice. But Daley wasn't quite as

> "Without John Daley, there wouldn't be any hockey in Johnstown. He's the man who rammed it home."
>
> — *former Chiefs majority owner Henry Brabham in 1994.*

enthusiastic as the other men attending the meeting.

"It wasn't a good time for me because I had just buried my (first) wife right after Christmas," said Daley, who in 1990 married the former Fran Raymond, then the team's sales manager. "This was like the second or third of January. The first game was the 13th. We had less than two weeks to get ready."

After some convincing, Daley accepted the challenge.

"We started from scratch, with no equipment and no players," Daley said.

A long list of duties awaited Daley, among those were hiring a coach, filling a roster in mid-season and purchasing uniforms and equipment. Joe Selenski was named coach. Daley set up a makeshift office in the arena. Things began to fall in place.

"We had Joe Selenski, which was a break at that time because he was trying to put a junior team together out of the state of Washington," Daley said. "He had a list of players to contact. He picked up guys like Rick Boyd and Brock Kelly. He picked up some players from the team he coached in Staten Island the year before. We filled in the rest."

'Black and gold'

The team adopted the nickname used in the motion picture "Slap Shot" filmed in Johnstown in 1976. Daley even got a break with uniforms. "Everybody thought we came out with the black and gold uniforms because of the Penguins, Steelers and Pirates," Daley said. "It was purely accidental. The only place we could find a full set of uniforms was in Niagara Falls, Ontario. The only full set they had available was the Boston Bruins. We took credit for the colors anyway."

The Chiefs debuted successfully, beating the Carolina Thunderbirds, 5-3, before 3,620 fans at the War Memorial on Jan. 13, 1988. "As far as the Chiefs, one of my most special memories is getting the team off the ground on such short notice in 1988 and winning the first game against a much heavily favored Carolina team," Daley said.

The Chiefs went 13-13 in an abbreviated All-American Hockey League season in 1988 and were 0-3 in the round-robin playoffs.

The next year, Daley and Brabham were instrumental in establishing the five-team ECHL, a league that has grown to 19 teams with future expansion looming.

Daley teamed with Brabham and became the minority owner of the Chiefs, as well as GM. The Chiefs went 157-141-40 in their first five ECHL seasons. This year's team was 35-27-4 as of Friday night.

Daley is one of the league officials who helped the ECHL evolve into a developmental league for NHL clubs. The Chiefs have had affiliations with the Boston Bruins and New Jersey Devils. This season the team is affiliated with the American Hockey League Hershey Bears. "Without John, the ECHL wouldn't have survived," Brabham said. "John was very instrumental in getting the ECHL off the ground, not just the Johnstown team. He's a legend."

"Since the inception of the league, John has meant an awful lot to the ECHL," added league commissioner Pat Kelly. "He turned it around in Johnstown and got the fans interested. His dedication to hockey is a life-long effort."

Daley became involved in professional hockey in 1962, when John Mitchell, known as Mr. Hockey in Johnstown, left the Jets to accept a front-office position with the Detroit Red Wings. The Jets needed a new GM.

"I worked for the Chamber of Commerce, and my forte back then was promotions," Daley said. "Charlie Kunkle (then the president of the Johnstown Hockey Co.) called and asked if I'd be interested. I said I didn't know anything about hockey. He said they needed somebody to generate some revenue for the team. They were in bad shape. I said no because I was ready to take another job in Point Pleasant, N.J., at another Chamber of Commerce that would have been a big step up."

Daley, however, was swayed into accepting a GM job. The Jets finished third three times with Daley as GM, and the 1963-64 team coached by Butch Martin finished first during the regular season. "We had some pretty respectable teams," Daley said.

"I'll never forget that I personally recruited three guys who made the National Hockey League," Daley said. "Larry Johnston, Andy Brown and Ralph MacSweyn."

The Jets struggled financially in the mid-1960s, and Daley resigned in April 1966. He took a job with Penelec and didn't return to hockey until 1988.

'It kept me young'

After five ECHL seasons and six years with the Chiefs, Daley and Brabham sold the team to three Latrobe attorneys, including current managing partner Ned Nakles Jr. Nakles kept Daley on to smooth the transition, but Daley announced he would step down after this season. His contract runs through May.

"The thing I'm going to miss the most is dealing with the kids," Daley said. "I think it kept me young. Also I'll miss the hockey people you meet. I'll miss people like Henry Brabham and Pat Kelly."

"The hockey world respects John," Kelly said. "Not just in the minor leagues, but in all of professional hockey. That's why Johnstown has had some pretty good players and some pretty good teams. We'll miss him because of his hockey knowledge."

Daley hasn't ruled out another job in hockey, but for now he intends to "take a couple months off."

"It's been a lot of work," Daley said. "But it's been rewarding. It's come a long way."

Coach Joe Selenski paces the locker room as the Chiefs prepare for the team's first game on Jan. 13, 1988 at the War Memorial.

Where Are They Now? - Scott Gordon

When the 1992 Winter Olympiad begins this February, a little bit of Johnstown will be skating on the ice in France. Former Johnstown Chief Scott Gordon will be one of three goaltenders for Team USA.

Gordon came to the Chiefs in 1988 and earned top goaltending honors in the inaugural season of the East Coast Hockey League. He posted a 3.82 goals against average in 31 games. He faced 1,048 shots for an 88.8% save average. His record in the net was 18-9-3, good enough to be named to the first team of the E.C.H.L.'s all-star squad.

Gordon went on to play in the National Hockey League for the Quebec Nordiques. He remains Nordique property and will resume his NHL career after the Olympics.

It's been 12 years since the USA captured the gold medal in hockey at the Olympic games, and with Scott Gordon in the net it might just happen again.

Above: Scott Gordon went from the Chiefs to the NHL and the Olympic Games. He was the first ECHL player to advance to the NHL.

Left: Chiefs defenseman Brock Kelly (5) blocks a shot in front of goalie Steve Averill against the Carolina Thunderbirds in the first ECHL game on Oct. 28, 1988 at Cambria County War Memorial Arena.

CHIEFS IN THE EIGHTIES

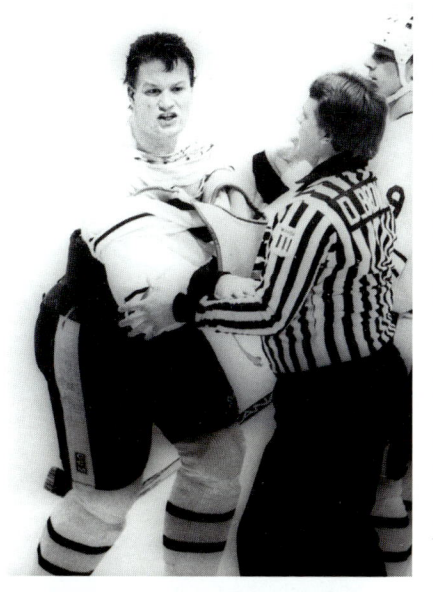

Top left: Chiefs enforcer Brock Kelly looks for trouble in a 1988 game.

Bottom left: Trainer Dana Heinze, a Johnstown native, was pressed into duty as an emergency goaltender on Jan. 4, 1989.

Middle: This 1989 championship series ticket couldn't be used due to the ice mysteriously melting at the Winston-Salem Memorial Coliseum.

Top right: The 1989 Riley Cup runner-up Chiefs were honored by hundreds of fans during a Central Park pep rally.

221

1987-88 Johnstown Chiefs

(Front, from left) Bob Deraney, Rob Hrytsak, Darren Servatius, head coach Joe Selenski, Scott Rettew, general manager John Daley, Sam Farace, Dwight Boss, Toby O'Brien. (Back) Assistant trainer Scott Sroka, Mike Black, Joe DeMitchell, Boyd Lomow, Brock Kelly, Harold Ochs, Rick Boyd, Rod Olver, Dan Pineau, head trainer Galen Head Jr.

1987-88 FINAL ALL-AMERICAN HOCKEY LEAGUE STANDINGS

	Games played	Won	Lost	Overtime losses	Points	Pct.	Goals for	Goals against
Virginia Lancers	43	7	5	1	75	0.872	321	129
Carolina Thunderbirds	49	34	15	0	68	0.694	355	182
Johnstown Chiefs *	26	13	13	0	26	0.500	157	115
Miami Valley Sabres	37	17	19	1	35	0.473	217	260
Danville Fighting Saints	35	15	20	0	30	0.429	240	317
Jackson All-Americans	40	14	21	5	33	0.413	227	318
Port Huron Clippers	38	9	28	1	19	0.250	212	347
Michigan Stars **	14	2	12	0	4	0.143	68	130

* Johnstown Chiefs were mid-season entry and standings were therefore based on percentage of points

** Michigan Stars ceased operations Nov. 30, 1987

Johnstown Chiefs
General Manager - John Daley
Coach - Joe Selenski
Trainer - Galen Head, Jr.
Assistant Trainer - Scott Sroka
Colors - Black, White and Gold

CHIEFS IN THE EIGHTIES

1987-88 Game Results

Preseason Results
No preseason games

Regular Season Results

Day	Date	Opponent	Johnstown	Opponent	Attendance	Record
Wed.	13-Jan	Carolina	5	3	3,620	1-0-0
Fri.	15-Jan	at Carolina	1	6		1-1-0
Sat.	16-Jan	at Virginia	1	7		1-2-0
Sun.	17-Jan	Danville	11	6	4,332	2-2-0
Wed.	20-Jan	at Jackson	17	2		3-2-0
Fri.	22-Jan	at Carolina	5	6		3-3-0
Sun.	24-Jan	Virginia	2	5	4,132	3-4-0
Thur.	28-Jan	at Danville	10	3		4-4-0
Fri.	29-Jan	at Jackson	9	1		5-4-0
Sat.	30-Jan	at Virginia	4	6		5-5-0
Tues.	2-Feb	Virginia	1	3	3,537	5-6-0
Fri.	5-Feb	at Virginia	3	5		5-7-0
Sun.	7-Feb	Jackson	15	0	4,072	6-7-0
Thur.	11-Feb	at Carolina	4	6		6-8-0
Fri.	12-Feb	at Miami Valley	9	4		7-8-0
Sat.	13-Feb	at Danville	6	3		8-8-0
Sun.	14-Feb	at Port Huron	14	5		9-8-0
Fri.	19-Feb	at Virginia	4	7		9-9-0
Sun.	21-Feb	at Carolina	6	5		10-9-0
Wed.	24-Feb	Carolina	4	6	3,571	10-10-0
Fri.	26-Feb	at Jackson	10	4		11-10-0
Sun.	28-Feb	Carolina	6	4	4,032	12-10-0
Wed.	2-Mar	Virginia	3	2	2,500	13-10-0
Fri.	5-Mar	Carolina	2	5	4,000	13-11-0
Sat.	6-Mar	Virginia	2	4	4,032	13-12-0
Thur.	10-Mar	at Carolina	3	7		13-13-0

Playoff Results

Day	Date	Opponent	Johnstown	Opponent	Attendance	Record
Sat.	12-Mar	at Virginia	5	6 (ot)		
Sun.	13-Mar	Carolina	2	4	4,032	
Mon.	15-Mar	Virginia	3	5	3,750	

Attendance Figures

	Dates	Totals	Average
Regular Season Attendance Totals	10	37,828	3,783
Playoff Attendance Totals	2	7,782	3,891
TOTAL ATTENDANCE	12	45,610	3,801

1987-88 Player Statistics

	Regular Season Scoring					Playoff Scoring				
	Games	G	A	Pts	PIM	Games	G	A	Pts	PIM
14 Scott Rettew	25	36	25	61	66					
9 Rob Hrytsak	25	16	45	61	39	3	0	4	4	4
10 Dan Pineau	26	16	22	38	57	3	0	0	0	0
19 Joe DeMitchell	19	17	18	35	48	3	2	1	3	0
4 Darren Servatius	26	10	23	33	154	3	1	1	2	21
17 Larry Rusconi	15	13	18	31	42					
7 Rick Boyd	24	7	21	28	154	3	1	0	1	24
18 Boyd Lomow	18	9	15	24	77	3	2	2	4	16
5 Brock Kelly	25	5	19	24	247	3	2	1	3	19
16 Rod Olver	26	5	11	16	127	2	0	0	0	0
2 Harold Ochs	19	3	10	13	45					
6 Dwight Boss	24	4	8	12	91	3	0	0	0	4
15 Sam Farace	26	3	9	12	27	1	0	0	0	2
11 Mike Black	8	3	5	8	4					
12 Todd Delveaux	6	4	1	5	17	3	1	2	3	0
17 Greg Neish	5	1	2	3	34	3	1	1	2	5
8 Gerry Zaccaria	11	1	2	3	11					
22 Paul Castron	1	2	0	2	0	3	0	1	1	2
11 Tommi Skaggs	6	1	0	1	2	3	0	0	0	2
11 Pat Antongiovanni	7	1	0	1	13					

30 Toby O'Brien (g)	14	0	1	1	17	1	0	0	0
12 Ken Bain	1	0	0	0	0				
22 Kurt Krolak	1	0	0	0	0				
3 Andy Martone	3	0	0	0	0	3	0	2	2	2
1 Bob Deraney (g)	13	0	0	0	4	2	0	0	0	0
TOTALS	26	157	255	412	1,276	3	10	15	25	101

Regular Season Goaltending

	G	Min	GA	ENG	SO	GAA	W	L	T	Saves	Save %
3 Toby O'Brien	14	806	55	1	1	4.10	7	6	0	396	0.878
1 Bob Deraney	13	751	58	1	0	4.64	6	7	0	420	0.879
TOTALS	26	1,560	113	2	1	4.42	13	13	0	816	0.878

Playoff Goaltending

	G	Min	GA	ENG	SO	GAA	W	L	Saves	Save %
30 Toby O'Brien	1	60	4	0	0	4.00	0	1		
1 Bob Deraney	2	120	11	0	0	5.50	0	2		
TOTALS	3	180	15	0	0	5.00	0	3		

DeMitchell also wore No. 12; Olver also wore No. 30; Oaks also wore No. 3.

Players on roster who did not play: 8 Jeff Vilac, Center; 30 Peter Maro, Goal.

The 1988-89 Chiefs gather after a win at the War Memorial.

CHIEFS IN THE EIGHTIES

1988-89 Johnstown Chiefs

(Front, from left) Scott Gordon, Joe Gurney, general manager John Daley, Darren Servatius, head coach Steve Carlson, Ed Harding, Lance Carlsen. (Middle) Quintin Brickley, Jeff Salzbrunn, Scott Brown, Jamie Evans, Rob Hrytsak, head trainer Dana Heinze. (Back) Mike Marcinkiewicz, Tom Sasso, Jean-Francois Nault, Brock Kelly, Ron Servatius, Bob Kennedy.

1988-89 FINAL EAST COAST HOCKEY LEAGUE STANDINGS

	Games played	Won	Lost	Shootout losses	Points	Goals for	Goals against
Erie Panthers	60	37	20	3	77	327	256
Johnstown Chiefs	60	32	22	6	70	295	251
Knoxville Cherokees	60	32	27	1	65	266	286
Carolina Thunderbirds	60	27	32	1	55	266	329
Virginia Lancers	60	22	30	8	52	266	298

Johnstown Chiefs
General Manager - John Daley
Coach - Steve Carlson
Trainer - Dana Heinze
Stickboy - Dave Erb
Colors - Black, White and Gold

1988-89 Game Results

Preseason Results
Score

Day	Date	Opponent	Johnstown	Opponent	Attendance	Record
Sun.	23-Oct	Knoxville	6	1	1,600	
Wed.	26-Oct	Erie	5	7	1,200	

Regular Season Results

Day	Date	Opponent	Johnstown	Opponent	Attendance	Record
Fri.	28-Oct	Carolina	6		2,728	0-1-0
Sat.	29-Oct	Virginia	7	0	2,412	1-1-0
Sun.	30-Oct	at Erie	1	2 (sol)		1-1-1
Wed.	2-Nov	at Virginia	10	6		2-1-1
Sat.	5-Nov	Carolina	2	4	3,442	2-2-1
Sun.	6-Nov	Erie	8	6	2,646	3-2-1
Wed.	9-Nov	Virginia	1	2	2,400	3-3-1
Sat.	12-Nov	Erie	5	3	3,561	4-3-1
Sun.	13-Nov	at Erie	6	4		5-3-1
Sat.	19-Nov	at Carolina	2	5		5-4-1
Sun.	20-Nov	at Knoxville	3	4		5-5-1
Wed.	23-Nov	Virginia	3	5	3,094	5-6-1
Thur.	24-Nov	at Erie	4	2		6-6-1
Fri.	25-Nov	at Virginia	4	1		7-6-1
Sat.	26-Nov	Carolina	7	2	4,058	8-6-1
Wed.	30-Nov	Knoxville	5	6 (sol)	2,320	8-6-2
Sat.	3-Dec	Erie	6	4	3,060	9-6-2
Sun.	4-Dec	Erie	5	3	2,399	10-6-2
Thur.	8-Dec	at Erie	3	5		10-7-2
Sat.	10-Dec	Knoxville	1	4	3,157	10-8-2
Wed.	14-Dec	at Carolina	7	6		11-8-2
Thur.	15-Dec	at Virginia	3	4 (sol)		11-8-3
Fri.	16-Dec	at Knoxville	5	6 (sol)		11-8-4
Sat.	17-Dec	Virginia	9	6	2,442	12-8-4
Fri.	30-Dec	at Carolina	6	5		13-8-4
Sat.	31-Dec	at Knoxville	3	4		13-9-4
Wed.	4-Jan	Erie	3	8	2,700	13-10-4
Fri.	6-Jan	Virginia	3	5	3,007	13-11-4
Sat.	7-Jan	at Knoxville	4	6		13-12-4
Sun.	8-Jan	at Knoxville	6	0		14-12-4
Wed.	11-Jan	Carolina	3	4 (sol)	2,402	14-12-5
Fri.	13-Jan	at Virginia	6	4		15-12-5
Sat.	14-Jan	at Carolina	2	4		15-13-5
Fri.	20-Jan	Carolina	7	0	3,340	16-13-5
Sat.	21-Jan	Carolina	8	3	3,912	17-13-5
Wed.	25-Jan	Knoxville	2	1	2,728	18-13-5
Fri.	27-Jan	at Knoxville	5	2		19-13-5
Sat.	28-Jan	at Virginia	5	4(sow)		20-13-5
Sun.	29-Jan	at Erie	0	8		20-14-5
Wed.	1-Feb	Knoxville	1	5	3,099	20-15-5
Sat.	4-Feb	Erie	7	4	4,066	21-15-5
Sun.	5-Feb	Carolina	5	2	3,481	22-15-5
Wed.	8-Feb	at Erie	4	8		22-16-5
Fri.	10-Feb	at Carolina	6	7		22-17-5
Sat.	11-Feb	Knoxville	3	4 (sol)	4,016	22-17-6
Sun.	12-Feb	Virginia	3	4	2,887	22-18-6
Fri.	17-Feb	at Virginia	7	4		23-18-6
Sat.	18-Feb	at Virginia	4	7		23-19-6
Sun.	19-Feb	at Knoxville	9	2		24-19-6
Wed.	22-Feb	Erie	7	5	3,400	25-19-6
Sun.	26-Feb	Knoxville	14	3	4,009	26-19-6
Wed.	1-Mar	Carolina	7	1	3,082	27-19-6
Fri.	3-Mar	at Carolina	3	7		27-20-6
Sun.	5-Mar	Erie	8	4	4,034	28-20-6
Fri.	10-Mar	at Erie	6	8		28-21-6
Sat.	11-Mar	at Virginia	5	4		29-21-6
Sun.	12-Mar	at Carolina	1	7		29-22-6
Wed.	15-Mar	Virginia	7	4	3,171	30-22-6
Fri.	17-Mar	at Erie	6	4		31-22-6
Sun.	19-Mar	Knoxville	6	1	4,042	32-22-6

Playoff Results

Day	Date	Opponent	Johnstown	Opponent	Attendance	Record
Thur.	23-Mar	Knoxville	6	1	3,269	1-0
Sat.	25-Mar	Knoxville	5	2	4,038	2-0

CHIEFS IN THE EIGHTIES

Tues.	28-Mar	at Knoxville	7	2		3-0
Thur.	30-Mar	at Knoxville	10	2		4-0
Sat.	1-Apr	Carolina	8	1	4,036	1-0
Sun.	2-Apr	Carolina	6	1	3,361	2-0
Wed.	5-Apr	at Carolina	4	7		2-1
Sat.	8-Apr	Carolina	3	5	4,055	2-2
Sun.	9-Apr	at Carolina	1	7		2-3
Mon.	10-Apr	at Carolina	7	4		3-3
Wed.	12-Apr	Carolina	4	7	4,146	3-4

Attendance Figures

	Dates	Totals	Average
Preseason Attendance Totals	2	2,800	1,400
Regular Season Attendance Totals	30	95,095	3,170
Playoff Attendance Totals	6	22,905	3,818
TOTAL ATTENDANCE	38	120,800	3,179

1988-89 Player Statistics

	Regular Season Scoring					Playoff Scoring				
	Games	G	A	Pts	PIM	Games	G	A	Pts	PIM
7 Tom Sasso	60	36	65	101	4	11	5	19	24	2
9 Rob Hrytsak	56	40	49	89	86	11	8	10	18	18
10 Joe Gurney	57	38	43	81	149	11	7	5	12	32
12 Jean-Francois Nault	52	24	54	78	148	11	4	11	15	22
32 Mike Marcinkiewicz	53	32	41	73	171	10	8	7	15	43
14 Jeff Salzbrunn	49	32	23	55	117	11	2	6	8	48
4 Darren Servatius	59	8	45	53	177	11	5	3	8	22
18 Ed Harding	58	14	25	39	151	11	3	5	8	36
5 Brock Kelly	54	5	26	31	365	10	0	2	2	47
2 Jamie Evans	32	10	20	30	33	10	2	4	6	45
19 Ron Servatius	59	5	25	30	199	10	0	6	6	26
8 Scott Brown	30	16	13	29	52	11	8	8	16	19
15 Quintin Brickley	21	5	19	24	6	11	7	8	15	15
18 Dan Pineau	15	8	7	15	16					
6 Bob Kennedy	21	5	7	12	13	11	2	3	5	12
3 Todd Morgan	27	2	9	11	91					
17 Tim Skaggs	30	5	4	9	48					
6 Frank O'Brien	33	1	8	9	36					
16 Dan Mercrones	7	3	5	8	2					
6 Mike Hiltner	4	2	5	7	7					
11 Tony Lopilato	5	2	4	6	0					
11 Mike Black	15	2	1	3	6					
6 Doug Stromback	3	0	2	2	0					
1 Lance Carlsen (g)	25	0	2	2	29	1	0	0	0	0
30 Scott Gordon (g)	31	0	2	2	8	11	0	1	1	8
30 Dana Heinze (g)	1	0	0	0	0					
8 Gary Brush	2	0	0	0	0					
17 E.J. Sauer	2	0	0	0	0					
20 Sylvain Lajeunesse	4	0	0	0	0					
30 Steve Averill (g)	6	0	0	0	4					
Bench					32					
TOTALS	60	295	504	799	1,950	11	61	98	159	395

Regular Season Goaltending

	G	Min	GA	ENG	SO	GAA	W	L	SOL	Saves	Save %
30 Dana Heinze	1	4	0	0	0	0.00	0	0	0	1	1.000
30 Scott Gordon	31	1,839	117	2	2	3.82	18	9	3	931	0.888
1 Lance Carlsen	25	1,447	102	2	1	4.23	11	10	3	805	0.888
30 Steve Averill	6	339	27	1	0	4.77	3	3	0	189	0.875
TOTALS	60	3,629	246	5	3	4.15	32	22	6	1,926	0.887

Playoff Goaltending

	G	Min	GA	ENG	SO	GAA	W	L	Saves	Save
30 Scott Gordon	11	647	36	2	0	3.34	7	4	296	0.892
1 Lance Carlsen	1	10	1	0	0	5.82	0	0	8	0.800
TOTALS	11	660	37	2	0	3.55	7	4	304	0.891

1989-90 Johnstown Chiefs

(Front, from left) Rich Burchill, Darren Servatius, general manager John Daley, Rick Boyd, head coach Steve Carlson, John Messuri, Mike Jeffrey. (Middle) Dean Hall, Mark Bogoslowski, Doug Weiss, Mitch Molloy, Sean Finn, Danny Williams, Jean-Francois Nault, head trainer Dana Heinze. (Back) Mike Rossetti, Bob Goulet, Bob Bennett, Greg Parks, Marc Vachon, Darren Schwartz.

1989-90 FINAL EAST COAST HOCKEY LEAGUE STANDINGS

	Games played	Won	Lost	Overtime losses	Points	Goals for	Goals against
Winston-Salem Thunderbirds	60	38	16	6	82	312	257
Erie Panthers	60	38	16	6	82	357	251
Virginia Lancers	60	36	18	6	78	261	218
Greensboro Monarchs	60	29	27	4	62	263	283
Hampton Roads Admirals	60	29	29	2	60	252	267
Nashville Knights	60	26	30	4	56	248	289
Johnstown Chiefs	60	23	31	6	52	233	291
Knoxville Cherokees	60	21	33	6	48	230	300

Johnstown Chiefs
General Manager - John Daley
Coach - Steve Carlson
Assistant Coach - Michael A. Berger
Player/Assistant Coach - Rick Boyd
Trainers - Dana Heinze, Mic Midderhoff
Colors - Black, White and Gold

* Note: Rick Boyd coached team Jan. 14, 1990 while Carlson was suspended by league – Dean Hall (injured) served as bench coach that game.

1989-90 Game Results

Preseason Results
Score

Day	Date	Opponent	Johnstown	Opponent	Attendance	Record
Sat.	21-Oct	at Erie	7	8		
Sun.	22-Oct	Hampton Roads	7	2	2,585	
Tues.	24-Oct	Hampton Roads *	3	2		

* Game played in Richmond, Va.

CHIEFS IN THE EIGHTIES

Regular Season Results

Day	Date	Opponent	Score Johnstown	Opponent	Attendance	Record
Fri.	27-Oct	at Erie	5	6		0-1-0
Sat.	28-Oct	Erie	1	3	4,042	0-2-0
Sun.	29-Oct	Hampton Roads	2	5	3,360	0-3-0
Sat.	4-Nov	Winston-Salem	5	4 (sow)	3,995	1-3-0
Sun.	5-Nov	Greensboro	4	5 (sol)	3,304	1-3-1
Fri.	10-Nov	at Winston-Salem	1	7		1-4-1
Sat.	11-Nov	at Greensboro	0	2		1-5-1
Fri.	17-Nov	Greensboro	5	2	4,002	2-5-1
Sat.	18-Nov	at Hampton Roads	1	6		2-6-1
Sun.	19-Nov	Erie	2	6	3,585	2-7-1
Thur.	23-Nov	at Winston-Salem	4	7		2-8-1
Fri.	24-Nov	at Virginia	4	3		3-8-1
Sat.	25-Nov	Winston-Salem	7	5	4,048	4-8-1
Sun.	26-Nov	Hampton Roads	6	1	3,396	5-8-1
Fri.	1-Dec	at Winston-Salem	6	5		6-8-1
Sat.	2-Dec	Hampton Roads	12	3	3,553	7-8-1
Sun.	3-Dec	Nashville	4	1	3,202	8-8-1
Fri.	8-Dec	at Greensboro	4	5 (sol)		8-8-2
Sat.	9-Dec	Knoxville	3	1	3,644	9-8-2
Sun.	10-Dec	Knoxville	10	4	3,414	10-8-2
Fri.	15-Dec	at Nashville	7	3		11-8-2
Sat.	16-Dec	at Knoxville	3	4 (otl)		11-8-3
Sun.	17-Dec	Virginia	5	4 (sow)	3,634	12-8-3
Fri.	22-Dec	at Hampton Roads	4	3 (sow)		13-8-3
Sat.	23-Dec	at Winston-Salem	4	9		13-9-3
Fri.	29-Dec	at Knoxville	5	3		14-9-3
Sat.	30-Dec	at Virginia	2	6		14-10-3
Sun.	31-Dec	Erie	7	4	4,052	15-10-3
Wed.	3-Jan	Erie	5	6	3,845	15-11-3
Thur.	4-Jan	at Greensboro	2	7		15-12-3
Fri.	5-Jan	at Hampton Roads	2	8		15-13-3
Sun.	7-Jan	at Virginia	4	0		16-13-3
Fri.	12-Jan	at Hampton Roads	3	2		17-13-3
Sat.	13-Jan	Winston-Salem	2	3 (sol)	4,063	17-13-4
Sun.	14-Jan	Winston-Salem	4	7	4,041	17-14-4
Fri.	19-Jan	at Virginia	0	2		18-14-4
Sat.	20-Jan	at Winston-Salem	3	2 (sow)		19-14-4
Wed.	24-Jan	Greensboro	1	2 (sol)	3,081	19-14-5
Fri.	26-Jan	Nashville	4	0	3,865	20-14-5
Sat.	27-Jan	Nashville	5	7	4,053	20-15-5
Mon.	29-Jan	at Erie	1	6		20-16-5
Wed.	31-Jan	Virginia	0	6	2,942	20-17-5
Fri.	2-Feb	at Nashville	3	5		20-18-5
Sat.	3-Feb	Hampton Roads	4	3	4,054	21-18-5
Sun.	4-Feb	Virginia	3	4	3,379	21-19-5
Fri.	9-Feb	at Erie	3	7		21-20-5
Sat.	10-Feb	Nashville	7	4	4,055	22-20-5
Sun.	11-Feb	Knoxville	2	5	3,983	22-21-5
Wed.	14-Feb	Virginia	2	3	2,817	22-22-5
Fri.	16-Feb	at Knoxville	8	10		22-23-5
Sat.	17-Feb	at Nashville	5	8		22-24-5
Sun.	18-Feb	at Knoxville	4	3		23-24-5
Wed.	21-Feb	Erie	8	9 (otl)	3,371	23-24-6
Sat.	24-Feb	at Erie	5	12		23-25-6
Sat.	3-Mar	Knoxville	1	3	4,049	23-26-6
Sun.	4-Mar	Erie	5	13	4,009	23-27-6
Fri.	9-Mar	at Nashville	2	1		24-27-6
Sat.	10-Mar	at Greensboro	3	11		24-28-6
Sun.	11-Mar	Greensboro	4	6	3,989	24-29-6
Wed.	14-Mar	at Erie	5	9		24-30-6

Attendance Figures

	Dates	Totals	Average
Preseason Attendance Figures	1	2,585	2,585
Regular Season Attendance Figures	30	110,827	3,694
TOTAL ATTENDANCE	31	113,412	3,658

1989-90 Player Statistics

Regular Season Scoring

	Games	G	A	Pts	PIM
3 John Messuri	55	25	47	72	45
10 Mike Rossetti	60	35	32	67	67
18 Darren Schwartz	50	28	27	55	270
19 Doug Weiss	40	19	23	42	32
20 Marc Vachon	58	18	21	39	38
16 Dean Hall	38	11	22	33	27
4 Darren Servatius	53	7	24	31	192
12 Dan Williams	50	11	18	29	251
6 Vince Guidotti	46	5	17	22	61
17 Mitch Molloy	18	10	10	20	102
2 Bob Goulet	52	6	14	20	57
15 Tim Hanley	16	6	12	18	28
7 Rick Boyd	45	5	12	17	284
14 Mark Bogoslowski	47	4	13	17	138
15 Greg Parks	8	5	9	14	7
44 Jean-Francois Nault	14	8	5	13	24
44 Mark Ziliotto	20	5	7	12	40
31 Shawn Byram	8	5	5	10	35
17 Rick Stromback	20	6	2	8	44
90 Rob Hrytsak	10	1	7	8	33
7 Gord Cruickshank	5	3	4	7	2
15 Rick McCarthy	6	2	3	5	10
32 Mike Marcinkiewicz	9	2	3	5	42
5 Lee Odelein	24	1	4	5	60
8 Sean Finn	6	0	5	5	16
14 Bob Bennett	9	2	2	4	20
44 Jamie Kelly	10	2	2	4	0
1 Richard Burchill (g)	33	0	3	3	16
8 Ryan Schiff	5	0	2	2	2
90 Todd Lalonde	1	1	0	1	2
3 Dave Mellen	6	0	1	1	8
5 Brock Kelly	7	0	1	1	68
90 Bill Birks	8	0	1	1	12
31 Mike Jeffrey (g)	16	0	1	1	12
20 Rocky Johnson	1	0	0	0	0
32 E.J. Sauer	1	0	0	0	0
15 Doug Smith	3	0	0	0	29
14 Will Putnam	4	0	0	0	0
35 Mark Bernard (g)	7	0	0	0	4
35 Darren McCluskey (g)	7	0	0	0	8
31 Tim Flanagan (g)	8	0	0	0	2
Bench					10
TOTALS	60	233	359	592	2,098

Regular Season Goaltending

	G	Min	GA	ENG	SO	GAA	W	L	OTL	SOL
31 Mike Jeffrey	17	918	56	0	0	3.66	8	6	1	1
1 Richard Burchill	32	1,723	134	1	0	4.67	13	13	1	1
31 Tim Flanagan	8	346	28	0	0	4.86	0	4	0	2
35 Darren McCluskey	5	259	23	0	0	5.33	1	3	0	0
35 Mark Bernard	9	400	45	0	0	6.75	1	5	0	0
Shootout Goals			4							
TOTALS	60	3,646	290	1	0	4.79	23	31	2	4

Note: Burchill played forward Jan. 20 vs. Winston-Salem.

Ziliotto also wore No. 8; Cruickshank also wore No. 17; Bernard also wore No. 30; Hanley also wore Nos. 16 and 6; Finn also wore No. 30; Flanagan also wore No. 35; Bennett also wore No. 19.

Players who were on roster, but did not play: 30 Dana Heinze, Goal.

CHIEFS IN THE EIGHTIES

Top: The Chiefs bench keeps an eye on the action in 1989-90 with coach Steve Carlson (center) and assistant coach Mike Berger (right) calling the shots.

Bottom left: Coach Joe Selenski hastily assembled the 1988 AAHL Chiefs in mid-season.

Bottom right: Even the Chiefs' dining habits attracted attention in 1988-89.

231

Future NHL player Peter Skudra guards the Chiefs net in 1995-96.

1990s Overview:
A Decade of Ups and Downs

By Mike Mastovich

Peaks and valleys? Highs and lows? Rollercoaster ride? The decade of the 1990s featured some of the most memorable moments in Johnstown professional hockey history. The East Coast Hockey League Chiefs captured the hearts and minds of the city's fans as the "honeymoon" stage of this relationship still loomed at the decade's outset.

The Chiefs were winners on the ice and popular at the box office. A hockey night in Johnstown was a highlight of the weekend, the thing to do, the place to be.

But somewhere in the middle of the 1990s, the Chiefs lost some of their allure. There were coaching changes, an affiliation lost, disgruntled players who would not report to a small-town franchise and sports agents who spread the word that Johnstown was a dead end that prospects should avoid.

Then, just as the situation appeared too bleak to rectify, something special occurred. Local owners Richard and Connie Mayer provided financial and moral support to a trio of "rebuilders." A young, enthusiastic general manager named Toby O'Brien teamed with a somewhat unknown, young and energetic head coach named Scott Allen to begin a lengthy, sometimes frustrating rebuilding process. Chiefs President James M. Edwards Sr. oversaw the campaign to reshape the Chiefs' image in minor league hockey circles. Part of that mission was to assemble a winning team in a city where most of the sport's naysayers said such a feat was virtually impossible. As the decade concluded, the Chiefs were competitive again. The foundation was built for future playoff success in an ECHL that had expanded to as many as 31 teams before finally settling at 25 members.

The '90s actually began with mixed reviews. The 1989-90 squad had a miserable 23 wins and missed the playoffs. Those Chiefs, however, collected a whopping 2,098 penalty minutes as fan-favorites such as Rick Boyd (284 PIM), Darren Schwartz (270), Dan Williams (251), Darren Servatius (192) and Mark Bogoslowski (138) led the hit parade.

Even though statistically, the 1990 Chiefs were among the least successful groups all-time locally, there is no disputing the popularity of the team known as "The Fightin' Chiefs." A total of 110,827 fans attended home games that season, an average of 3,694 a night in the 4,040-seat War Memorial.

Puck tossed into press box

Coach Steve Carlson led the 1991 and 1992 teams to the postseason, with the '92 Chiefs posting what was then a club-record 36 victories. Carlson was voted runner-up for 1991-92 ECHL Coach of the Year honors, and his team won a first-round playoff series against intra-state rival Erie. He already had 123 wins and three playoff appearances as coach of the Chiefs. But Carlson still lost his job amid controversy after the infamous Brian Ferreira puck-throwing incident in the Chiefs' final game of the 1992 playoff series against Cincinnati at the War Memorial.

The Cyclones were well on their way to winning the game (7-1) and the best-of-3 series (2-0) as 3,019 fans watched. Chiefs players and the local crowd were obviously upset with a string of officiating calls that, right or wrong, went against the home team. As the game progressed and the one-sided margin ballooned, matters on the ice deteriorated.

During one stoppage of play, Ferreira slowly skated toward the face-off circle, where a puck lay on the ice. He slipped off his glove, scooped up the disc and used a side-arm delivery to toss the puck into the press box, where ECHL Commissioner Pat Kelly was watching. Kelly sat in the auxiliary box adjacent to the main box. Ferreira's throw was wide right, nearly hitting a reporter. The puck caromed off the wall, leaving a scuff mark that remained years later.

Ferreira and forward Matt Glennon, who had briefly played for the Boston Bruins prior to joining the Chiefs, made their ascent to the press box in a scene straight from "Slap Shot." Glennon had received a game misconduct earlier and was in street clothes. He also had skate guards for Ferreira. Once upstairs, the two players yelled to Kelly, who only stared coldly at them. A statistician had closed the door to the auxiliary box and prevented the players from crossing the small metal bridge to reach Kelly.

Had this been a movie, it would have been hilarious. In real life, Ferreira and Glennon each received 30-game suspensions. The oddest part of the ordeal was that Ferreira was one of the most respected and productive Chiefs.

"We watched it all and just couldn't believe it. It felt like we were in the movies," said former Chiefs captain Perry Florio. "After the second period, we were getting our butts kicked. Brian and I were sitting in the locker room. We were griping about the refs. I remember his exact words, 'I'd like to kick that guy's butt.' He wasn't talking about the ref. He was talking about the commissioner. I remember saying, 'He's up in the press box.' I threw it out there. I didn't think he'd do it.

"Brian got thrown out of a face-off. I remember the puck was still on the ice. Brian grabbed the puck and side-armed it up there. I couldn't believe it. Then Matty Glennon was standing there with his skate guards. It had to be all planned out. I felt so bad because I felt like I threw it out there."

Eddie's boys

Former New York Rangers and Detroit Red Wings player Eddie Johnstone was named coach in 1992-93. He won 102 games in three seasons. Johnstone's teams advanced to three playoffs, but never won a postseason series. The 1992-93 Chiefs did win one of the most dramatic postseason games in team history. Defenseman Jeff Ricciardi, who netted only seven goals in 61 regular-season games, scored 8:47 into overtime as the Chiefs defeated the visiting Richmond Renegades 5-4 in a one-game play-in.

Ricciardi skated end to end after the goal, waving his right fist in a circle as he moved while almost kneeling on one leg. Players mobbed goaltender John Bradley. Florio jubilantly hugged coach Johnstone, forgetting that only days earlier in practice, Johnstone had separated his shoulder.

"I remember that just before he scored the goal the play was down our end. They shot the puck. I got a piece of it and it started rolling toward the goal line," netminder Bradley recalled. "Someone was just able to stop it as the puck was about to get across the line."

Richmond star Phil Huber snapped a shot from just inside the blue line that hit Bradley's glove, popped out and crept within an inch of the goal line. Bradley also made two point-blank saves just before the game-winner.

"The whistle blew. We ended up going down to the other end and a minute or so after that, he got the game-winner," Bradley said. "Within seconds, it turned around. We were on the verge of going home, and then seconds later we won the game."

Streaks and stumbles

The 1993-94 team had a colorful season that included hockey history when Knoxville Cherokees goaltender Manon Rheaume defeated the Chiefs 9-6 at the Coliseum on Nov. 6, 1993. Rheaume earlier had become the first woman to start a professional hockey game. But she wasn't the first female goalie to win a game. Erin Whitten, with the ECHL's Toledo Storm, won in relief over Dayton on Oct. 30 and posted her first win as a starter a day before Rheaume won the high-scoring game against the Chiefs.

That same season, Johnstown had a franchise-record, 10-game winning streak from Dec. 12, 1993 to Jan. 7, 1994. The Chiefs outscored opponents by a combined 71-31 in those 10 straight wins. Goaltenders Bradley and Rob Laurie were on top of their respective games. High-scoring wing Bruce Coles joined the team in mid-December and provided a spark. Players such as Dennis Purdie, Ted Dent, Gord Christian, Pittsburgh native Jamie Adams and Matt Hoffman provided offense during a run that tied the 1967-68 Johnstown Jets for the city's longest winning streak (Dec. 30, 1967 to Jan. 21, 1968).

Later that same season, Four players and a Johnstown resident were injured during a two-car crash on an icy road in Richland Township. Leading scorer Purdie, fifth-leading scorer Christian and defensemen Campbell Blair, the driver, and Ben Wyzansky all suffered varying degrees of injuries that sidelined them. The other car's driver also was injured. Fortunately, there were no fatalities in the Feb. 18, 1994 accident.

"We had a 10-game winning streak. We went back and forth for a while after that, then we got another winning streak and were back on track," said Ned Nakles Jr., who was an owner of the team then. "Before the wreck we had a really stirring comeback in Wheeling. We were really back to playing dominant hockey. Then there was the wreck.

"It was just so senseless. It really took the wind out of our sails. But thank God nobody was killed. It was scary."

The loss of four players left Johnstone and Daley scrambling to fill a roster.

With only 12 skaters the Chiefs somehow beat the visiting Birmingham Bulls 9-7 on Feb. 19 behind Matt Hoffman's two-goal, four-point night. An emotional Nakles shook every player's hand in the quiet home locker room after that win.

The Chiefs' misfortune did enable Johnstown native David Murphy to become the first local native to score a goal for the Chiefs. The Westmont Hilltop High School graduate had attended Johnstown's training camp but was a late cut. He briefly played with the ECHL's Charlotte Checkers before returning home. Murphy scored in the second period of an 8-3 loss to Raleigh at the War Memorial on Feb. 20.

Away from the ice, the Chiefs also underwent changes, as four different ownership groups took the reigns during the decade. Majority owner Henry Brabham and minority owner-GM John Daley, who had been with the team since its inception, sold the Chiefs to a group of Latrobe attorneys on April 1, 1993.

New ownership

Managing partner Nakles Jr., his father, Ned Nakles Sr., and Leonard Reeves owned the team for two seasons before selling to local WJAC-TV on April 6, 1995.

When WJAC-TV was bought by out-of-town owners two years later, Richard Mayer, former operator of the television station, took ownership of the Chiefs, with his wife, Connie. The Mayers put Edwards in charge of the day-to-day operations.

Johnstone was fired prior to the 1995-96 season. After a string of candidates turned down offers to coach the Chiefs, Nick Fotiu was hired in mid-July, late in the recruiting season. Fotiu, a popular coach and fan favorite as a player with the New York Rangers, brought many of his former players from the ECHL's Nashville Knights, including high-scoring forward Trevor Jobe, obtained in a trade involving the Chiefs' Purdie.

But the Chiefs never clicked under Fotiu, who lost too much of the recruiting season to assemble a quality club. Jobe did become the ECHL's all-time leading scorer while wearing a Chiefs' uniform, but his offense-first, self-centered style of play didn't sit well with blue-collar fans in Johnstown. Jobe was traded away by midseason.

Fotiu also brought in goaltender Peter Skudra, an outcast in Erie whom Fotiu developed in 1995-96 and briefly in 1996-97. With Fotiu's help, Skudra eventually played in the NHL beginning in 1997 with the Pittsburgh Penguins.

But after two straight losing seasons and a dismal start in 1997-98, Fotiu was fired. His assistant coach, Scott Allen, was promoted and began a rebuilding project that showed promise once the Calgary Flames were brought aboard as an affiliate. "We discovered that we couldn't get people to come to Johnstown," Edwards said. "The movie 'Slap Shot' was a negative. It was not a positive for us. Out there in the hockey world, the hockey players, their agents and everyone else said, 'Don't go to Johnstown. It's a dump. Everybody is trying to leave. It's a rusted out mill town. You saw it in 'Slap Shot.' "

Edwards said firing Johnstone was a mistake based upon the recommendation of former team president Les Crooks. Cutting Fotiu loose, he said, was the right move but one of the most difficult decisions Edwards made. Fotiu was popular in the community as well as the locker room. "I brought in Toby O'Brien as general manager (in 1996). We decided that we were going to change our philosophy," Edwards said. "First of all, we would never lie to a player in the recruiting process. If you're going to be a role player, we're going to tell you that. We told the truth up front.

"The second thing was that we would never lie and cheat on the salary cap. We're not going to tell you we're going to pay you $500 a week and then when it comes to training camp tell you we're only going to give you $350. The third thing was that if you're chasing the dream, we will never hold you back regardless of what's happening at the local level. We will let you go to the next level."

Outsiders began to notice Johnstown's approach under O'Brien and Allen. Players began to report. Agents suddenly were calling the Chiefs instead of refusing to take phone calls from Johnstown.

Prospects wanted to skate in Johnstown, and they became active in the community.

Times were about to change.

CHIEFS IN THE NINETIES

Top: Chiefs wing Jeff Beaudin provided grit in 1991-92.

Bottom: Chiefs goaltender Neil Little stops a shot against the Hampton Roads Admirals in 1994-95.

237

Chiefs defenseman Perry Florio in front of the War Memorial net against the Columbus Chill.

CHIEFS IN THE NINETIES

Perry Florio

'It Was a Family'

Former Chiefs Captain Florio Played Five Seasons in Johnstown

By Mike Mastovich

The way Perry Florio viewed the situation, he was a Johnstowner, specifically, a Johnstown Chief. The Chiefs and the team's fans were his family. The city was home.

Florio played 305 of his 358 career ECHL regular-season games with the Chiefs. At the time of his 1995 retirement, the defenseman had appeared in the most games in Chiefs history, a mark that has been passed twice since then.

"What made Johnstown special was the unity with the teammates and the fans," said Florio, who coached teams in Roanoke, Va., Florence, S.C., Elmira, N.Y., and Anchorage, Alaska, after retiring as a player. "To me it was a family. It wasn't always a happy family, but it was a family all the time. Before Johnstown, I had played in college and on a lot of teams. I never felt the unity that I felt in Johnstown. It was like having 19 brothers and 3,500 moms and dads (as fans). I never could believe how close you could get to the fans by playing pro hockey.

"I go back there now, 17 years later, and I still see some of the same people who remember me and call me by my first name. It was like having a huge extended family. That meant a lot to me. I'm a people person. I didn't keep to myself. I love getting out and basking in the community."

Cat calls on the road

Florio entered the ECHL in 1989-90 with the Knoxville Cherokees. A trade brought him to Johnstown the next season. His steady play and vocal presence made Florio a natural choice for the Chiefs captaincy, a role he held multiple seasons. A fan favorite in Johnstown, Florio also was well-known in opposing rinks. He often was taunted in cities such as Erie, Norfolk, Va., Charleston, S.C., and Nashville, Tenn.

"Hampton Roads hates me. Erie hates me. Toledo hates me. In a lot of cities I hear the cat calls about being around so long," Florio said in an October 1993 interview on the eve of his breaking the East Coast Hockey League record for career regular-season games played, another mark that since has been broken. "If I was invisible on the ice, they wouldn't be yelling. I must be getting under their skin for some reason."

Florio was an emotional player. After Johnstown defenseman Jeff Ricciardi's overtime goal won a 1993 play-in postseason game over Richmond at Cambria County War Memorial Arena, Florio wept openly in the locker room.

"The Richmond playoff game was one of the highest highlights," Florio said. "It was a play-in game to get into the playoffs. It wasn't winning the Cup. There was so much tension and we cared about each other and we cared about winning. That's why internally we put a lot of pressure on ourselves to win.

"Teams that I played on or coached on the last 20 years, there wasn't that caring by all 20 guys. We had an urgency to not let the other 19 or 20 guys down. We had leaders, whether they wore a letter on their uniform or not."

Time to 'pick up the slack'

In a 1995 first-round playoff against South Carolina, Florio was suspended for Game 3 of a best-of-5 series. The Chiefs lost a controversial contest at the War Memorial that night and faced elimination in Game 4 at home.

Florio returned to the lineup and had four points in a 7-5 win that forced Game 5 in Charleston.

"I remember being suspended in the South Carolina series for banging my stick off the glass," Florio said. "I was in tears when they told me. I was so upset that I let my teammates down. Here I am the captain of the team and I had to sit and watch. The next game I had a goal and three assists in the win at home. That was my way of telling the guys that I'm sorry and I'm going to pick up the slack."

Florio wasn't about to let the season end on his account. At least not that night.

Florio tallied 44 goals and 215 points in five seasons with the Chiefs. He also had 803 penalty minutes. His leadership qualities and willingness to be active in the local community were intangible assets.

He grew up on Long Island, N.Y., but Florio quickly took to Johnstown.

His parents, Perry Sr. and Maureen, relocated to Johnstown from New York and remained in the city years after the younger Florio's retirement from the Chiefs.

The Florios formed a bond with the city and its residents.

"I've moved on to other cities that didn't come close to meeting Johnstown in that regard," Perry Jr. said. "People ask me now where I'm from. I tell them I was born in New York but I'm from Pennsylvania. We have more friends there and more ties there than anywhere else."

> "People ask me now where I'm from. I tell them I was born in New York but I'm from Pennsylvania. We have more friends there and more ties there than anywhere else."
>
> — *Perry Florio*

CHIEFS IN THE NINETIES

Top: Chiefs captain Rick Boyd slows down a Peoria Rivermen player at the War Memorial.

Middle: Chiefs forward Trevor Jobe broke the ECHL career scoring mark in 1995-96.

Bottom left: John Tripp was a productive forward who helped Johnstown reach the playoffs in 1999-2000.

Bottom right: Eddie Johnstone was the Chiefs coach from 1992 to 1995.

241

Mark Green celebrates with Bob Woods after Green scored his 50th goal in his 50th game of the 1991-92 season. The rookie left wing was the first Johnstown professional hockey player to accomplish the feat.

CHIEFS IN THE NINETIES

REPRINT

Johnstown Chiefs rookie left wing Mark Green needed two goals during a Feb. 15, 1992 game against Raleigh to become the first player in Johnstown professional hockey history to net 50 goals in the first 50 games of a season. Green accomplished the feat at Cambria County War Memorial Arena. Sadly, he died at age 36 on Oct. 4, 2004. The Tribune-Democrat's Feb. 16, 1992 account of Green's milestone game follows:

Chiefs' Green on target in 5-4 victory
Rookie achieves 50-50 goal

By Mike Mastovich

Fifty games into his rookie East Coast Hockey League season, Johnstown Chiefs left winger Mark Green experienced a different sensation.

"I was pretty nervous actually," said Green, who made Johnstown hockey history Saturday night at the War Memorial Arena. "After 50 games, you shouldn't be nervous. I hadn't been nervous for so long, but this time I could feel the butterflies."

Prior to Johnstown's 5-4 shootout victory over the Raleigh IceCaps, Green had carried the monumental burden of being two goals shy of 50, while playing in his 50th game. That Green could become the first 50-50 player in Johnstown franchise history only added to the accomplishment's significance.

"I just wanted to get it over with as quick as possible," Green said.

Green accomplished his objective 8:22 into the second period, when he scored his second goal and sent a sellout crowd of 4,040 into hockey euphoria.

Green scored his first goal at 11:40 of the opening period on an assist from center Brian Ferreira, who was in his first game back with the Chiefs after a nine-game stay with the AHL Maine Mariners.

Initially, Ferreira was credited with the goal, which prompted a round of boos from the crowd. Referee Joe Ernst realized the mistake and quickly had the score credited to Green. The 50th goal was highlight film material. Defenseman Dave MacIntyre played the puck off the boards in the Chiefs defensive zone and sent a pass cross-ice toward Green, who was just inside the red line.

> "I just wanted to get it over with as quick as possible."
>
> — *Mark Green, Chiefs left winger.*

243

"It would've been a two-line pass, but Brian Ferreira tipped it up after Mac made the initial pass," Green said.

"I knew Mark was there and I wanted to tip it to him to avoid the two-line pass," Ferreira said. "Mark did the rest."

Green then skated toward the left circle, where he put a fake on Raleigh defenseman Kris Miller. Once past Miller, Green beat IceCaps goalie Mike Mudd with a shot high on the right side.

"I saw Bruce Coles breaking for the net, and I was actually getting ready to pass it to him when I saw the defenseman come out," Green said. "I walked around the defenseman and the goalie was reading me to pass the puck. I looked at Bruce, and the goalie slid just enough to give me enough room to score."

The packed arena gave Green a standing ovation. The officials allowed extra time before the next face-off to let Green and the Chiefs savor the moment.

"I was just excited," said Green, who immediately was surrounded by his teammates. "It was pretty emotional."

"This is a milestone," said Ferreira. "This doesn't happen often in any league."

"Mark's earned it all year," added linemate Coles. "I was just glad to be on his line."

Green's second goal gave the Chiefs a 4-1 lead. Ferreira had made it 1-0 with his 25th goal of the season at 4:28 of the first. Green and Coles assisted. But Raleigh's Brad Gratton tied the game two minutes later. Green's first goal put Johnstown ahead 2-1 after one period. MacIntyre scored on the power play at 2:33 of the second period on assists from Matt Glennon and newcomer Chuck Wiegand.

After Green's 50th goal, the Chiefs played flat, as Raleigh scored three unanswered goals — by Kirby Lindal, Trevor Pochipinski and Mike Chighisola — to force overtime.

Johnstown goaltender Smokey Reddick was impressive in the final period and opening minutes of overtime, stopping several shots from point-blank range.

Reddick saved his best saves for last, stopping all four Raleigh shootout attempts. Coles and Green scored shootout goals for Johnstown, and Coles was credited with the game-winner.

Green is the third ECHL player to score 50 goals this year and the second to reach the plateau in 50 games or less.

Top left: Chiefs defenseman Bob Woods (8) celebrates a goal.

Top right: Defenseman Jason Courtemanche.

Bottom: Chiefs Rival Fullum (21) and Dennis Purdie (19) cover a Columbus Chill player in 1992-93.

CHIEFS IN THE NINETIES

The Chiefs introduced a new logo in 1996-97 that was used for one season.

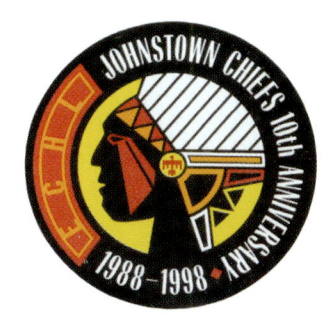

The Chiefs commemorated their 10th year in the ECHL with this logo during the 1997-98 season.

245

Chiefs prolific goal scorer and all-star Bruce Coles (10).

CHIEFS IN THE NINETIES

Bruce Coles

Fan-Favorite Coles Kept Coming Back to Johnstown

By Mike Mastovich

The puck landed squarely on Bruce Coles' stick just inside the blue line.

The veteran forward had a clear path to the net. At age 31, and in his second stint with the Johnstown Chiefs, Coles had perhaps lost a step since he had first donned a black and gold jersey at Cambria County War Memorial Arena almost a decade earlier.

But Coles still had that flair for the dramatic. He still possessed that uncanny knack for scoring the big goal. As time wound down with the Chiefs trailing the first-place Roanoke Express by one, Coles made a cut in front of goaltender Dave Gagnon and flipped the puck into the net for a short-handed goal that tied the game with 29 seconds left.

Air horns blared from above the War Memorial press box. The crowd was on its feet. Fans were screaming, clapping and jumping up and down.

"I felt like I was 20 years old again," Coles said after that Feb. 18, 2000 game that the Chiefs eventually dropped 3-2 in an overtime shootout.

That stellar goal turned out to be the last of Coles' distinguished professional career — one that included five seasons with the Chiefs, five years in the American Hockey League and two in the International Hockey League. Coles only played eight games in 1999-2000. He scored three goals and eight points.

When he stepped aside, Coles held the Chiefs career record with 106 goals in 132 regular-season games. Chiefs wing Lukas Smital later broke the record with 107 goals.

That final goal against Roanoke was classic Coles. He hadn't played in Johnstown since 1995, but immediately revived memories of his ability to seemingly score at will, if only for one night.

"That whole team and that whole experience in Johnstown was awesome."

— *Bruce Coles*

From Winston-Salem to Johnstown

Coles originally joined the Chiefs on Dec. 10, 1991. Coach Steve Carlson acquired him in a trade with Winston-Salem. His college teammate Brian Ferreira was a center for the Chiefs and highly recommended Coles, who had 175 points in four seasons at Rensselaer Polytechnic Institute in Troy, N.Y.

Coles made an immediate impact. He played on a line with Ferreira and 6-foot-4 wing Mark Green. A rookie from Clarkson University, Green eventually was the first player in Johnstown hockey history to net 50 goals in the first 50 games of a season.

The line of center Ferreira, right wing Coles and left wing Green combined for 126 goals and 270 points during the 1991-92 regular season. In the '92 playoffs, Johnstown beat Erie in the first round before falling to a powerhouse Cincinnati squad in the division semifinals. "I always say there are guys on the first line of any ECHL team that could play in the American Hockey League, and the first line in the AHL who could play in the NHL," said Coles, who became a pharmaceutical salesman after hockey. "That line we had could have been competitive in the AHL given the opportunity. Mark Green was a great player with a great shot. Brian had great passing. It was a lot of fun. It was a close team.

"I don't know if you have those types of teams any more. The ECHL now is a big business. Give credit to Mr. Daley (GM John Daley). We were a tight-knit group of players."

His role as a member of the Canadian National Team forced Coles to miss the opening of the 1992-93 ECHL season. He returned to the Chiefs on Dec. 16, 1992.

Coach Eddie Johnstone's team was 10-10-2 when Coles arrived. The Chiefs went 18-6-4 in the 28 games Coles played. He scored 28 goals and 54 points, helping the Chiefs advance to the playoffs, where they lost to newcomer Wheeling. Coles began the 1993-94 season playing for the Durham Wasps in the British Hockey League, but once again provided the Chiefs with a spark when he returned to Johnstown on Dec. 17, 1993.

'Warm and fuzzy feeling'

Whether he came back to the Chiefs never really was a question for Coles. It was just a matter of when he'd return. "That whole team and that whole experience in Johnstown was awesome — whether it was the townspeople, or the local restaurants. It was a warm and fuzzy feeling and the team responded," Coles said. "It was a well-respected team in the community and the community respected what we were doing on the ice."

A trend reversed in 1994-95. Coles began the season in Johnstown but earned a Dec. 19, 1994 call-up to the AHL's Hershey Bears. Coles had two solid seasons with Hershey, and then joined the AHL's Philadelphia Phantoms for two more productive years, including a Calder Cup-winning run in 1997-98. Injuries and contract issues slowed Coles during his final two seasons. But he had one last shot with the Chiefs and made the most of his short stay on a team that eventually ended a four-year playoff drought.

"For me, Johnstown was really a large part of my career and who I am. If that league wasn't there or the players that I played with weren't there, things might be different right now," he said. "I always go back to the fact that it was always a place to hone my skills and feel really welcome whether it was at the beginning of a season, the middle of the season or the end of the season," Coles added. "It was a great place for me to end my career because of the warmth of the fans and the people in the community. They were always positive from the first year that I played there until the 10th year."

CHIEFS IN THE NINETIES

Top: Chiefs wing Martin Masa (18) challenges a Peoria goaltender.

Middle left: The Chiefs bus was stuck on the Ohio Turnpike during a 1999 ice storm.

Middle right: The Iron Dog was a popular Chiefs mascot throughout the 1990s.

Right: All is in order inside the Chiefs 1998-99 locker room.

249

Top: Forward Chuck Wiegand fights for control against the Greensboro Monarchs.

Above: Chiefs forward Ryan Petz was a team captain in the mid-1990s.

Right: Coach Nick Fotiu led the Chiefs from 1995 to 1997.

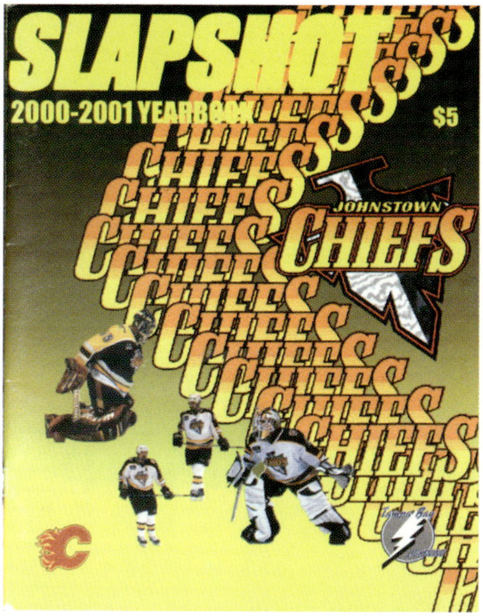

CHIEFS IN THE NINETIES

SLAPSHOT 2000-2001 YEARBOOK $5

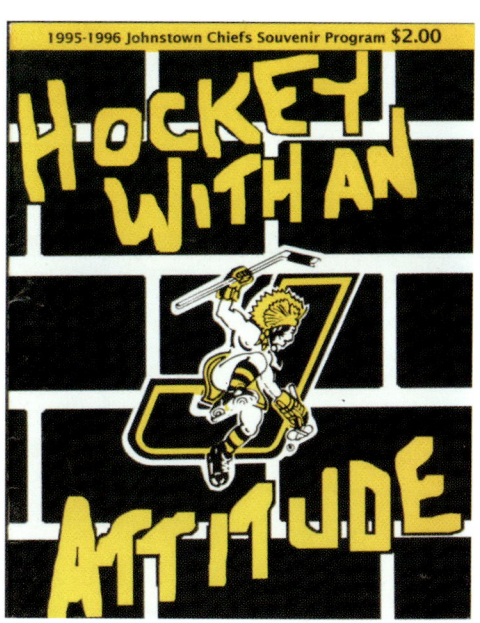

1995-1996 Johnstown Chiefs Souvenir Program $2.00

HOCKEY WITH AN ATTITUDE

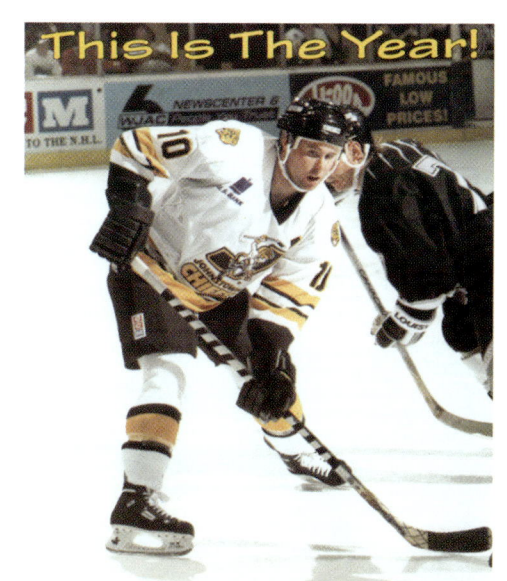

This Is The Year!
1994 - 95 Johnstown Chiefs

"IRON DOG"

251

1990-91 Johnstown Chiefs

(Front, from left) Stan Reddick, Dave Buda, general manager John Daley, Rick Boyd, head coach Steve Carlson, John Messuri, Chris Harvey. (Middle) Bob Woods, Darren Schwartz, Perry Florio, Mike Rossetti, Bob Goulet, Rob Hrytsak, head trainer Dana Heinze. (Back) Assistant trainer Eric Millinder, Andrew MacVicar, Rick Allain, Ian Ferguson, Brian Ferreira, Chris Grassie, equipment manager Mic Midderhoff.

1990-91 FINAL EAST COAST HOCKEY LEAGUE STANDINGS

	Games played	Won	Lost	Overtime losses	Points	Goals for	Goals against
East Division							
Hampton Roads Admirals	64	38	20	6	82	300	248
Johnstown Chiefs	64	32	29	3	67	324	287
Erie Panthers	64	1	30	3	65	302	302
Richmond Renegades	64	29	29	6	64	300	307
Roanoke Valley Rebels	64	26	31	7	59	218	295
West Division							
Knoxville Cherokees	64	46	13	5	97	377	230
Cincinnati Cyclones	64	37	24	3	77	285	281
Greensboro Monarchs	64	34	27	3	71	275	268
Louisville Icehawks	64	31	29	4	66	251	309
Nashville Knights	64	29	31	4	62	307	317
Winston-Salem Thunderbirds	64	20	41	3	43	228	323

Johnstown Chiefs
General Manager - John Daley
Coach - Steve Carlson
Trainers - Dana Heinze, Mic Midderhoff, Eric Millinder
Colors - Black, White and Gold

1990-91 Game Results

Preseason Results

Day	Date	Opponent	Johnstown	Opponent	Attendance	Record
Thur.	18-Oct	Cincinnati	6	5	1,801	
Sat.	20-Oct	Louisville	8	7	2,018	

Regular Season Results

Day	Date	Opponent	Johnstown	Opponent	Attendance	Record
Wed.	24-Oct	at Winston-Salem	6	7 (sol)		0-0-1
Fri.	26-Oct	Nashville	6	1	3,475	1-0-1
Sat.	27-Oct	Winston-Salem	3	4	3,474	1-1-1
Wed.	31-Oct	Knoxville	4	8	2,573	1-2-1

CHIEFS IN THE NINETIES

Day	Date	Opponent	Johnstown	Opponent	Attendance	Record
Sat.	3-Nov	Winston-Salem	5	7	3,493	1-3-1
Sun.	4-Nov	Greensboro	4	7	2,806	1-4-1
Fri.	9-Nov	Erie	6	5 (sow)	3,588	2-4-1
Sat.	10-Nov	Cincinnati	12	3	3,456	3-4-1
Thur.	15-Nov	at Greensboro	2	4		3-5-1
Fri.	16-Nov	at Winston-Salem	1	4		3-6-1
Sat.	17-Nov	at Erie	5	3		4-6-1
Wed.	21-Nov	at Hampton Roads	3	2		5-6-1
Fri.	23-Nov	at Richmond	5	4 (otw)		6-6-1
Sat.	24-Nov	Roanoke Valley	6	4	4,065	7-6-1
Sun.	25-Nov	Winston-Salem	7	8	2,838	7-7-1
Tues.	27-Nov	at Cincinnati	4	5		7-8-1
Fri.	30-Nov	at Hampton Roads	4	5		7-9-1
Sat.	1-Dec	Greensboro	5	2	3,857	8-9-1
Tues.	4-Dec	at Greensboro	3	0		9-9-1
Wed.	5-Dec	Roanoke Valley	7	1	2,475	10-9-1
Sat.	8-Dec	Louisville	6	2	3,263	11-9-1
Sun.	9-Dec	Louisville	2	4	2,630	11-10-1
Tues.	11-Dec	at Hampton Roads	7	5		12-10-1
Fri.	14-Dec	Richmond	11	3	3,004	13-10-1
Sat.	15-Dec	at Richmond	2	5		13-11-1
Sun.	16-Dec	Nashville	8	3	2,645	14-11-1
Fri.	21-Dec	at Erie	4	9		14-12-1
Sat.	22-Dec	Hampton Roads	6	7 (sol)	3,508	14-12-2
Sun.	23-Dec	Hampton Roads	12	5	3,408	15-12-2
Wed.	26-Dec	at Erie	3	5		15-13-2
Sat.	29-Dec	at Knoxville	5	3		16-13-2
Mon.	31-Dec	Erie	5	4	4,055	17-13-2
Thur.	3-Jan	at Roanoke Valley	5	3		18-13-2
Fri.	4-Jan	at Greensboro	2	7		18-14-2
Sat.	5-Jan	at Knoxville	4	6		18-15-2
Tues.	8-Jan	at Nashville	5	4		19-15-2
Fri.	11-Jan	at Richmond	6	3		20-15-2
Sat.	12-Jan	Richmond	6	1	4,052	21-15-2
Sun.	13-Jan	Cincinnati	4	5	3,364	21-16-2
Wed.	16-Jan	Knoxville	10	1	2,945	22-16-2
Fri.	18-Jan	at Knoxville	4	7		22-17-2
Sat.	19-Jan	at Nashville	4	7		22-18-2
Wed.	23-Jan	Greensboro	5	4	2,893	23-18-2
Sat.	26-Jan	Erie	6	5	4,039	24-18-2
Wed.	30-Jan	Roanoke Valley	4	5	2,685	24-19-2
Fri.	1-Feb	at Roanoke Valley	5	3		25-19-2
Sat.	2-Feb	Erie	3	5	4,006	25-20-2
Sun.	3-Feb	Erie	7	2	3,550	26-20-2
Tues.	5-Feb	at Cincinnati	4	5		26-21-2
Fri.	8-Feb	at Cincinnati	9	3		27-21-2
Sun.	10-Feb	at Nashville	8	6		28-21-2
Fri.	15-Feb	at Roanoke Valley	6	5 (sow)		29-21-2
Sat.	16-Feb	Knoxville	6	4	4,035	30-21-2
Sun.	17-Feb	Hampton Roads	3	9	4,009	30-22-2
Wed.	20-Feb	at Louisville	6	7		30-23-2
Fri.	22-Feb	at Louisville	3	4		30-24-2
Sat.	23-Feb	at Louisville	3	4		30-25-2
Sun.	24-Feb	at Erie	1	6		30-26-2
Wed.	27-Feb	Nashville	3	6	2,986	30-27-2
Sat.	2-Mar	Cincinnati	3	4 (sol)	4,035	30-27-3
Sun.	3-Mar	Richmond	6	2	3,288	31-27-3
Thur.	7-Mar	at Winston-Salem	7	6		32-27-3
Fri.	8-Mar	at Erie	2	3		32-28-3
Sun.	10-Mar	Louisville	5	6	3,899	32-29-3

Playoff Results
Score

Day	Date	Opponent	Johnstown	Opponent	Attendance	Record
Thur.	14-Mar	Erie	5	3	2,276	1-0
Fri.	15-Mar	Erie	2	4	3,033	1-1
Sat.	16-Mar	at Erie	1	6		1-2
Tues.	19-Mar	at Erie	4	3		2-2
Wed.	20-Mar	Erie	6	2	3,039	3-2
Fri.	22-Mar	at Hampton Roads	4	3		1-0
Sun.	24-Mar	at Hampton Roads	4	5		1-1
Tues.	26-Mar	Hampton Roads	3	4	3,303	1-2
Wed.	27-Mar	Hampton Roads	2	3	3,807	1-3
Fri.	29-Mar	at Hampton Roads	0	10		1-4

253

Attendance Figures

	Dates	Totals	Average
Preseason Attendance Figures	2	3,819	1,910
Regular Season Attendance Figures	32	108,399	3,387
Playoff Attendance Figures	5	15,458	3,092
TOTAL ATTENDANCE	39	127,676	3,274

1990-91 Player Statistics

	Regular Season Scoring					Playoff Scoring				
	Games	G	A	Pts	PIM	Games	G	A	Pts	PIM
3 John Messuri	61	26	64	90	40	10	4	7	11	10
17 Gord Cruickshank	57	44	33	77	112	8	2	3	5	10
22 Dave Buda	54	45	31	76	41					
18 Darren Schwartz	62	33	34	67	254	10	2	0	2	74
20 Andy MacVicar	55	27	34	61	72	10	2	6	8	18
10 Mike Rossetti	43	17	36	53	60					
19 Rob Hrytsak	40	22	28	50	58	10	4	5	9	10
4 Ian Ferguson	64	9	41	50	42	8	0	2	2	4
31 Brian Ferreira	38	25	22	47	47	8	9	2	11	14
16 Chris Grassie	60	10	35	45	78	10	0	8	8	23
35 Perry Florio	57	8	36	44	179	9	1	4	5	30
8 Bob Woods	23	12	25	37	32					
2 Bob Goulet	44	8	17	25	96	10	0	2	2	14
12 Chris Palmer	25	3	20	23	13	1	0	0	0	7
6 Jason Simon	22	11	9	20	55					
7 Rick Boyd	26	5	10	15	128					
23 Rick Allain	36	2	12	14	100	10	0	0	0	50
14 Brennan Maley	24	6	7	13	40					
19 Kurt Lackten	12	2	7	9	18					
23 Tom Multon	16	3	4	7	31					
14 Jeff Salzbrunn	5	2	4	6	11	10	6	4	10	17
19 Tony Bobbitt	6	1	3	4	6					
6 Craig Shepherd	3	1	2	3	0					
21 Steve Chelios	7	0	3	3	8					
15 Brad James	1	1	0	1	2					
44 Mike Tinkham	4	1	0	1	5					
12 Mark Montanari	1	0	1	1	2					
21 Todd Lalonde	2	0	1	1	2					
12 Wayne Strip	4	0	1	1	9					
15 Jeff Thompson	4	0	1	1	4					
5 Lee Odelein	9	0	1	1	34					
1 Stan Reddick (g)	36	0	1	1	16	10	0	0	0	2
21 Rob Chadwick	1	0	0	0	0					
44 Jacques Mailhot	2	0	0	0	21	9	1	3	4	46
44 Chris Kiene	3	0	0	0	0					
8 Brad Courteau	6	0	0	0	0					
14 Steve Huff	6	0	0	0	2					
31 Mike Parson (g)	6	0	0	0	0					
32 Chris Harvey (g)	31	0	0	0	6	2	0	0	0	0
8 Scott Brown						1	0	0	0	2
21 Brian Horan						1	0	0	0	2
7 Dave MacIntyre						7	0	4	4	0
21 Ted Miskolczi						6	0	0	0	4
Bench					22					
TOTALS	64	324	523	847	1,646	10	31	50	81	337

Regular Season Goaltending

	G	Min	GA	ENG	SO	GAA	W	L	OTL	SOL	Saves	Save %
31 Mike Parson	6	333	23	0	0	4.14	4	2	0	0	199	0.896
32 Chris Harvey	31	1,606	113	2	1	4.22	11	13	0	2	985	0.897
1 Stan Reddick	36	1,957	143	6	0	4.38	17	14	0	1	1,187	0.892
TOTALS	64	3,896	279	8	1	4.42	32	29	0	3	2,371	0.892

Playoff Goaltending

	G	Min	GA	ENG	SO	GAA	W	L	Saves	Save %
1 Stan Reddick	10	542	34	1	0	3.76	4	6	293	0.896
32 Chris Harvey	2	68	8	0	0	7.06	0	0	40	0.833
TOTALS	10	610	42	1	0	4.23	4	6	333	0.886

Mailhot also wore No.8.

Players on roster who did not play: 31 Peter Harris, Goal; 30 Dana Heinze, Goal.

CHIEFS IN THE NINETIES

1991-92 Johnstown Chiefs

(Front, from left) Mike Parson, Doug Weiss, Brian Ferreira, general manager John Daley, Bob Woods, head coach Steve Carlson, Perry Florio, Stan Reddick. (Middle) Stickboy Sean Raymond, head trainer Dana Heinze, Rob Hrytsak, Jeff Beaudin, Doug Sinclair, Mark Green, Ted Miskolczi, Mike McCormick, Mike Roberts, Matt Glennon, broadcaster Dave Mishkin. (Back) Assistant trainer Matt Koeck, Bruce Coles, Scott McCrady, Christian Lariviere, Chuck Wiegand, Dave MacIntyre, Mike Rossetti, equipment manager Mic Midderhoff, assistant equipment manager Derek Craft.

1991-92 FINAL EAST COAST HOCKEY LEAGUE STANDINGS

	Games played	Won	Lost	Overtime losses	Points	Goals for	Goals against
East Division							
Greensboro Monarchs	64	43	17	4	90	297	252
Hampton Roads Admirals	64	42	20	2	86	298	220
Winston-Salem Thunderbirds	64	36	24	4	76	270	245
Richmond Renegades	64	30	27	7	67	263	263
Raleigh Icecaps	64	25	33	6	56	228	284
Roanoke Valley Rebels	64	21	36	7	49	236	313
Knoxville Cherokees	64	20	36	8	48	265	355
West Division							
Toledo Storm	64	46	15	3	95	367	240
Cincinnati Cyclones	64	36	20	8	80	329	284
Johnstown Chiefs	64	36	23	5	77	294	248
Erie Panthers	64	33	27	4	70	284	309
Dayton Bombers	64	32	26	6	70	305	300
Louisville Icehawks	64	31	25	8	70	315	30
Columbus Chill	64	25	30	9	59	298	341
Nashville Knights	64	24	36	4	52	246	335

Johnstown Chiefs
General Manager - John Daley
Coach - Steve Carlson
Training Staff - Dana Heinze, Mic Midderhoff, Derek Craft, Matt Koeck
Stickboy - Sean Raymond
Colors - Black, White and Gold

1991-92 Game Results

Preseason Results

			Score			
Day	Date	Opponent	Johnstown	Opponent	Attendance	Record
Sat.	19-Oct	Roanoke Valley	5	7	1,647	
Sun.	20-Oct	Knoxville	3	2	1,421	

Regular Season Results

			Score			
Day	Date	Opponent	Johnstown	Opponent	Attendance	Record
Fri.	25-Oct	at Richmond	5	7		0-1-0

Day	Date	Opponent	Johnstown	Opponent	Attendance	Record
Sat.	26-Oct	Hampton Roads	8	6	3,402	1-1-0
Wed.	30-Oct	Roanoke Valley	2	6	2,503	1-2-0
Fri.	1-Nov	at Toledo	5	6 (otl)		1-2-1
Sat.	2-Nov	Dayton	7	5	3,440	2-2-1
Tues.	5-Nov	at Columbus	6	3		3-2-1
Wed.	6-Nov	at Dayton	3	5		3-3-1
Fri.	8-Nov	at Erie	4	3 (otw)		4-3-1
Sun.	10-Nov	Louisville	7	3	3,174	5-3-1
Fri.	15-Nov	at Cincinnati	4	3 (otw)		6-3-1
Sun.	17-Nov	Columbus	6	4	2,954	7-3-1
Fri.	22-Nov	at Cincinnati	6	5		8-3-1
Sat.	23-Nov	Toledo	4	5 (sol)	4,041	8-3-2
Thur.	28-Nov	Dayton	7	5	3,345	9-3-2
Fri.	29-Nov	at Richmond	4	2		10-3-2
Sat.	30-Nov	Richmond	5	7	4,081	10-4-2
Thur.	5-Dec	at Roanoke Valley	4	5		10-5-2
Fri.	6-Dec	at Hampton Roads	2	4		10-6-2
Sun.	8-Dec	Winston-Salem	2	5	2,667	10-7-2
Tues.	10-Dec	at Louisville	2	0		11-7-2
Wed.	11-Dec	at Dayton	5	4 (otw)		12-7-2
Sat.	14-Dec	at Dayton	6	2		13-7-2
Sun.	15-Dec	Knoxville	1	3	2,685	13-8-2
Fri.	20-Dec	at Richmond	4	3		14-8-2
Sat.	21-Dec	Richmond	3	4	2,964	14-9-2
Sun.	22-Dec	Cincinnati	6	5	2,928	15-9-2
Thur.	26-Dec	at Erie	1	4		15-10-2
Sat.	28-Dec	Erie	4	3 (otw)	3,852	16-10-2
Sun.	29-Dec	at Columbus	5	2		17-10-2
Tues.	31-Dec	Erie	6	3	4,041	18-10-2
Fri.	3-Jan	at Louisville	4	3		19-10-2
Sat.	4-Jan	at Cincinnati	2	4		19-11-2
Wed.	8-Jan	at Dayton	6	1		20-11-2
Fri.	10-Jan	at Toledo	5	3		21-11-2
Sat.	11-Jan	Greensboro	9	3	3,941	22-11-2
Sun.	12-Jan	Greensboro	12	2	3,009	23-11-2
Sat.	18-Jan	Dayton	4	6	4,055	23-12-2
Sun.	19-Jan	Dayton	5	4 (otw)	3,289	24-12-2
Wed.	22-Jan	Roanoke Valley	6	1	2,388	25-12-2
Fri.	24-Jan	at Nashville	7	2		26-12-2
Sat.	25-Jan	at Nashville	2	4		26-13-2
Wed.	29-Jan	Nashville	4	1	2,829	27-13-2
Fri.	31-Jan	at Richmond	8	2		28-13-2
Sat.	1-Feb	Richmond	4	2	3,803	29-13-2
Sun.	2-Feb	Erie	5	3	3,988	30-13-2
Wed.	5-Feb	Louisville	6	5 (sow)	3,263	31-13-2
Fri.	7-Feb	at Roanoke Valley	2	6		31-14-2
Sat.	8-Feb	at Hampton Roads	5	6 (otl)		31-14-3
Sun.	9-Feb	at Roanoke Valley	1	3		31-15-3
Sat.	15-Feb	Raleigh	5	4 (sow)	4,040	32-15-3
Sun.	16-Feb	Columbus	7	3	3,965	33-15-3
Fri.	21-Feb	at Knoxville	4	9		33-16-3
Sat.	22-Feb	at Winston-Salem	6	2		34-16-3
Sun.	23-Feb	at Greensboro	1	6		34-17-3
Fri.	28-Feb	at Erie	3	4		34-18-3
Sat.	29-Feb	Erie	9	2	4,056	35-18-3
Sun.	1-Mar	Toledo	2	4	4,034	35-19-3
Fri.	6-Mar	at Raleigh	10	4		36-19-3
Sat.	7-Mar	Hampton Roads	3	4 (otl)	3,874	36-19-4
Sun.	8-Mar	Hampton Roads	2	4	3,353	36-20-4
Fri.	13-Mar	at Erie	4	5 (sol)		36-20-5
Sat.	14-Mar	Cincinnati	2	5	3,720	36-21-5
Sun.	15-Mar	Cincinnati	3	6	3,771	36-22-5
Wed.	18-Mar	Toledo	2	3	2,760	36-23-5

Playoff Results

Day	Date	Opponent	Johnstown	Opponent	Attendance	Record
Fri.	20-Mar	Erie	2	4	2,285	0-1
Sat.	21-Mar	Erie	4	0	3,012	1-1
Sun.	22-Mar	at Erie	5	2		2-1
Wed.	25-Mar	at Erie	5	3		3-1
Sat.	28-Mar	at Cincinnati	1	8		0-1
Sun.	29-Mar	Cincinnati	1	7	3,019	0-2

CHIEFS IN THE NINETIES

Attendance Figures

	Dates	Totals	Average
Preseason Attendance Totals	2	3,068	1,534
Regular Season Attendance Totals	32	110,215	3,444
Playoff Totals	3	8,316	2,772
TOTAL ATTENDANCE	37	121,599	3,286

1991-92 Player Statistics

	Regular Season Scoring					Playoff Scoring				
	Games	G	A	Pts	PIM	Games	G	A	Pts	PIM
22 Mark Green	64	68	49	117	44	6	2	3	5	4
5 Bruce Coles	43	32	45	77	113	6	3	1	4	12
17 Brian Ferreira	39	26	50	76	94	6	1	5	6	53
8 Bob Woods	63	18	43	61	44	6	4	1	5	14
7 Dave MacIntyre	63	21	37	58	84	6	1	2	3	4
23 Matt Glennon	30	9	46	55	77	6	2	4	6	25
21 Rob Hrytsak	47	19	27	46	68					
35 Perry Florio	63	10	35	45	247	6	0	0	0	21
6 Doug Weiss	64	14	30	44	23	5	0	0	0	9
19 Ted Miskolczi	38	25	15	40	71	4	0	1	1	2
14 Andy Bezeau	28	11	10	21	142					
2 Mark Krys	43	8	12	20	73					
18 Christian Lariviere	62	3	16	19	142	6	1	3	4	24
31 Mike Rossetti	14	10	8	18	29	6	3	2	5	12
20 Mike McCormick	19	4	9	13	22	5	1	0	1	2
20 Eric Reisman	32	0	12	12	50					
44 Scott McCrady	10	0	7	7	44	3	0	1	1	4
10 John Mooney	8	3	3	6	15					
3 Chuck Wiegand	14	3	2	5	19					
15 Jeff Beaudin	31	2	3	5	72	6	0	1	1	18
12 Mike Roberts	40	1	4	5	24	6	0	2	2	8
15 Pat Penner	7	2	1	3	0					
16 Mike Sanderson	6	1	2	3	4					
14 Dan Poirier	3	1	1	2	9					
5 Steve Beadle	4	1	1	2	4					
4 Everton Blackwin	11	1	1	2	17					
4 Doug Sinclair	18	1	0	1	142					
31 Mike Parson (g)	17	0	1	1	2	5	0	0	0	0
32 Stan Reddick (g)	42	0	1	1	8	4	0	1	1	0
44 Sean Callanan (g)	1	0	0	0	0					
16 Craig Shepherd	2	0	0	0	0					
14 Phil Esposito	3	0	0	0	4					
16 Chris Grassie	3	0	0	0	10					
44 Chris Harvey (g)	4	0	0	0	4					
16 Tony Silvestri	5	0	0	0	0					
23 Mark Cascagnette	6	0	0	0	17					
1 John Fletcher (g)	6	0	0	0	0					
Bench					32					
TOTALS	64	294	471	765	1,750	6	18	27	45	212

Regular Season Goaltending

	G	Min	GA	ENG	SO	GAA	W	L	OTL	SOL	Saves	Save %
1 John Fletcher	6	318	13	0	0	2.45	3	2	0	0	159	0.924
31 Mike Parson	17	994	61	5	1	3.68	6	7	1	2	474	0.886
32 Stan Reddick	42	2,352	151	2	0	3.85	25	12	2	0	1,260	0.893
44 Chris Harvey	4	193	12	0	0	4.04	2	2	0	0	86	0.878
44 Sean Callanan	1	6	1	0	0	10.00	0	0	0	0	2	0.667
Shootout Goals			3									
TOTALS	64	3,863	241	7	1	3.85	6	23	3	2	1,981	0.889

Playoff Goaltending

	G	Min	GA	ENG	SO	GAA	W	L	Saves	Save %
32 Stan Reddick	4	136	9	0	1	3.97	1	2	70	0.886
31 Mike Parson	5	224	15	0	0	4.02	2	1	101	0.871
TOTALS	6	360	24	0	1	4.00	3	3	171	0.877

Parson also wore No. 1; Silvestri also wore No. 14.

Players on roster who did not play: 30 Dana Heinze, Goal; 31 Joe Matty, Goal; 30 Nick Sereggla, Goal.

1992-93 Johnstown Chiefs

(Front, from left) John Bradley, Chuck Wiegand, Matt Robbins, general manager John Daley, Perry Florio, head coach Eddie Johnstone, Tim Hanus, Derry Menard, Scott Bailey. (Middle) Christian Lariviere, Mark Krys, Bob Woods, Jeff Massey, Shayne Antoski, Chris Crombie, Paul Ohman, Joey McTamney. (Back) Equipment manager Mic Midderhoff, trainer Matt Koeck, Rival Fullum, Jeff Ricciardi, Trevor Forsythe, Tommi Virkkunen, Scott Longstaff, broadcaster Dave Mishkin, equipment manager Derek Craft.

1992-93 FINAL EAST COAST HOCKEY LEAGUE STANDINGS

	Games played	Won	Lost	Overtime losses	Points	Goals for	Goals against
East Division							
Wheeling Thunderbirds	64	40	16	8	88	314	223
Hampton Roads Admirals	64	37	21	6	80	294	235
Raleigh Icecaps	64	37	22	5	79	289	262
Johnstown Chiefs	64	34	23	7	75	281	264
Richmond Renegades	64	34	28	2	70	292	292
Greensboro Monarchs	64	33	29	2	68	256	261
Roanoke Valley Rampage	64	14	49	1	29	227	387
West Division							
Toledo Storm	64	36	17	11	83	316	238
Dayton Bombers	64	35	23	6	76	282	270
Nashville Knights	64	36	25	3	75	312	305
Erie Panthers	64	35	25	4	74	305	307
Louisville Icehawks	64	30	27	7	67	302	293
Birmingham Bulls	64	30	29	5	65	290	313
Columbus Chill	64	30	30	4	64	257	256
Knoxville Cherokees	64	19	39	6	44	212	323

Johnstown Chiefs
General Manager - John Daley
Coach - Eddie Johnstone
Training Staff - Matt Koeck, Derek Craft, Mic Midderhoff
Colors - Black, White and Gold

1992-93 Game Results

Preseason Results
Score

Day	Date	Opponent	Johnstown	Opponent	Attendance	Record
Fri.	9-Oct	Wheeling	5	3	1,275	

CHIEFS IN THE NINETIES

Day	Date				
Sat.	10-Oct	at Wheeling	4	5	
Sun.	11-Oct	Richmond	11	4	1,190
Tues.	13-Oct	Knoxville	11	5	1,040

Regular Season Results

Day	Date	Opponent	Johnstown	Opponent	Attendance	Record
Sat.	17-Oct	Dayton	5	4 (otw)	3,439	1-0-0
Fri.	23-Oct	at Richmond	5	8		1-1-0
Sat.	24-Oct	Louisville	5	4	3,070	2-1-0
Sat.	31-Oct	Roanoke Valley	2	4	3,079	2-2-0
Fri.	6-Nov	at Wheeling	2	3 (sol)		2-2-1
Sat.	7-Nov	Wheeling	6	5 (sow)	3,230	3-2-1
Wed.	11-Nov	Hampton Roads	4	3 (sow)	2,238	4-2-1
Sat.	14-Nov	Greensboro	10	7	3,248	5-2-1
Sat.	21-Nov	at Roanoke Valley	3	1		6-2-1
Sun.	22-Nov	Wheeling	4	7	2,721	6-3-1
Wed.	25-Nov	Greensboro	1	3	2,643	6-4-1
Fri.	27-Nov	Wheeling	2	4	3,547	6-5-1
Sat.	28-Nov	at Wheeling	3	4 (sol)		6-5-2
Sun.	29-Nov	at Columbus	2	3		6-6-2
Wed.	2-Dec	Erie	6	3	1,915	7-6-2
Sat.	5-Dec	at Erie	2	4		7-7-2
Sun.	6-Dec	Wheeling	4	6	2,084	7-8-2
Tues.	8-Dec	at Raleigh	3	4		7-9-2
Wed.	9-Dec	at Hampton Roads	3	1		8-9-2
Fri.	11-Dec	at Columbus	4	3 (otw)		9-9-2
Sat.	12-Dec	Hampton Roads	2	3	2,313	9-10-2
Tues.	15-Dec	at Greensboro	5	4		10-10-2
Fri.	18-Dec	at Erie	5	8		10-11-2
Sat.	19-Dec	Columbus	6	5	2,461	11-11-2
Sun.	20-Dec	Erie	7	2	2,214	12-11-2
Sat.	26-Dec	at Erie	6	3		13-11-2
Thur.	31-Dec	Erie	3	4 (otl)	4,041	13-11-3
Sat.	2-Jan	Hampton Roads	6	4	3,143	14-11-3
Wed.	6-Jan	at Richmond	5	3		15-11-3
Fri.	8-Jan	at Hampton Roads	6	2		16-11-3
Sat.	9-Jan	Richmond	3	5	3,272	16-12-3
Sun.	10-Jan	Richmond	7	8	2,484	16-13-3
Tues.	12-Jan	at Birmingham	6	2		17-13-3
Wed.	13-Jan	at Nashville	7	4		18-13-3
Fri.	15-Jan	Erie	3	4	2,805	18-14-3
Sat.	16-Jan	Hampton Roads	1	7	3,466	18-15-3
Tues.	19-Jan	at Wheeling	3	9		18-16-3
Fri.	22-Jan	at Richmond	6	7 (sol)		18-16-4
Sat.	23-Jan	Raleigh	10	1	3,213	19-16-4
Sun.	24-Jan	Raleigh	4	3 (otw)	3,167	20-16-4
Thur.	28-Jan	at Wheeling	7	6		21-16-4
Fri.	29-Jan	at Erie	5	6		21-17-4
Sat.	30-Jan	Roanoke Valley	4	1	3,855	22-17-4
Wed.	3-Feb	Nashville	5	3	2,265	23-17-4
Fri.	5-Feb	at Greensboro	6	0		24-17-4
Sat.	6-Feb	at Raleigh	4	5		24-18-4
Wed.	10-Feb	Knoxville	6	3	2,579	25-18-4
Sat.	13-Feb	Raleigh	6	3	3,253	26-18-4
Sun.	14-Feb	Greensboro	7	3	3,582	27-18-4
Wed.	17-Feb	at Dayton	3	6		27-19-4
Fri.	19-Feb	at Louisville	4	5 (otl)		27-19-5
Sat.	20-Feb	at Knoxville	5	4		28-19-5
Wed.	24-Feb	Toledo	5	3	2,125	29-19-5
Fri.	26-Feb	at Roanoke Valley	5	4		30-19-5
Sat.	27-Feb	Roanoke Valley	5	6 (otl)	3,985	30-19-6
Sun.	28-Feb	at Toledo	1	8		30-20-6
Wed.	3-Mar	Raleigh	4	3	2,369	31-20-6
Fri.	5-Mar	at Roanoke Valley	2	3		31-21-6
Sat.	6-Mar	Toledo	4	7	4,059	31-22-6
Sun.	7-Mar	at Wheeling	1	0		32-22-6
Tues.	9-Mar	at Raleigh	6	5 (otw)		33-22-6
Wed.	10-Mar	at Hampton Roads	1	5		33-23-6
Fri.	12-Mar	at Greensboro	3	4 (sol)		33-23-7
Mon.	15-Mar	Birmingham	5	2	3,307	34-23-7

259

Playoff Results

Day	Date	Opponent	Johnstown	Opponent	Attendance	Record
Wed.	17-Mar	Richmond	5	4 (ot)	1,938	1-0
Fri.	19-Mar	at Wheeling	2	3		0-1
Sat.	20-Mar	at Wheeling	3	4		0-2
Sun.	21-Mar	Wheeling	4	1	2,879	1-2
Tues.	23-Mar	Wheeling	0	5	2,750	1-3

Attendance Figures

	Dates	Totals	Average
Preseason Attendance Totals	3	3,505	1,168
Regular Season Attendance Totals	32	95,172	2,974
Playoff Attendance Totals	3	7,567	2,522
TOTAL ATTENDANCE	38	106,244	2,796

1992-93 Player Statistics

	Regular Season Scoring					Playoff Scoring				
	Games	G	A	Pts	PIM	Games	G	A	Pts	PIM
18 Chris Crombie	63	29	35	64	267	5	1	1	2	2
17 Matt Robbins	56	23	41	64	37	5	0	5	5	2
15 Tim Hanus	47	26	34	60	77					
10 Bruce Coles	28	28	26	54	61	5	1	3	4	29
21 Rival Fullum	57	28	23	51	31	5	5	0	5	2
4 Bob Woods	61	11	36	47	72	5	1	1	2	8
35 Perry Florio	61	11	32	43	162	5	0	1	1	25
16 Mark Karpen	38	17	25	42	22	5	1	4	5	4
5 Jeff Ricciardi	61	7	29	36	248	5	2	2	4	6
20 Chuck Wiegand	37	15	15	30	10	5	0	2	2	0
7 Derry Menard	38	7	23	30	22	3	0	1	1	2
22 Jeff Massey	56	17	12	29	38					
23 Christian Lariviere	51	4	20	24	93	5	1	3	4	4
19 Tommi Virkkunen	25	7	15	22	8					
30 Brent Thurston	20	5	17	22	63					
16 Scott Longstaff	19	6	14	20	0					
3 Mark Krys	25	4	14	18	18					
19 Dennis Prudie	17	10	7	17	38	5	1	3	4	38
19 Yevgeny Pavlov	24	8	9	17	40					
2 Paul Ohman	42	3	10	13	31	5	0	0	0	14
32 Joey McTamney	27	3	8	11	26					
44 Ted Miskolczi	6	6	3	9	27					
8 Trevor Forsythe	25	2	6	8	92					
12 David Earn	9	2	2	4	15					
12 Shayne Antoski	8	1	3	4	2					
1 John Bradley (g)	36	0	3	3	26	5	0	0	0	2
14 Phil Esposito	6	1	1	2	40					
17 John Craighead	1	0	2	2	17					
31 Scott Bailey (g)	36	0	2	2	6					
32 Troy Frederick	8	0	1	1	0					
14 Chic Pojar	1	0	0	0	0					
4 Tyler Green	2	0	0	0	0					
30 Dan Ryder (g)	4	0	0	0	26					
14 Steve Gibson						3	0	1	1	2
12 Dusty McLellan						4	1	0	1	0
Bench					32					
TOTALS	64	281	468	749	1,647	5	14	27	41	140

Regular Season Goaltending

	G	Min	GA	ENG	SO	GAA	W	L	OTL	SOL	Saves	Save %
31 Scott Bailey	36	1,750	112	6	1	3.84	13	15	2	1	785	0.875
1 John Bradley	36	1,910	127	0	1	3.99	20	7	1	2	823	0.866
30 Dan Ryder	4	214	15	0	0	4.21	1	1	0	1	107	0.877
Shootout Goals			4									
TOTALS	64	3,874	258	6	2	4.09	34	23	3	4	1,715	0.867

Playoff Goaltending

	G	Min	GA	ENG	SO	GAA	W	L	Saves	Save %
1 John Bradley	5	307	17	0	0	3.32	2	3	158	0.903
TOTALS	5	307	17	0	0	3.32	2	3	158	0.903

Players on roster who did not play: 6 Kyle Galloway, Defense; 30 Darren Hersh, Goal (playoff back-up).

CHIEFS IN THE NINETIES

1993-94 Johnstown Chiefs

(Front, from left) John Bradley, Rob Leask, Bob Woods, general manager John Daley, Perry Florio, head coach Eddie Johnstone, Ted Dent, Dennis Purdie, Adam Thompson. (Middle) Tim Hanus, Francois Bourdeau, Jan Beran, Gord Christian, Matt Hoffman, Dusty McLellan, Chuck Wiegand, Jason Jennings. (Back) Trainer Matt Koeck, equipment manager Derek Craft, Cory Banika, Campbell Blair, Phil Soukoroff, Rival Fullum, Jamie Adams, director of sales Jim Brazill, broadcaster Dave Mishkin.

1993-94 FINAL EAST COAST HOCKEY LEAGUE STANDINGS

	Games played	Won	Lost	Overtime losses	Points	Goals for	Goals against
North Division							
Toledo Storm	68	44	20	4	92	338	289
Columbus Chill	68	41	20	7	89	344	285
Wheeling Thunderbirds	68	38	23	7	83	327	289
Johnstown Chiefs	68	37	27	4	78	323	308
Dayton Bombers	68	29	31	8	66	316	308
Erie Panthers	68	27	36	5	59	264	334
East Division							
Hampton Roads Admirals	68	41	19	8	90	298	246
Raleigh Icecaps	68	41	20	7	89	296	221
Greensboro Monarchs	68	41	21	6	88	319	262
Charlotte Checkers	68	39	25	4	82	281	271
Roanoke Express	68	37	28	3	77	300	290
South Carolina Stingrays	68	33	26	9	75	294	291
Richmond Renegades	68	34	29	5	73	286	293
West Division							
Knoxville Cherokees	68	44	18	6	94	325	246
Birmingham Bulls	68	44	20	4	92	340	268
Nashville Knights	68	26	36	6	58	255	289
Huntsville Blast	68	20	39	9	49	241	315
Louisville Icehawks	68	16	44	8	40	236	356
Huntington Blizzard	68	14	49	5	33	191	413

Johnstown Chiefs
General Manager - John Daley
Coach - Eddie Johnstone
Training Staff - Matt Koeck, Derek Craft, Mic Midderhoff
Colors - Black, White and Gold
Note: Team wore white Jets jerseys with Blue trim (Toronto style, worn 1964-1972) for one game vs. Erie.

1993-94 Game Results

Preseason Results

Day	Date	Opponent	Score Johnstown	Opponent	Attendance	Record
Wed.	13-Oct	Knoxville	6	9	2,200	
Fri.	15-Oct	Huntington	11	5	1,800	
Sat.	16-Oct	Erie	2	4	1,321	

Regular Season Results

Day	Date	Opponent	Score Johnstown	Opponent	Attendance	Record
Fri.	22-Oct	at Toledo	2	12		0-1-0
Sat.	23-Oct	Columbus	4	7	3,712	0-2-0
Sun.	24-Oct	Erie	5	6 (otl)	2,306	0-2-1
Tues.	26-Oct	at Hampton Roads	4	9		0-3-1
Fri.	29-Oct	Dayton	1	3		0-4-1
Sat.	30-Oct	at Erie	7	1		1-4-1
Sun.	31-Oct	Dayton	6	3	2,453	2-4-1
Fri.	5-Nov	at Huntington	6	2		3-4-1
Sat.	6-Nov	at Knoxville	6	9		3-5-1
Sun.	7-Nov	at Nashville	4	8		3-6-1
Tues.	9-Nov	at Birmingham	5	7		3-7-1
Fri.	12-Nov	al Wheeling	6	5		4-7-1
Sat.	13-Nov	Wheeling	7	6 (otw)	3,230	5-7-1
Sun.	14-Nov	Louisville	7	5	2,329	6-7-1
Fri.	19-Nov	Charlotte	4	5	3,504	6-8-1
Sun.	21-Nov	Nashville	4	2	2,321	7-8-1
Tues.	23-Nov	at Columbus	2	9		7-9-1
Thur.	25-Nov	at Erie	6	2		8-9-1
Fri.	26-Nov	at Dayton	3	1		9-9-1
Sat.	27-Nov	Toledo	10	3	4,049	10-9-1
Fri.	3-Dec	at Dayton	4	7		10-10-1
Sat.	4-Dec	at Toledo	1	3		10-11-1
Sun.	5-Dec	Columbus	6	4	2,234	11-11-1
Fri.	10-Dec	at Columbus	1	6		11-12-1
Sat.	11-Dec	Wheeling	2	8	2,592	11-13-1
Sun.	12-Dec	Knoxville	3	2	2,774	12-13-1
Fri.	17-Dec	at Columbus	6	3		13-13-1
Sat.	18-Dec	Wheeling	10	4	2,747	14-13-1
Sun.	19-Dec	Dayton	11	5	2,147	15-13-1
Sun.	26-Dec	at Erie	6	4		16-13-1
Tues.	28-Dec	Huntington	13	3	3,194	17-13-1
Wed.	29-Dec	at Dayton	5	3		18-13-1
Fri.	31-Dec	Erie	8	1	4,045	19-13-1
Sun.	2-Jan	at Toledo	5	3		20-13-1
Fri.	7-Jan	at Richmond	4	3		21-13-1
Sat.	8-Jan	Roanoke	4	5 (otl)	3,251	21-13-2
Tues.	11-Jan	at Raleigh	5	6 (sol)		21-13-3
Wed.	12-Jan	at South Carolina	7	9		21-14-3
Fri.	14-Jan	at Wheeling	3	4 (sol)		21-14-4
Sat.	15-Jan	Wheeling	4	2	3,240	22-14-4
Mon.	17-Jan	at Columbus	2	5		22-15-4
Tues.	18-Jan	at Roanoke	6	2		23-15-4
Sat.	22-Jan	Columbus	3	5	4,101	23-16-4
Sun.	23-Jan	at Wheeling	5	7		23-17-4
Fri.	28-Jan	South Carolina	3	5	3,020	23-18-4
Sat.	29-Jan	Huntsville	4	0	3,257	24-18-4
Wed.	2-Feb	at Greensboro	4	6		24-19-4
Thur.	3-Feb	at Charlotte	4	3		25-19-4
Sun.	6-Feb	at Wheeling	5	4 (sow)		26-19-4
Tues.	8-Feb	at Toledo	6	3		27-19-4
Wed.	9-Feb	Erie	4	2	2,650	28-19-4
Fri.	11-Feb	at Erie	3	2 (otw)		29-19-4
Sat.	12-Feb	Toledo	3	4	3,414	29-20-4
Sun.	13-Feb	Greensboro	7	5	2,833	30-20-4
Wed.	16-Feb	Hampton Roads	7	4	2,314	31-20-4
Sat.	19-Feb	Birmingham	9	7	3,702	32-20-4
Sun.	20-Feb	Raleigh	3	8	2,994	32-21-4
Wed.	23-Feb	Columbus	4	7	2,267	32-22-4
Sat.	26-Feb	Dayton	3	7	3,429	32-23-4
Sun.	27-Feb	Toledo	1	5	3,169	32-24-4
Sat.	5-Mar	Richmond	3	6	3,202	32-25-4
Sun.	6-Mar	Erie	4	3 (sow)	3,185	33-25-4
Thur.	10-Mar	at Huntsville	4	2		34-25-4
Fri.	11-Mar	at Louisville	3	5		34-26-4
Sun.	13-Mar	Toledo	6	1	3,202	35-26-4
Fri.	18-Mar	at Erie	3	5		35-27-4
Sat.	19-Mar	Wheeling	3	2 (sow)	4,077	36-27-4
Sun.	20-Mar	Erie	4	3	3,221	37-27-4

CHIEFS IN THE NINETIES

Playoff Results

Wed.	23-Mar	Columbus	2	1	2,201	1-0
Fri.	25-Mar	at Columbus	4	9		1-1
Sat.	26-Mar	at Columbus	1	4		1-2

Attendance Figures

	Dates	Totals	Average
Preseason Attendance Totals	3	5,321	1,774
Regular Season Attendance Totals	34	104,165	3,064
Playoff Attendance Totals	1	2,201	2,201
TOTAL ATTENDANCE	38	111,687	2,939

1993-94 Player Statistics

	Regular Season Scoring					Playoff Scoring				
	Games	G	A	Pts	PIM	Games	G	A	Pts	PIM
10 Ted Dent	67	30	54	84	161	3	0	0	0	21
19 Dennis Purdie	57	36	46	82	171	3	3	2	5	8
12 Matt Hoffman	58	33	40	73	85	3	1	0	1	2
8 Bob Woods	43	18	37	55	57	3	1	3	4	4
14 Gord Christian	45	29	25	54	95	3	0	0	0	4
35 Perry Florio	62	12	40	52	117	3	0	1	1	42
17 Jason Jennings	44	19	26	45	38	3	0	1	1	0
30 Bruce Coles	24	23	20	43	56	3	0	1	1	10
22 Jamie Adams	43	16	21	37	16					
20 Chuck Wiegand	46	18	18	36	36					
44 Rob Leask	52	11	25	36	137	3	1	2	3	14
32 Cory Banika	48	16	14	30	262					
4 Campbell Blair	52	5	22	27	56					
2 Martin D'Orsonnens	53	5	22	27	94	3	1	0	1	0
15 Tim Hanus	20	9	14	23	28	3	0	0	0	6
7 Francois Bourdeau	63	6	17	23	61	3	0	1	1	0
23 Jan Beran	18	10	6	16	15					
6 Glen Lang	31	4	8	12	14					
16 Phil Soukoroff	13	2	9	11	9					
21 Rival Fullum	12	4	6	10	11					
18 Yannick Frechette	15	5	3	8	57	3	0	0	0	5
3 Ben Wyzansky	9	1	7	8	8	3	0	1	1	0
18 Dusty McLellan	10	2	5	7	39					
22 Randy Skarda	9	1	6	7	6					
32 Jeff Grant	10	1	6	7	15					
5 Kevin Quinn	26	1	5	6	128					
16 Matt Yingst	6	2	3	5	10					
21 Helmut Karel	6	1	4	5	31					
1 John Bradley (g)	36	0	3	3	55	1	0	0	0	0
21 Eric Dandenault	2	1	1	2	6					
31 Shayne Antoski	3	0	2	2	2					
20 Shawn Bourgeois	7	0	2	2	7	3	0	0	0	0
23 Stephen Sangermano	2	1	0	1	0					
20 David Murphy	4	1	0	1	5					
31 Rob Laurie (g)	35	0	1	1	6	3	0	0	0	0
16 Gord Law	2	0	0	0	2					
5 Garry Gulash	3	0	0	0	60					
21 Kyle Blacklock	8	0	0	0	10					
30 Adam Thompson (g)	8	0	0	0	0					
Bench					12					
TOTALS	68	323	518	841	1,978	3	7	12	19	116

Regular Season Goaltending

	G	Min	GA	ENG	SO	GAA	W	L	OTL	SOL	Saves	Save%
31 Rob Laurie	34	1,942	128	4	0	3.96	18	13	1	0	1,083	0.894
1 John Bradley	36	1,834	143	3	1	4.68	16	13	1	1	966	0.871
30 Adam Thompson	8	333	28	0	0	5.05	3	1	1	0	137	0.830
Shootout Goals			2									
TOTALS	68	4,109	301	7	1	4.50	37	27	3	1	2,186	0.877

Playoff Goaltending

	G	Min	GA	ENG	SO	GAA	W	L	Saves	Save%
31 Rob Laurie	3	153	11	0	0	4.31	1	2	78	0.876
1 John Bradley	1	27	3	0	0	6.70	0	0	12	0.800
TOTALS	3	180	14	0	0	4.67	1	2	90	0.865

Murphy also wore No. 12; Antoski also wore No. 15.

1994-95 Johnstown Chiefs

(Front, from left) Aaron Israel, general manager/coach Eddie Johnstone, owner Ned Nakles Sr., owner Ned Nakles Jr., Perry Florio, owner Leonard Reeves, president Les Crooks, Neil Little. (Middle) Justin Duberman, Martin D'Orsonnes, Jason Brousseau, Brian McCarthy, Steve Foster, Steve Norton, Matt Hoffman, Jason Jennings, Ben Wyzansky. (Back) Trainer Matt Koeck, equipment manager Derek Craft, Dan Sawyer, Anton Federov, Rod Hinks, Mike Dennis, Jay Ness, director of sales Jim Brazill, broadcaster Gregg DeVitto.

1994-95 FINAL EAST COAST HOCKEY LEAGUE STANDINGS

	Games played	Won	Lost	Overtime losses	Points	Goals for	Goals against
North Division							
Wheeling Thunderbirds	68	46	17	5	97	313	243
Dayton Bombers	68	42	17	9	93	307	224
Toledo Storm	68	41	22	5	87	287	230
Columbus Chill	68	31	32	5	67	282	315
Johnstown Chiefs	68	31	32	5	67	256	297
Erie Panthers	68	18	46	4	40	256	356
East Division							
Richmond Renegades	68	41	20	7	89	271	232
Roanoke Express	68	39	19	10	88	255	223
Charlotte Checkers	68	37	22	9	83	274	261
Hampton Roads Admirals	68	37	23	8	82	255	239
Greensboro Monarchs	68	31	28	9	71	277	293
Raleigh Icecaps	68	23	39	6	52	239	295
West Division							
South Carolina Stingrays	68	42	19	7	91	255	215
Tallahassee Tiger Sharks	68	36	25	7	79	268	227
Nashville Knights	68	32	30	6	70	263	279
Knoxville Cherokees	68	30	30	8	68	241	267
Huntington Blizzard	68	28	37	3	59	224	275
Birmingham Bulls	68	26	38	4	56	273	325

Johnstown Chiefs
General Manager - Eddie Johnstone
Coach - Eddie Johnstone
Training Staff - Matt Koeck, Derek Craft, Mic Midderhoff
Colors - Black, White and Gold
Team wore third jersey — Gold with black and red trim for Sunday home games
Team wore Jets blue jersey on "Turn Back the Clock Night" — 1964-72 version vs. Toledo

1994-95 Game Results

Preseason Results

Day	Date	Opponent	Johnstown	Opponent	Attendance	Record
Wed.	12-Oct	at Roanoke Valley	3	8		
Thur.	13-Oct	at Hampton Roads	3	4		

CHIEFS IN THE NINETIES

Regular Season Results

Day	Date	Opponent	Johnstown	Opponent	Attendance	Record
Sat.	15-Oct	Hampton Roads	3	2	970	
Sun.	16-Oct	Richmond	5	4	1,100	
Thur.	20-Oct	Columbus	7	4	3,421	1-0-0
Fri.	21-Oct	at Toledo	5	6 (otl)		1-0-1
Sat.	22-Oct	at Dayton	5	8		1-1-1
Fri.	28-Oct	at Erie	6	4		2-1-1
Sat.	29-Oct	Columbus	3	6	3,241	2-2-1
Wed.	2-Nov	at Hampton Roads	4	5		2-3-1
Fri.	4-Nov	at Columbus	3	5		2-4-1
Sat.	5-Nov	Toledo	4	2	3,711	3-4-1
Fri.	11-Nov	at Erie	4	6		3-5-1
Sat.	12-Nov	Columbus	5	6 (sol)	3,727	3-5-2
Sun.	13-Nov	Erie	6	4	2,347	4-5-2
Wed.	16-Nov	at Wheeling	6	5		5-5-2
Fri.	18-Nov	at Toledo	4	3 (sow)		6-5-2
Sun.	20-Nov	at Columbus	1	3		6-6-2
Thur.	24-Nov	at Erie	8	6		7-6-2
Fri.	25-Nov	at Toledo	2	6		7-7-2
Sat.	26-Nov	Toledo	5	1	4,068	8-7-2
Tues.	29-Nov	at Columbus	4	6		8-8-2
Sat.	3-Dec	Dayton	8	3	3,301	9-8-2
Sun.	4-Dec	Erie	6	5	2,561	10-8-2
Fri.	9-Dec	at Wheeling	3	5		10-9-2
Sat.	10-Dec	at Erie	5	4		11-9-2
Sun.	11-Dec	Erie	3	2	2,594	12-9-2
Fri.	16-Dec	at Wheeling	4	5		12-10-2
Sat.	17-Dec	Wheeling	4	3 (sow)	3,403	13-10-2
Sun.	18-Dec	at Toledo	4	7		13-11-2
Fri.	23-Dec	at Dayton	0	5		13-12-2
Mon.	26-Dec	at Wheeling	2	4		13-13-2
Tues.	27-Dec	Dayton	2	1	3,117	14-13-2
Thur.	29-Dec	Columbus	6	5 (sow)	2,942	15-13-2
Sat.	31-Dec	Erie	4	5 (sol)	4,070	15-13-3
Wed.	4-Jan	at Erie	Postponed snow - rescheduled for Feb. 15			
Fri.	6-Jan	at Wheeling	2	4		15-14-3
Sat.	7-Jan	Dayton	4	5 (otl)	2,761	15-14-4
Sun.	8-Jan	Dayton	2	3	2,580	15-15-4
Fri.	13-Jan	Wheeling	2	5	2,967	15-16-4
Sat.	14-Jan	at Columbus	2	7		15-17-4
Sun.	15-Jan	Richmond	6	5	2,543	16-17-4
Wed.	18-Jan	at Toledo	2	9		16-18-4
Fri.	20-Jan	Wheeling	6	5 (sow)	2,514	17-18-4
Sat.	21-Jan	Roanoke	3	5	3,307	17-19-4
Wed.	25-Jan	at Richmond	2	11		17-20-4
Sat.	27-Jan	at Roanoke	4	3 (sow)		18-20-4
Sun.	28-Jan	Erie	5	3	3,786	19-20-4
Fri.	3-Feb	at Charlotte	5	4 (sow)		20-20-4
Sat.	4-Feb	at Raleigh	4	9		20-21-4
Sun.	5-Feb	at Greensboro	1	9		20-22-4
Sat.	11-Feb	Toledo	5	4 (sow)	3,064	21-22-4
Sun.	12-Feb	Greensboro	5	4	2,879	22-22-4
Tues.	14-Feb	Columbus	2	3	1,830	22-23-4
Wed.	15-Feb	at Erie	3	2 (sow)		23-23-4
Fri.	17-Feb	at Roanoke	1	4		23-24-4
Sat.	18-Feb	Huntington	6	2	3,442	24-24-4
Sun.	19-Feb	Richmond	1	4	2,652	24-25-4
Wed.	22-Feb	Toledo	0	4	2,730	24-26-4
Sat.	25-Feb	Hampton Roads	3	2	4,045	25-26-4
Sun.	26-Feb	Wheeling	5	6 (sol)	2,696	25-26-5
Wed.	1-Mar	at Dayton	1	2		25-27-5
Thur.	2-Mar	Hampton Roads	1	2	1,822	25-28-5
Sat.	4-Mar	Roanoke	1	4	3,449	25-29-5
Sun.	5-Mar	Toledo	1	2	3,265	25-30-5
Wed.	8-Mar	at Richmond	3	4		25-31-5
Fri.	10-Mar	Dayton	5	4 (otw)	2,705	26-31-5
Sat.	11-Mar	at Erie	4	1		27-31-5
Sun.	12-Mar	Erie	8	6	3,043	28-31-5
Fri.	17-Mar	at Toledo	3	6		28-32-5
Sat.	18-Mar	at Dayton	4	1		29-32-5
Sun.	19-Mar	at Columbus	5	0		30-32-5

265

Day	Date	Opponent			Score	Attendance	Record
Tues.	21-Mar	Columbus	6	3		2,626	31-32-5

Playoff Results

Day	Date	Opponent				Attendance	Record
Thur.	23-Mar	at South Carolina	6	5 (otw)			1-0
Sat.	25-Mar	at South Carolina	1	6			1-1
Tues.	28-Mar	South Carolina	3	4		2,114	1-2
Wed.	29-Mar	South Carolina	7	5		1,626	2-2
Fri.	31-Mar	at South Carolina	3	5			2-3

Attendance Figures

	Games	Totals	Average
Preseason Attendance Totals	2	2,070	1,035
Regular Season Attendance Totals	34	103,209	3,036
Playoff Attendance Totals	2	3,740	1,870
TOTAL ATTENDANCE	38	109,019	2,869

1994-95 Player Statistics

	Regular Season Scoring					Playoff Scoring				
	Games	G	A	Pts	PIM	Games	G	A	Pts	PIM
21 Rod Hinks	66	30	46	76	90	5	4	1	5	4
20 Jason Brousseau	57	35	26	61	74	5	1	2	3	6
12 Matt Hoffman	55	25	36	61	113	5	2	4	6	10
44 Rob Leask	60	16	45	61	110	1	0	0	0	0
19 Dennis Purdie	36	27	33	60	125	5	5	3	8	12
17 Jason Jennings	67	23	31	54	57	5	0	3	3	2
30 Bruce Coles	29	20	25	45	56					
10 Ted Dent	46	9	24	33	125					
35 Perry Florio	62	3	28	31	94	4	0	6	6	12
27 Justin Duberman	24	13	14	27	30	5	0	7	7	20
24 Mike Dennis	59	5	18	23	86	5	0	1	1	28
23 Brandon Christian	39	7	12	19	226					
14 Jay Ness	38	6	11	17	12	5	2	2	4	6
7 Ben Wyzansky	64	4	12	16	66					
2 Steve Norton	31	4	10	14	12					
3 Martin D'Orsonnens	39	5	7	12	79	5	1	5	6	4
15 Paul MacLean	40	5	7	12	26					
16 Anton Federov	13	5	6	11	2	5	1	1	2	0
22 Dan Sawyer	58	2	9	11	111	5	0	0	0	2
16 Matt Yingst	41	5	5	10	27					
10 Brian McCarthy	12	4	4	8	2	5	4	1	5	2
4 Steve Foster	21	1	6	7	14	5	0	1	1	2
18 Peter Romeo	11	0	4	4	16					
1 Aaron Israel (g)	30	0	4	4	16	3	0	0	0	2
14 Gord Christian	4	1	2	3	29					
18 Ryan Sittler	1	1	1	2	0					
18 Jeff Connelly	4	0	2	2	0					
31 Rob Laurie (g)	26	0	2	2	2					
5 Kevin Quinn	7	0	1	1	36					
4 Philippe Boudreault	2	0	0	0	2					
4 Joel Eagan	3	0	0	0	2					
2 Jason Richard	4	0	0	0	4					
31 Neil Little (g)	16	0	0	0	2	3	0	0	0	4
Bench					10					
TOTALS	68	256	431	687	1,656	5	20	37	57	116

Regular Season Goaltending

	G	Min	GA	ENG	SO	GAA	W	L	OTL	SOL	Saves	Save%
31 Neil Little	16	897	55	0	0	3.68	7	6	0	1	475	0.896
1 Aaron Israel	30	1,775	119	1	1	4.02	17	10	1	1	978	0.892
31 Rob Laurie	26	1,456	113	6	0	4.66	7	16	1	1	782	0.874
Shootout Goals			3									
TOTALS	68	4,128	290	7	1	4.32	31	32	2	3	2,235	0.883

Playoff Goaltending

	G	Min	GA	ENG	SO	GAA	W	L	Saves	Save%
31 Neil Little	3	145	11	0	0	4.55	0	2	70	0.864
1 Aaron Israel	3	157	14	0	0	5.35	2	1	63	0.818
TOTALS	5	302	25	0	0	4.97	2	3	133	0.842

Brousseau also wore No.2; Sawyer also wore No. 23; Brandon Christian also wore No. 20; Little also wore No. 1.

Players on roster who did not play: 1 Jim Slazyk, Goal; 1 Chad Black, Goal; 1 John Bradley, Goal; 30 Dana Heinze, Goal; 30 George Bozak, Goal.

CHIEFS IN THE NINETIES

1995-96 Johnstown Chiefs

(Front, from left) Peter Skudra, Jason Weinrich, head coach Nick Fotiu, Rick Boyd, general manager Les Crooks, president Jim Edwards Sr., Don Parsons, Joakim Wiberg. (Middle) Rick Emmett, Martin Woods, Chuck Wiegand, Billy Tibbetts, Rob Mencunas, Brandon Christian, Nick Jones, Sean Perry, Ryan Petz, Alex Savchenkov. (Back) Head trainer Dana Heinze, assistant trainer Rick Hilbrecht, equipment manager Mic Midderhoff, Ted Russell, Jim Krayer, Brent Wilde, Jeff Mead, director of sales Jim Brazill, broadcaster Gregg DeVitto.

1995-96 FINAL EAST COAST HOCKEY LEAGUE STANDINGS

	Games played	Won	Lost	Shootout losses	Points	Goals for	Goals against
North Division							
Toledo Storm	70	48	14	8	104	301	240
Wheeling Thunderbirds	70	42	23	5	89	289	261
Louisville River Frogs	70	39	24	7	85	266	237
Columbus Chill	70	37	28	5	79	285	268
Dayton Bombers	70	35	28	7	77	247	237
Erie Panthers	70	25	40	5	55	227	293
Johnstown Chiefs	70	21	38	11	53	249	322
Huntington Blizzard	70	21	39	10	52	232	309
South Division							
Louisiana Ice Gators	70	43	21	6	92	312	261
Nashville Knights	70	42	22	6	90	368	307
Tallahassee Tiger Sharks	70	42	22	6	90	283	260
Knoxville Cherokees	70	37	29	4	78	323	303
Jacksonville Lizard Kings	70	33	29	8	74	267	288
Birmingham Bulls	70	26	39	5	57	258	360
Mobile Mysticks	70	22	37	11	55	265	325
East Division							
Richmond Renegades	70	46	11	13	105	314	225
Charlotte Checkers	70	45	21	4	94	294	250
South Carolina Stingrays	70	40	22	8	88	284	251
Roanoke Express	70	36	28	6	78	231	260
Hampton Roads Admirals	70	32	25	13	77	278	265
Raleigh Icecaps	70	23	34	13	59	215	266

Johnstown Chiefs
General Manager - Les Crooks
Coach - Nick Fotiu (Note: Les Crooks coached team Dec. 29 vs. Toledo when Fotiu was suspended.)
Player/Assistant Coach - Trevor Jobe
Training Staff - Dana Heinze, Mic Midderhoff, Rick Hilbrecht
Colors - Black, White and Gold

1995-96 Game Results

Preseason Results

Day	Date	Opponent	Score Johnstown	Opponent	Attendance	Record
Fri.	6-Oct	Richmond	6	4	968	

267

Day	Date	Opponent			Attendance	
Sat.	7-Oct	Erie	5	4 (ot)	857	
Sun.	8-Oct	at Erie	1	10		

Regular Season Results

Day	Date	Opponent	Score Johnstown	Opponent	Attendance	Record
Sat.	14-Oct	Wheeling	3	7	3,547	0-1-0
Tues.	17-Oct	Erie	4	2	1,875	1-1-0
Fri.	20-Oct	Columbus	3	4 (sol)	1,936	1-1-1
Sat.	21-Oct	Huntington	1	5	2,534	1-2-1
Fri.	27-Oct	Toledo	4	5 (sol)	2,636	1-2-2
Sat.	28-Oct	Dayton	7	8	2,384	1-3-2
Tues.	31-Oct	at Raleigh	7	5		2-3-2
Wed.	1-Nov	at South Carolina	3	2 (sow)		3-3-2
Sat.	4-Nov	at Charlotte	4	5		3-4-2
Fri.	10-Nov	at Wheeling	6	7 (sol)		3-4-3
Sat.	11-Nov	Dayton	2	4	2,855	3-5-3
Sun.	12-Nov	Toledo	4	5 (sol)	2,134	3-5-4
Thur.	16-Nov	Louisville	3	6	1,964	3-6-4
Fri.	17-Nov	at Erie	2	3 (sol)		3-6-5
Sat.	18-Nov	at Toledo	5	4 (sow)		4-6-5
Wed.	22-Nov	Wheeling	3	5	2,005	4-7-5
Fri.	24-Nov	at Columbus	2	6		4-8-5
Sat.	25-Nov	Columbus	6	5	3,715	5-8-5
Sat.	2-Dec	Dayton	3	5	3,077	5-9-5
Sun.	3-Dec	at Wheeling	6	3		6-9-5
Fri.	8-Dec	at Huntington	7	3		7-9-5
Sat.	9-Dec	at Louisville	1	7		7-10-5
Sun.	10-Dec	at Toledo	2	3 (sol)		7-10-6
Thur.	14-Dec	Erie	4	7	1,885	7-11-6
Fri.	15-Dec	at Toledo	2	5		7-12-6
Sat.	16-Dec	at Dayton	2	5		7-13-6
Sat.	23-Dec	Richmond	4	7	2,607	7-14-6
Tues.	26-Dec	at Huntington	3	5		7-15-6
Wed.	27-Dec	Wheeling	4	5 (sol)	2,707	7-15-7
Fri.	29-Dec	Toledo	7	6	2,603	8-15-7
Sat.	30-Dec	Toledo	1	7	2,730	8-16-7
Wed.	3-Jan	at Louisville	3	6		8-17-7
Thur.	4-Jan	at Knoxville	4	6		8-18-7
Sat.	6-Jan	Huntington	6	2	2,559	9-18-7
Tues.	9-Jan	at Erie	3	4 (sol)		9-18-8
Fri.	12-Jan	Columbus	3	2	1,996	10-18-8
Sat.	13-Jan	at Columbus	2	10		10-19-8
Sun.	14-Jan	at Huntington	3	6		10-20-8
Tues.	16-Jan	at Louisville	3	8		10-21-8
Wed.	17-Jan	at Dayton	3	5		10-22-8
Sat.	20-Jan	Louisville	1	2	2,916	10-23-8
Sun.	21-Jan	Louisville	5	4	2,671	11-23-8
Fri.	26-Jan	at Huntington	2	4		11-24-8
Sat.	27-Jan	at Toledo	3	6		11-25-8
Fri.	2-Feb	at Columbus	2	3		11-26-8
Sat.	3-Feb	Knoxville	2	6	2,662	11-27-8
Sun.	4-Feb	Dayton	1	5	2,199	11-28-8
Wed.	7-Feb	at Dayton	4	7		11-29-8
Fri.	9-Feb	at Erie	6	5 (sow)		12-29-8
Sat.	10-Feb	Raleigh	2	4	2,519	12-30-8
Sun.	11-Feb	Huntington	3	4	1,962	12-31-8
Wed.	14-Feb	at Columbus	5	2		13-31-8
Sat.	17-Feb	Hampton Roads	3	1	2,678	14-31-8
Sun.	18-Feb	Erie	4	2	2,782	15-31-8
Fri.	23-Feb	at Richmond	4	6		15-32-8
Sat.	24-Feb	Roanoke	7	2	3,059	16-32-8
Sun.	25-Feb	Louisville	5	3	2,227	17-32-8
Fri.	1-Mar	Nashville	3	4 (sol)	2,573	17-32-9
Sat.	2-Mar	at Hampton Roads	1	3		17-33-9
Sun.	3-Mar	Huntington	10	2	2,490	18-33-9
Wed.	6-Mar	Tallahassee	1	5	2,509	18-34-9
Fri.	8-Mar	at Louisville	5	2		19-34-9
Sat.	9-Mar	at Dayton	2	3		19-35-9
Sun.	10-Mar	at Wheeling	3	5		19-36-9
Tues.	12-Mar	at Roanoke	1	4		19-37-9

CHIEFS IN THE NINETIES

Fri.	15-Mar	Columbus	5	6 (sol)	2,461	19-37-10
Sat.	16-Mar	Wheeling	4	1	2,771	20-37-10
Fri.	22-Mar	at Wheeling	1	7		20-38-10
Sat.	23-Mar	at Erie	4	5 (sol)		20-38-11
Sun.	24-Mar	Erie	5	4	3,605	21-38-11

Attendance Figures

	Dates	Totals	Average
Preseason Attendance Totals	2	1,825	913
Regular Season Attendance Totals	35	89,833	2567
TOTAL ATTENDANCE	37	91,658	2477

1995-96 Player Statistics

Regular Season Scoring

	Games	G	A	Pts	PIM
31 Don Parsons	66	50	39	89	104
16 Trevor Jobe	36	33	37	70	72
10 Billy Tibbetts	58	37	31	68	300
22 Greg Burke	52	11	31	42	135
17 Jeff Mead	61	15	25	40	31
4 Steve Foster	44	3	30	33	64
21 Chuck Wiegand	43	17	14	31	14
44 Ryan Petz	31	15	13	28	38
23 Jason Weinrich	68	3	22	25	115
15 Brent Wilde	70	10	13	23	86
24 Marquis Mathieu	25	4	17	21	89
19 Jason Courtemanche	60	5	15	20	363
24 Craig Lutes	20	7	11	18	12
7 Rick Boyd	50	3	15	18	253
6 Rick Emmett	24	2	15	17	12
18 Alex Savchenkov	16	6	9	15	42
3 Martin Woods	22	4	8	12	95
5 Yvan Corbin	9	5	6	11	4
8 Sean Perry	45	5	6	11	96
12 Jim Krayer	36	3	7	10	19
4 Ted Russell	18	2	6	8	4
20 Malcolm Cameron	20	2	5	7	25
6 Scott MacDonald	32	0	7	7	38
20 Brandon Christian	37	1	4	5	219
20 Brandon Coates	13	1	3	4	16
35 Peter Skudra (g)	30	0	4	4	14
44 Jason Renard	10	2	1	3	43
14 Rich Rerrie	16	2	1	3	13
12 Gerry Daley	4	1	0	1	2
44 Sergei Olympiev	3	0	1	1	0
21 Rob Mencunas	10	0	1	1	8
35 Aaron Israel (g)	17	0	1	1	8
5 Bill Brewer	1	0	0	0	2
1 Joakim Wiberg (g)	1	0	0	0	0
14 Brad Turcotte	4	0	0	0	0
1 John Bradley (g)	5	0	0	0	0
1 Mike Parson (g)	24	0	0	0	2
5 Nick Jones	29	0	0	0	91
Bench					52
TOTALS	70	249	398	647	2,481

Regular Season Goaltending

	G	Min	GA	ENG	SO	GAA	W	L	SOL	Saves	Save%
35 Peter Skudra	30	1,657	98	2	0	3.55	12	11	4	964	0.908
1 Joakim Wiberg	1	60	4	0	0	4.00	0	0	0	35	0.897
1 John Bradley	5	258	19	0	0	4.40	1	3	0	107	0.849
35 Aaron Israel	17	979	81	1	0	4.96	5	7	5	541	0.870
1 Mike Parson	24	1,226	103	3	0	5.04	3	17	2	683	0.869
Shootout Goals			11								
TOTALS	70	4,200	316	6	0	4.60	21	38	11	2,330	0.879

Burke also wore No. 7; Coates also wore No. 44.

Players on roster who did not play: 30 George Bozak, Goal.

269

1996-97 Johnstown Chiefs

(Front, from left) Klemen Mohoric, Ryan Petz, Martin Woods, assistant coach Scott Allen, head coach Nick Fotiu, Rick Boyd, president Jim Edwards Sr., general manager Toby O'Brien, Ryan Savoia, Alex Chunchukov, Beau Reidel. (Middle) Jaynen Rissling, Lukas Smital, Martin Masa, Denis Lamoureux, Kam White, Brandon Christian, Greg Callahan, Kelly Leroux, Carl Fleury, Trevor Converse. (Back) Head trainer Dana Heinze, athletic trainer Chris Stewart, equipment manager Mic Midderhoff, Dan Harrison, Jim Krayer, Ted Russell, Jon Mahoney, sales Bill Stuart, sales Jim Brazill, broadcaster Gregg DeVitto, secretary Helen Buchan.

1996-97 FINAL EAST COAST HOCKEY LEAGUE STANDINGS

	Games played	Won	Lost	Shootout losses	Points	Goals for	Goals against
North Division							
Columbus Chill	70	44	21	5	93	303	257
Peoria Rivermen	70	43	21	6	92	308	219
Dayton Bombers	70	36	26	8	80	253	258
Wheeling Nailers	70	36	29	5	77	298	291
Toledo Storm	70	32	28	10	74	258	248
Huntington Blizzard	70	33	33	4	70	273	296
Louisville River Frogs	70	29	31	10	68	234	290
Johnstown Chiefs	70	24	39	7	55	253	354
South Division							
Tallahassee Tiger Sharks	70	39	23	8	86	263	236
Birmingham Bulls	70	36	25	9	81	291	296
Louisiana Ice Gators	70	38	28	4	80	292	244
Mobile Mysticks	70	34	25	11	79	257	263
Mississippi Sea Wolves	70	34	26	10	78	241	245
Pensacola Ice Pilots	70	36	31	3	75	275	275
Baton Rouge Kingfish	70	31	33	6	68	222	238
Jacksonville Lizard Kings	70	21	37	12	54	220	299
East Division							
South Carolina Stingrays	70	45	15	10	100	345	253
Hampton Roads Admirals	70	46	19	5	97	286	223
Richmond Renegades	70	41	25	4	86	252	235
Roanoke Express	70	38	26	6	82	262	250
Charlotte Checkers	70	35	28	7	77	271	267
Raleigh Icecaps	70	30	33	7	67	256	293
Knoxville Cherokees	70	24	43	3	51	260	343

Johnstown Chiefs
General Manager - Toby O'Brien
Coach - Nick Fotiu
Assistant Coach - Scott Allen
Goaltender Coach - Fred Quistgard
Training Staff - Dana Heinze, Chris Stewart, Mic Midderhoff
Locker Room Attendants - John Brezovic, Sean McTighe, Jesse Shoff
Colors - Black, White and Gold
Note: Brad Park worked as special advisor during season – coached five games from Dec. 15-21 when Fotiu was suspended

CHIEFS IN THE NINETIES

1996-97 Game Results

Preseason Results

Day	Date	Opponent	Johnstown	Opponent	Attendance	Record
Thur.	10-Oct	at Wheeling	4	3		
Sat.	12-Oct	Raleigh	5	1	900	
Sun.	13-Oct	Richmond	2	5	710	

Regular Season Results

Day	Date	Opponent	Johnstown	Opponent	Attendance	Record
Thur.	17-Oct	Peoria	2	7	2,850	0-1-0
Fri.	25-Oct	at Wheeling	2	5		0-2-0
Sat.	26-Oct	Wheeling	5	4	2,932	1-2-0
Fri.	1-Nov	at Columbus	2	5		1-3-0
Sat.	2-Nov	Baton Rouge	2	6	2,821	1-4-0
Wed.	6-Nov	at Peoria	2	3		1-5-0
Fri.	8-Nov	at Toledo	5	4 (sow)		2-5-0
Sun.	10-Nov	at Richmond	2	5		2-6-0
Wed.	13-Nov	Toledo	4	2	2,250	3-6-0
Fri.	15-Nov	at Huntington	1	4		3-7-0
Sat.	16-Nov	at Knoxville	3	6		3-8-0
Sun.	17-Nov	at Raleigh	2	5		3-9-0
Wed.	20-Nov	at Columbus	2	3 (sol)		3-9-1
Fri.	22-Nov	at Huntington	4	6		3-10-1
Sat.	23-Nov	Columbus	4	1	4,138	4-10-1
Wed.	27-Nov	Columbus	3	9	2,290	4-11-1
Fri.	29-Nov	at Dayton	0	3		4-12-1
Sat.	30-Nov	Toledo	2	1	3,369	5-12-1
Fri.	6-Dec	Huntington	5	6	2,049	5-13-1
Sat.	7-Dec	Wheeling	6	5 (sow)	2,629	6-13-1
Fri.	13-Dec	at Wheeling	3	9		6-14-1
Sat.	14-Dec	Dayton	6	4	3,265	7-14-1
Sun.	15-Dec	at Toledo	6	5 (sow)		8-14-1
Tues.	17-Dec	at Roanoke	3	6		8-15-1
Thur.	19-Dec	at Hampton Roads	3	7		8-16-1
Fri.	20-Dec	at South Carolina	1	9		8-17-1
Sat.	21-Dec	at Charlotte	1	9		8-18-1
Fri.	27-Dec	Wheeling	2	6	3,430	8-19-1
Sat.	28-Dec	Columbus	3	7	2,955	8-20-1
Mon.	30-Dec	at Dayton	3	4		8-21-1
Tues.	31-Dec	Peoria	5	3	3,554	9-21-1
Fri.	3-Jan	at Louisville	3	4 (sol)		9-21-2
Sat.	4-Jan	at Louisville	4	5		9-22-2
Fri.	10-Jan	Huntington	5	4	2,098	10-22-2
Sat.	11-Jan	Columbus	3	5	2,912	10-23-2
Fri.	17-Jan	at Richmond	Postponed due to electrical problems - rescheduled for March 4			
Sat.	18-Jan	Jacksonville	3	4 (sol)	2,968	10-23-3
Fri.	24-Jan	Louisville	3	4	2,048	10-24-3
Sat.	25-Jan	Louisville	4	5	3,375	10-25-3
Tues.	28-Jan	Dayton	7	3	1,681	11-25-3
Fri.	31-Jan	at Huntington	5	6 (sol)		11-25-4
Sat.	1-Feb	Mobile	8	3	3,168	12-25-4
Sun.	2-Feb	Wheeling	6	5 (sow)	3,088	13-25-4
Sat.	8-Feb	Louisville	1	6	2,942	13-26-4
Sun.	9-Feb	Louisville	4	3 (sow)	2,925	14-26-4
Tues.	11-Feb	at Columbus	1	5		14-27-4
Wed.	12-Feb	at Dayton	7	8		14-28-4
Sat.	15-Feb	Huntington	5	4	2,890	15-28-4
Sun.	16-Feb	Huntington	6	5 (sow)	2,760	16-28-4
Wed.	19-Feb	at Toledo	2	3		16-29-4
Sat.	22-Feb	Dayton	4	5 (sol)	3,154	16-29-5
Sun.	23-Feb	Pensacola	7	5	3,408	17-29-5
Thur.	27-Feb	at Peoria	3	8		17-30-5
Fri.	28-Feb	Toledo	5	4 (sow)	2,096	18-30-5
Sat.	1-Mar	Birmingham	1	4	2,933	18-31-5
Tues.	4-Mar	at Richmond	3	4 (sol)		18-31-6
Wed.	5-Mar	Richmond	5	3	2,435	19-31-6
Fri.	7-Mar	Tallahassee	7	3	2,348	20-31-6
Sat.	8-Mar	Toledo	1	5	3,184	20-32-6
Tues.	11-Mar	at Peoria	0	6		20-33-6
Fri.	14-Mar	Peoria	3	9	2,564	20-34-6
Sat.	15-Mar	Peoria	2	7	3,178	20-35-6

Day	Date	Opponent	GF	GA	Att	Record
Sun.	16-Mar	at Wheeling	5	10		20-36-6
Tues.	18-Mar	at Louisville	4	3 (sow)		21-36-6
Fri.	21-Mar	at Huntington	3	4		21-37-6
Sat.	22-Mar	at Columbus	6	5 (sow)		22-37-6
Sun.	23-Mar	at Toledo	5	4		23-37-6
Wed.	26-Mar	at Peoria	5	10		23-38-6
Fri.	28-Mar	at Dayton	3	4		23-39-6
Sat.	29-Mar	Dayton	4	5 (sol)	4,061	23-39-7
Sun.	30-Mar	at Wheeling	6	5		24-39-7

Attendance Figures

	Dates	Totals	Average
Preseason Attendance Totals	2	1,610	805
Season Attendance Totals	35	100,748	2,879
TOTAL ATTENDANCE	37	102,358	2,766

1996-97 Player Statistics

Regular Season Scoring

	Games	G	A	Pts	PIM
12 Alex Chunchukov	70	34	58	92	75
8 Ryan Savoia	60	35	44	79	100
18 Martin Masa	59	36	32	68	114
10 Carl Fleury	68	30	37	67	102
44 Ryan Petz	69	25	27	52	90
4 Martin Woods	67	16	34	50	233
21 Ted Russell	64	9	41	50	92
24 Lukas Smital	68	19	29	48	62
27 Jim Krayer	56	10	13	23	14
25 Dan Harrison	26	3	20	23	91
16 Denis Lamoureux	29	8	9	17	4
19 Trevor Converse	42	6	8	14	160
22 Greg Callahan	47	2	10	12	156
15 Jaynen Rissling	20	2	7	9	23
7 Rick Boyd	23	3	4	7	141
17 Jon Mahoney	15	1	6	7	39
23 Jeramie Heistad	16	1	5	6	42
8 Sean Perry	31	3	2	5	58
2 Kam White	47	0	5	5	261
17 Dan Reimann	33	1	3	4	34
20 Brandon Christian	49	1	3	4	140
19 Brian Scott	7	2	1	3	4
35 Beau Reidel (g)	27	0	3	3	2
3 Chad Dameworth	4	2	0	2	4
23 Evan Anderson	12	2	0	2	6
3 Alexei Krivchenkov	5	1	1	2	24
16 Matt McElwee	17	1	1	2	32
31 Klemen Mohoric (g)	15	0	1	1	0
35 Olie Sundstrom (g)	24	0	1	1	43
6 Kelly Leroux	27	0	1	1	57
14 Scott Allen	1	0	0	0	0
3 James Mooney	1	0	0	0	0
5 Jon Pirrong	1	0	0	0	0
23 Rok Rojsek	1	0	0	0	0
14 Peter Cermak	3	0	0	0	0
22 Chad Michalchuk	4	0	0	0	30
35 Peter Skudra (g)	4	0	0	0	2
5 Jason Richard	6	0	0	0	6
31 Marc Seigel (g)	10	0	0	0	2
Bench					44
TOTALS	70	253	406	659	2,287

Regular Season Goaltending

	G	Min	GA	ENG	SO	GAA	W	L	SOL	Saves	Save%
35 Peter Skudra	4	200	11	0	0	3.30	2	1	1	111	0.910
35 Beau Reidel	27	1,452	117	1	0	4.83	9	12	4	714	0.859
35 Olie Sundstrom	24	1,349	110	4	0	4.89	8	15	1	658	0.857
31 Klemen Mohoric	15	736	63	0	0	5.13	5	5	1	345	0.846
31 Marc Seigel	10	440	39	2	0	5.31	0	6	0	265	0.872
Shootout Goals			7								
TOTALS	70	4,200	347	7	0	5.06	24	39	7	2,093	0.855

Players on roster who did not play: 31 Steve Wachter, Goal; 31 Scott Galt, Goal.

CHIEFS IN THE NINETIES

1997-98 Johnstown Chiefs

(Front, from left) Dan Dennis, Dan Harrison, Carl Fleury, head coach Scott Allen, Harold Hersh, chairman Jim Edwards Sr., general manager Toby O'Brien, Iouri (Yuri) Krivokhija, Jon Sorg, Steve Plouffe. (Middle) Dean Campanale, Chris Fawcett, Fredrik Svensson, Kelly Leroux, Tim O'Brien, Chad Richard, Greg Callahan, Mike Rusk, Lukas Smital, Brian Callahan, Francois Archambault, Dave Tremblay. (Back) Head trainer Dana Heinze, athletic trainer Chris Stewart, assistant trainer Sean McTighe, assistant equipment manager Sean Raymond, head equipment manager Mic Midderhoff, Reg Cardinal, Scott Stephens, Ian Smith, sales Jim Brazill, sales Bill Stuart, media John Patterson, administrative assistant Tom Gramling, broadcaster Bob McElligott, secretary Helen Buchan.

1997-98 FINAL EAST COAST HOCKEY LEAGUE STANDINGS

	Games played	Won	Lost	Shootout losses	Points	Goals for	Goals against
Northeast Division							
Roanoke Express	70	42	21	7	91	235	208
Wheeling Nailers	70	37	24	9	83	255	255
Chesapeake Icebreakers	70	34	28	8	76	252	239
Hampton Roads Admirals	70	32	28	10	74	222	225
Richmond Renegades	70	30	33	7	67	218	277
Johnstown Chiefs	70	23	41	6	52	219	297
Northwest Division							
Peoria Rivermen	70	44	19	7	95	296	213
Toledo Storm	70	41	21	8	90	251	210
Dayton Bombers	70	36	26	8	80	255	256
Huntington Blizzard	70	34	29	7	75	230	259
Columbus Chill	70	33	30	7	73	221	220
Louisville River Frogs	70	32	31	7	71	228	257
Southeast Division							
South Carolina Stingrays	70	41	23	6	88	246	218
Charlotte Checkers	70	35	24	11	81	251	237
Pee Dee Pride	70	34	25	11	79	214	215
Jacksonville Lizard Kings	70	35	29	6	76	243	239
Raleigh Icecaps	70	32	33	5	69	236	254
Tallahassee Tiger Sharks	70	24	44	2	50	210	320
Southwest Division							
Louisiana Ice Gators	70	43	17	10	96	298	232
Birmingham Bulls	70	39	23	8	86	293	257
Pensacola Ice Pilots	70	36	24	10	82	276	262
New Orleans Brass	70	36	24	10	82	278	263
Mobile Mysticks	70	35	27	8	78	236	233
Mississippi Sea Wolves	70	34	27	9	77	225	224
Baton Rouge Kingfish	70	33	27	10	76	220	238

Johnstown Chiefs
General Manager - Toby O'Brien
Coach - Nick Fotiu (until Dec. 26 – 6-20-2); Scott Allen (from Dec. 26 – 17-21-4)
Assistant Coach - Scott Allen – until Dec. 26; Galen Head.
Training Staff - Dana Heinze, Chris Stewart, Mic Midderhoff
Locker Room Attendants - Sean Raymond, John Brezovic, Sean McTighe, Jesse Shoff
Colors - Black, White and Gold
Team wore third jerseys that were red, white, black and gold

1997-98 Game Results

Preseason Results

Day	Date	Opponent	Johnstown	Opponent	Attendance	Record
Thur.	9-Oct	Chesapeake	1	7	580	
Sat.	11-Oct	Wheeling	1	2	724	
Sun.	12-Oct	Wheeling	6	2		

Regular Season Results

Day	Date	Opponent	Johnstown	Opponent	Attendance	Record
Thur.	16-Oct	Toledo	4	2	2,468	1-0-0
Sat.	18-Oct	Wheeling	2	7	2,631	1-1-0
Thur.	23-Oct	at Richmond	3	4		1-2-0
Fri.	24-Oct	at Hampton Roads	3	4		1-3-0
Sat.	25-Oct	Hampton Roads	5	4 (sow)	2,709	2-3-0
Fri.	31-Oct	at Columbus	0	2		2-4-0
Sat.	1-Nov	Chesapeake	5	4 (sow)	2,724	3-4-0
Sun.	2-Nov	Louisville	2	3	2,238	3-5-0
Fri.	7-Nov	at Huntington	3	7		3-6-0
Sat.	8-Nov	at Toledo	3	4		3-7-0
Tues.	11-Nov	Peoria	1	2 (sol)	2,265	3-7-1
Wed.	12-Nov	at Columbus	4	3 (sow)		4-7-1
Sat.	15-Nov	at Roanoke	2	3		4-8-1
Sun.	16-Nov	at Dayton	1	5		4-9-1
Wed.	19-Nov	at Hampton Roads	2	5		4-10-1
Fri.	21-Nov	at Dayton	4	6		4-11-1
Sat.	22-Nov	Wheeling	3	4	3,778	4-12-1
Sun.	23-Nov	at Toledo	2	5		4-13-1
Fri.	28-Nov	Pee Dee	5	2	4,107	5-13-1
Sat.	29-Nov	at Roanoke	2	3 (sol)		5-13-2
Sat.	6-Dec	Huntington	3	6	2,721	5-14-2
Wed.	10-Dec	at Hampton Roads	2	8		5-15-2
Fri.	12-Dec	at Dayton	5	4 (sow)		6-15-2
Sat.	13-Dec	at Peoria	1	7		6-16-2
Sun.	14-Dec	at Peoria	2	5		6-17-2
Wed.	17-Dec	at Louisville	2	4		6-18-2
Fri.	19-Dec	at Columbus	5	7		6-19-2
Sat.	20-Dec	Hampton Roads	4	7	2,373	6-20-2
Fri.	26-Dec	Toledo	1	0	2,922	7-20-2
Sat.	27-Dec	at Chesapeake	3	6		7-21-2
Sun.	28-Dec	at Wheeling	5	6 (sol)		7-21-3
Wed.	31-Dec	Peoria	6	3	2,970	8-21-3
Fri.	2-Jan	Richmond	4	07	2,709	8-22-3
Sat.	3-Jan	Columbus	4	2	2,583	9-22-3
Fri.	9-Jan	at Hampton Roads	4	3 (sow)		10-22-3
Sat.	10-Jan	Columbus	3	2	3,084	11-22-3
Sun.	11-Jan	at Wheeling	4	3		12-22-3
Fri.	16-Jan	at Richmond	6	2		13-22-3
Sat.	17-Jan	at Chesapeake	3	1		14-22-3
Sun.	18-Jan	Hampton Roads	1	3	3,316	14-23-3
Thur.	22-Jan	at Peoria	5	6		14-24-3
Fri.	23-Jan	at Columbus	3	4		14-25-3
Sat.	24-Jan	Richmond	8	2	3,846	15-25-3
Sat.	31-Jan	at Wheeling	4	3		16-25-3
Sun.	1-Feb	Chesapeake	1	4	3,716	16-26-3
Tues.	3-Feb	Louisville	3	4	2,018	16-27-3
Thur.	5-Feb	at Chesapeake	2	7		16-28-3
Fri.	6-Feb	at Richmond	4	1		17-28-3
Sat.	7-Feb	Hampton Roads	3	2	3,028	18-28-3
Fri.	13-Feb	Peoria	4	7	3,334	18-29-3
Sat.	14-Feb	Wheeling	4	3 (sow)	2,955	19-29-3
Thur.	19-Feb	at Chesapeake	1	8		19-30-3
Sat.	21-Feb	Chesapeake	1	6	2,964	19-31-3
Sun.	22-Feb	Roanoke	2	4	2,288	19-32-3
Tues.	24-Feb	at Roanoke	2	5		19-33-3
Sat.	28-Feb	Toledo	4	5 (sol)	2,808	19-33-4
Sun.	1-Mar	Dayton	3	4 (sol)	2,009	19-33-5
Fri.	6-Mar	Richmond	2	5	2,189	19-34-5
Sat.	7-Mar	Dayton	7	3	2,008	20-34-5
Sun.	8-Mar	at Roanoke	2	3		20-34-6
Wed.	11-Mar	Columbus	1	4	1,679	20-35-6

CHIEFS IN THE NINETIES

Sat.	14-Mar	Dayton	3	5	2,375	20-36-6
Sun.	15-Mar	Roanoke	4	6	2,310	20-37-6
Tues.	17-Mar	Louisville	8	7	1,829	21-37-6
Thur.	19-Mar	at Louisville	1	4		21-38-6
Sat.	21-Mar	at Richmond	5	2		22-38-6
Sun.	22-Feb	Richmond	1	5	2,685	22-39-6
Fri.	27-Mar	at Wheeling	0	6		22-40-6
Sat.	28-Mar	Roanoke	1	4	2,404	22-41-6
Sun.	29-Mar	Wheeling	6	3	2,661	23-41-6

Attendance Figures

	Dates	Totals	Average
Preseason Attendance Totals	2	1,304	652
Regular Season Attendance Totals	35	94,704	2,706
TOTAL ATTENDANCE	37	96,008	2,595

1997-98 Player Statistics

Regular Season Scoring

	Games	G	A	Pts	PIM
24 Lukas Smital	62	39	26	65	95
18 Martin Masa	59	23	42	65	183
10 Carl Fleury	46	21	30	51	89
44 Harold Hersh	49	20	23	43	55
2 Ian Smith	51	10	33	43	47
27 Scott Stephens	66	13	18	31	50
25 Dan Harrison	66	7	23	30	153
12 Francois Archambault	49	14	14	28	51
15 Reg Cardinal	49	13	12	25	55
14 Brian Callahan	49	8	13	21	91
3 Iouri (Yuri) Krivokhija	28	4	17	21	34
22 Greg Callahan	63	4	16	20	214
5 Jon Sorg	70	6	10	16	119
23 Marcus Draxler	40	8	7	15	56
16 Dave Tremblay	19	7	8	15	2
6 Kelly Leroux	62	5	5	10	160
13 Ivo Jan	20	3	6	9	23
19 Eric Hallman	24	0	9	9	23
4 Mike Rusk	28	2	5	7	31
55 Chad Richard	10	0	7	7	77
8 Ryan Savoia	6	1	5	6	0
3 Mark Yannetti	21	1	5	6	20
35 Steve Plouffe (g)	44	0	6	6	4
20 Brett Bruininks	8	3	2	5	35
4 Martin Woods	15	1	3	4	54
23 Chris Fawcett	7	3	0	3	0
17 Greg Foulidis	9	1	2	3	8
8 Brian Scott	12	1	1	2	2
55 Garrett Burnett	34	1	1	2	331
17 Dean Campanale	9	0	2	2	2
19 Fredrik Svensson	15	0	1	1	2
31 Dan Dennis (g)	36	0	1	1	0
26 Jerry Petrucci	1	0	0	0	0
31 Marc Seigel (g)	1	0	0	0	0
16 Chris Bowen	2	0	0	0	0
17 Jeff Frankel	2	0	0	0	2
12 Quinten Van Horlick	2	0	0	0	14
16 Denis Lamoureux	5	0	0	0	0
21 Sergei Olympiev	6	0	0	0	6
20 Tim O'Brien	9	0	0	0	14
Bench					16
TOTALS	70	219	353	572	2,118

Regular Season Goaltending

	G	Min	GA	ENG	SO	GAA	W	L	SOL	Saves	Save%
35 Steve Plouffe	44	2,355	153	5	1	3.90	11	23	4	1,229	0.889
31 Dan Dennis	36	1,765	122	4	0	4.15	12	17	2	873	0.877
31 Marc Seigel	1	60	7	0	0	7.00	0	1	0	29	0.806
Shootout Goals			6								
TOTALS		4,200	288	9	1	4.24	23	41	6	2,131	0.878

Players on roster who did not play: 1 Mike Wincer, Goal; 1 Jim Mock, Goal; 30 Dana Heinze, Goal.

1998-99 Johnstown Chiefs

(Front, from left) Matt Eisler, Aaron Cain, assistant coach Galen Head, head coach Scott Allen, Shawn Frappier, president Jim Edwards Sr., general manager Toby O'Brien, Martin Masa, Rob Gropp. (Middle) Jeremy Thompson, Jakub Ficenec, Steve Duke, Matt Eldred, David Ficenec, Joel Irving, Jody Shelley, Casey Kesselring, Bryan McKinney, Brad Englehart, E.J. Bradley. (Back) Head trainer Dana Heinze, medical trainer Chris Stewart, assistant trainer Holly Hill, equipment manager Mic Midderhoff, Kent Simpson, Pavel Nestak, Dmitri Tarabrin, Ian Smith, E.J. Bradley, administrative assistant Tom Gramling, media John Patterson, assistant general manager Jim Brazill, sales Tom Menna, broadcaster Bob McElligott.

1998-99 FINAL EAST COAST HOCKEY LEAGUE STANDINGS

	Games played	Won	Lost	Shootout losses	Points	Goals for	Goals against
Northeast Division							
Roanoke Express	70	38	22	10	86	224	201
Hampton Roads Admirals	70	38	24	8	84	215	213
Richmond Renegades	70	40	27	3	83	239	196
Chesapeake Icebreakers	70	34	25	11	79	229	206
Johnstown Chiefs	70	27	34	9	63	218	265
Northwest Division							
Columbus Chill	70	39	24	7	85	257	242
Peoria Rivermen	70	39	25	6	84	243	230
Toledo Storm	70	39	26	5	83	256	246
Dayton Bombers	70	34	27	9	77	239	241
Huntington Blizzard	70	31	33	6	68	221	253
Wheeling Nailers	70	27	37	6	60	206	249
Southeast Division							
Pee Dee Pride	70	51	15	4	106	289	191
Florida Everblades	70	45	20	5	95	253	180
South Carolina Stingrays	70	40	20	10	90	235	216
Augusta Lynx	70	38	27	5	81	235	233
Jacksonville Lizard Kings	70	35	33	2	72	235	255
Charlotte Checkers	70	29	30	11	69	221	262
Miami Matadors	70	28	32	10	66	208	266
Greenville Grrrowl	70	26	33	11	63	208	241
Southwest Division							
Louisiana Ice Gators	70	46	18	6	98	297	205
Mississippi Sea Wolves	70	41	22	7	89	251	215
Birmingham Bulls	70	37	29	4	78	251	267
New Orleans Brass	70	30	27	13	73	244	261
Mobile Mysticks	70	31	31	8	70	231	259
Baton Rouge Kingfish	70	30	30	10	70	222	228
Tallahassee Tiger Sharks	70	27	34	9	63	212	250
Pensacola Ice Pilots	70	25	41	4	54	199	267

Johnstown Chiefs
General Manager - Toby O'Brien
Coach - Scott Allen
Assistant Coach - Galen Head
Scout - Dennis Miller
Training Staff - Dana Heinze, Chris Stewart, Mic Midderhoff, Holly Hill, Breanne Godfrey
Locker Room Attendants - Sean McTighe, Jesse Shoff

CHIEFS IN THE NINETIES

Colors - Black, White and Gold
Wore white home Charlestown Chiefs jerseys Dec. 31, 1998
* Note: Galen Head and Dennis Miller coached team during exhibition games while Scott Allen watched from press box

1998-99 Game Results

Preseason Results

Day	Date	Opponent	Johnstown	Opponent	Attendance	Record
Thur.	8-Oct	Wheeling	6	5	543	
Fri.	9-Oct	at Wheeling	4	5		
Sat.	10-Oct	at Columbus	5	0		

Regular Season Results

Day	Date	Opponent	Johnstown	Opponent	Attendance	Record
Thur.	15-Oct	Chesapeake	0	4	2,344	0-1-0
Sat.	17-Oct	Richmond	6	2	2,214	1-1-0
Sun.	18-Oct	at Richmond	5	3		2-1-0
Sat.	24-Oct	Hampton Roads	1	4	2,416	2-2-0
Fri.	30-Oct	at Hampton Roads	4	9		2-3-0
Sat.	31-Oct	Dayton	2	4	2,112	2-4-0
Fri.	6-Nov	at Chesapeake	3	5		2-5-0
Sat.	7-Nov	at Roanoke	3	4 (sol)		2-5-1
Wed.	11-Nov	Roanoke	2	3 (sol)	2,200	2-5-2
Sat.	14-Nov	Toledo	4	3	2,790	3-5-2
Fri.	20-Nov	Roanoke	6	4	2,838	4-5-2
Sat.	21-Nov	at Dayton	2	3		4-6-2
Thur.	26-Nov	at Wheeling	3	0		5-6-2
Fri.	27-Nov	Chesapeake	4	5 (sol)	3,419	5-6-3
Sat.	28-Nov	Richmond	3	2	2,752	6-6-3
Sat.	5-Dec	Columbus	7	0	2,359	7-6-3
Fri.	11-Dec	at Columbus	2	5		7-7-3
Sat.	12-Dec	at Huntington	4	3		8-7-3
Sun.	13-Dec	at Wheeling	3	5		8-8-3
Fri.	18-Dec	at Columbus	1	6		8-9-3
Sat.	19-Dec	Chesapeake	1	4	2,068	8-10-3
Sun.	20-Dec	at Richmond	3	4 (sol)		8-10-4
Sat.	26-Dec	Wheeling	5	6	2,566	8-11-4
Sun.	27-Dec	at Wheeling	1	4		8-12-4
Tues.	29-Dec	Hampton Roads	2	5	2,095	8-13-4
Wed.	30-Dec	at Chesapeake	5	4 (sow)		9-13-4
Thur.	31-Dec	Chesapeake	3	0	4,063	10-13-4
Sat.	2-Jan	at Toledo	4	3 (sow)		11-13-4
Sun.	3-Jan	at Huntington	Postponed due to snow - rescheduled for March 19			
Sat.	9-Jan	Columbus	3	5	2,120	11-14-4
Fri.	15-Jan	at Chesapeake	1	3		11-15-4
Mon.	18-Jan	at Huntington	6	5		12-15-4
Wed.	20-Jan	at Richmond	0	4		12-16-4
Fri.	22-Jan	at Columbus	3	5		12-17-4
Sat.	23-Jan	Hampton Roads	5	2	2,912	13-17-4
Sun.	24-Jan	Peoria	6	2	2,237	14-17-4
Tues.	26-Jan	at Roanoke	3	7		14-18-4
Fri.	29-Jan	at Chesapeake	6	7 (sol)		14-18-5
Sat.	30-Jan	Roanoke	2	3 (sol)	2,791	14-18-6
Wed.	3-Feb	Wheeling	4	3 (sow)	1,759	15-18-6
Fri.	5-Feb	at Roanoke	6	5 (sow)		16-18-6
Sat.	6-Feb	Wheeling	3	6	2,453	16-19-6
Sun.	7-Feb	Chesapeake	1	4	2,103	16-20-6
Fri.	12-Feb	at Hampton Roads	2	0		17-20-6
Sat.	13-Feb	Huntington	1	3	2,099	17-21-6
Sun.	14-Feb	Richmond	0	3	2,016	17-22-6
Wed.	17-Feb	at Hampton Roads	2	4		17-23-6
Fri.	19-Feb	at Wheeling	0	6		17-24-6
Sat.	20-Feb	Wheeling	3	5	2,582	17-25-6
Sun.	21-Feb	Huntington	5	4	2,640	18-25-6
Tues.	23-Feb	at Roanoke	1	4		18-26-6
Fri.	26-Feb	Dayton	6	5 (sow)	2,060	19-26-6
Sat.	27-Feb	Toledo	3	4 (sol)	2,473	19-26-7
Wed.	3-Mar	Hampton Roads	7	4	1,589	20-26-7
Fri.	5-Mar	Roanoke	3	2 (sow)	2,054	21-26-7
Sat.	6-Mar	Columbus	3	4 (sol)	2,293	21-26-8
Sun.	7-Mar	at Hampton Roads	3	4		21-27-8

Day	Date	Opponent	GF	GA	Att	Record
Thur.	11-Mar	at Wheeling	1	3		21-28-8
Fri.	12-Mar	Huntington	3	2 (sow)	2,110	22-28-8
Sat.	13-Mar	Peoria	4	1	2,633	23-28-8
Wed.	17-Mar	Richmond	2	4	1,680	23-29-8
Fri.	19-Mar	at Huntington	6	4		24-29-8
Sat.	20-Mar	at Dayton	3	6		24-30-8
Sun.	21-Mar	Wheeling	5	4	2,611	25-30-8
Wed.	24-Mar	at Chesapeake	0	3		25-31-8
Fri.	26-Mar	at Peoria	4	5		25-32-8
Sat.	27-Mar	at Peoria	4	5 (sol)		25-32-9
Sun.	28-Mar	at Toledo	2	1		26-32-9
Fri.	2-Apr	at Richmond	1	5		26-33-9
Sat.	3-Apr	at Roanoke	1	2		26-34-9
Sun.	4-Apr	Roanoke	5	3	2,433	27-34-9

Attendance Figures

	Dates	Totals	Average
Preseason Attendance Totals	1	543	543
Regular Season Attendance Totals	35	83,884	2,397
TOTAL ATTENDANCE	36	84,427	2,345

1998-99 Player Statistics

Regular Season Scoring

	Games	G	A	Pts	PIM
28 Martin Mesa	64	27	30	57	83
26 Joel Irving	65	26	20	46	112
19 Casey Kesselring	46	18	25	43	21
23 Jakub Ficenec	59	18	23	41	54
12 E.J. Bradley	66	13	22	35	36
24 Lukas Smital	34	12	21	33	38
2 Ian Smith	60	4	28	32	72
15 Jody Shelley	52	12	17	29	325
16 Brad Englehart	50	15	13	28	63
20 Kent Simpson	55	6	21	27	56
5 Steve Duke	54	4	23	27	58
44 Aaron Cain	68	14	12	26	100
27 Shawn Frappier	58	4	21	25	48
10 Eric Normandin	31	9	11	20	30
4 Derrick Walser	24	8	12	20	29
3 Jon Sorg	38	4	13	17	99
6 Mike Vellinga	45	1	14	15	22
22 Carl Fleury	22	7	7	14	31
17 Dmitri Tarabrin	31	7	6	13	6
21 Jeremy Thompson	54	3	6	9	224
8 Bryan McKinney	29	1	7	8	28
25 Etienne Drapeau	14	2	4	6	4
10 Matt Eldred	22	1	4	5	68
14 John Tripp	7	2	0	2	12
1 Rob Gropp (g)	7	0	2	2	2
55 Igor Karpenko (g)	7	0	2	2	0
31 Matt Eisler (g)	43	0	2	2	10
55 Mikhail Strelkov	8	0	1	1	67
7 David Ficenec	21	0	1	1	2
1 Mike Beale (g)	1	0	0	0	0
18 Eric Hamlet	1	0	0	0	2
25 Kevin Hill	1	0	0	0	0
35 Pavel Nestak (g)	19	0	0	0	10
Bench					22
TOTALS	70	218	368	586	1,734

Regular Season Goaltending

	G	Min	GA	ENG	SO	GAA	W	L	SOL	Saves	Save%
1 Mike Beale	1	8	0	0	0	0.00	0	0	0	8	1.000
55 Igor Karpenko	7	369	20	1	0	3.25	4	3	0	174	0.897
31 Matt Eisler	43	2,457	145	2	2	3.54	14	20	7	1,192	0.892
35 Pavel Nestak	19	1,061	65	2	2	3.68	7	9	2	456	0.875
1 Rob Gropp	7	303	21	0	0	4.15	2	2	0	140	0.870
Shootout Goals			9								
TOTALS	70	4,200	260	5	4	3.79	27	34	9	1,970	0.881

Players on roster who did not play: 1 Benoit Thibert, Goal; 1 Mike Sherman, Goal.

CHIEFS IN THE NINETIES

1999-2000 Johnstown Chiefs

(Front, from left) Frederic Deschenes, Joel Irving, Carl Fleury, assistant general manager Jim Brazill, head coach Scott Allen, Shawn Frappier, president Jim Edwards Sr., general manager Toby O'Brien, treasurer Dennis Vickroy, Andrew Dale, Brent Bilodeau, Tyrone Garner. (Middle) Ryan Chaytors, E.J. Bradley, Bryan McKinney, Kevin Kellett, Mike Vellinga, Ryan Tocher, Kris Porter, Jason Spence, Brett Gibson, Chuck Mindel, Andrew Clark, Mikko Sivonen. (Back) Locker room attendant Cory Mesteller, locker room attendant Chuck Lamberson, medical trainer Chris Stewart, locker room attendant Doug Mesteller, equipment manager Mic Midderhoff, Dmitri Tarabrin, Mike Thompson, public relations director Kevin McGeehan, broadcaster Keith Gerhart, administrative assistant Tom Gramling, sales Tom Menna, bookkeeper Marge Moehler, secretary Helen Buchan.

1999-2000 FINAL EAST COAST HOCKEY LEAGUE STANDINGS

	Games played	Won	Lost	Shootout losses	Points	Goals for	Goals against
Northeast Division							
Roanoke Express	70	44	20	6	94	221	181
Richmond Renegades	70	44	21	5	93	258	205
Hampton Roads Admirals	70	44	22	4	92	241	198
Trenton Titans	70	37	29	4	78	233	199
Charlotte Checkers	70	25	38	7	57	186	254
Greensboro Generals	70	20	43	7	47	229	337
Northwest Division							
Peoria Rivermen	70	45	20	5	95	273	216
Huntington Blizzard	70	35	25	10	80	230	238
Johnstown Chiefs	70	33	28	9	75	235	234
Dayton Bombers	70	32	28	10	74	230	226
Wheeling Nailers	70	25	40	5	55	202	246
Toledo Storm	70	22	41	7	51	214	306
Southeast Division							
Florida Everblades	70	53	15	2	108	277	181
Pee Dee Pride	70	47	18	5	99	233	175
Greenville Grrrowl	70	46	18	6	98	277	198
South Carolina Stingrays	70	35	25	10	80	253	242
Augusta Lynx	70	34	31	5	73	243	248
Tallahassee Tiger Sharks	70	31	33	6	68	256	261
Jacksonville Lizard Kings	70	27	34	9	63	246	291
Southwest Division							
Louisiana Ice Gators	70	43	18	9	95	281	241
Mobile Mysticks	70	40	28	2	82	275	230
New Orleans Brass	70	36	27	7	79	230	219
Mississippi Sea Wolves	70	35	27	8	78	241	221
Pensacola Ice Pilots	70	35	29	6	76	215	216
Baton Rouge Kingfish	70	33	32	5	71	253	277
Jackson Bandits	70	32	32	6	70	201	227
Birmingham Bulls	70	29	37	4	62	255	297
Arkansas Riverblades	70	18	49	3	39	192	316

Johnstown Chiefs
General Manager - Toby O'Brien
Coach - Scott Allen
Assistant Coach - Galen Head
Training Staff - Mic Midderhoff, Chris Stewart
Locker Room Attendants - Chuck Lamberson, Doug Mesteller, Cory Mesteller, Jesse Shoff
Colors - Black, White and Gold

1999-2000 Game Results

Preseason Results

Day	Date	Opponent	Score Johnstown	Opponent	Attendance	Record
Wed.	6-Oct	Trenton	3	12	422	
Fri.	8-Oct	at Wheeling	0	2		
Sat.	9-Oct	Wheeling	7	1	634	

Regular Season Results

Day	Date	Opponent	Johnstown	Opponent	Attendance	Record
Thur.	14-Oct	Trenton	6	3	2,239	1-0-0
Fri.	15-Oct	at Trenton	0	3		1-1-0
Sat.	16-Oct	Huntington	6	2	2,115	2-1-0
Fri.	22-Oct	at Pee Dee	3	1		3-1-0
Sat.	23-Oct	at Charlotte	8	1		4-1-0
Sun.	24-Oct	at Greenville	5	4		5-1-0
Wed.	27-Oct	at Greensboro	3	0		6-1-0
Sat.	30-Oct	Huntington	4	5	2,437	6-2-0
Sun.	31-Oct	Louisiana	2	4	2,095	6-3-0
Fri.	5-Nov	at Toledo	4	0		7-3-0
Sat.	6-Nov	Wheeling	6	5	2,464	8-3-0
Thur.	11-Nov	Greenville	3	4 (sol)	2,178	8-3-1
Sat.	13-Nov	Hampton Roads	4	2	2,464	9-3-1
Wed.	17-Nov	at Hampton Roads	1	4		9-4-1
Fri.	19-Nov	Tallahassee	2	3	3,424	9-5-1
Sat.	20-Nov	at Toledo	1	5		9-6-1
Thur.	25-Nov	Greensboro	3	6	2,058	9-7-1
Fri.	26-Nov	Wheeling	2	4	3,612	9-8-1
Sat.	27-Nov	at Huntington	3	7		9-9-1
Fri.	3-Dec	at Greensboro	3	5		9-10-1
Sat.	4-Dec	Roanoke	3	2 (sow)	2,107	10-10-1
Sun.	5-Dec	at Roanoke	2	1		11-10-1
Fri.	10-Dec	at Peoria	2	4		11-11-1
Sat.	11-Dec	at Peoria	2	1		12-11-1
Fri.	17-Dec	at Hampton Roads	3	4		12-12-1
Sat.	18-Dec	Dayton	4	3	2,156	13-12-1
Sun.	19-Dec	at Wheeling	3	4 (sol)		13-12-2
Sun.	26-Dec	at Dayton	2	3 (sol)		13-12-3
Tues.	28-Dec	at Trenton	4	5 (sol)		13-12-4
Fri.	31-Dec	Wheeling	4	3 (sow)	3,070	14-12-4
Sat.	1-Jan	Richmond	5	3	2,179	15-12-4
Wed.	5-Jan	at Hampton Roads	2	3 (sol)		15-12-5
Fri.	7-Jan	at Roanoke	2	3		15-13-5
Sat.	8-Jan	Dayton	5	2	2,648	16-13-5
Sun.	9-Jan	at Richmond	5	4 (sow)		17-13-5
Fri.	14-Jan	at Huntington	6	4		18-13-5
Sat.	15-Jan	Trenton	1	2 (sol)	2,802	18-13-6
Fri.	21-Jan	at Richmond	4	6		18-14-6
Sat.	22-Jan	Wheeling	4	1	2,640	19-14-6
Sun.	23-Jan	Toledo	4	7	1,586	19-15-6
Fri.	28-Jan	at Dayton	3	2 (sow)		20-15-6
Sat.	29-Jan	Greensboro	5	3	2,600	21-15-6
Sat.	5-Feb	Peoria	5	1	2,642	22-15-6
Sun.	6-Feb	Trenton	7	2	3,151	23-15-6
Wed.	9-Feb	at Wheeling	1	3		23-16-6
Fri.	11-Feb	Dayton	2	3 (sol)	2,082	23-16-7
Sat.	12-Feb	Hampton Roads	3	6	3,033	23-17-7
Wed.	16-Feb	at Trenton	2	3		23-18-7
Fri.	18-Feb	at Huntington	3	7		23-19-7
Sat.	19-Feb	Dayton	3	1	2,859	24-19-7
Sun.	20-Feb	Huntington	3	4	1,995	24-20-7
Fri.	25-Feb	at Wheeling	5	3		25-20-7
Sun.	27-Feb	Richmond	3	7	2,475	25-21-7
Wed.	1-Mar	Charlotte	6	5	1,762	26-21-7
Fri.	3-Mar	at Dayton	6	4		27-21-7
Sat.	4-Mar	Trenton	1	2	2,359	27-22-7
Sun.	5-Mar	Toledo	3	2	1,821	28-22-7
Fri.	10-Mar	at Roanoke	2	3		28-23-7
Sat.	11-Mar	Huntington	7	2	2,545	29-23-7
Fri.	17-Mar	at Dayton	0	4		29-24-7
Sat.	18-Mar	Roanoke	2	3 (sol)	2,488	29-24-8
Sun.	19-Mar	Peoria	8	5	1,948	30-24-8
Tues.	21-Mar	at Trenton	1	3		30-25-8
Fri.	24-Mar	at Roanoke	3	2		31-25-8
Sat.	25-Mar	at Hampton Roads	2	4		31-26-8

CHIEFS IN THE NINETIES

Day	Date	Opponent	GF	GA	Att	Record
Sun.	26-Mar	Richmond	3	4 (sol)	2,077	31-26-9
Wed.	29-Mar	at Richmond	2	5		31-27-9
Fri.	31-Mar	at Wheeling	2	1		32-27-9
Sat.	1-Apr	Roanoke	2	1	2,315	33-27-9
Sun.	2-Apr	Trenton	4	6	1,975	33-28-9

Playoff Results

Day	Date	Opponent	GF	GA	Att	Record
Tues.	4-Apr	at Roanoke	3	0		1-0
Wed.	5-Apr	Roanoke	3	4	1,390	1-1
Fri.	7-Apr	Roanoke	4	0	2,194	2-1
Sat.	8-Apr	at Roanoke	4	1		3-1
Sun.	16-Apr	at Peoria	3	4 (otl)		0-1
Tues.	18-Apr	at Peoria	4	7		0-2
Fri.	21-Apr	Peoria	1	2	2,411	0-3

Attendance Figures	Dates	Totals	Average
Preseason Attendance Totals	2	1,056	528
Regular Season Attendance Totals	35	84,401	2,411
Playoff Attendance Totals	3	5,995	1,998
TOTAL ATTENDANCE	40	91,452	2,286

1999-2000 Player Statistics

Regular Season Scoring / Playoff Scoring

Player	Games	G	A	Pts	PIM	Games	G	A	Pts	PIM
7 Andrew Dale	64	26	42	68	73	7	3	2	5	8
22 Carl Fleury	55	18	38	56	93	7	3	4	7	12
26 Joel Irving	61	25	28	53	152	7	2	2	4	20
14 Andrew Clark	65	26	21	47	41	5	2	2	4	13
4 Derrick Walser	54	17	26	43	104	7	3	3	6	8
5 Brent Bilodeau	70	8	26	34	94	7	0	4	4	8
27 Shawn Frappier	58	8	25	33	51	7	0	3	3	8
6 Mike Thompson	37	14	16	30	55	7	1	2	3	6
16 Ryan Chaytors	54	13	16	29	45	4	1	2	3	0
38 Kris Porter	30	13	13	26	16	7	4	1	5	8
15 Jody Shelley	36	9	17	26	256					
25 John Tripp	38	13	11	24	64					
18 Bryan McKinney	57	5	16	21	140					
17 Dmitri Tarabrin	67	5	14	19	95	7	3	1	4	21
10 Mike Vellinga	69	2	17	19	144	7	0	1	1	18
12 E.J. Bradley	35	5	13	18	14	1	0	0	0	0
19 Chuck Mindel	41	9	8	17	18	4	0	1	1	12
28 Brett McLean	8	4	7	11	6					
8 Jeff Sullivan	58	2	8	10	181	7	0	2	2	32
33 Bruce Coles	8	3	5	8	8					
2 Ryan Tocher	11	2	4	6	23	2	0	0	0	2
3 Kevin Kellett	37	1	3	4	53	7	0	4	4	14
20 Jason Spence	36	2	1	3	106					
23 Brett Gibson	6	1	2	3	0	6	0	0	0	12
24 Brent Dodginghorse	17	1	2	3	62					
33 Matt Eldred	11	0	3	3	33					
31 Frederic Deschenes (g)	49	0	3	3	2	6	0	0	0	2
38 Frank Littlejohn	1	2	0	2	4					
55 Tyrone Garner (g)	17	0	2	2	2	1	0	0	0	0
21 Yauheni Kurylin	5	1	0	1	0					
21 Mikko Sivonen	3	0	0	0	0	6	0	3	3	2
44 Craig Hillier (g)	5	0	0	0	2					
35 Pavel Nestak (g)	5	0	0	0	0					
23 Tom Field	8	0	0	0	0					
Bench					22					2
TOTALS	70	235	387	622	1,959	7	22	37	59	208

Regular Season Goaltending

	G	Min	GA	ENG	SO	GAA	W	L	SOL	Saves	Save %
35 Pavel Nestak	5	210	10	0	0	2.85	1	1	0	105	0.913
55 Tyrone Garner	17	971	48	2	0	2.97	8	6	3	424	0.898
31 Frederic Deschenes	49	2,786	146	3	2	3.14	23	19	6	1,244	0.895
44 Craig Hillier	5	212	15	1	0	4.24	1	2	0	106	0.876
Shootout Goals			9								
TOTALS	70	4,200	228	6	2	3.34	33	28	9	1,879	0.889

Playoff Goaltending

	G	Min	GA	ENG	SO	GAA	W	L	Saves	Save%
55 Tyrone Garner	1	59	2	0	0	2.03	0	1	23	0.920
31 Frederic Deschenes	6	369	15	1	2	2.44	3	3	172	0.920
TOTALS	7	428	17	1	2	2.52	3	4	195	0.915

Players on roster who did not play: 1 Mark Scally, Goal; 1 Shane Clifford, Goal; 44 Jeff Mathias, Goal; 55 Troy Baxter, Goal; 1 Rob Murdoch, Goal Mathias also wore No. 55.

281

Chiefs left wing Jason Spence splits the Dayton Bombers defense.

2000s Overview: Beating the Odds

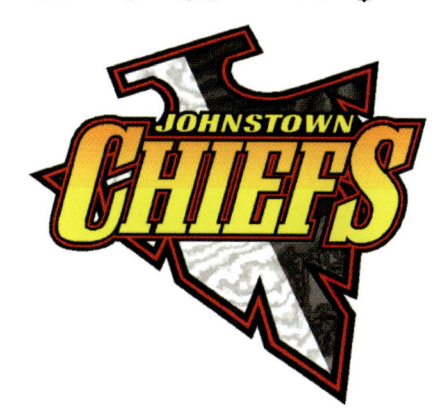

By Mike Mastovich

It simply can't be done. At least that was the perception outside of Johnstown.

There was no way a Chiefs team that suffered through miserable times in the 1990s could reclaim the franchise's spot as a competitive Kelly Cup playoff squad. Had the ownership group, front office or coach Scott Allen believed such talk, there probably wouldn't be ECHL hockey in Johnstown. Instead, the Chiefs evolved into the "little franchise that could" by clawing their way back into the playoffs during the 2000s, as the team enjoyed notable success — winning three series under coaches Allen and Frank Anzalone.

"I think a ton of credit has to go to the three main people who believed in us and kept that team floating," said Allen, the Chiefs' head coach for five seasons, an assistant one season, and now part of the AHL staff in Quad City. "That was (former Tribune-Democrat publisher) Dick and Connie Mayer and (former WJAC-TV executive director) Jim Edwards.

"Those three people deserve probably the most credit out of anybody because that team is still operating in Johnstown as a direct result of those three people."

Lighting a Flame

In the early years of the ECHL, the Chiefs had a solid affiliation with the Boston Bruins and a productive working agreement with the New Jersey Devils. Later, the American Hockey League's Hershey Bears spent two seasons as primary affiliate, and the International League's Kansas City Blades worked with coach Eddie Johnstone. Links to the Pittsburgh Penguins and Philadelphia Flyers later in the decade had mixed results.

One of the keys to the Chiefs' resurgence in the new millennium was an affiliation deal struck with the NHL's Calgary Flames in 1998-99. General Manager Toby O'Brien and Allen had roles in securing the affiliation, and Allen immediately began attending training camps with the Flames and their AHL club in Saint John, New Brunswick.

The affiliation brought to Johnstown future NHL players such as enforcer Jody Shelley, defenseman Derrick Walser, forwards Brett McLean and John Tripp, and goaltenders Dany Sabourin and Tyrone Garner. Some contract players who didn't advance to the NHL still were among the best at the ECHL level. They included defensemen Mike Vellinga and Jeff Sullivan, and forwards Joel Irving and Shaun Sutter.

The Calgary affiliation materialized after the Chiefs made a sacrifice late in the 1997-98 season. Allen had replaced the fired Nick Fotiu as head coach. He and O'Brien stood by the team's decision to allow players to advance regardless of the Chiefs' on-ice situation. "Nick Polano, the assistant general manager of the Flames at the time, called me at about the time when we were in a little resurgence after the coaching change late in the 1997-98 season," O'Brien said. "Calgary asked for Martin Masa, one of our best players, and he went up to Saint John and played extremely well. A week later, Polano called again and asked for another player, Lukas Smital. Those were two of our top players at the time. We let them go. I told Nick Polano that I'd let them have both guys if at the end of the season Calgary would have a meeting involving me and Al Coates, the general manager at Calgary at the time."

O'Brien got his meeting, but he had to drive to Portland, Maine.

"I was sitting in the office one night and Nick Polano called and said he was going to be out our way and maybe we could meet," O'Brien said. "They were going to be in Portland. I thought, 'Out our way?' I looked up plane flights. They were $1,200 to $1,400. So I went home, showered, got in my car and drove 14 hours. We met. We had a long discussion. A week later he said he wanted to be affiliated with us.

"We let our two best players go, but in turn we secured the Calgary affiliation which I think was the absolutely key next step to get where we needed to go to re-establish ourselves in the hockey world and become a competitive contender in the ECHL."

Playoff drama

Tangible results were evident during the 1999-2000 ECHL season. The addition of franchise goaltender Frederic Deschenes and the leadership of Brent Bilodeau, Dmitri Tarabrin and Jason Spence combined with the arrival of many of the aforementioned Calgary-Saint John contract players to make the Chiefs a formidable group.

The Chiefs won six of their first seven games and swept through a tough four-game trip through the Carolinas with victories over Pee Dee (3-1), Charlotte (8-1), Greenville (5-4) and Greensboro (3-0). After Johnstown beat his team by seven goals at Independence Hall on Oct. 23, 1999, Charlotte coach Shawn Wheeler, a former star player, proclaimed that these Chiefs were the best ECHL team he had ever seen.

The Chiefs cooled off after some key players such as McLean, Tripp and Shelley were called up to the AHL. But Johnstown still finished with 33 wins, 75 points and third place in the Northwest Division.

The 2000 Kelly Cup playoffs brought the Chiefs their first postseason series victory since 1992. Behind Deschenes' two shutouts, Johnstown upset highly regarded Roanoke, twice winning on the road, including the series-clinching fourth game.

Johnstown lost the next series to eventual Kelly Cup champion Peoria.

In 2001, the Chiefs placed fourth in the Northwest and dropped a 3-1 series to Trenton in the playoffs. The next season, the Chiefs produced one of the most dramatic playoff turnarounds in league history.

After placing third in the regular season, the Chiefs faced division runner-up Peoria in the first round in '02. The Rivermen, always among the Chiefs' toughest foes, jumped out to a 2-0 advantage in the best-of-5 series by winning twice at Carver Arena. The games were close, 2-1 in the opener and 1-0 in Game 2.

Allen's Peoria promise

Allen vowed that the Chiefs would return to Peoria for a decisive fifth game. That bold promise meant that Johnstown had to win a pair at the War Memorial.

The Chiefs responded with a 6-1 victory in Game 3 and a 3-1 win in Game 4 as the War Memorial rocked with fans who understood the significance of those two wins.

"I still have guys talk to me about being down 2-0 to Peoria and coming back," Allen said. The Chiefs shocked the Rivermen with a 4-0 shutout in Game 5 at Carver Arena.

The magic didn't last long. Division champion Dayton defeated the Chiefs 4-3 in a double overtime game at Hara Arena to open the Northwest Division Final series. The Chiefs dropped three straight to the eventual Kelly Cup runner-up Bombers.

The 2001-02 season ended an era in Chiefs hockey. Allen left to accept an assistant coaching position with the American Hockey League's San Antonio Rampage.

The Mayers sold the Chiefs to a group fronted by majority owner Neil Smith, the former New York Rangers Stanley Cup-winning general manager, and Richard Adams, the ECHL's former president and CEO.

In seven seasons as part of the Chiefs' ownership team, including five years as sole owners, Richard and Connie Mayer reportedly lost more than $1 million but still kept the team operating in Johnstown. Part of the sales agreement included a guarantee that Smith and Adams not move the Chiefs for an unspecified number of years.

"To me, Mr. Mayer is my hero and the city of Johnstown's unsung hero," said Ned Nakles Jr., who led a group that owned the Chiefs from 1993-95 and remains a minority owner. "He never looked for publicity. He never asked for accolades. He shied away from the spotlight. But he's probably done more for Chiefs hockey and the city of Johnstown than anyone else. Through it all he never asked for a word of thanks."

Smith and Adams moved O'Brien from general manager to head coach. Jim Brazill, who had been with the Chiefs in a number of front office positions since 1992, was named general manager.

The Chiefs missed the playoffs in 2003 and 2005 under O'Brien. But the 2003-04 team produced a special season — the best regular season in Chiefs' history — only to see their playoff hopes squashed in a one-game, play-in upset loss to visiting Reading.

"The entire 2003-04 season was just something special," said Brazill, who started as a Chiefs intern before holding titles as director of sales, ticket manager, director of operations, assistant GM, vice president of operations and vice president/GM in 13 years. "Off the ice, we had the Save Our Sports grass-roots effort to save the Chiefs. We had the Message Board Crusaders and the Chiefs Fan Club in our corner. We got the two-year lease extension to save the team.

"On the ice, for so many years it seemed that we were on the short end of the stick and the puck bounced the other way. That year everything we did was right and the puck was bouncing our way almost every night. Then that final play-in game against Reading the puck hit the post twice and the puck didn't bounce our way."

The 2003-04 Chiefs posted single-season records for wins (45), home wins (26), road wins (19), fewest regulation losses (20) and team shutouts (seven). The fourth-place Chiefs had eight more wins and 13 more points than fifth-place Reading.

But at the season's outset, Johnstown was among the teams that voted for the wild-card playoff format. The Chiefs probably wished for another vote after Reading's David Masse scored twice against Johnstown goalie Dmitri Patzold, and Royals goaltender Cody Rudkowsky played a phenomenal game in a 2-1 win. Further adding to the irony was that Johnstown had a 6-3-0 record against Reading that season and was 4-0-0 at home against the Royals.

The Chiefs' most successful regular season was followed by one of the most crushing playoff losses, one ranking second perhaps only to the 1989 Game 7 setback to Carolina in the Riley Cup Final. Before that playoff setback, the Chiefs' special season included a lengthy stay by former NHL all-star goaltender Arturs Irbe, who won 10 games and the hearts of Chiefs fans. There also was a surge that followed the additions of veteran Larry Courville and Jeff Zehr. After Jan. 7, 2004, the Chiefs went 28-6-4, with a 10-1-1 mark in the final 12 games.

Community support

The community rallied behind the Chiefs, who had six sellout crowds at the War Memorial for the first time since the 1991-92 season. The average attendance soared to 2,551, an increase of 307 a night from the previous year. Much of that had to do with the team's play. But an aggressive grass roots campaign to support the team and the Chiefs' willingness to be active in the community also were significant.

Mainstays such as Randy Rowe, Jean Desrochers, Morgan Cey, Tarabrin and Doug Andress were the faces of the franchise from 2005-07.

"My first year as an intern there still was that, 'Open the doors and they'll come era.' On a Saturday night it was average for us to get 3,200 or 3,300 people in the building and on a good Saturday it was even better just by opening the doors," said Brazill, whose first day with the Chiefs was Dec. 26, 1992. "The honeymoon ended. Ownership changed hands a couple times. It was in a downward spin until some stability came in Dick Mayer and Jim Edwards. There still were always the rumors that 'this' is the last year of the team, but the community always rallied around the team. The attendance numbers never did get back up to those numbers of the early days but they've consistently been around 2,500. Louisiana was averaging 9,000 or 10,000 a night when they were in their honeymoon period. When their honeymoon period was over, they not only flattened out, they were gone. For Johnstown to still have 2,500 a night says something about the community."

> "I want hockey to survive in Johnstown. That's my first priority, and it always has been."
>
> — Neil Smith

The ECHL did its share to keep Johnstown as an historic and viable operation. The league did its best to provide weekend dates. Leaders such as Adams and current Commissioner Brian McKenna have supported the Chiefs and Johnstown hockey in general. The ECHL grew from five to 25 members with large market cities such as Las Vegas, Fresno, Stockton, Trenton, Charlotte and Phoenix, among others. Teams moved into southern markets with beaches or winter golf available to players. The league appeared to have outgrown Johnstown. But ECHL leaders felt otherwise.

"Johnstown is very much the Green Bay of minor-league hockey," McKenna said. "It's a long-standing market, a small market by some standards. But in terms of pride and support of the fans, knowledge of the game and tradition of the sport, it is right up there in the minor-league markets in all of North America."

The Chiefs' ownership was restructured prior to the 2005-06 season. Lancaster businessman Jim Weber joined the group and touted himself as primary owner. Adams was out of the picture, and Smith quietly faded into the background despite the fact that it was later learned he remained the majority owner under a complex agreement.

Weber soon brought in the Tampa Bay Lightning as a part-owner and affiliate. Tampa and its AHL club in Springfield, Mass., supplied the majority of players to Johnstown and had a hand in virtually every on-ice decision.

Brazill left to take a job at nearby St. Francis University before the 2005-06 season. O'Brien moved back to the general manager position, and Anzalone was hired by Tampa to coach the Chiefs and implement the Lightning's systems.

Anzalone's teams were respectable, if not spectacular. The Chiefs finished fourth in 2005-06 and swept a best-of-3 playoff series against Trenton before falling in three straight to Toledo in the division semifinals. The 2006-07 squad placed fifth, but eliminated Reading on the final day of the regular season to claim the division's last playoff berth. Johnstown won 6-3 at the Sovereign Center as goalie Ryan Munce made 49 saves to quiet 7,072 mostly Royals fans. The surprising push to the postseason was followed by a pair of losses to Trenton in a best-of-3 series.

Soon after the season, Weber and the Lightning parted ways, which meant Anzalone, who was under contract to Tampa, was out as coach.

Weber hired coach Ian Herbers on June 18, 2007, and named 10-year front office member Kevin McGeehan as director of hockey operations. Herbers, a former NHL player, had been an associate coach with Saginaw in the OHL.

On July 5, 2007 the Chiefs' future was clouded as Weber unexpectedly announced that a sudden change in his financial situation forced him to leave the team's ownership group.

Smith reasserted himself as the team's majority owner and vowed that the Chiefs would play their 20th anniversary season in the ECHL. League commissioner Brian McKenna provided his support and reinforced Smith's assessment.

"I want hockey to survive in Johnstown. That's my first priority, and it always has been," Smith said after Weber's abrupt announcement. "Make sure the fans and the good people that have supported the team so long know my heart is in this. This is my own money. This isn't a corporation or a way to write off taxes. I'm a traditionalist. I don't want to see hockey move out of Johnstown. I've been very committed to the ECHL. We're going to do everything we can to keep that team there. I'm the majority owner and I think that message should carry some weight."

Chiefs goaltender Frederic Deschenes fights for position against the Wheeling Nailers.

Frederic Deschenes

'Great Memories'
Deschenes Stood Tall in Goal for Chiefs

By Mike Mastovich

Standing 5-foot, 9-inches tall and weighing about 165 pounds, Frederic Deschenes hardly resembled the prototypical franchise player when he signed with the Johnstown Chiefs during the summer of 1999.

The goaltender Johnstown fans eventually knew simply as "Freddie" didn't have the intimidating presence of a 6-foot-5 checking-line forward who spent three hours a day in the gym and 15 minutes a game in the penalty box. But the size of Deschenes' heart and the weight carried on his figuratively broad shoulders made him a formidable player in front of the net. Quick, agile and possessing uncanny reflexes and reaction time, Freddie was tough to beat once he got into a mental zone.

"He wasn't the biggest guy in the world. That being said, he knew he had to use everything else to his advantage," former Chiefs coach Scott Allen said. "Freddie was solid with his angles. He was a strong reaction goalie. He had quick limbs and was tough to beat upstairs. He was a battler and a worker and he'd do whatever it took to keep the puck out of the net."

His dedication and work ethic made the goalie from Quebec City even more effective. Deschenes put in the time and effort to improve. Labeled an ironman or a work horse, he played incredible stretches of consecutive games at a position where most goaltenders prefer to rotate with a back-up every couple of nights.

Deschenes needed all of those skills and intangible qualities when he joined the Chiefs for the 1999-2000 season.

'Franchise goaltender'

Johnstown had missed the playoffs four consecutive years, an unheard of drought for a franchise that had enjoyed so much success in the early years of the ECHL.

Near the end of the 1990s, Johnstown had received a bad rap from players and their agents. Trades fell through when players refused to report. It was difficult to sign top-notch talent. General Manager Toby O'Brien and Coach Allen changed that image while working with experienced team president James Edwards Sr., who also served as ECHL Chairman.

Signing Deschenes was hailed as one of the most important transactions in the team's history. Freddie immediately was labeled a "franchise goaltender," and the front office made no secret that he was one of the Chiefs' highest-paid players ever.

Deschenes had led the Granby Predateurs of the Quebec Major Junior Hockey League to the Canadian Hockey League's coveted Memorial Cup in 1996. He had American Hockey League experience with Rochester in 1996-97 and was in the IHL with Quebec in 1997-98. Deschenes split 1998-99 between Orlando in the IHL and Birmingham in the ECHL. With the Bulls, he was leading the ECHL in minutes played (2,224) and saves (1,161) prior to his late-January 1999 call-up to the IHL.

"When Toby and Scott Allen came to Quebec City the summer before my first year in Johnstown, they told me about the team and the city," Deschenes said. "I decided to sign a contract with Johnstown. I didn't know what my time would be like there.

"But after I played three seasons there, it was a great situation for me. I was treated real well by the organization and everybody in the town. I only have great memories about it."

The feeling was mutual as far as Chiefs followers were concerned. Deschenes helped the Chiefs end that four-year playoff drought. In fact, he was in net for three straight playoff appearances and two postseason series wins from 2000 to 2002.

> "I don't think we could have found a better guy than Freddie Deschenes. He was a true professional from Day 1. ... He worked as hard as anybody on the ice. The players had confidence in him."
>
> — *Scott Allen, Chiefs coach*

With three consecutive 20-win seasons, Deschenes had 69 regular-season victories, the most by a Chiefs goaltender. He had a record-tying seven playoff victories.

Deschenes played a Chiefs' single-season record 54 games in 2000-01 and appeared in 49 regular season games in both of his other two years here. In 2001-02, Deschenes tied Stan "Smokey" Reddick's single-season win mark at 25. That postseason, he and the Chiefs fell behind 0-2 in a first-round, best-of-5 playoff series with Peoria.

In one of the most dramatic turnarounds in league history, the Chiefs stormed back with three straight wins to advance to the division finals. "We lost the first two games in Peoria," Deschenes said. "Allen said in the room after the second game that the series wasn't over and we'd be back for Game 5 in Peoria, and we'd win it.

"We won Game 3 in Johnstown (6-1), came back and won Game 4 (3-1). We went back to Peoria and won by a shutout (4-0) but I had nothing to do with that. We played as a team that night and beat a pretty good team."

At the time, the Chiefs were only the 11th ECHL squad to overcome an 0-2 playoff series deficit and only the fourth to do so in a five-game series.

"That's a long bus ride, but it was great to be there," Deschenes said of the 13-hour drive to Peoria for Game 5. "We worked so hard during the season. Finally, when things like that happen, it's always a fun time."

CHIEFS IN THE 2000s

'We really put everything together'

That 2002 playoff series win capped Deschenes' stellar run in Johnstown. The team fell to Dayton in the division finals, and Freddie retired soon after the final game.

The diminutive goaltender had come full circle in Johnstown.

"When I got there the team had a losing experience. We came with a good group," said Deschenes of teammates such as Brent Bilodeau, Jeff Sullivan, Jason Spence, Mike Vellinga and Ryan Chaytors. "We really put everything together. That started with Toby O'Brien and Scott Allen, who did a great job as a coach. We put all the pieces together. Every player was pretty proud of what we did when we went through the first round of the playoffs that year in 2000.

"If you went back to the seasons they had before, that was huge for the organization at that time."

Freddie made a huge impact once the Chiefs finally reached the playoffs in April 2000. The seventh-seeded Chiefs upset a second-seeded Roanoke team that had 44 regular-season wins. Deschenes had a 3-0 shutout at the Roanoke Civic Center in Game 1. With the series even at 1-1, Freddie recorded a 4-0 shutout in Game 3 at Johnstown. Only a late Roanoke 5-on-3 goal prevented Deschenes from posting his third shutout of the series in the clinching fourth game at the Civic Center. He stopped 105 of 110 Express shots as the Chiefs won their first playoff series since 1992.

"Of all the years I've been a head coach, the only year I haven't made the playoffs was my first year in Johnstown in 1998-99," said Allen, now an AHL assistant coach. "I knew the reason why at the end of the season. We had inconsistent goaltending. We had to go out and find a guy who was going to give us a chance to win every night.

"I don't think we could have found a better guy than Freddie Deschenes," Allen added. "He was a true professional from Day 1. Freddie showed up to work every day. You didn't have to worry about him as far as his being prepared. He worked as hard as anybody on the ice. The players had confidence in him."

Even standing at 5-9, Freddie was a giant as far as his teammates and Chiefs fans were concerned.

Jeff Sullivan, left, and Brent Bilodeau played six seasons together with the Chiefs.

Bilodeau, Sullivan

'Solid Leaders'

Defensemen Bilodeau and Sullivan Were Friends, Fan Favorites

By Mike Mastovich

As difficult as it might be for Johnstown Chiefs followers to imagine, Brent Bilodeau and Jeff Sullivan didn't sign with the ECHL team as part of a package deal.

Instead, Bilodeau, a former first-round draft pick of the storied Montreal Canadiens franchise, and Sullivan, then under contract with the NHL's Calgary Flames' affiliate in Saint John, New Brunswick, arrived in Johnstown from different directions in 1999.

But once in the city, the two defensemen formed an alliance on the ice, in the locker room and away from the arena. They remained Johnstown Chiefs for six seasons, collecting record numbers of games played and penalty minutes along the way.

Both solid players, Bilodeau and Sullivan earned the respect of their teammates and coaches. The duo was well-known among Chiefs fans.

On game nights, captain Bilodeau was introduced over the public address system as, "Brent ... Bill-A-Dooooooo." Sullivan was so popular the team held a Jeff Sullivan bobble head promotion on an afternoon when fans lined up in two directions, encircling Cambria County War Memorial Arena while waiting for their "Sully" doll.

"They brought leadership and accountability. They showed up every day prepared and they were solid leaders," said former Chiefs coach Scott Allen, who coached Bilodeau and Sullivan during their first three seasons in Johnstown. "Brent Bilodeau was a first-round pick who never made it to the National Hockey League, but still wanted to be a player. Jeff Sullivan was a mid-round pick of Ottawa. He had some tough times during his last year of juniors when his dad got sick and he lost his dad.

"He was the type of guy who would leave it on the ice every night and do the little things. He'd block shots. He would do the work in the hard areas. He'd make it difficult on the opposing players.

"Both of those guys, when they spoke, players listened and respected them. Those two guys had the respect of their peers. They were both committed to the Chiefs organization and to Johnstown. Guys like that we thought were the foundation of our team that we could build around."

The Chiefs had struggled through four consecutive seasons of missing the playoffs. The 1995-96, 1996-97 and 1997-98 teams posted some of the worst records in team history, combining for only 68 wins in 210 games. The franchise faced the challenge of rebuilding its reputation on the ice and image off the ice. General Manager Toby O'Brien and coach Allen gradually assembled a group that at first was competitive, then eventually made three straight playoff appearances, winning two series.

Signing Bilodeau and adding Sullivan were two key moves in the lengthy process.

Bilodeau signed with the Chiefs hoping to restart an injury-plagued career. Blood clots in his leg had not only threatened his hockey career, but also his health in general. Sullivan was among a group of contract players assigned to Johnstown by the NHL Flames. Players such as future NHL skaters Jody Shelley, Brett McLean, Derrick Walser and John Tripp were other prospects sent to the Chiefs.

The addition of "franchise" goaltender Frederic Deschenes that same 1999-2000 season was another piece of the puzzle.

'We brought that attitude'

"I didn't know much of the history of Johnstown not making the playoffs, and my thought process of every year was that it wasn't about just making the playoffs, but to win a championship," Bilodeau said. "Not making the playoffs was not an option.

"I thought we brought that attitude when we came in. Right from the start I remember our first year, I told Scott Allen it was a championship that we wanted."

The championship was elusive. But the Chiefs' rebuilding project was a success.

Johnstown advanced to the playoffs in 2000, ending the four-year drought. The Chiefs surprised second-seeded Roanoke by winning the best-of-5 series, 3 games to 1.

"To see the diehard fans and the people that really support the team watch us win a playoff round like that, the excitement, was a lot of fun," said Bilodeau, who played in what was a then-Chiefs' record 414 regular season games. "The whole city really built around that and rallied around that. It was a great thing to be a part of."

The 6-foot-4, 230-pound Bilodeau beat the injury bug during his time in Johnstown. He appeared in 70, 64, 72, 71, 70 and 67 games. "I was banged up quite a bit when I was playing in the American Hockey League and the IHL," said Bilodeau, a native of Clyde, Alberta. "Once I got to Johnstown, they fixed my knee after the first season. A lot of it was luck. Some people play 15 years without an injury. Some guys played a couple years and are too injured to go on. Sometimes I shouldn't have been playing. I had a broken foot, a broken wrist, broken fingers, but I played."

At 6-1 and a solid 215 pounds, Sullivan brought a no-nonsense approach to his game. The defenseman wasn't known for scoring goals. But he stood his ground on the blue line. When the situation merited such action, Sullivan was willing to drop the gloves and fight. His Johnstown hockey record 1,205 career penalty minutes in 315 regular-season games with the Chiefs reinforce that fact.

"I just played hard and whatever happened, happened," the soft-spoken Sullivan said. "I worked hard and played hard. When you're at the rink, you're there to do a job and you do it the best you can. That's how I always approached the game."

That approach stemmed from Sullivan's off-season job as a commercial fisherman on the North Atlantic Ocean. The native of Brigus South, Newfoundland, was part of a five-man crew on a 49-foot long boat that traveled 12 to 15 hours and spent nearly a week at sea during most fishing excursions for shrimp and crabs.

"I've been out in some pretty bad weather," Sullivan said. "We have to be aware of icebergs when we're steaming at night. It's pretty tough work."

Sullivan returned to land, working in the construction business after his retirement as a Chief. "He was an old-school hockey player," Allen said.

'Everything started in Johnstown'

Appropriately, Bilodeau and Sullivan retired together on April 9, 2005 after the Chiefs' season finale. The players and their wives remain close friends years later.

"Everything started in Johnstown," Bilodeau said. "I didn't know Sully at all. I just got to know him when we both got to Johnstown. Our love of the game made us close friends. We love hockey and we wanted to win. We're both low-maintenance kind of guys. We both just appreciated our gift to be able to play hockey."

Even the typically low-key Sullivan grasped the significance of his and Bilodeau's final game that April day at the War Memorial.

"It was emotional. After the fact it kind of clicked in that we're not going to play pro hockey anymore," Sullivan said. "It was nice going out together. The fans appreciated the way we played."

Dmitri Tarabrin has skated in more games than any player in Chiefs history.

Dmitri Tarabrin

'Whatever it Takes to be a Chief'
Hard-Working Tarabrin Makes Johnstown His Home

By Mike Mastovich

The 2001-02 ECHL season might have been the most important year in Dmitri Tarabrin's lengthy and distinguished professional hockey career.

Ironically, Tarabrin never laced up the skates in '01-02. The feisty 5-foot-8 right wing from Moscow, Russia, didn't make the Johnstown Chiefs' roster after training camp that season despite previously appearing in 159 games with the Chiefs from 1999-01.

Tarabrin had a reputation as a blue-collar player, one who didn't shy away from taking the body — even fighting opponents sometimes six inches taller and outweighing him by 50 pounds. A fan favorite, Tarabrin seemed to furiously skate full-speed up the ice each shift. His passion for the game was obvious.

That's why the 2001-02 season was so pivotal for the forward who eventually appeared in more games with the Chiefs than any other player.

Tarabrin realized how much hockey meant to him after he was cut by the Chiefs that season. It might be a cliché, but he loved the game and missed it badly during a year in which he instead labored for a Johnstown construction company.

"I worked with Major Builders. It's heavy work. It's not easy," Tarabrin said of his "other" job. "It's a great group of guys. I met a lot of people. I worked in a different environment. I spent the year there building and I met a lot of great people. I tried to stay in shape as much as I could, and hopefully, that chance would come."

Fate intervened in October 2002. Toby O'Brien was in his first year as head coach of the Chiefs after serving as the team's general manager the previous six years.

O'Brien offered Tarabrin a spot in training camp. Few gave the veteran good odds of sticking with the club after sitting out a year. He had veteran status and ECHL teams only are permitted four vets. Plus, the Chiefs had their share of contract players from their American League affiliate in Saint John, New Brunswick.

But once the season opened, there was Tarabrin, on the official roster.

He scored two goals and had a four-point night in the Chiefs' 6-2 victory at Dayton, Ohio, on Oct. 20 — the third game of the season. Those were Tarabrin's first goals and points since March 28, 2001.

"It was totally different. I wasn't playing one year. I was working in the real world, real life," Tarabrin said. "That taught me a lot about the appreciation of the game and the love of the game. To tell the truth I didn't watch one hockey game that whole year. I wasn't on skates for about seven or eight months. I told Toby O'Brien I was thinking about playing again. I said we were going to give it a hell of a try."

Tarabrin responded by posting the best numbers of his pro career to that point: 17 goals, 25 assists, 42 points and 101 penalty minutes in 71 games. "I pushed myself to the limit," Tarabrin said. "When you're out of the game for seven or eight months, that's a hell of a hole to come out of. This is a serious business and I needed to do what I had to do. When I came out of training camp, I was a happy camper.

"I went full-out and it's a 100 percent thing," he said. "I could not have done it alone. Great players played with me that year and I had a blast. Every game I play, I appreciate the ice. I understand it's not going to last forever."

Tarabrin made the most of that second chance. Entering the 2007-08 season, he had played a Chiefs-record 474 regular season games and appeared in 493 games overall, including 19 postseason contests. Tarabrin began the '07-08 season with 99 career goals — trailing only Lukas Smital (107) and Bruce Coles (106) on the team's all-time list. His 232 points ranked second behind Rob Hrytsak (254).

"Every year, Dmitri comes to camp and there's been a job that he has to earn," O'Brien said during a 2005 interview. "Every year — except for that one — he finds a way to make our hockey team. When he gets his chance, he performs.

"There were a number of guys we had in camp who were in Dmitri's situation," O'Brien recalled. "They all wanted to play. So does Dmitri. But Dmitri told me after a lot of thought, 'Toby, I'll do whatever it takes to be a Chief.' We wanted a guy who will do whatever it takes to be a Chief."

Tarabrin's road to Johnstown was filled with obstacles most North American players typically don't face. "When I left Russia, I was 17 years old," Tarabrin said. "I went to junior hockey in Canada. I was a member of the Russian National Team and they wouldn't let me play in Canada. Finally, I got my release and played."

He spent two seasons with the North Battleford North Stars in the SJHL. Tarabrin made his professional debut with the ECHL's Wheeling Nailers in 1997-98 and remained with the team until a trade to Johnstown midway through the 1998-99 campaign. "I didn't know what to expect in junior hockey. I decided to play and see what would happen," Tarabrin said. "Lucky for me a couple scouts saw me. I went to Detroit and had a good tryout. I went to Baton Rouge for ECHL training camp. But all the spots were taken. Wheeling called and Johnstown called.

"It was a flip of a coin. I ended up in Wheeling or I could have been in Johnstown a year and a half earlier."

Tarabrin has become a transplanted Johnstowner. He and his wife, Deena, and daughter, Sasha, reside in the city year-round.

"I met a lot of people," he said. "I got the job in the summertime. I know how the town lives and breathes and works. It's not just the hockey side, but the living side, too. It's suitable for me. I've grown to love the town over the years."

The town and its hockey fans have returned the favor.

CHIEFS IN THE 2000s

Left and above: Chiefs captain Randy Rowe won over fans with his blue-collar game.

Below: Coach Scott Allen on the Chiefs bench. Allen has the most wins of any Chiefs head coach.

299

Arturs Irbe, a former NHL all-star who appeared in the Stanley Cup Final with the Carolina Hurricanes, played much of the 2003-04 season in Johnstown.

REPRINT

Former NHL all-star goaltender Arturs Irbe was on the Johnstown Chiefs roster for much of the 2003-04 ECHL season. The goalie known as "Archie" created a stir and attracted a crowd when he played. After his return to the NHL later that season, Irbe still followed the Chiefs. A Tribune-Democrat article on March 20, 2004, when Irbe and the Carolina Hurricanes played the Penguins in Pittsburgh, follows:

Irbe checks on Chiefs during Pittsburgh trip

By Mike Mastovich

PITTSBURGH — Arturs Irbe stood outside the Carolina Hurricanes' locker room at Mellon Arena yesterday afternoon, a couple hours before the start of a game against the Pittsburgh Penguins.

Geographically speaking, Irbe landed about 70 miles west of Johnstown during his first trip back to Pennsylvania since his much-heralded stay with the Johnstown Chiefs. In hockey terminology, Irbe and the Hurricanes might as well have been a million miles from the ECHL. But don't think that the likable goaltender has erased the Chiefs or the city from his memory.

"They are playing on the road tonight? They played Wednesday?" Irbe asked, referring to the Chiefs. "Who's hurt? How many games are left? They are within three points of Peoria?" In fact, Irbe reeled off almost as many questions about the Chiefs as those he fielded regarding his return to the NHL last month. "It's going all right. I can't complain," said Irbe, who is 3-1-1 with a 1.97 goals against average and .912 save percentage in five games with Carolina.

Last night, Kevin Weekes started in goal for the 'Canes and Irbe was the backup. That didn't bother Irbe, who appreciates his place on Carolina's roster after a tumultuous contract dispute that lasted about a year and ultimately led to his demotion to the ECHL Chiefs. "It's worked out," Irbe said. "Human nature lets you adapt pretty quickly to things. When I was in Johnstown, I adapted. I was fine and settled into the situation. Obviously everyone in Johnstown made the transition as easy as possible."

Irbe joined the Chiefs in Toledo a day before the regular season opened.

He treated the team, coaches and training staff to dinner at a steak house, picking up a tab reportedly more than $900. Not a bad off-ice introduction.

At the rink, Irbe was just as popular, going 10-3-1 with a 2.13 GAA and .927 save percentage. A 12-year NHL player and two-time all-star, Irbe won his first six games, earned an ECHL Goaltender of the Week honor and eventually was named the starter for the ECHL All-Star Game. But a wrist injury that eventually required surgery and an extensive rehabilitation period sidelined him for 11 weeks.

After returning to the lineup, he won games on Feb. 13 at Toledo and Feb. 17 at home against Peoria. Carolina recalled him after the victory over the Rivermen.

Irbe played his 300th game with the Hurricanes and stopped 18 of 19 shots in a 2-1 win at Washington in his first game back in the NHL on Feb. 25.

"Everything was smooth except it took me probably a good three or four real practices to get back in the swing of things," Irbe said. "The ECHL is two tiers down and it's a little bit different. But it wasn't that rough."

But Irbe said it doesn't really feel as if he spent more than half a season out of the NHL.

"I'm back to what I had been doing the previous 12 years," said Irbe, who has a 216-235-79 record and 33 shutouts in 563 NHL games. "The adjustment didn't really need to be made. I don't feel like I have been missing. It was a quick adjustment."

It also was an adjustment Irbe once feared he might not have to make this season.

In 2002-03, Irbe and the Hurricanes went head-to-head after Weekes took over the starting job.

Irbe wanted a trade. The Hurricanes unsuccessfully attempted to deal him. Carolina later waived him, but Irbe went unclaimed. His salary, which included $2.7 million this season and another $2.5 next year, made Irbe a tough sell.

Irbe briefly played in the AHL late last season. At this season's outset, he was on the outs in the Hurricanes organization and General Manager Jim Rutherford made no secret of that fact. To buy out Irbe prior to this season, Carolina would have had to pay him $3.467 million. Instead, the Hurricanes offered $1.8 million, and Irbe declined.

Rather than send the goalie to the AHL, Rutherford contacted Chiefs majority owner Neil Smith about the possibility of placing Irbe in Johnstown.

Carolina coach Peter Laviolette, the former Wheeling Nailers coach, took over for fired coach Paul Maurice on Dec. 15.

Eventually, Laviolette asked about the possibility of bringing Irbe back into the NHL mix. Since his call-up, Irbe has put the past differences with the organization out of mind. So has Laviolette.

"He said, 'Basically, you have a clean slate with me and I don't care about your past,'" Irbe said of his coach. "He said that in a good way. 'You just have to do things the way you can. If you can deliver, that's all I'm asking you. Nothing else.' "

Irbe has made two appearances in Carolina's past six games. "I sat the first week back," Irbe said. "I have played one third or 40 percent of the games. Kevin gets a couple and I get one. That's fine. The team keeps getting points. That's all you can ask for."

When asked if he still glances at the ECHL standings, Irbe smiled.

"I check on the Chiefs," he said. "I have kept in touch with (coach Toby O'Brien) every week. It's great to see the team is doing well. The foundation is right and the playoffs are right around the corner. Good luck to everybody there. That's all I can say right now."

CHIEFS IN THE 2000s

Top: Coach Toby O'Brien confers with forward Steve Hildenbrand and Johnstown native Josh Piro (23) in 2003-04.

Middle: Chiefs forward Joe Tallari works the puck along the boards against the Dayton Bombers.

Bottom left: Chiefs all-star Jean Desrochers.

Bottom right: Chiefs coach Frank Anzalone led the team to two playoff berths in 2006 and 2007.

303

Johnstown hockey fans line up to catch a glimpse of the Stanley Cup after Dana Heinze brought hockey's coveted trophy to the War Memorial in July 2004.

REPRINT

CHIEFS IN THE 2000s

Former Chiefs trainer Dana Heinze used his time in Johnstown as a stepping stone to the National Hockey League. Heinze was assistant equipment manager of the Tampa Bay Lightning when the team won the Stanley Cup in 2004. He remembered his hockey roots and brought the Cup to Johnstown, where more than 1,800 people unexpectedly packed the War Memorial Arena. The Tribune-Democrat's July 10, 2004 article follows:

City goes Cup crazy
Nearly 2,000 turn out for glimpse of Lord Stanley's Cup

By Mike Mastovich

Mary Miller awoke early yesterday, quickly went through her morning routine and headed downtown to Cambria County War Memorial Arena.

The emergency medical technician from Dale Borough made certain she was the first person in a line that eventually included more than 1,800 people — some of whom waited two hours to catch a brief glimpse of the Stanley Cup.

"I was here at 9 o'clock and I was excited," said Miller, a Johnstown Chiefs fan who has had season tickets for 10 years. "This is the first time the Cup's been in Johnstown and I really wanted to see it. It's great to have Dana Heinze bring it here. I'm also happy for the Tampa Bay Lightning."

Heinze, 36, is a Westmont Hilltop High School graduate and former trainer-equipment manager of the ECHL Chiefs. He capped his fifth season with the NHL's Tampa Bay Lightning which won the Stanley Cup last month. As part of a long NHL tradition, each member of the Stanley Cup-winning team is entitled to take possession of the Cup for a day. Heinze opted to bring one of sports' most historic trophies to his hometown.

Neither Heinze, the War Memorial staff nor the Chiefs, who coordinated the event, could have imagined Johnstown hockey fans' response to the Cup's visit. "You couldn't have asked for a better turnout," Heinze said, wearing a Lightning shirt and a big smile.

"This is wonderful. I'm glad everyone stayed patient and stayed with us for this. This is something. I got choked up emotionally. I walked in the building with the Cup and thought I was going to cry for a minute. I'm just so happy and proud to be able to share this with everyone."

The event was scheduled from 11 a.m. to 1:30 p.m. But a wide line formed near Section

3 and stretched 15 sections to the opposite side of the building. Even as people crossed the red carpet placed in front of the Cup to pose for photos or touch the trophy, additional fans entered the building.

The line never really shrunk until late in the afternoon. The concourse gates were lowered at 1:15 to prevent more people from entering the building because Heinze and Walt Neubrand, the Cup caretaker provided by the Hockey Hall of Fame in Toronto, had a 3 p.m. deadline to depart for other scheduled stops.

The last fan photographed the Cup at 2:43 p.m., more than an hour later than anticipated.

The historic event had people talking about hockey at a time when the Tour de France and upcoming Major League Baseball All-Star game take center stage in sports.

The Chiefs collected donations of more than $1,000 for the Galen Head Jr. Memorial Scholarship presented annually to area high school players. Team officials said that Cup enthusiasts from at least seven different states visited the arena.

The War Memorial concession stand sold about 300 hot dogs as part of a lunchtime businessman's special.

Chiefs videographer Doug Heck snapped 416 photos of fans posing beside the Cup. Other people used their own cameras to capture the moment.

"Swamped, totally swamped," Heck's son Matt, 15, said as he frantically tried to keep pace while making computer prints of the photos.

Chiefs fan Mark Kadas held his 1-month-old daughter, Kylie, above the Cup as his wife Christine watched. Kylie was born on June 7, the same day Tampa beat Calgary 2-1 to win the Cup at St. Pete Times Forum. The baby fit almost perfectly inside the chalice atop the trophy, sleeping quietly the whole time.

"She was born at 3:19 in the afternoon and we watched the game that night," Mr. Kadas, a West End resident, said. "We saw Dana sew up (a cut on) Martin St. Louis' face at the end of the game."

Hockey fans altered their work schedules and lunch breaks. Christopher Brett, 15, ended his vacation at an uncle's home a few days early to return to Johnstown from Newark, New Jersey. "He's been rooting for the Lightning to win the whole time," said Maryann Brett, Christopher's mother and Chiefs season ticket holder. "He already had the vacation planned to spend a week with his uncle. He wanted to come back. That's how big of a deal this is."

Matthew Papinchak, 12, a Harrisburg youth hockey player, persuaded his grandfather to travel across the state to see the Cup. "I love hockey and it's great to see one of my favorite teams win it," Papinchak said.

Chiefs coach Toby O'Brien soaked up the atmosphere as the long line slowly filed into the rink. "Any time you can see the pinnacle of your sport, whether you're a player, coach, staff member or most importantly, a fan, it's just great," O'Brien said. "We have lines around the building in the middle of July. It shows how dedicated the hockey fans are here in Johnstown."

"I couldn't be happier for the Chiefs and for Dana Heinze. He achieved what we all try to achieve. I want to thank Dana for remembering where his roots are."

As the Cup finally was loaded into a van with a seat belt strapped across the trophy, Heinze held his wife Kathy's hand and headed toward the exit. He appeared both relieved and content.

"We did the right thing," Heinze said, nodding in the affirmative. Those who spent the afternoon in line waiting to be a small part of hockey history couldn't have agreed more.

CHIEFS IN THE 2000s

Top: Former Chiefs athletic trainer Chris Stewart continued the "Stanley Cup roll" in Johnstown. The city native was part of the Carolina Hurricanes' Stanley Cup run in 2006 and brought the Cup to Johnstown that September.

Top: Future NHL player Jody Shelley reacts after scoring a goal for the Chiefs against the Greensboro Generals.

Middle: Chiefs captain Brent Bilodeau (5), defenseman Mike Vellinga (10) and forward Ryan Chaytors (16) crunch a Huntington Blizzard player. Goalie Frederic Deschenes (31) watches the action.

Bottom: Chiefs right wing Lukas Smital nets his club-record 107th career goal on March 14, 2003 against Atlantic City at Cambria County War Memorial Arena.

CHIEFS IN THE 2000s

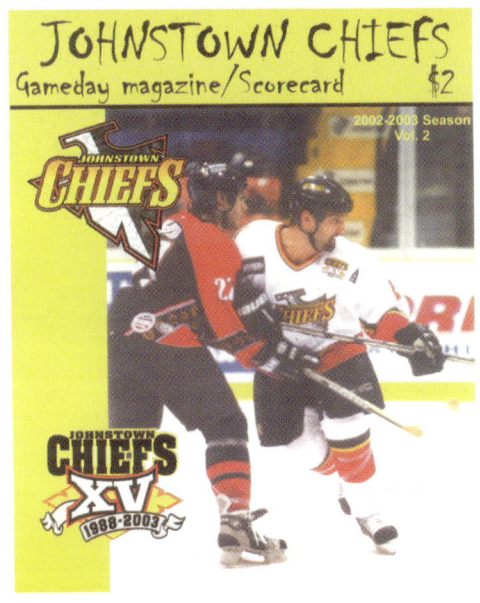

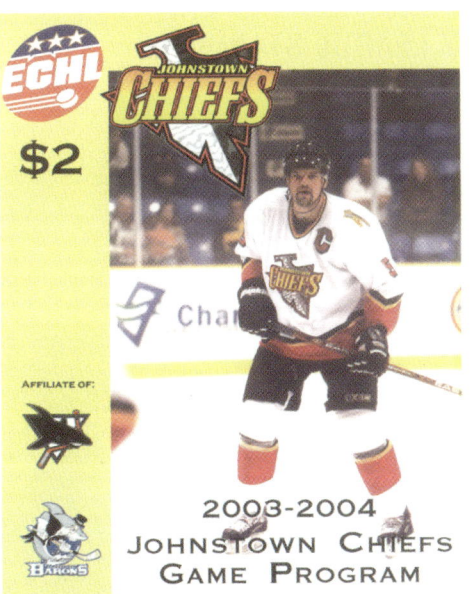

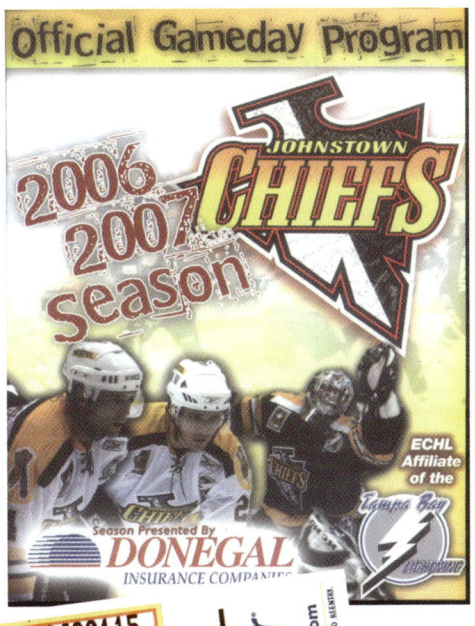

309

2000-01 Johnstown Chiefs

(Front, from left) Frederic Deschenes, Andrew Clark, Jeff Sullivan, head coach Scott Allen, Brent Bilodeau, president Jim Edwards Sr., bookkeeper Dennis Vickroy, Jason Spence, Andrew Dale, Dany Sabourin. (Middle) Equipment manager Mic Midderhoff, Mike Rodrigues, Jim Shepherd, Kenny Corupe, Roman Marakhovski, Blair Stayzer, Ryan Tocher, Ted Laviolette, Edo Terglav, medical trainer Chris Stewart. (Back) Locker room attendant Cory Mesteller, locker room attendant Chuck Lamberson, locker room attendant Jesse Shoff, locker room attendant Doug Mesteller, Mike Rodrigues, Jim Leger, Eric Schneider, Ryan Chaytors, Dmitri Tarabrin. Missing from photo: General manager Toby O'Brien, assistant general manager Jim Brazill.

2000-01 FINAL EAST COAST HOCKEY LEAGUE STANDINGS

	Games played	Won	Lost	Overtime losses	Points	Goals for	Goals against
Northeast Division							
Trenton Titans	72	50	18	4	104	236	164
Roanoke Express	72	38	30	4	80	231	195
Charlotte Checkers	72	34	26	12	80	247	252
Richmond Renegades	72	35	31	6	76	223	228
Greensboro Generals	72	26	39	7	59	215	277
Northwest Division							
Peoria Rivermen	72	45	17	10	100	238	182
Dayton Bombers	72	45	21	6	96	247	194
Toledo Storm	72	37	27	8	82	262	259
Johnstown Chiefs	72	28	36	8	64	207	238
Wheeling Nailers	72	24	40	8	56	192	277
Southeast Division							
South Carolina Stingrays	72	42	23	7	91	240	210
Florida Everblades	72	38	26	8	84	236	242
Tallahassee Tiger Sharks	72	38	27	7	83	248	219
Pee Dee Pride	72	38	28	6	82	242	231
Augusta Lynx	72	36	29	7	79	259	253
Greenville Grrrowl	72	34	33	5	73	219	239
Southwest Division							
Louisiana Ice Gators	72	42	24	6	90	237	209
Jackson Bandits	72	39	24	9	87	206	209
Mobile Mysticks	72	38	28	6	82	240	233
New Orleans Brass	72	35	25	12	82	247	239
Arkansas Riverblades	72	34	24	14	82	237	232
Baton Rouge Kingfish	72	35	26	11	81	216	225
Mississippi Sea Wolves	72	34	33	5	73	221	218
Birmingham Bulls	72	28	40	4	60	224	296
Pensacola Ice Pilots	72	27	40	5	59	201	250

Johnstown Chiefs
General Manager - Toby O'Brien
Coach - Scott Allen
Assistant Coach - Galen Head
Training Staff - Mic Midderhoff, Chris Stewart
Locker Room Attendants - Chuck Lamberson, Doug Mesteller, Corey Mesteller, Jesse Shoff
Colors - Black, White, Gold and Red

CHIEFS IN THE 2000s

2000-01 Game Results

Preseason Results

Day	Date	Opponent	Johnstown	Opponent	Attendance	Record
Fri.	6-Oct	Dayton	4	6	678	
Sat.	7-Oct	Toledo	5	4 (ot)	963	
Sun.	8-Oct	Wheeling	7	3	571	

Regular Season Results

Day	Date	Opponent	Johnstown	Opponent	Attendance	Record
Thur.	12-Oct	Wheeling	5	1	2,006	1-0-0
Sat.	14-Oct	Richmond	4	3 (otw)	2,318	2-0-0
Tues.	17-Oct	at Roanoke	1	2		2-1-0
Wed.	18-Oct	at Richmond	4	1		3-1-0
Fri.	20-Oct	at Dayton	1	2		3-2-0
Sat.	21-Oct	Wheeling	3	4 (otl)	2,204	3-2-1
Fri.	27-Oct	at Dayton	1	2 (otl)		3-2-2
Sat.	28-Oct	at Peoria	2	4		3-3-2
Fri.	3-Nov	at Greensboro	3	2		4-3-2
Sat.	4-Nov	Roanoke	5	1	2,567	5-3-2
Wed.	8-Nov	at Toledo	2	5		5-4-2
Fri.	10-Nov	at Toledo	0	5		5-5-2
Sat.	11-Nov	Toledo	2	3 (sol)	2,877	5-5-3
Tues.	14-Nov	at Trenton	1	2		5-6-3
Fri.	17-Nov	Dayton	4	3 (otw)	3,142	6-6-3
Sat.	18-Nov	at Richmond	6	4		7-6-3
Wed.	22-Nov	Charlotte	6	3	1,768	8-6-3
Fri.	24-Nov	Arkansas	5	6	2,970	8-7-3
Sat.	25-Nov	Arkansas	2	3	2,904	8-8-3
Sun.	26-Nov	at Toledo	1	3		8-9-3
Fri.	1-Dec	Peoria	1	4	1,750	8-10-3
Sat.	2-Dec	Peoria	3	4	2,082	8-11-3
Fri.	8-Dec	at Charlotte	1	5		8-12-3
Sat.	9-Dec	at Roanoke	2	3		8-13-3
Sun.	10-Dec	at Roanoke	1	4		8-14-3
Fri.	15-Dec	at Wheeling	1	2		8-15-3
Sat.	16-Dec	Wheeling	5	3	2,097	9-15-3
Fri.	22-Dec	at Richmond	2	6		9-16-3
Sat.	23-Dec	Wheeling	3	0	2,064	10-16-3
Wed.	27-Dec	Roanoke	3	0	2,083	11-16-3
Fri.	29-Dec	Dayton	4	2	2,037	12-16-3
Sat.	30-Dec	at Trenton	3	2 (sow)		13-16-3
Sun.	31-Dec	Trenton	0	1	2,828	13-17-3
Wed.	3-Jan	at Toledo	1	5		13-18-3
Sat.	6-Jan	Greensboro	9	4	2,371	14-18-3
Sun.	7-Jan	at Roanoke	6	3		15-18-3
Tues.	9-Jan	at Greensboro	4	5 (otl)		15-18-4
Wed.	10-Jan	at Charlotte	3	8		15-19-4
Fri.	12-Jan	Dayton	3	2	2,038	16-19-4
Sat.	13-Jan	at Wheeling	3	4		16-20-4
Fri.	19-Jan	Peoria	2	1 (sow)	2,032	17-20-4
Sat.	20-Jan	Peoria	1	3	2,783	17-21-4
Fri.	26-Jan	at Wheeling	2	3 (otl)		17-21-5
Sat.	27-Jan	at Wheeling	3	2 (sow)		18-21-5
Wed.	31-Jan	Richmond	3	1	1,672	19-21-5
Fri.	2-Feb	Roanoke	4	2	2,004	20-21-5
Sat.	3-Feb	Trenton	2	3	2,649	20-22-5
Wed.	7-Feb	at Trenton	2	4		20-23-5
Fri.	9-Feb	Toledo	2	7	2,092	20-24-5
Sat.	10-Feb	Toledo	7	9	2,837	20-25-5
Wed.	14-Feb	at Toledo	3	2		21-25-5
Thur.	15-Feb	Richmond	1	2	1,550	21-26-5
Sat.	17-Feb	at Dayton	0	4		21-27-5
Sun.	18-Feb	at Peoria	3	2 (otw)		22-27-5
Tues.	20-Feb	at Peoria	0	4		22-28-5
Thur.	22-Feb	Greensboro	2	3 (sol)	2,353	22-28-6
Sun.	25-Feb	Wheeling	5	3	3,616	23-28-6
Fri.	2-Mar	Toledo	4	2	1,912	24-28-6
Sat.	3-Mar	Dayton	3	4	2,758	24-29-6
Sun.	4-Mar	Trenton	1	3	2,193	24-30-6
Fri.	9-Mar	Wheeling	7	2	2,153	25-30-6
Sat.	10-Mar	Peoria	2	6	2,684	25-31-6
Fri.	16-Mar	at Dayton	2	4		25-32-6
Sat.	17-Mar	Dayton	6	2	2,333	26-32-6
Sun.	18-Mar	Richmond	4	3 (sow)	2,070	27-32-6
Wed.	21-Mar	at Trenton	4	6		27-33-6
Fri.	23-Mar	at Peoria	2	4		27-34-6

311

Sat.	24-Mar	at Peoria	3	4 (sol)			27-34-7
Wed.	28-Mar	at Toledo	2	5			27-35-7
Fri.	30-Mar	at Wheeling	4	5 (sol)			27-35-8
Sat.	31-Mar	Toledo	5	4		3,532	28-35-8
Sun.	1-Apr	at Dayton	0	3			28-36-8
		Playoff Results					
Sat.	7-Apr	at Trenton	0	2			0-1
Sun.	8-Apr	at Trenton	3	4 (ot)			0-2
Fri.	13-Apr	Trenton	3	1		2,009	1-2
Sat.	14-Apr	Trenton	1	5		1,562	1-3

Attendance Figures

	Dates	Totals	Average
Preseason Attendance Totals	3	2,212	737
Regular Season Attendance Totals	36	85,329	2,370
Playoff Attendance Totals	2	3,571	1,786
TOTAL ATTENDANCE	41	91,112	2,222

2000-01 Player Statistics

	Regular Season Scoring					Playoff Scoring				
	Games	G	A	Pts	PIM	Games	G	A	Pts	PIM
72 Eric Schneider	66	33	37	70	32	4	0	1	1	6
14 Andrew Dale	71	23	38	61	72	4	1	0	1	0
16 Ryan Chaytors	50	20	30	50	28	4	1	0	1	4
26 Jim Shepherd	44	14	26	40	135	4	1	2	3	10
13 Dorian Anneck	47	15	20	35	32					
10 Mike Vellinga	66	5	25	30	85	4	0	2	2	0
5 Brent Bilodeau	64	7	22	29	123	4	1	1	2	7
17 Dmitri Tarabrin	61	14	11	25	61	4	0	0	0	0
19 Andrew Clark	42	12	13	25	35	4	1	1	2	2
18 Jan Sulc	54	6	17	23	41					
24 Ryan Tocher	70	2	19	21	75	4	0	0	0	4
27 Chris Brassard	25	11	8	19	83					
4 Mike Rodrigues	61	4	13	17	78					
12 Jim Leger	40	9	7	16	48	4	0	0	0	2
27 John McNabb	25	9	6	15	20					
8 Jeff Sullivan	69	2	9	11	302	4	0	0	0	9
12 Maxim Potapov	15	4	4	8	2					
7 Kenny Corupe	12	2	6	8	20					
27 Samuel St. Pierre	6	3	2	5	2	4	2	1	3	2
26 Benoit Dusablon	11	2	3	5	4					
6 Mark Thompson	41	2	3	5	82					
22 Mikko Kuparinen	13	1	4	5	10					
44 Mike Kiesman	30	1	3	4	56	3	0	0	0	17
67 Blair Stayzer	37	1	3	4	104					
20 Jason Spence	47	1	3	4	217	4	0	1	1	2
44 Jeff Lukasak	12	1	2	3	17					
22 Kenton Smith	13	0	3	3	12	4	0	1	1	2
13 Ted Laviolette	7	1	1	2	6	4	0	0	0	18
18 Edo Terglav	6	1	0	1	0	1	0	0	0	0
26 Brent Ozarowski	11	1	0	1	4					
2 Karl Infanger	2	0	1	1	0					
33 Tyrone Garner (g)	5	0	1	1	0					
2 Roman Marakhovski	9	0	1	1	6					
30 Dany Sabourin (g)	19	0	1	1	17	1	0	0	0	0
22 Ryan Moynihan	1	0	0	0	0					
2 Rick Boyd	2	0	0	0	6					
7 Pat Glenday	3	0	0	0	4					
2 D.J. Maracle	3	0	0	0	2					
31 Frederic Deschenes (g)	54	0	0	0	8	4	0	0	0	0
Bench					36					
TOTALS	72	207	342	549	1,865	4	7	10	17	85

Regular Season Goaltending

	G	Min	GA	ENG	SO	GAA	W	L	OTL	SOL	Saves	Save%
33 Tyrone Garner	5	306	15	0	0	2.94	3	1	1	0	157	0.913
31 Frederic Deschenes	54	3,158	157	4	2	2.98	21	26	2	4	1,515	0.906
30 Dany Sabourin	19	903	56	2	0	3.72	4	9	1	0	408	0.879
Shootout Goals					4							
TOTALS	72	4,367	232	6	2	3.27	28	36	4	4	2,080	0.897

Playoff Goaltending

	G	Min	GA	ENG	SO	GAA	W	L	Saves	Save%
31 Frederic Deschenes	4	207	9	1	0	2.61	1	3	97	.915
30 Dany Sabourin	1	40	2	0	0	3.00	0	0	8	.800
TOTALS	4	247	11	1	0	2.91	1	3	105	.897

Terglav also wore No. 44; Anneck also wore No. 7.
Players on roster who did not play: 1 Shane Clifford, Goal; 33 Chris Cuppett, Goal; 1 Vinny Prestinary, Goal.

CHIEFS IN THE 2000s

2001-02 Johnstown Chiefs

(Front, from left) Frederic Deschenes, Chad Onufrechuk, assistant general manager Jim Brazill, head coach Scott Allen, Brent Bilodeau, president Jim Edwards Sr., general manager Toby O'Brien, Jeff Sullivan, Dany Sabourin. (Middle) Andrew Clark, Jim Leger, Rob Sandrock, Eric Schneider, Mark White, Lukas Smital, Kevin Baker, Kevin Clauson, Blair Stayzer, Jason Spence, Shaun Sutter, Vladimir Nemec, J.F. Boutin, Mike Rodrigues, Ryan Townsend. (Back) Locker room attendant Josh Kush, locker room attendant Corey Mesteller, locker room attendant Chuck Lamberson, medical trainer Chris Stewart, locker room attendant Doug Mesteller, equipment manager Mic Midderhoff, David Gove, Philippe Roy, Dan Carlson, broadcaster Matt Dimperio, broadcaster Matt Jordan, public relations director Kevin McGeehan, administrative assistant Tom Gramling, bookkeeper Marge Moehler, administrative assistant Darla Polyac

2001-02 FINAL EAST COAST HOCKEY LEAGUE STANDINGS

	Games played	Won	Lost	Overtime losses	Points	Goals for	Goals against
Northeast Division							
Trenton Titans	72	46	16	10	102	238	178
Charlotte Checkers	72	41	20	11	93	256	207
Atlantic City Boardwalk Bullies	72	42	22	8	92	233	209
Roanoke Express	72	35	26	11	81	242	223
Richmond Renegades	72	32	30	10	74	191	225
Reading Royals	72	27	36	9	63	182	215
Greensboro Generals	72	23	41	8	54	188	278
Northwest Division							
Dayton Bombers	72	40	20	12	92	222	196
Peoria Rivermen	72	41	23	8	90	206	179
Johnstown Chiefs	72	39	31	2	80	220	232
Cincinnati Cyclones	72	36	30	6	78	210	207
Wheeling Nailers	72	36	32	4	76	213	208
Toledo Storm	72	28	34	10	66	225	265
Southeast Division							
Greenville Grrrowl	72	43	23	6	92	231	198
Pee Dee Pride	72	41	25	6	88	236	218
Columbia Inferno	72	36	22	14	86	211	197
South Carolina Stingrays	72	39	26	7	85	235	225
Florida Everblades	72	37	27	8	82	207	221
Augusta Lynx	72	36	26	10	82	218	224
Macon Whoopee	72	29	31	12	70	194	228
Columbus Cottonmouths	72	24	37	11	59	197	242
Southwest Division							
Louisiana Ice Gators	72	56	12	4	116	261	156
Mississippi Sea Wolves	72	41	26	5	87	251	232
Pensacola Ice Pilots	72	38	28	6	82	247	242
Jackson Bandits	72	34	29	9	77	187	202
New Orleans Brass	72	36	32	4	76	211	209
Mobile Mysticks	72	28	26	18	74	215	237
Arkansas Riverblades	72	31	31	10	72	189	206
Baton Rouge Kingfish	72	29	35	8	66	187	244

Johnstown Chiefs
General Manager - Toby O'Brien
Coach - Scott Allen
Assistant Coach - Galen Head
Training Staff - Mic Midderhoff, Chris Stewart

Locker Room Attendants - Chuck Lambeson, Doug Mesteller, Cory Mesteller, Josh Kush
Colors - Black, White, Gold and Red

2001-02 Game Results

Preseason Results

Day	Date	Opponent	Johnstown	Opponent	Attendance	Record
Fri.	5-Oct	Wheeling *	3	4		
Sat.	6-Oct	Wheeling	3	2	889	

* Game played at Iceoplex – Pittsburgh, Pa.

Regular Season Results

Day	Date	Opponent	Johnstown	Opponent	Attendance	Record
Fri.	12-Oct	at Toledo	3	9		0-1-0
Sat.	13-Oct	Atlantic City	4	3 (sow)	3,096	1-1-0
Wed.	17-Oct	Trenton	1	2	1,358	1-2-0
Fri.	19-Oct	at Atlantic City	2	4		1-3-0
Sat.	20-Oct	at Richmond	4	2		2-3-0
Fri.	26-Oct	at Reading	1	3		2-4-0
Sat.	27-Oct	Cincinnati	3	5	2,217	2-5-0
Sun.	28-Oct	at Wheeling	2	6		2-6-0
Wed.	31-Oct	Wheeling	2	1	1,603	3-6-0
Fri.	2-Nov	at Peoria	4	3 (sow)		4-6-0
Sat.	3-Nov	at Peoria	2	1		5-6-0
Fri.	9-Nov	Richmond	2	3 (sol)	1,818	5-6-1
Sat.	10-Nov	Dayton	4	3 (sow)	2,697	6-6-1
Fri.	16-Nov	Toledo	5	4	3,243	7-6-1
Wed.	21-Nov	Reading	4	2	1,741	8-6-1
Fri.	23-Nov	Wheeling	3	5	3,189	8-7-1
Sat.	24-Nov	Richmond	2	3	2,612	8-8-1
Sun.	25-Nov	at Cincinnati	3	2		9-8-1
Wed.	28-Nov	at Reading	2	1 (sow)		10-8-1
Fri.	30-Nov	at Richmond	2	1		11-8-1
Sat.	1-Dec	at Roanoke	2	5		11-9-1
Fri.	7-Dec	at Toledo	3	5		11-10-1
Sat.	8-Dec	Dayton	5	6	2,286	11-11-1
Sun.	9-Dec	Trenton	4	2	1,606	12-11-1
Tues.	11-Dec	at Trenton	6	5 (sow)		13-11-1
Fri.	14-Dec	at Wheeling	2	6		13-12-1
Sat.	15-Dec	at Dayton	2	5		13-13-1
Sun.	16-Dec	at Cincinnati	4	2		14-13-1
Fri.	21-Dec	Reading	5	2	1,874	15-13-1
Sat.	22-Dec	Reading	5	3	2,044	16-13-1
Sun.	23-Dec	at Roanoke	3	6		16-14-1
Thur.	27-Dec	at Dayton	3	2 (otw)		17-14-1
Sat.	29-Dec	Toledo	1	3	2,575	17-15-1
Sun.	30-Dec	at Trenton	1	4		17-16-1
Mon.	31-Dec	Dayton	5	6	3,000	17-17-1
Fri.	4-Jan	at Trenton	2	5		17-18-1
Sun.	6-Jan	at Cincinnati	1	0		18-18-1
Fri.	11-Jan	at Reading	2	6		18-19-1
Sat.	12-Jan	Roanoke	3	1	2,427	19-19-1
Fri.	18-Jan	at Dayton	4	7		19-20-1
Sat.	19-Jan	Cincinnati	5	1	2,044	20-20-1
Sun.	20-Jan	Toledo	5	2	1,638	21-20-1
Fri.	25-Jan	at Wheeling	3	1		22-20-1
Sun.	27-Jan	at Richmond	3	2 (otw)		23-20-1
Fri.	1-Feb	Peoria	3	2 (otw)	1,845	24-20-1
Sat.	2-Feb	Peoria	2	1	2,632	25-20-1
Fri.	8-Feb	at Dayton	1	4		25-21-1
Sat.	9-Feb	at Dayton	1	3		25-22-1
Sun.	10-Feb	Reading	5	1	2,101	26-22-1
Wed.	13-Feb	at Trenton	2	5		26-23-1
Fri.	15-Feb	at Toledo	2	5		26-24-1
Sat.	16-Feb	Dayton	2	4	2,732	26-25-1
Sun.	17-Feb	Toledo	4	3 (sow)	1,970	27-25-1
Fri.	22-Feb	Atlantic City	2	1 (otw)	2,142	28-25-1
Sat.	23-Feb	Dayton	3	2 (otw)	2,332	29-25-1
Sun.	24-Feb	Trenton	3	2	1,798	30-25-1
Fri.	1-Mar	Cincinnati	6	5 (sow)	1,690	31-25-1
Sat.	2-Mar	Toledo	6	3	2,304	32-25-1
Wed.	6-Mar	at Wheeling	2	3		32-26-1
Fri.	8-Mar	Cincinnati	3	4 (sol)	2,366	32-26-2
Sat.	9-Mar	Wheeling	4	3 (otw)	2,716	33-26-2
Sun.	10-Mar	Wheeling	2	5	1,793	33-27-2
Thur.	14-Mar	at Cincinnati	2	4		33-28-2

314

CHIEFS IN THE 2000s

Day	Date	Opponent			Att.	Record
Fri.	15-Mar	Atlantic City	1	3	1,862	33-29-2
Sat.	16-Mar	Reading	4	2	2,644	34-29-2
Wed.	20-Mar	at Toledo	5	2		35-29-2
Fri.	22-Mar	at Peoria	3	1		36-29-2
Sat.	23-Mar	at Peoria	4	3 (sow)		37-29-2
Wed.	27-Mar	at Cincinnati	4	6		37-30-2
Fri.	29-Mar	at Toledo	2	1 (otw)		38-30-2
Sat.	30-Mar	Greensboro	6	1	2,798	39-30-2
Sun.	31-Mar	Atlantic City	2	3	1,965	40-30-2

Playoff Results

Day	Date	Opponent			Att.	Record
Tues.	2-Apr	at Peoria	1	2		0-1
Wed.	3-Apr	at Peoria	0	1		0-2
Fri.	5-Apr	Peoria	6	1	2,041	1-2
Sat.	6-Apr	Peoria	3	1	2,548	2-2
Tues.	9-Apr	at Peoria	4	0		3-2
Fri.	12-Apr	at Dayton	3	4 (ot)		0-1
Sat.	13-Apr	at Dayton	1	3		0-2
Thur.	18-Apr	Dayton	1	5	2,229	0-3

Attendance Figures

	Dates	Totals	Average
Preseason Attendance Figures	1	889	889
Regular Season Attendance Figures	36	80,758	2,243
Playoff Attendance Figures	3	6,818	2,273
TOTAL ATTENDANCE	40	88,465	2,212

2001-02 Player Statistics

Regular Season Scoring / Playoff Scoring

Player	Games	G	A	Pts	PIM	Games	G	A	Pts	PIM
16 Eric Schneider	65	38	40	78	40	8	4	4	8	2
26 Dan Carlson	61	28	33	61	63	8	2	5	7	8
33 David Gove	54	17	32	49	32	8	1	3	4	4
7 J.F. Boutin	52	14	27	41	95	8	1	4	5	16
12 Philippe Roy	63	5	33	38	43	8	4	3	7	4
24 Jim Leger	59	20	17	37	74	8	0	1	1	15
21 Lukas Smital	62	19	18	37	55	8	1	0	1	6
5 Brent Bilodeau	72	3	30	33	95	8	0	2	2	19
10 Jim Shepherd	52	16	16	32	112					
14 Chad Onufrechuk	49	9	17	26	22	8	1	12	8	
10 Rob Sandrock	19	3	18	21	10	8	0	4	4	28
4 Mike Rodrigues	71	2	19	21	86	8	0	2	2	13
25 Shaun Sutter	34	13	7	20	34	8	0	1	1	4
19 Andrew Clark	36	7	10	17	39					
44 Kevin Baker	18	6	10	16	26	5	4	1	5	6
20 Jason Spence	55	8	6	14	181	6	0	0	0	6
6 Kevin Clauson	72	0	11	11	79	3	0	0	0	2
28 Blair Stayzer	41	1	8	9	100	5	1	0	1	9
8 Jeff Sullivan	36	3	5	8	155	5	0	1	1	20
18 Vladimir Nemec	39	3	5	8	18					
23 Ryan Townsend	32	3	2	5	75					
27 Ryan Shmyr	29	2	3	5	174					
55 Mark White	62	0	4	4	52	8	0	0	0	10
31 Frederic Deschenes (g)	49	0	3	3	0	6	0	1	1	0
15 Sergei Skrobot	15	0	2	2	4					
32 Dany Sabourin (g)	27	0	1	1	2	3	0	0	0	0
1 Bill Ruggiero (g)	2	0	0	0	0					
25 David Vychodil	2	0	0	0	2					
22 Rick Gorman	4	0	0	0	2					
Bench					18					
TOTALS	72	220	377	597	1,688	8	19	33	52	180

Regular Season Goaltending

	G	Min	GA	ENG	SO	GAA	W	L	OTL	SOL	Saves	Save %
31 Frederic Deschenes	49	2,760	135	4	1	2.93	25	21	0	1	1,264	0.904
32 Dany Sabourin	27	1,539	84	3	0	3.28	14	10	0	1	695	0.892
1 Bill Ruggeiro	2	60	4	0	0	4.00	0	0	0	0	26	0.867
Shootout Goals			2									
TOTALS	72	4,359	225	7	1	3.19	39	31	0	2	1,985	0.895

Playoff Goaltending

	G	Min	GA	ENG	SO	GAA	W	L	Saves	Save %
31 Frederic Deschenes	6	361	11	0	1	1.83	3	3	162	0.936
32 Dany Sabourin	3	137	5	1	0	2.18	0	2	73	0.936
TOTALS	8	498	16	1	1	2.05	3	5	235	0.933

Players on roster who did not play: 1 Shane Clifford, Goal; 1 Mark Scally, Goal; 1 Grant Van Laar, Goal.

315

2002-03 Johnstown Chiefs

(Front, from left) Peter Aubry, Ryan Shmyr, goaltending coach Shane Clifford, assistant coach Nick Pappas, head coach Toby O'Brien, Brent Bilodeau, president Jim Edwards Sr., general manager Jim Brazill, Lukas Smital, Jeff Sullivan, Mark Scally. (Middle) Andy Doktorchik, Vladimir Nemec, Pierre-Luc Courchesne, Ian Manzano, Samuel St. Pierre, Jason Shmyr, Mike Varhaug, Tim Branham, Jay Langager, Shaun Sutter, Matt Doman, Shawn Mather. (Back) Locker room attendant Cory Mesteller, medical trainer Chris Stewart, equipment manager Mic Midderhoff, Ryan Townsend, Dmitri Tarabrin, Dominic Forget, Steve Hildenbrand, locker room attendant Doug Mesteller, locker room attendant Chuck Lamberson, locker room attendant Josh Kush.

2002-03 FINAL EAST COAST HOCKEY LEAGUE STANDINGS

	Games played	Won	Lost	Overtime losses	Points	Goals for	Goals against
Northeast Division							
Atlantic City Boardwalk Bullies	72	41	19	12	94	268	224
Greensboro Generals	72	42	21	9	93	235	211
Roanoke Express	72	42	24	6	90	265	239
Trenton Titans	72	38	24	10	86	229	207
Charlotte Checkers	72	41	28	3	85	262	234
Richmond Renegades	72	35	31	6	76	240	239
Reading Royals	72	32	35	5	69	261	303
Northwest Division							
Toledo Storm	72	47	15	10	104	247	196
Peoria Rivermen	72	48	17	7	103	241	181
Cincinnati Cyclones	72	36	29	7	79	257	236
Lexington Men O' War	72	34	31	7	75	188	212
Johnstown Chiefs	72	28	33	11	67	214	243
Wheeling Nailers	72	28	41	3	59	193	261
Dayton Bombers	72	24	38	10	58	191	247
Southeast Division							
Columbia Inferno	72	47	23	2	96	265	202
South Carolina Stingrays	72	42	22	8	92	248	225
Pee Dee Pride	72	40	26	6	86	244	213
Florida Everblades	72	35	23	14	84	239	243
Greenville Grrrowl	72	28	36	8	64	217	262
Augusta Lynx	72	27	39	6	60	203	256
Columbus Cottonmouths	72	25	39	8	58	197	270
Southwest Division							
Mississippi Sea Wolves	72	44	24	4	92	250	211
Louisiana Ice Gators	72	40	20	12	92	249	210
Arkansas Riverblades	72	37	24	11	85	238	236
Jackson Bandits	72	38	26	8	84	210	195
Pensacola Ice Pilots	72	33	30	9	75	228	241
Baton Rouge Kingfish	72	20	43	9	49	184	266

Johnstown Chiefs
General Manager - Jim Brazill
Coach - Toby O'Brien
Assistant Coaches - Galen Head, Nick Pappas
Goaltender Coach - Shane Clifford
Consultant - Reg Kent

CHIEFS IN THE 2000s

Training Staff - Mic Midderhoff, Chris Stewart
Locker Room Attendants - Chuck Lamberson, Doug Mesteller, Cory Mesteller, Josh Kush
Colors - Black, White, Gold and Red
Wore White, Blue and Gold Charlestown Chiefs jerseys six times during season.

2002-03 Game Results

Preseason Results

Day	Date	Opponent	Johnstown	Opponent	Attendance	Record
Fri.	4-Oct	Wheeling *	1	4		
Sat.	5-Oct	Wheeling	3	1	958	

* Game played at Iceoplex – Pittsburgh, Pa.

Regular Season Results

Day	Date	Opponent	Johnstown	Opponent	Attendance	Record
Fri.	11-Oct	at Dayton	5	1		1-0-0
Sat.	12-Oct	Toledo	5	4 (otw)	2,718	2-0-0
Fri.	18-Oct	at Toledo	2	4		2-1-0
Sat.	19-Oct	Cincinnati	2	5	2,431	2-2-0
Sun.	20-Oct	at Dayton	6	2		3-2-0
Fri.	25-Oct	at Peoria	2	3		3-3-0
Sat.	26-Oct	at Peoria	1	0 (sow)		4-3-0
Thur.	31-Oct	Lexington	3	4	1,384	4-4-0
Fri.	1-Nov	at Toledo	2	5		4-5-0
Sat.	2-Nov	Dayton	4	3 (sow)	2,085	5-5-0
Fri.	8-Nov	Wheeling	1	4	1,871	5-6-0
Sat.	9-Nov	Reading	2	4	2,272	5-7-0
Sun.	10-Nov	at Lexington	2	3 (sol)		5-7-1
Wed.	13-Nov	at Cincinnati	1	5		5-8-1
Fri.	15-Nov	Toledo	5	4	3,042	6-8-1
Sat.	16-Nov	at Lexington	3	1		7-8-1
Fri.	22-Nov	Peoria	3	4	2,287	7-9-1
Sat.	23-Nov	Peoria	3	6	2,108	7-10-1
Sun.	24-Nov	at Dayton	5	2		8-10-1
Thur.	28-Nov	at Wheeling	4	1		9-10-1
Fri.	29-Nov	Wheeling	4	2	2,575	10-10-1
Sat.	30-Nov	Greensboro	2	3 (sol)	1,909	10-10-2
Wed.	4-Dec	at Cincinnati	2	8		10-11-2
Sat.	7-Dec	Dayton	4	3	1,952	11-11-2
Sun.	8-Dec	at Richmond	0	3		11-12-2
Tues.	10-Dec	at Roanoke	3	4 (sol)		11-12-3
Fri.	13-Dec	Peoria	6	4	1,379	12-12-3
Sat.	14-Dec	Peoria	2	3	1,672	12-13-3
Fri.	20-Dec	Cincinnati	3	4	1,552	12-14-3
Sat.	21-Dec	Reading	2	6	1,797	12-15-3
Sun.	22-Dec	at Lexington	2	4		12-16-3
Thur.	26-Dec	at Trenton	1	3		12-17-3
Fri.	27-Dec	at Wheeling	0	1 (sol)		12-17-4
Sat.	28-Dec	at Toledo	0	3		12-18-4
Tues.	31-Dec	Richmond	2	1 (sow)	3,078	13-18-4
Fri.	3-Jan	at Atlantic City	3	4 (sol)		13-18-5
Sat.	4-Jan	at Trenton	3	2		14-18-5
Fri.	10-Jan	at Wheeling	3	4		14-19-5
Sat.	11-Jan	Lexington	4	5 (sol)	1,888	14-19-6
Sun.	12-Jan	at Dayton	3	4 (otl)		14-19-7
Wed.	15-Jan	Toledo	2	5	1,547	14-20-7
Fri.	17-Jan	at Peoria	4	5		14-21-7
Sat.	18-Jan	at Peoria	2	3		14-22-7
Sun.	19-Jan	at Dayton	1	3		14-23-7
Fri.	24-Jan	Reading	9	4	1,912	15-23-7
Sat.	25-Jan	Dayton	3	0	2,492	16-23-7
Wed.	29-Jan	Augusta	8	2	1,877	17-23-7
Fri.	31-Jan	at Atlantic City	3	7		17-24-7
Sat.	1-Feb	at Richmond	4	2		18-24-7
Sun.	2-Feb	Greensboro	4	3 (sow)	2,225	19-24-7
Wed.	5-Feb	Lexington	3	2 (otw)	1,770	20-24-7
Fri.	7-Feb	Cincinnati	2	3 (sol)	1,869	20-24-8
Sat.	8-Feb	Wheeling	0	3	2,676	20-25-8

317

Day	Date	Opponent	GF	GA	Att	Record
Fri.	14-Feb	at Reading	2	3		20-26-8
Sat.	15-Feb	at Trenton	4	3 (otw)		21-26-8
Wed.	19-Feb	at Toledo	3	4		21-27-8
Fri.	21-Feb	Trenton	1	6	1,926	21-28-8
Sat.	22-Feb	Toledo	2	4	4,074	21-29-8
Fri.	28-Feb	at Lexington	1	2 (otl)		21-29-9
Sat.	1-Mar	Wheeling	3	2	2,402	22-29-9
Sun.	2-Mar	Dayton	4	2	2,195	23-29-9
Sat.	8-Mar	at Reading	5	4 (sow)		24-29-9
Sun.	9-Mar	Atlantic City	5	1	2,699	25-29-9
Tues.	11-Mar	at Cincinnati	5	2		26-29-9
Fri.	14-Mar	Atlantic City	1	3	2,184	26-30-9
Sat.	15-Mar	Trenton	4	3 (sow)	2,595	27-30-9
Wed.	19-Mar	Lexington	3	4 (sol)	2,106	27-30-10
Fri.	21-Mar	at Cincinnati	3	4 (otl)		27-30-11
Sun.	23-Mar	at Toledo	4	5		27-31-11
Fri.	28-Mar	at Wheeling	0	4		27-32-11
Sat.	29-Mar	Wheeling	6	4	2,984	28-32-11
Sun.	30-Mar	Cincinnati	3	5	3,259	28-33-11

Attendance Totals	Dates	Totals	Average
Preseason Attendance Totals	1	958	958
Regular Season Attendance Totals	36	80,792	2,244
TOTAL ATTENDANCE	37	81,750	2,209

2002-03 Player Statistics   Regular Season Scoring

	Games	G	A	Pts	PIM
26 Dominic Forget	70	23	39	62	47
22 Samuel St. Pierre	59	23	35	58	38
7 J.F. Boutin	47	20	38	58	144
17 Dmitri Tarabrin	71	17	25	42	101
15 Steve Hildenbrand	72	11	30	41	120
42 Lukas Smital	52	18	16	34	52
44 Philippe Roy	56	11	19	30	68
18 Vladimir Nemec	70	12	17	29	38
28 Pierre-Luc Courchesne	67	14	14	28	68
5 Brent Bilodeau	71	10	17	27	62
24 Jim Leger	30	12	9	21	20
25 Jay Langager	61	1	15	16	57
8 Jeff Sullivan	58	5	11	16	196
14 Ian Manzano	43	3	12	15	34
16 Andy Doktorchik	62	4	7	11	74
19 Shaun Sutter	9	7	3	10	4
4 Mike Rodrigues	40	1	8	9	32
10 Shawn Mather	16	3	5	8	12
21 Tim Branham	30	1	7	8	32
33 Matt Doman	16	2	4	6	20
6 Jason Shmyr	12	3	2	5	53
27 Ryan Shmyr	45	2	3	5	129
20 Jason Spence	23	2	2	4	91
55 Mike Varhaug	24	1	3	4	157
23 Ryan Townsend	32	1	2	3	27
30 Peter Aubry (g)	48	0	3	3	4
19 Gavin Hodgson	10	1	0	1	10
1 Dany Dallaire (g)	8	0	1	1	0
1 Shane Clifford (g)	1	0	0	0	0
12 Josh Piro	1	0	0	0	0
31 Mark Scally (g)	20	0	0	0	0
Bench		6		6	10
TOTALS	72	214	347	561	1,700

Regular Season Goaltending

	G	Min	GA	ENG	SO	GAA	W	L	OTL	SOL	Saves	Save %
1 Shane Clifford	1	1	0	0	0	0.00	0	0	0	0	0	0
30 Peter Aubry	48	2,870	140	2	3	2.93	21	18	2	6	1,459	0.912
1 Dany Dallaire	8	402	23	1	0	3.43	2	5	0	0	153	0.869
31 Mark Scally	20	1,116	69	0	0	3.71	5	10	1	2	477	0.874
Shootout Goals			8									
TOTALS	72	4,389	240	3	3	3.32	28	33	3	8	2,089	0.896

2003-04 Johnstown Chiefs

(Front, from left) David Currie, Shawn Mather, Dmitri Tarabrin, head coach Toby O'Brien, Brent Bilodeau, general manager Jim Brazill, Steve Hildenbrand, Jeff Sullivan, Dmitri Patzold. (Middle) Mike James, Chad Cavanagh, Dan Growden, Ian Manzano, Richard Paul, Jeff Zehr, Larry Courville, Jay Langager, Pierre-Luc Courchesne, Brent Kelly. (Back) Locker room attendant Zach Aman, locker room attendant Chuck Lamberson, locker room attendant Josh Kush, equipment manager Mic Midderhoff, Chris Leinweber, Dominic Forget, Jason Notermann, locker room attendant Doug Mesteller, locker room attendant Cory Mesteller, medical trainer Chris Stewart.

2003-04 FINAL ECHL STANDINGS

	Games played	Won	Lost	Overtime losses	Points	Goals for	Goals against
Northern Division							
Wheeling Nailers	72	51	17	4	106	259	188
Atlantic City Boardwalk Bullies	72	47	19	6	100	242	159
Peoria Rivermen	72	45	18	9	99	244	177
Johnstown Chiefs	72	45	20	7	97	223	195
Reading Royals	72	37	25	10	84	212	189
Trenton Titans	72	37	28	7	81	222	193
Dayton Bombers	72	26	41	5	57	187	271
Toledo Storm	72	23	38	11	57	183	258
Cincinnati Cyclones	72	25	43	4	54	175	223
Southern Division							
Columbia Inferno	72	44	20	8	96	275	217
Roanoke Express	72	38	26	8	84	219	232
Florida Everblades	72	37	25	10	84	239	221
South Carolina Stingrays	72	39	28	5	83	205	202
Greensboro Generals	72	40	30	2	82	241	240
Charlotte Checkers	72	31	32	9	71	206	230
Florence Pride	72	30	33	9	69	210	254
Greenville Grrrowl	72	14	53	5	33	177	281
Central Division							
Louisiana Ice Gators	72	48	22	2	98	235	167
Mississippi Sea Wolves	72	45	20	7	97	256	200
Gwinnett Gladiators	72	42	22	8	92	248	193
Pensacola Ice Pilots	72	40	23	9	89	240	239
Columbus Cottonmouths	72	37	27	8	82	214	197
Augusta Lynx	72	32	33	7	71	203	234
Texas Wildcatters	72	22	44	6	50	196	287
Pacific Division							
San Diego Gulls	72	49	13	10	108	240	177
Las Vegas Wranglers	72	43	22	7	93	227	186
Idaho Steelheads	72	40	23	9	89	219	208
Alaska Aces	72	38	28	6	82	220	210
Bakersfield Condors	72	25	38	9	59	201	236
Fresno Falcons	72	23	43	6	52	187	275
Long Beach Ice Dogs	72	23	44	5	51	191	257

Johnstown Chiefs
General Manager - Jim Brazill
Coach - Toby O'Brien
Assistant Coach - Galen Head
Goaltender Coach - Shane Clifford
Consultant - Reggie Kent
Trainers - Mic Midderhoff, Chris Stewart
Locker Room Attendants - Chuck Lamberson, Doug Mesteller, Cory Mesteller, Josh Kush, Zach Aman
Colors - Black, White, Gold and Red

2003-04 Game Results

Preseason Results

Day	Date	Opponent	Johnstown	Opponent	Attendance	Record
Fri.	10-Oct	Roanoke *	5	2		
Sat.	11-Oct	Roanoke**	4	1	600**	
Sat.	11-Oct	Wheeling**	1	3		

* Game played in Altoona, Pa.
** Two games played with 3 - 15 minute periods – Tickets sold as package.

Regular season results

Day	Date	Opponent	Johnstown	Opponent	Attendance	Record
Fri.	17-Oct	at Toledo	1	4		0-1-0
Sat.	18-Oct	Long Beach	4	1	4,011	1-1-0
Sun.	19-Oct	Cincinnati	6	1	1,673	2-1-0
Wed.	22-Oct	Texas	5	2	1,750	3-1-0
Fri.	24-Oct	at Dayton	6	1		4-1-0
Fri.	31-Oct	Dayton	1	4	1,646	4-2-0
Sat.	1-Nov	Reading	3	1	2,307	5-2-0
Fri.	7-Nov	Toledo	4	1	2,783	6-2-0
Sat.	8-Nov	at Trenton	3	0		7-2-0
Sun.	9-Nov	at Atlantic City	0	5		7-3-0
Wed.	12-Nov	at Atlantic City	2	0		8-3-0
Fri.	14-Nov	Wheeling	3	1	4,191	9-3-0
Sat.	15-Nov	at Cincinnati	1	2 (sol)		9-3-1
Sun.	16-Nov	at Wheeling	3	1		10-3-1
Fri.	21-Nov	Wheeling	4	1	2,218	11-3-1
Sat.	22-Nov	Dayton	5	2	2,639	12-3-1
Wed.	26-Nov	at Wheeling	1	6		12-4-1
Fri.	28-Nov	Atlantic City	1	3	3,627	12-5-1
Sat.	29-Nov	Atlantic City	4	1	2,185	13-5-1
Fri.	5-Dec	Peoria	3	2 (otw)	1,506	14-5-1
Sat.	6-Dec	Peoria	3	4 (sol)	2,174	14-5-2
Wed.	10-Dec	at Cincinnati	2	6		14-6-2
Fri.	12-Dec	at Peoria	2	5		14-7-2
Sat.	13-Dec	at Peoria	2	0		15-7-2
Fri.	19-Dec	at Dayton	3	4		15-8-2
Sat.	20-Dec	at Dayton	2	5		15-9-2
Fri.	26-Dec	Toledo	2	3 (sol)	2,457	15-9-3
Sat.	27-Dec	Toledo	2	5	2,473	15-10-3
Sun.	28-Dec	at Dayton	3	1		16-10-3
Tues.	30-Dec	at Trenton	1	6		16-11-3
Wed.	31-Dec	Dayton	3	2 (sow)	4,015	17-11-3
Fri.	2-Jan	at Reading	1	2		17-12-3
Sat.	3-Jan	at Reading	1	4		17-13-3
Sun.	4-Jan	at Atlantic City	1	5		17-14-3
Wed.	7-Jan	at Trenton	4	2		18-14-3
Fri.	9-Jan	Cincinnati	4	2	2,141	19-14-3
Sat.	10-Jan	Reading	2	0	2,246	20-14-3
Fri.	16-Jan	at Peoria	3	2		21-14-3
Sat.	17-Jan	at Peoria	0	1 (sol)		21-14-4
Fri.	23-Jan	Roanoke	2	5	1,825	21-15-4
Sat.	24-Jan	Reading	4	2	2,088	22-15-4
Sun.	25-Jan	at Toledo	4	2		23-15-4
Fri.	30-Jan	Atlantic City	2	3 (sol)	1,925	23-15-5
Sat.	31-Jan	Reading	5	2	2,316	24-15-5
Wed.	4-Feb	Wheeling	3	0	1,863	25-15-5
Sun.	8-Feb	at Cincinnati	5	3		26-15-5
Fri.	13-Feb	at Toledo	4	3 (otw)		27-15-5
Sat.	14-Feb	at Reading	1	6		27-16-5
Mon.	16-Feb	Peoria	4	5 (sol)	2,307	27-16-6
Tues.	17-Feb	Peoria	5	4	2,375	28-16-6
Sat.	21-Feb	Trenton	4	2	3,728	29-16-6
Sun.	22-Feb	Dayton	4	0	1,920	30-16-6
Wed.	25-Feb	at Trenton	2	5		30-17-6
Fri.	27-Feb	at Toledo	3	2		31-17-6
Sat.	28-Feb	Toledo	6	5 (sow)	2,986	32-17-6
Sun.	29-Feb	Trenton	3	2	1,866	33-17-6
Wed.	3-Mar	at Reading	4	3		34-17-6
Fri.	5-Mar	Wheeling	3	4	2,248	34-18-6
Sat.	6-Mar	Atlantic City	4	0	2,835	35-18-6

320

CHIEFS IN THE 2000s

Sun.	7-Mar	at Wheeling	1	6			35-19-6
Fri.	12-Mar	at Reading	4	3			36-19-6
Sat.	13-Mar	Wheeling	6	2		3,752	37-19-6
Sun.	14-Mar	Trenton	6	2		1,853	38-19-6
Wed.	17-Mar	at Atlantic City	3	2 (sow)			39-19-6
Sat.	20-Mar	at Cincinnati	3	2			40-19-6
Sun.	21-Mar	Dayton	1	5		3,346	40-20-6
Wed.	24-Mar	at Atlantic City	5	2			41-20-6
Fri.	26-Mar	at Wheeling	5	3			42-20-6
Sat.	27-Mar	Trenton	6	4		3,703	43-20-6
Sun.	28-Mar	Cincinnati	4	3 (otw)		2,859	44-20-6
Fri.	2-Apr	at Reading	2	3 (sol)			44-20-7
Sat.	3-Apr	at Trenton	4	2			45-20-7

Playoff Result

Mon.	5-Apr	Reading	1	2	1,941	0-1

Attendance Figures	Dates	Totals	Average
Preseason Attendance Totals	1	600	600
Regular Season Attendance Totals	36	91,837	2,551
Playoff Attendance Totals	1	1,941	1,941
TOTAL ATTENDANCE	38	94,378	2,484

2003-04 Player Statistics

	Regular Season Scoring					Playoff Scoring				
	Games	G	A	Pts	PIM	Games	G	A	Pts	PIM
26 Dominic Forget	72	26	37	63	49	1	0	1	1	0
15 Steve Hildenbrand	70	28	34	62	115	1	1	0	1	2
22 Jason Notermann	68	25	29	54	73	1	0	0	0	0
10 Shawn Mather	68	23	31	54	38	1	0	0	0	0
19 Brent Kelly	68	25	25	50	33	1	0	0	0	0
6 Jay Langager	70	8	32	40	42	1	0	0	0	0
28 Pierre-Luc Courchesne	70	17	22	39	57	1	0	0	0	2
25 Larry Courville	38	12	20	32	67	1	0	0	0	4
5 Brent Bilodeau	70	7	23	30	81	1	0	0	0	2
12 Chad Cavanagh	69	10	18	28	64	1	0	0	0	0
17 Dmitri Tarabrin	70	11	15	26	67	1	0	0	0	0
14 Ian Manzano	71	3	20	23	41	1	0	0	0	0
44 Jeff Zehr	22	7	14	21	72	1	0	1	1	0
2 Jeff Sullivan	66	0	15	15	282	1	0	0	0	0
4 Chris Leinweber	35	6	6	12	27	1	0	0	0	0
21 Willie Levesque	31	5	6	11	27					
23 Josh Piro	38	2	4	6	4					
55 Richard Paul	67	2	4	6	182					
18 Mike James	20	1	3	4	73	1	0	0	0	0
24 Dan Growden	34	1	2	3	28					
7 Ryan Crane	6	0	3	3	16					
1 Arturs Irbe (g)	14	0	2	2	2					
7 Bill Downey	4	1	0	1	18					
7 Mike Dombkiewicz	2	0	0	0	2					
16 Curtiss Patrick	8	0	0	0	11					
33 Dmitri Patzold (g)	8	0	0	0	2	1	0	0	0	0
30 Cory Campbell (g)	19	0	0	0	8					
31 David Currie (g)	34	0	0	0	2					
Bench			3	3	8					
Total	72	223	365	588	1,491					

Regular Season Goaltending

	G	Min	GA	ENG	SO	GAA	W	L	OTL	SOL	Saves	Save %
30 Cory Campbell	19	1,117	38	3	4	2.04	9	7	0	3	447	0.922
1 Arturs Irbe	14	847	30	0	1	2.13	10	3	0	1	381	0.927
33 Dmitri Patzold	8	443	20	0	0	2.71	7	0	0	0	197	0.908
31 David Currie	34	1,963	96	1	3	2.93	19	10	0	3	919	0.905
Shootout Goals			7									
TOTALS	72	4,370	191	4	8	2.68	45	20	0	7	1,944	0.909

Playoff Goaltending

	G	Min	GA	ENG	SO	GAA	W	L	Saves	Save %
33 Dmitri Patzold	1	59	2	0	0	2.02	0	1	30	0.938
TOTALS	1	60	2	0	0	2.00	0	1	30	0.938

Players on roster who did not play: 1 Joe Inman, Goal; 1 Shane Clifford, Goal; Tom Draper, Goal (claimed off waivers - did not report - Jan. 7, 2004.).

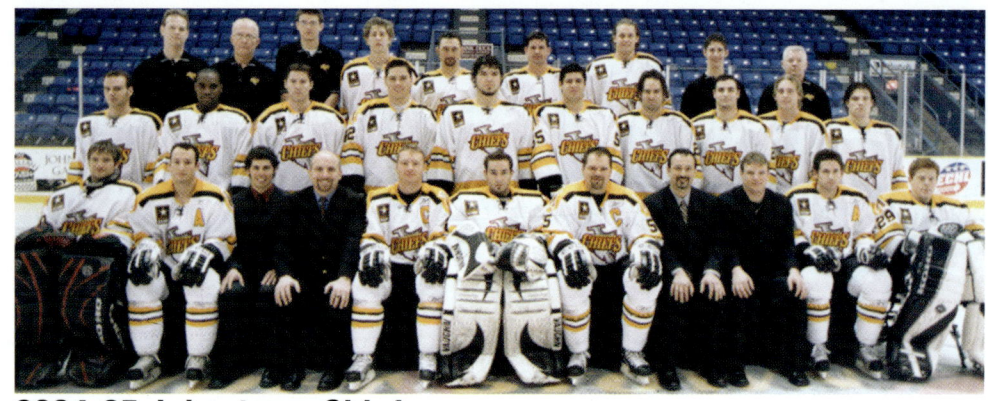

2004-05 Johnstown Chiefs

(Front, from left) Mark Scally, Ian Manzano, assistant coach Matt Bertani, head coach Toby O'Brien, Jeff Sullivan, David Currie, Brent Bilodeau, general manager Jim Brazill, goaltending coach Shane Clifford, Brian Collins, David Cann. (Middle) Chris Leinweber, Brett Peterson, Brent Kelly, Jean Desrochers, Jonathan Tremblay, Chester Gallant, Pierre-Luc Courchesne, Peter Trovato, Chad Cavanagh, David Bowman. (Back) Assistant trainer Terry Aman, equipment manager Mic Midderhoff, head trainer Doug Bennett, Jay Latulippe, Dmitri Tarabrin, Joe Gerbe, Matt Reid, locker room attendant Josh Kush, locker room attendant Chuck Lamberson.

2004-05 FINAL ECHL STANDINGS

	Games played	Won	Lost	Overtime losses	Points	Goals for	Goals against
NATIONAL CONFERENCE							
Northern Division							
Reading Royals	72	43	22	7	93	220	161
Trenton Titans	72	42	21	9	93	213	197
Atlantic City Boardwalk Bullies	72	42	22	8	92	205	189
Toledo Storm	72	41	26	5	87	203	194
Peoria Rivermen	72	38	26	8	84	213	177
Wheeling Nailers	72	38	29	5	81	171	173
Johnstown Chiefs	72	22	36	14	58	191	258
Dayton Bombers	72	23	40	9	55	175	225
Western Division							
Alaska Aces	72	45	19	8	98	233	187
Long Beach Ice Dogs	72	43	20	9	95	220	181
Idaho Steelheads	72	42	23	7	91	223	183
Bakersfield Condors	72	40	22	10	90	232	205
Fresno Falcons	72	39	25	8	86	204	217
San Diego Gulls	72	35	29	8	78	206	222
Las Vegas Wranglers	72	31	33	8	70	201	199
Victoria Salmon Kings	72	15	52	5	35	178	298
AMERICAN CONFERENCE							
Southern Division							
Pensacola Ice Pilots	72	51	16	5	107	248	178
Florida Everblades	72	42	20	10	94	237	192
Gwinnett Gladiators	72	40	24	8	88	241	202
Mississippi Sea Wolves	72	39	24	9	87	223	215
Louisiana Ice Gators	72	26	40	6	58	192	266
Texas Wildcatters	72	17	44	11	45	178	260
Eastern Division							
Columbia Inferno	72	38	22	12	88	199	186
South Carolina Stingrays	72	39	24	9	87	230	219
Charlotte Checkers	72	39	26	7	85	226	219
Greenville Grrrowl	72	39	28	5	83	210	204
Pee Dee Pride	72	31	36	5	67	203	219
Augusta Lynx	72	28	35	9	65	188	237

Johnstown Chiefs
General Manager - Jim Brazill
Coach - Toby O'Brien
Assistant Coach - Matt Bertani, Galen Head

Player/Coach - Brent Bilodeau
Goaltending Coach - Shane Clifford
Trainer - Mic Midderhoff, Doug Bennett, Terry Aman, Chris Stewart – until Dec. 2004
Locker Room Attendants - Chuck Lamberson, Doug Mesteller, Cory Mesteller, Josh Kush, Zach Aman
Colors - Black, White, Gold and Red

2004-05 Game Results

Preseason Results

Day	Date	Opponent	Johnstown	Opponent	Attendance	Record
Thur.	14-Oct	Wheeling *	1	3		
Sat.	16-Oct	at Wheeling	4	3		

* Game played in Harmorville, Pa.

Regular Season Results

Day	Date	Opponent	Johnstown	Opponent	Attendance	Record
Sat.	23-Oct	Wheeling	4	3	3,317	1-0-0
Sun.	24-Oct	Dayton	3	4 (sol)	2,055	1-0-1
Fri.	29-Oct	Pee Dee	2	3 (otl)	1,707	1-0-2
Sat.	30-Oct	Pee Dee	4	5 (sol)	1,855	1-0-3
Fri.	5-Nov	Reading	2	1	1,985	2-0-3
Sat.	6-Nov	at Trenton	2	3 (sol)		2-0-4
Wed.	10-Nov	at Trenton	2	3 (sol)		2-0-5
Fri.	12-Nov	Peoria	6	5	3,351	3-0-5
Sat.	13-Nov	Peoria	5	2	2,335	4-0-5
Wed.	17-Nov	at Wheeling	1	3		4-1-5
Fri.	19-Nov	Dayton	5	1	3,140	5-1-5
Sat.	20-Nov	at Dayton	4	5		5-2-5
Sun.	21-Nov	at Toledo	1	4		5-3-5
Wed.	24-Nov	Trenton	1	2 (otl)	1,929	5-3-6
Fri.	26-Nov	Toledo	3	2	3,104	6-3-6
Sat.	27-Nov	Long Beach	5	1	2,635	7-3-6
Fri.	3-Dec	at Dayton	1	4		7-4-6
Sat.	4-Dec	Atlantic City	1	6	2,475	7-5-6
Sun.	5-Dec	at Trenton	3	4 (sol)		7-5-7
Fri.	10-Dec	at Reading	3	4 (sol)		7-5-8
Sat.	11-Dec	at Atlantic City	5	4 (otw)		8-5-8
Fri.	17-Dec	at Dayton	3	0		9-5-8
Sat.	18-Dec	Dayton	3	1	2,132	10-5-8
Sun.	19-Dec	Atlantic City	2	3 (sol)	1,727	10-5-9
Fri.	31-Dec	Toledo	4	3	3,799	11-5-9
Sat.	1-Jan	Fresno	4	5	2,090	11-6-9
Sun.	2-Jan	at Trenton	5	2		12-6-9
Fri.	7-Jan	Trenton	2	5	1,885	12-7-9
Sat.	8-Jan	Bakersfield	1	4	2,339	12-8-9
Sun.	9-Jan	Reading	4	1	2,543	13-8-9
Fri.	14-Jan	at Wheeling	2	4		13-9-9
Sat.	15-Jan	Toledo	2	5	1,775	13-10-9
Sun.	16-Jan	Wheeling	1	5	1,660	13-11-9
Tues.	18-Jan	at South Carolina	3	4		13-12-9
Thur.	20-Jan	at Charlotte	1	2 (otl)		13-12-10
Sat.	22-Jan	at Pee Dee	4	2		14-12-10
Sun.	23-Jan	at South Carolina	2	4		14-13-10
Sun.	30-Jan	at Atlantic City	4	1		15-13-10
Fri.	4-Feb	Atlantic City	1	3	1,962	15-14-10
Sat.	5-Feb	San Diego	2	3 (sol)	3,011	15-14-11
Sun.	6-Feb	Peoria	3	6	2,108	15-15-11
Wed.	9-Feb	at Trenton	2	5		15-16-11
Sat.	12-Feb	at Toledo	0	3		15-17-11
Sun.	13-Feb	at Peoria	1	7		15-18-11
Tues.	15-Feb	at Peoria	3	2 (sow)		16-18-11
Fri.	18-Feb	at Dayton	2	1 (otw)		17-18-11
Sat.	19-Feb	Dayton	4	2	3,237	18-18-11
Sun.	20-Feb	Trenton	3	2	1,746	19-18-11
Tues.	22-Feb	at Reading	1	3		19-19-11
Fri.	25-Feb	at Toledo	1	4		19-20-11
Sat.	26-Feb	at Toledo	3	4		19-21-11
Sun.	27-Feb	Trenton	2	3 (sol)	2,004	19-21-12
Tues.	1-Mar	at Reading	1	5		19-22-12
Fri.	4-Mar	at Wheeling	2	3		19-23-12
Sat.	5-Mar	at Atlantic City	4	5 (otl)		19-23-13
Sun.	6-Mar	Reading	1	4	2,113	19-24-13
Fri.	11-Mar	Atlantic City	1	3	1,831	19-25-13
Sat.	12-Mar	Wheeling	2	3 (otl)	3,844	19-25-14

Day	Date	Opponent	GF	GA	Attendance	Record
Sun.	13-Mar	Toledo	3	4	3,285	19-26-14
Thur.	17-Mar	Peoria	0	7	1,446	19-27-14
Fri.	18-Mar	at Wheeling	4	1		20-27-14
Sat.	19-Mar	at Dayton	4	7		20-28-14
Tues.	22-Mar	at Peoria	3	5		20-29-14
Wed.	23-Mar	at Peoria	2	6		20-30-14
Fri.	25-Mar	at Reading	1	5		20-31-14
Sat.	26-Mar	at Atlantic City	3	5		20-32-14
Sun.	27-Mar	at Atlantic City	4	5		20-33-14
Tues.	1-Apr	at Toledo	1	4		20-34-14
Wed.	2-Apr	Dayton	7	6 (sow)	2,329	21-34-14
Thur.	3-Apr	Wheeling	6	4	1,822	22-34-14
Tues.	8-Apr	Trenton	2	5	1,812	22-35-14
Wed.	9-Apr	Atlantic City	2	3	2,442	22-36-14

Attendance Figures	Dates	Totals	Average
Regular Season Attendance Figures	36	84,830	2,356
TOTAL ATTENDANCE	36	84,830	2,356

2004-05 Player Statistics   Regular Season Scoring

	Games	G	A	Pts	PIM
22 Jean Desrochers	72	19	33	52	29
16 Joe Tallari	66	32	19	51	56
10 Shawn Mather	56	19	24	43	26
19 Brent Kelly	37	15	25	40	15
26 Chad Cavanagh	72	16	21	37	106
28 Pierre-Luc Courchesne	72	9	25	34	78
15 Steve Hildenbrand	37	11	20	31	66
7 Mike James	58	11	19	30	207
17 Dmitri Tarabrin	65	8	17	25	53
14 Ian Manzano	71	1	21	22	31
27 David Bowman	71	5	16	21	73
32 Matt Reid	62	11	9	20	27
12 Jeremy Van Hoof	59	3	16	19	56
24 Chris Leinweber	47	3	12	15	46
5 Brent Bilodeau	67	2	13	15	87
25 Brian Collins	29	6	6	12	28
25 Peter Trovato	13	1	7	8	14
33 Dennis Packard	15	3	4	7	6
2 Jeff Sullivan	28	2	4	6	89
18 Jonathan Tremblay	46	2	3	5	136
19 Scott Dobben	14	3	1	4	10
4 Brett Peterson	13	1	3	4	8
55 Adam Henrich	6	2	1	3	15
25 Evgeny Lazarev	5	1	2	3	12
44 Jean-Francois Soucy	14	1	2	3	49
23 Joe Gerbe	11	0	2	2	2
29 John Kororiz	2	1	0	1	2
23 Grant Stevenson	2	1	0	1	2
12 Jay Latulippe	5	0	1	1	2
55 Chester Gallant	5	0	1	1	33
30 Mark Scally (g)	7	0	1	1	0
44 Paul Lynch	14	0	1	1	18
31 David Currie (g)	30	0	1	1	0
25 Bill Downey	2	0	0	0	0
1 Brian Gratz (g)	2	0	0	0	0
6 Doug O'Brien	3	0	0	0	2
55 Glenn Olson	4	0	0	0	9
29 David Cann (g)	44	0	0	0	4
Bench				2	24
TOTALS	72	191	330	521	1,421

Regular Season Goaltending

	G	Min	GA	ENG	SO	GAA	W	L	OTL	SOL	Saves	Save %
1 Brian Gratz	2	26	1	0	0	2.29	0	1	0	0	17	0.944
31 David Currie	30	1,708	86	4	1	3.02	10	12	1	6	778	0.900
29 David Cann	41	2,281	129	2	0	3.39	11	19	4	3	1,117	0.896
30 Mark Scally	7	361	27	0	0	4.48	1	4	0	0	188	0.874
Shootout goals			9									
TOTALS	72	4,376	252	6	1	3.54	22	36	5	9	2,100	0.891

Players on roster who did not play: 1 Scott Graham, Goal; 1 Tyler Mittlestead, Goal; 1 David Marlin, Goal.

CHIEFS IN THE 2000s

2005-06 Johnstown Chiefs

(Front, from left) Morgan Cey, Dmitri Tarabrin, public relations director Kevin McGeehan, Jason Spence, head coach Frank Anzalone, Randy Rowe, general manager Toby O'Brien, Ian Manzano, Josh Disher, Mike Betz. (Middle) John Toffey, Ben Wallace, Jim Hakewill, Adam Henrich, Dennis Packard, Andre Deveaux, Justin Kelly, Brandon Elliott, Doug Andress, Jake Heller, Brad Sullivan. (Back) Medical trainer Scott Adams, Jean Desrochers, Jon Hedberg, Brad Thompson, Brett Peterson, Steve Cygan, equipment manager Mic Midderhoff.

2005-06 FINAL ECHL STANDINGS

	Games played	Won	Lost	Overtime losses	Shootout losses	Points	Goals for	Goals against
NATIONAL CONFERENCE								
North Division								
Toledo Storm	72	46	21	3	2	97	244	189
Wheeling Nailers	72	45	21	3	3	96	247	186
Reading Royals	72	42	23	3	4	91	249	209
Johnstown Chiefs	72	30	26	4	12	76	223	243
Trenton Titans	72	31	36	2	3	67	166	214
Dayton Bombers	72	20	46	4	2	46	193	275
South Division								
Gwinnett Gladiators	72	50	15	0	7	107	304	208
Florida Everblades	72	48	20	3	1	100	267	208
Greenville Grrrowl	72	45	24	0	3	93	248	203
South Carolina Stingrays	72	32	25	7	8	79	230	237
Charlotte Checkers	72	33	34	2	3	71	232	254
Augusta Lynx	72	30	36	1	5	66	16	255
Columbia Inferno	72	25	39	3	5	58	209	290
Pensacola Ice Pilots	72	21	44	5	2	49	194	293
AMERICAN CONFERENCE								
West Division								
Alaska Aces	72	53	12	5	2	13	289	168
Las Vegas Wranglers	72	53	13	4	2	112	267	176
Idaho Steelheads	72	43	21	4	4	94	268	221
Utah Grizzlies	72	36	30	5	1	78	235	236
Victoria Salmon Kings	72	26	37	5	4	61	204	261
Phoenix Roadrunners	72	20	47	1	4	45	156	263
Pacific Division								
Fresno Falcons	72	43	15	5	9	100	230	205
Bakersfield Condors	72	40	26	2	4	86	221	222
Long Beach Ice Dogs	72	36	27	4	5	81	210	217
San Diego Gulls	72	34	30	4	4	76	213	214
Stockton Thunder	72	18	40	7	7	50	192	260

Johnstown Chiefs
General Manager - Toby O'Brien
Coach - Frank Anzalone
Trainers - Mic Midderhoff, Scott Adams
Locker Room Attendants - Doug Mesteller, Cory Mesteller, Josh Kush, Will Page, Zach Aman, Dave Zeigler
Colors - Black, White, Gold and Red

2005-06 Game Results

Preseason Results

Day	Date	Opponent	Johnstown	Opponent	Attendance	Record
Thur.	13-Oct	Wheeling *	3	2 (sow)		
Sat.	15-Oct	at Wheeling	4	3 (sow)		

* Game played in Greensburg, Pa.

325

Regular Season Results

Day	Date	Opponent	GF	GA	Att.	Record
Fri.	21-Oct	at Columbia	2	4		0-1-0
Sat.	22-Oct	Reading	2	3	3,130	0-2-0
Wed.	26-Oct	Toledo	4	5 (otl)	1,796	0-2-1
Fri.	28-Oct	Trenton	2	3 (sol)	2,375	0-2-2
Sat.	29-Oct	at Toledo	2	6		0-3-2
Fri.	4-Nov	at Trenton	2	3 (sol)		0-3-3
Sat.	5-Nov	Wheeling	2	4	2,827	0-4-3
Fri.	11-Nov	Trenton	2	3 (sol)	3,461	0-4-4
Sat.	12-Nov	Wheeling	2	4	2,405	0-5-4
Sun.	13-Nov	at Wheeling	1	4		0-6-4
Fri.	18-Nov	South Carolina	4	1	2,212	1-6-4
Sat.	19-Nov	at Toledo	5	2		2-6-4
Wed.	23-Nov	at Trenton	1	2		2-7-4
Fri.	25-Nov	Trenton	5	1	3,002	3-7-4
Sat.	26-Nov	at Wheeling	4	3 (otw)		4-7-4
Tues.	29-Nov	at Las Vegas	4	5 (sol)		4-7-5
Wed.	30-Nov	at Bakersfield	1	2 (sol)		4-7-6
Fri.	2-Dec	at Fresno	3	2 (sow)		5-7-6
Sat.	3-Dec	at San Diego	1	7		5-8-6
Sun.	4-Dec	at San Diego	5	4 (sow)		6-8-6
Tues.	6-Dec	at Las Vegas	0	4		6-9-6
Fri.	9-Dec	Reading	2	7	1,793	6-10-6
Sat.	10-Dec	Dayton	4	0	2,084	7-10-6
Sun.	11-Dec	at Toledo	1	7		7-11-6
Wed.	14-Dec	Trenton	1	0	1,443	8-11-6
Fri.	16-Dec	Fresno	2	3 (sol)	1,732	8-11-7
Sat.	17-Dec	at Wheeling	1	2		8-12-7
Tues.	20-Dec	Charlotte	3	2	1,677	9-12-7
Fri.	30-Dec	at Trenton	2	1		10-12-7
Sat.	31-Dec	Columbia	7	4	3,907	11-12-7
Fri.	6-Jan	Reading	3	4	1,837	11-13-7
Sat.	7-Jan	Dayton	3	4 (sol)	2,420	11-13-8
Sun.	8-Jan	at Dayton	5	3		12-13-8
Tues.	10-Jan	at Dayton	5	1		13-13-8
Wed.	11-Jan	Dayton	4	3	1,501	14-13-8
Fri.	13-Jan	Reading	3	4	2,033	14-14-8
Sat.	14-Jan	Toledo	3	7	2,705	14-15-8
Wed.	18-Jan	Reading	5	1	1,591	15-15-8
Fri.	20-Jan	at Toledo	4	6		15-16-8
Sat.	21-Jan	at Reading	2	7		15-17-8
Fri.	27-Jan	at Dayton	8	6		16-17-8
Sat.	28-Jan	at Wheeling	4	2		17-17-8
Wed.	1-Feb	Trenton	5	0	1,435	18-17-8
Fri.	3-Feb	at Dayton	2	3 (sol)		18-17-9
Sat.	4-Feb	Dayton	3	4 (sol)	2,775	18-17-10
Tues.	7-Feb	at Reading	5	4 (sow)		19-17-10
Fri.	10-Feb	Toledo	5	3	1,962	20-17-10
Sat.	11-Feb	Dayton	4	5 (sol)	2,176	20-17-11
Sun.	12-Feb	at Dayton	3	4		20-18-11
Fri.	17-Feb	at Trenton	4	3		21-18-11
Sat.	18-Feb	at Trenton	2	5		21-19-11
Sun.	19-Feb	Wheeling	3	4	2,581	21-20-11
Fri.	24-Feb	Toledo	1	0	2,228	22-20-11
Sat.	25-Feb	Dayton	5	4 (sow)	2,843	23-20-11
Sun.	26-Feb	Trenton	4	3	2,055	24-20-11
Fri.	3-Mar	at Reading	6	2		25-20-11
Sun.	5-Mar	Greenville	2	3	3,107	25-21-11
Fri.	10-Mar	Trenton	2	1	2,131	26-21-11
Sat.	11-Mar	Wheeling	5	6 (otl)	3,081	26-21-12
Sun.	12-Mar	Reading	1	0	2,851	27-21-12
Fri.	17-Mar	at Reading	5	6 (otl)		27-21-13
Sat.	18-Mar	Toledo	2	0	3,189	28-21-13
Sun.	19-Mar	Wheeling	6	2	2,878	29-21-13
Wed.	22-Mar	Wheeling	0	4	2,116	29-22-13
Fri.	24-Mar	at Reading	4	5 (otl)		29-22-14
Sat.	25-Mar	at Toledo	3	4		29-23-14
Sun.	26-Mar	at Wheeling	2	5		29-24-14
Wed.	29-Mar	at Trenton	3	4 (sol)		29-24-15
Fri.	31-Mar	at Dayton	5	2		30-24-15
Sat.	1-Apr	at Wheeling	2	5		30-25-15
Fri.	7-Apr	at Toledo	1	3		30-26-15
Sat.	8-Apr	Toledo	2	3 (sol)	3,742	30-26-16

Playoff Results

Day	Date	Opponent	GF	GA	Att.	Record
Mon.	10-Apr	Trenton	2	1 (otw)	1,069	1-0

Tues.	11-Apr	at Trenton	4	3		2-0	
Fri.	14-Apr	at Toledo	2	3		0-1	
Sat.	15-Apr	at Toledo	1	4		0-2	
Wed.	19-Apr	Toledo	3	5	1,277	0-3	

Attendance Figures	Dates	Totals	Average
Regular Season Attendance Totals	36	87,081	2,419
Playoff Attendance Totals	2	2,346	1,173
TOTAL ATTENDANCE	38	89,427	2,353

2005-06 Player Statistics

	Regular Season Scoring					Playoff Scoring				
	Games	G	A	Pts	PIM	Games	G	A	Pts	PIM
27 Justin Kelly	59	31	40	71	45	5	2	2	4	2
17 Dmitri Tarabrin	62	21	29	50	35	5	1	0	1	4
18 Randy Rowe	45	28	15	43	28	5	2	2	4	2
22 Jean Desrochers	72	19	24	43	45	5	2	0	2	2
33 Adam Henrich	51	18	23	41	78	5	2	4	6	8
29 J.B. Bittner	51	10	29	39	37					
7 Joe Tallari	55	18	19	37	34	4	0	1	1	8
4 Doug Andress	64	6	31	37	47	5	0	1	1	6
24 Brett Peterson	72	5	19	24	69	5	1	0	1	4
19 Steve Cygan	48	7	16	23	16					
14 Ian Manzano	72	0	18	18	34	5	0	0	0	10
26 Brandon Elliott	68	10	7	17	207	5	0	0	0	0
37 Paul Caponigri	30	7	10	17	51					
28 Brad Thompson	32	6	11	17	8	2	0	0	0	0
23 Gerard Dicaire	27	4	10	14	14					
13 Tyler Kindle	32	2	10	12	18					
42 Zbynek Hrdel	15	6	5	11	10	4	1	2	3	8
49 John Toffey	61	6	5	11	46					
15 Andre Deveaux	11	4	7	11	36	5	1	1	2	2
16 Dennis Packard	16	2	9	11	12	5	0	1	1	4
6 Brady Greco	29	5	5	10	65					
12 Ben Wallace	58	0	10	10	16	5	0	0	0	2
55 Mike Egener	18	2	2	4	66					
6 Jon Hedberg	16	1	3	4	4					
20 Jason Spence	8	1	1	2	8					
25 Jim Hakewill	35	0	2	2	41	5	0	1	1	2
23 Brad Sullivan	14	0	1	1	4					
30 Josh Disher (g)	2	0	0	0	0					
31 Brian Eklund (g)	2	0	0	0	0					
23 Jereny Downs	3	0	0	0	2					
31 David Currie (g)	5	0	0	0	0					
44 Jay Rosehill	5	0	0	0	13	5	0	0	0	4
31 Gabe Winer (g)	6	0	0	0	0					
1 Mike Betz (g)	7	0	0	0	0					
3 Jake Heller	7	0	0	0	6					
35 Jonathan Boutin (g)	19	0	0	0	4	3	0	0	0	0
40 Morgan Cey (g)	36	0	0	0	4	3	0	0	0	0
Bench				4	16					2
TOTALS	72	223	361	584	1,119	5	12	15	27	70

Regular Season Goaltending

	G	Min	GA	ENG	SO	GAA	W	L	OTL	SOL	Saves	Save %
30 Josh Disher	2	113	4	0	0	2.13	1	1	0	0	79	0.952
40 Morgan Cey	35	2,032	93	5	3	2.75	17	9	0	7	1,092	0.922
35 Jonathan Boutin	19	1,145	56	3	2	2.93	8	9	0	2	642	0.920
31 Brian Eklund	2	130	7	0	0	3.23	1	0	0	1	73	0.913
31 David Currie	5	305	17	2	0	3.34	0	3	1	1	126	0.881
31 Gabe Winer	6	295	18	1	1	3.66	2	2	1	0	183	0.867
1 Mike Betz	7	365	25	0	0	4.10	1	2	2	1	186	0.882
Shootout goals			12									
TOTALS	72	4,385	232	11	6	3.32	30	26	4	12	2,381	0.907

Playoff Goaltending

	G	Min	GA	ENG	SO	GAA	W	L	Saves	Save %
40 Morgan Cey	3	134	6	0	0	2.68	1	1	84	0.933
35 Jonathan Boutin	3	170	10	0	0	3.53	1	2	92	0.902
TOTALS	5	304	16	0	0	3.16	2	3	176	0.917

Hedberg also wore No. 13; Packard also wore Nos. 16 and 55; Henrich also wore No. 23; Hrdel also wore Nos. 28 and 44; Betz also wore No. 35; Cey also wore No. 1

Players on roster who did not play: 1, Nick Rau, Goal; 1 Brian Gratz, Goal; 1 Craig Rehode, Goal; 31 Shane Clifford, Goal; 42 Mark Scally, Goal.

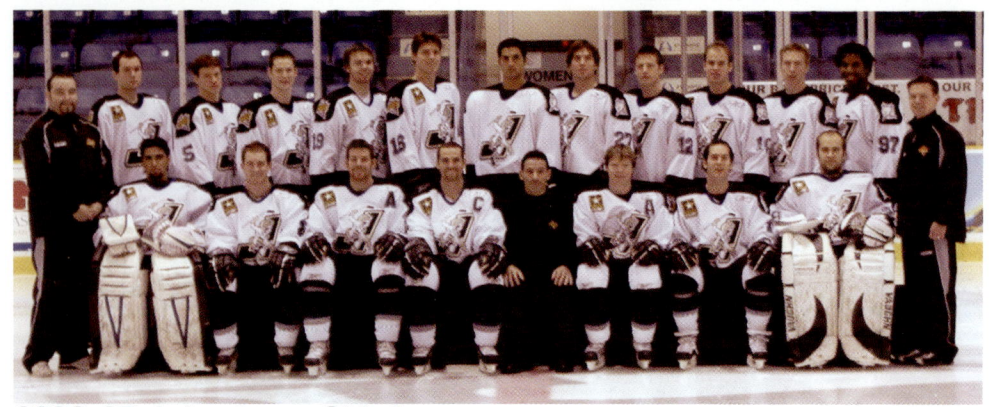

2006-07 Johnstown Chiefs

(Front, from left) Gerald Coleman, Ian MacLean, Brandon Elliott, Doug Andress, head coach Frank Anzalone, Randy Rowe, Gus Katsuras, Morgan Cey. (Back) Equipment manager Casey Taylor, John Toffey, Bryan Nathe, P.J. Atherton, Zbynek Hrdel, Ryan Gibbons, Andre Deveaux, Grant Jacobsen, Ben Wallace, Radek Smolenak, Andrew Martens, Maxime Boisclair, medical trainer Rodney Bogart.

2006-07 FINAL ECHL STANDINGS

	Games played	Won	Lost	Overtime losses	Shootout losses	Points	Goals for	Goals against
AMERICAN CONFERENCE								
North Division								
Dayton Bombers	72	37	26	2	7	83	213	191
Toledo Storm	72	39	30	1	2	81	211	220
Cincinnati Cyclones	72	37	29	4	2	80	213	198
Trenton Titans	72	36	31	1	4	77	252	242
Johnstown Chiefs	72	33	33	3	3	72	216	232
Reading Royals	72	32	33	2	5	71	221	235
Wheeling Nailers	72	32	34	2	4	70	215	255
South Division								
Florida Everblades	72	44	22	4	2	94	272	212
Texas Wildcatters	72	41	22	5	4	91	265	222
Gwinnett Gladiators	72	41	24	5	2	89	289	256
Charlotte Checkers	72	42	27	1	2	87	252	220
Augusta Lynx	72	39	29	1	3	82	258	265
South Carolina Stingrays	72	36	27	4	5	81	250	251
Columbia Inferno	72	29	34	4	5	67	217	256
Pensacola Ice Pilots	72	20	46	2	4	46	233	318
NATIONAL CONFERENCE								
West Division								
Alaska Aces	72	49	16	3	4	105	270	176
Idaho Steelheads	72	42	24	2	4	90	240	208
Victoria Salmon Kings	72	36	32	1	3	76	239	249
Phoenix Roadrunners	72	27	40	2	3	59	201	255
Utah Grizzlies	72	22	42	4	4	52	184	294
Pacific Division								
Las Vegas Wranglers	72	46	12	6	8	106	231	187
Bakersfield Condors	72	41	19	3	9	94	270	236
Stockton Thunder	72	38	24	5	5	86	225	197
Fresno Falcons	72	34	29	5	4	77	195	197
Long Beach Ice Dogs	72	27	42	0	3	57	209	267

Johnstown Chiefs
General Manager - Ryan Belec
Coach - Frank Anzalone
Training Staff - Casey Taylor, Rodney Bogart
Locker Room Attendants - Doug Mesteller, Cory Mesteller, Dave Zeigler
Colors - Black, White, Gold and Red
Team wore Jets blue road jersey three games during regular season (Style 74-77)

2006-07 Game Results

Preseason Results

Day	Date	Opponent	Johnstown	Opponent	Attendance	Record
Fri.	13-Oct	at Wheeling	4	5		
Sat.	14-Oct	Wheeling	5	3	450	

Regular Season Results

Day	Date	Opponent	Johnstown	Opponent	Attendance	Record
Sat.	21-Oct	Pensacola	5	2	2,429	1-0-0
Sun.	22-Oct	at Trenton	3	5		1-1-0
Wed.	25-Oct	Wheeling	3	2	1,928	2-1-0
Fri.	27-Oct	at Wheeling	3	7		2-2-0
Sat.	28-Oct	Cincinnati	1	3	1,963	2-3-0
Wed.	1-Nov	at Toledo	3	5		2-4-0
Fri.	3-Nov	Trenton	7	3	2,115	3-4-0
Sat.	4-Nov	Wheeling	5	2	2,398	4-4-0
Sun.	5-Nov	at Wheeling	2	4		4-5-0
Fri.	10-Nov	Charlotte	1	5	3,098	4-6-0
Sat.	11-Nov	Toledo	2	3 (otl)	2,235	4-6-1
Sun.	12-Nov	at Reading	5	3		5-6-1
Wed.	15-Nov	Trenton	3	4	1,536	5-7-1
Fri.	17-Nov	Wheeling	4	2	2,037	6-7-1
Sat.	18-Nov	at Dayton	3	1		7-7-1
Fri.	24-Nov	at Reading	7	5		8-7-1
Sat.	25-Nov	Trenton	3	6	2,406	8-8-1
Fri.	1-Dec	Trenton	4	3 (sow)	1,740	9-8-1
Sat.	2-Dec	Reading	3	2 (sow)	1,831	10-8-1
Fri.	8-Dec	at Dayton	1	3		10-9-1
Sat.	9-Dec	Reading	2	3 (otl)	2,225	10-9-2
Sun.	10-Dec	Bakersfield	2	3	1,675	10-10-2
Thur.	14-Dec	at Cincinnati	2	3 (sol)		10-10-3
Fri.	15-Dec	at Cincinnati	2	7		10-11-3
Sat.	16-Dec	Cincinnati	3	2 (otw)	2,217	11-11-3
Sat.	23-Dec	at Toledo	5	2		12-11-3
Wed.	27-Dec	at Toledo	2	4		12-12-3
Fri.	29-Dec	at Trenton	1	2		12-13-3
Sat.	30-Dec	at Wheeling	7	1		13-13-3
Sun.	31-Dec	Toledo	5	2	4,136	14-13-3
Fri.	5-Jan	at Gwinnett	3	4 (sol)		14-13-4
Sat.	6-Jan	at Augusta	2	7		14-14-4
Sun.	7-Jan	at South Carolina	2	7		14-15-4
Fri.	12-Jan	at Dayton	2	1 (sow)		15-15-4
Mon.	15-Jan	Wheeling	1	2	2,534	15-16-4
Fri.	19-Jan	Dayton	3	6	2,883	15-17-4
Sun.	21-Jan	at Toledo	0	3		15-18-4
Wed.	24-Jan	at Trenton	5	4 (sow)		16-18-4
Sat.	27-Jan	Augusta	4	6	3,503	16-19-4
Sun.	28-Jan	Dayton	1	3	3,022	16-20-4
Fri.	2-Feb	at Reading	3	2 (otw)		17-20-4
Sat.	3-Feb	Reading	4	1	3,644	18-20-4
Wed.	7-Feb	at Cincinnati	4	1		19-20-4
Sat.	10-Feb	Wheeling	5	2	2,748	20-20-4
Sun.	11-Feb	Reading	5	2	2,521	21-20-4
Wed.	14-Feb	at Trenton	0	5		21-21-4
Fri.	16-Feb	at Cincinnati	4	5 (otl)		21-21-5
Sat.	17-Feb	Cincinnati	4	7	2,721	21-22-5
Sun.	18-Feb	Trenton	3	2	2,342	22-22-5
Fri.	23-Feb	at Wheeling	4	1		23-22-5
Sat.	24-Feb	at Wheeling	4	3 (otw)		24-22-5
Wed.	28-Feb	Dayton	1	4	4,021	24-23-5
Fri.	2-Mar	at Reading	2	3		24-24-5
Sat.	3-Mar	at Wheeling	2	3 (sol)		24-24-6
Sun.	4-Mar	Toledo	3	1	2,184	25-24-6
Wed.	7-Mar	at Trenton	2	5		25-25-6
Fri.	9-Mar	Wheeling	5	2	2,814	26-25-6
Sat.	10-Mar	Cincinnati	1	4	3,224	26-26-6
Sun.	11-Mar	Toledo	2	4	2,226	26-27-6
Sat.	17-Mar	at Reading	1	3		26-28-6
Sun.	18-Mar	Trenton	2	5	2,217	26-29-6
Wed.	21-Mar	at Trenton	4	3		27-29-6
Fri.	23-Mar	at Dayton	1	4		27-30-6

Day	Date	Opponent		Score		Attendance	Record
Sat.	24-Mar	at Dayton	3	2 (sow)			28-30-6
Sun.	25-Mar	Dayton	2	3		2,833	28-31-6
Tues.	27-Mar	at Cincinnati	3	1			29-31-6
Fri.	30-Mar	Toledo	6	1		2,775	30-31-6
Sat.	31-Mar	Dayton	2	0		3,136	31-31-6
Sun.	1-Apr	Cincinnati	2	1 (otw)		2,891	32-31-6
Wed.	4-Apr	at Toledo	1	3			32-32-6
Fri.	6-Apr	Reading	3	4		2,982	32-33-6
Sat.	7-Apr	at Reading	6	3			33-33-6

Playoff Results

Day	Date	Opponent	Score		Attendance	Record
Tues.	9-Apr	at Trenton	2	4		0-1
Wed.	10-Apr	Trenton	5	7	1,163	0-2

Attendance Figures	Dates	Totals	Average
Preseason Attendance Totals	1	450	450
Regular Season Attendance Totals	36	93,190	2,589
Playoff Attendance Totals	1	1,163	1,163
TOTAL ATTENDANCE	38	94,803	2,495

2006-07 Player Statistics

	Regular Season Scoring					Playoff Scoring				
	Games	G	A	Pts	PIM	Games	G	A	Pts	PIM
97 Maxime Boisclair	59	17	34	51	92	2	0	2	2	0
22 Jean Desrochers	54	17	21	38	42	2	1	2	3	2
18 Randy Rowe	34	15	23	38	22					
19 Zbynek Hrdel	65	13	23	36	67	2	2	0	2	0
10 Radek Smolenak	43	15	20	35	35	1	0	0	0	0
17 Dmitri Tarabin	47	16	16	32	36	2	0	2	2	2
36 Adam Henrich	32	15	19	34	119	2	0	0	0	2
21 Gus Katsuras	48	12	22	34	30	2	1	1	2	2
55 Andrew Martens	70	6	24	30	50	2	0	0	0	0
41 P.J. Atherton	57	5	25	30	50					
4 Doug Andress	57	10	19	29	34					
71 Stanislav Lascek	25	12	15	27	26					
27 Grant Jacobsen	67	9	13	22	61	2	0	2	2	6
44 John Adams	41	5	13	18	38	2	0	1	1	0
26 Brandon Elliott	48	11	6	17	137					
15 Eric Przepiorka	40	7	8	15	22					
20 Andre Deveaux	21	6	8	14	51					
5 Bryan Nathe	54	2	11	13	440					
23 Geoff Waugh	56	1	12	13	91	2	1	0	1	4
16 Ryan Gibbons	57	4	8	12	38	1	0	0	0	0
12 Ben Wallace	71	1	11	12	16	1	0	0	0	0
6 Marek Kvapil	7	3	8	11	2	2	1	1	2	0
24 Ian MacLean	41	3	8	11	20	2	0	0	0	0
7 David Spina	6	4	2	6	4					
20 Rob Lehtinen	13	2	2	4	4	1	0	0	0	0
2 Jay Rosehill	1	0	0	0	2					
35 Jonathan Boutin (g)	2	0	0	0	0					
6 Brady Greco	5	0	0	0	12					
1 Ryan Munce (g)	14	0	0	0	2	1	0	0	0	0
37 Gerald Coleman (g)	17	0	0	0	2					
49 John Toffey	25	0	0	0	8					
29 Morgan Cey (g)	47	0	0	0	0	1	0	0	0	0
2 Nick Kuiper						2	0	0	0	0
Bench		5		5	22					
TOTALS	72	216	371	587	1,179	2	7	11	18	18

Regular Season Goaltending

	G	Min	GA	ENG	SO	GAA	W	L	OTL	SOL	Saves	Save %
1 Ryan Munce	14	652	28	1	0	2.58	6	3	1	0	323	0.920
29 Morgan Cey	47	2,662	130	5	1	2.93	20	19	2	3	1,424	0.916
35 Jonathan Boutin	2	117	6	2	0	3.07	0	2	0	0	68	0.919
37 Gerald Coleman	17	914	52	5	0	3.41	7	9	0	0	480	0.902
Shootout Goals				3								
TOTALS	72	4,345	219	13	1	3.20	33	33	3	3	2,295	0.908

Playoff Goaltending

	G	Min	GA	ENG	SO	GAA	W	L	Saves	Save %
1 Ryan Munce	1	59	4	0	0	4.08	0	1	38	.905
29 Morgan Cey	1	60	7	0	0	7.00	0	1	28	.800
TOTALS	2	120	11	0	0	5.50	0	2	66	.857

MISCELLANEOUS STATS

On to The Show

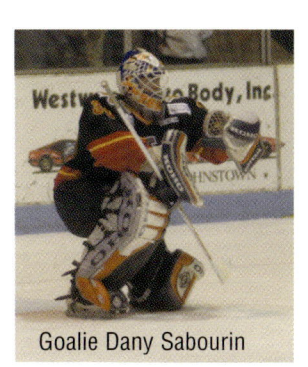

The following is a list of individuals who were part of Johnstown hockey teams and eventually made it to the National Hockey League or World Hockey Association:

Goalie Dany Sabourin

Goaltenders

Ross Brooks	Boston
Andy Brown	Detroit/Pittsburgh NHL// Indianapolis WHA
Dan Canney	Boston
Joe Daley	Pittsburgh/Buffalo/Detroit/ Winnipeg WHA
Nick Damore	Boston
Norm Defelice	Boston
Marv Edwards	Pittsburgh/Toronto/California
Ed Johnston	Boston/Toronto/St. Louis/Chicago
Claude Legris	Detroit
Norm Rocky Farr	Buffalo
Louie Levasseur	Minnesota North Stars NHL//Minnesota/Edmonton/ New England/Quebec WHA
Dan Olesevich	New York Rangers
Joe Schaefer	New York Rangers
Don Simmons	Boston/Toronto/ New York Rangers
Giles Villemure	New York Rangers/Chicago
Bob Sneddon	California
Jim McLeod	St. Louis NHL//Chicago New Jersey/Los Angeles/Michigan WHA
Wayne Wood	Birmingham/Vancouver/ Calgary/Toronto WHA
Lynn Zimmerman	Denver/Ottawa/Houston WHA
Mike Curran	Minnesota/WHA

Skaters

Lloyd Ailsby	New York
Claire Alexander	Toronto/Vancouver
Bill Anderson	Boston
Bruce Boudreau	Toronto/Chicago
Fred Burchell	Montreal
Wayne Bianchin	Pittsburgh/Edmonton
Ken Klirea	Detroit
Wally Kilra	Ottawa/Philadelphia/ Montreal/Detroit
Jack Carlson	Minnesota/St. Louis/Detroit NHL// Minnesota/Edmonton/New England WHA
Steve Carlson	Los Angles NHL//Minnesota/ New England/Edmonton WHA
Dwight Carruthers	Detroit/Philadelphia
Gary Collins	Toronto
Kevin Collins	Linesman
Mike Chernoff	Minnesota NHL/Vancouver WHA
Bob Dawes	Toronto/Montreal
Guy Delparte	Colorado
Hank Dyck	New York
Jack Dyte	Chicago
Harry Frost	Boston
Gary Gambucci	Minnesota NHL/Minnesota WHA
Lorry Gloeckner	Detroit
Dave Hanson	Detroit/Minnesota NHL// Minnesota/ New England/ Birmingham WHA
Galen Head	Detroit
Paul Holmgren	Philadelphia/Minnesota NHL// Minnesota WHA
Bob Gryp	Boston/Washington
John Hilworth	Detroit
Larry Johnston	Detroit/Los Angeles/Kansas City/ Colorado NHL//Michigan WHA
Ed Kachur	Chicago
Ted Lanyon	Pittsburgh
Dave Lucas	Detroit
Ralph MacSweyn	Philadelphia NHL//Los Angles / Vancouver WHA
Brian Marchinko	Toronto/Islanders
Jack McIntyre	Boston/Chicago/Detroit
Jim Mair	Philadelphia/Islanders/Vancouver
Jim Mikol	Toronto/New York Rangers
Don McLean	Washington
Tony Poeta	Chicago
Larry Regan	Boston/Toronto
Bill "Red" Mitchell	Chicago
Dick Sarrazin	Philadelphia NHL//New England/ Chicago WHA
Morris Stefaniw	Atlanta
Bob Warner	Toronto
Bob Whitlock	Minnesota NHL//Chicago/ Los Angles/Indianapolis WHA
Mike Wong	Detroit
Joe Zanussi	New York Rangers/Boston/ St. Louis NHL//Winnipeg WHA
Jim Adair	Vancouver WHA
Bob Boyd	Minnesota WHA
Jim Cardiff	Philadelphia/Vancouver WHA
Ray Delorenzi	Vancouver/Calgary WHA
Francois Ouimet	Minnesota/Cincinnati WHA
Dick Paradise	Minnesota WHA
Gene Peacosh	New York/Jersey/San Diego/ Edmonton/Indianapolis WHA

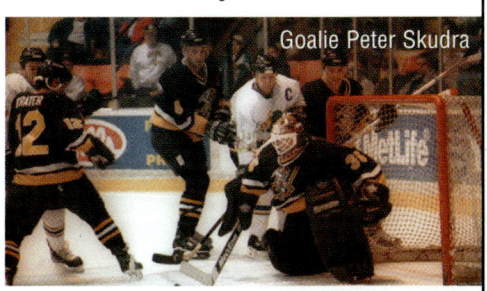

Goalie Peter Skudra

331

Bill Reed	Michigan/Calgary WHA
Craig Reichmuth	New York/Jersey/Michigan/San Diego WHA
Joe Robertson	Minnesota/Indianapolis WHA
Paul Steigerwald	Pittsburgh
Jean Tetreault	Vancouver/Minnesota WHA
Pierre Viau	Chicago WHA
Rob Walton	Minnesota/Vancouver/Calgary WHA
Pat Westrum	Minnesota/Calgary/Birmingham WHA
Jerry Zrymiak	Los Angles/Michigan/Toronto/Minnesota WHA

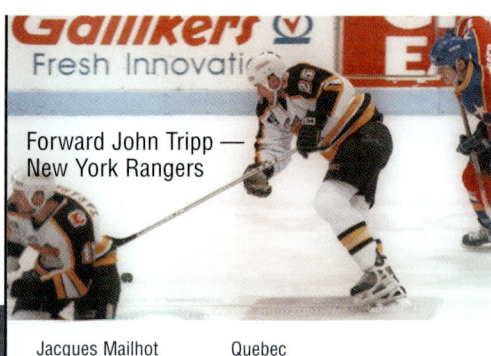

Forward John Tripp — New York Rangers

Goalie Andy Brown — Detroit and Pittsburgh (NHL)

Jacques Mailhot	Quebec
Marquis Mathieu	Boston
Bob McElligott	Columbus
Brett McLean	Chicago
Mic Midderhoff	Tampa Bay
Dave Mishkin	Tampa Bay
Mitch Molloy	Buffalo
Doug O'Brien	Tampa Bay
Greg Parks	Islanders
Dmitri Patzold	San Jose
Dany Sabourin	Calgary/Pittsburgh
Ryan Savoia	Pittsburgh
Jody Shelley	Columbus
Jason Simon	Islanders/Phoenix
Randy Skarda	St. Louis
Peter Skudra	Pittsburgh/Buffalo/Boston/Vancouver
Grant Stevenson	San Jose
Chris Stewart	Carolina/Pittsburgh
Billy Tibbetts	Pittsburgh/Philadelphia/New York
John Tripp	New York/Los Angeles
Derrick Walser	Columbus
Jeff Zehr	Boston

Chiefs

Scott Adams	Pittsburgh
Scott Bailey	Boston
Garrett Burnett	Anaheim
Shawn Byram	Islanders/Chicago
Larry Courville	Vancouver
John Craighead	Toronto
Justin Duberman	Pittsburgh
Benoit Dusablon	New York
Brian Eklund	Tampa Bay
Nick Fotiu	New York/Calgary/Philadelphia/Edmonton NHL//New England WHA
Tyrone Garner	Calgary
Matt Glennon	Boston
Scott Gordon	Quebec
David Gove	Carolina
Dana Heinze	Tampa/Pittsburgh
Artus Irbe	San Jose/Dallas/Carolina
Eddie Johnstone	New York/Detroit NHL//Michigan WHA
Neil Little	Philadelphia

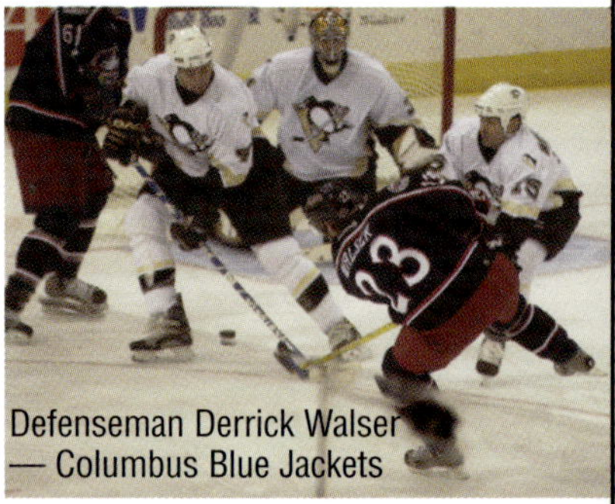

Goalie Artus Irbe — San Jose, Dallas, Carolina

Defenseman Derrick Walser — Columbus Blue Jackets

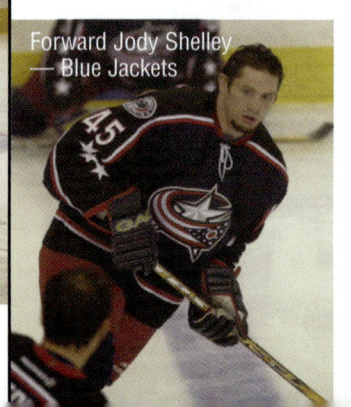

Forward Jody Shelley — Blue Jackets

332

JOHNSTOWN'S TOP CAREER SCORERS
Regular Season

	Years	Games	G	A	Pts
Dick Roberge	54-72	1159	737	962	1699
Don Hall	51-62	667	393	585	978
Reg Kent	65-74	601	274	544	818
Galen Head	67-76	561	312	292	604
Ken Coombes	55-61	388	162	345	507
Dave Lucas	56-67	733	142	364	506
Dan Patrick	61-69	443	176	291	467
Bill Ives	62-68	375	191	236	427
Gene Peacosh	68-72	294	187	239	426
Neil Forth	62-67	302	133	276	409
Vern Campigotto	71-79	481	120	248	368
John Gofton	64-76	305	172	157	329
John Horvath	50-55	244	102	226	328
John Lumley	59-62	196	138	151	289
Butch Martin	61-64	205	111	171	282

JETS INDIVIDUAL RECORDS
POINTS
Game ....8, Reg Bechtold (5g, 3a)
John Gofton (3g, 5a), Reggie Kent (3g, 5a)
Regular season ....Reggie Kent 145 (38g, 107a) 1967-68
Regular season + playoffs......Ken Laufman 149 (44g, 105a) 1961-62
Point streak ....19 games, John Gofton (1967-68)
(25 assists, Games 1-19)
Career (Regular season) ....1,624, Dick Roberge
979, Don Hall; 507, Ken Coombes

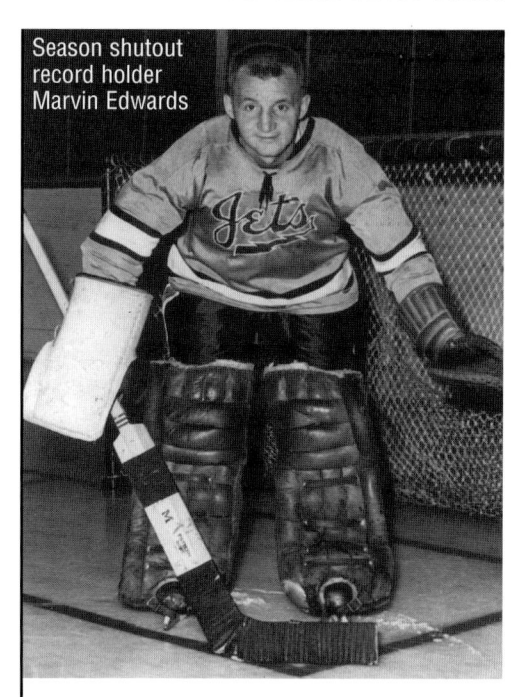

GOALS
Period........................4, Dick Roberge vs. Philadelphia (1/5/64)
Game ....5, seven times
(Arnie Schmautz, Don Hall, John Lumley, John Gofton,
Alan Cameron, Gene Peacosh, Reg Bechtold)
Regular season................................67, Galen Head (1968-69)
*Rookie year, EHL. NAHL record held by Henry Taylor
with 50 goals (1975-76)
Regular season + playoffs ....69, Galen Head (1968-69)
Hat-Tricks (Season)...6, four times
(Dick Roberge and
Don Hall 1955-56, Billy Ives and John Gofton 1966-67)
Goal streak ....14 games, John Gofton (1967-68)
(19 goals, Games 2-15)
Career (Regular season) ....708, Dick Roberge;
393, Don Hall; 191, Billy Ives;
131, Vern Campigotto

Jets top scorer 1962 and '67 Neil Forth

Season shutout record holder Marvin Edwards

ASSISTS
Game ....6, five times
(Ken McNally, Don Hall, Dan Patrick, Reg Kent,
Gene Peacosh)
Regular season............................Reggie Kent 107 (1967-68)
Regular season + playoffs ....Reggie Kent 107 (1967-68)
Assist streak ....12 games, Reggie Kent (1967-68)
(32 assists, Games 9-50)
Career (Regular season) ....916, Dick Roberge
586, Don Hall; 364, Dave Lucas; 251, Vern Campigotto

PENALTIES
Minutes (Period)..38, Dave Hanson vs. Binghamton (1/15/76)
*NAHL record (4 minors, 2 majors, misconduct and
game misconduct)
Minutes (Game).............. 48, Jim Mair at Syracuse (12/7/67)
Minutes (Season) ....405, Larry Johnson, (1963-64)
*Rookie year
Game ....Jim Mair, 10 at Syracuse (12-7-67)
(4 minors, 4 majors, misconduct and game misconduct)
Career (Minutes, Season) ....963, Dave Lucas (11 seasons)
652, Jim Mair; 587, Dave Hanson (2 seasons)

GOALTENDERS
Shutouts (Season) ....8, Marvin Edwards (1960-61)
Goals-against average (Reg. season + playoffs)
2.53, Ed Johnston (1959-60),
2.53, Ivan Walmsley (1951-52)
Goals-against average (Regular season)
2.65, Lynn Zimmerman (1968-69)
Goals-against average (Playoffs) ....1.50, Marvin Edwards

GAMES PLAYED
Seasons ....16, Dick Roberge
11, Don Hall and Dave Lucas
Regular season games .... 1,084, Dick Roberge
733, Dave Lucas; 667 Don Hall

333

CHIEFS CAREER RECORDS

Games played
1. Dmitri Tarabrin — 474
2. Brent Bilodeau — 414
3. Jeff Sullivan — 315
4. Perry Florio — 305
5. Lukas Smital — 278
6. Ian Manzano — 257
7. Jean Desrochers — 198
8. Bob Woods — 190
9. Martin Masa — 182
10. Mike Vellinga — 180

Goals
1. Lukas Smital — 107
2. Bruce Coles — 106
3. Dmitri Tarabrin — 99
4. Rob Hrystak — 98
5. Martin Masa — 86
6. Carl Fleury — 76
7. Dennis Purdie — 73
8. Eric Schneider — 71
9. Mark Green — 68
10. Mike Rossetti — 62

Assists
1. Perry Florio — 171
2. Rob Hyrtsak — 156
3. Bob Woods — 141
4. Dmitri Tarabrin — 133
5. Brent Bilodeau — 131
6. Bruce Coles — 121
7. Carl Fleury — 112
8. John Messuri — 111
9. Lukas Smital — 110
10. Martin Masa — 104

Points

Player	GP	G	A	PTS
1. Rob Hyrtsak	175	98	156	254
2. Dmitri Tarabrin	474	99	133	232
3. Bruce Coles	132	106	121	227
4. Lukas Smital	278	107	110	217
5. Perry Florio	305	44	171	215
6. Bob Woods	190	59	141	200
7. Martin Masa	182	86	104	190
8. Carl Fleury	191	76	112	188
9. Brent Bilodeau	414	37	131	168
10. John Messuri	116	51	111	162

Penalty minutes
1. Jeff Sullivan — 1105
2. Rick Boyd — 966
3. Perry Florio — 799
4. Brock Kelly — 680
5. Jason Spence — 603
6. Brandon Christian — 585
7. Jody Shelley — 581
8. Brent Bilodeau — 542
9. Darren Schwartz — 524
10. Darren Servatius — 523

Goalie wins
1. Frederic Deschenes — 69
2. Stan Reddick — 42
3. John Bradley — 37
   Morgan Cey — 37
5. David Currie — 29

Chiefs all-time points leader Rob Hrytsak (left) wasn't afraid to mix it up from time to time, as evidenced by the aftermath of one of his fights.

Until Frederic Deschenes passed him, Stan "Smokey" Reddick was the Chiefs' all-time wins leader with 42.

MISCELLANEOUS STATS

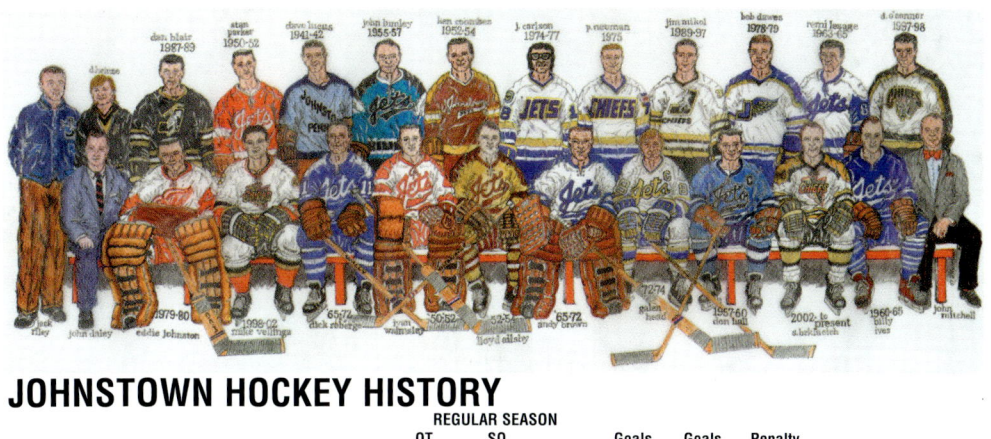

JOHNSTOWN HOCKEY HISTORY

Year	League	Games	Won	Lost	Tied	OT losses	SO losses	Points	Goals for	Goals against	Penalty minutes	Standings	Attendance
BLUEBIRDS													
41-42	EAHL	60	34	20	6			74	248	215	562	Tie-1	25,000+
JETS													
50-51	EAHL	54	26	25	3			55	195	194	809	Tie-1	90,298
51-52	EAHL	65	39	21	5			83	264	186	902	1st	112,170
52-53	EAHL	60	28	29	3			59	226	244	728	2nd	77,490
53-54	IHL	64	35	26	3			73	254	222	837	3rd	94,434
54-55	IHL	60	25	34	1			51	188	219	715	5th	58,792
55-56	EHL	64	32	32	0			64	312	298	676	4th	83,162
56-57	EHL	64	31	33	0			62	320	290	797	4th	92,375
57-58	EHL	64	31	30	3			65	228	225	482	4th	109,791
58-59	EHL	64	33	28	3			69	252	223	694	2nd	115,373
59-60	EHL	64	45	18	1			91	255	176	779	1st-S	111,845
60-61	EHL	64	40	22	2			82	273	215	757	Tie-1-S	86,711
61-62	EHL	68	41	26	1			83	296	255	619	2nd-N	96,061
62-63	EHL	68	34	31	3			71	254	309	735	3rd-N	71,101
63-64	EHL	72	41	26	5			87	297	245	1,032	1st-N	96,985
64-65	EHL	72	41	31	0			82	330	294	991	3rd-N	87,036
65-66	EHL	72	39	31	2			80	303	267	820	3rd-N	80,525
66-67	EHL	72	34	36	2			70	267	290	961	3rd-N	102,675
67-68	EHL	72	38	25	9			85	386	273	1,236	3rd-N	102,376
68-69	EHL	72	42	23	7			91	358	230	1,461	2nd-N	111,638
69-70	EHL	74	27	33	14			68	318	344	1,120	3rd-N	87,815
70-71	EHL	74	30	29	15			75	275	298	1,442	3rd-N	119,338
71-72	EHL	74	33	28	14			80	290	269	856	2nd-N	108,028
72-73	EHL	76	36	28	12			84	283	255	1,477	2nd-N	90,695
73-74	NAHL	74	32	38	4			68	265	303	1,002	5th	75,194
74-75	NAHL	74	38	32	4			80	274	255	1,594	4th	124,008
75-76	NAHL	76	47	25	2			96	346	257	1,479	1st-W	120,478
76-77	NAHL	73	22	49	2			46	253	334	1,118	7th	68,513
WINGS													
78-79	NEHL	70	25	42	3			53	251	315	1,186	5th	64,931
RED WINGS													
79-80	EHL	70	24	45	1			49	281	384	1,271	5th	83,804
CHIEFS													
87-88	AAHL	26	13	13		0	0	26	157	115	1,276	3rd	45,610
88-89	ECHL	60	32	22		0	6	70	295	251	1,950	2nd	120,800
89-90	ECHL	60	23	31		2	4	52	233	291	2,097	7th	113,412
90-91	ECHL	64	32	29		0	3	67	324	287	1,646	2nd-E	127,676
91-92	ECHL	64	36	23		3	2	77	294	248	1,750	3rd-W	121,599
92-93	ECHL	64	34	23		3	4	75	281	264	1,647	4th-E	106,244
93-94	ECHL	68	37	27		3	1	78	323	308	1,978	4th-N	111,687
94-95	ECHL	68	31	32		2	3	67	256	297	1,656	5th-N	109,019
95-96	ECHL	70	21	38		0	11	53	249	322	2,481	7th-N	91,658
96-97	ECHL	70	24	39		0	7	55	253	354	2,287	8th-N	102,358
97-98	ECHL	70	23	41		0	6	52	219	297	2,118	6th-NE	96,008
98-99	ECHL	70	27	34		0	9	63	218	265	1,734	5th-NE	84,427
99-00	ECHL	70	33	28		0	9	75	235	234	1,959	3rd-NW	91,452
00-01	ECHL	72	28	36		4	4	64	207	238	1,865	4th-NW	91,112
01-02	ECHL	72	39	31		0	2	80	220	232	1,688	3rd-NW	88,465
02-03	ECHL	72	28	33		3	8	67	214	243	1,700	5th-NW	81,750
03-04	ECHL	72	45	20		0	7	97	223	195	1,491	4th-NE	94,378
04-05	ECHL	72	22	36		5	9	58	191	258	1,421	7th-N	84,830
05-06	ECHL	72	30	26		4	12	76	223	243	1,119	4th-N	89,427
06-07	ECHL	72	33	33		3	3	72	216	232	1,179	5th-N	94,803
TOTALS		3378	1614	1492	130	32	110	3,500	13,173	13,058	26,231		4,670,357

335

				PLAYOFFS					
Year	League	Win	Losses	Goals for	Goals against	Penalty Minutes	Results	Home games	Attendance
BLUEBIRDS									
41-42	EAHL	5	3	35	37	57	Round-Robin	4	
JETS									
50-51	EAHL	2	4	20	27	85	Round-Robin	3	9,248
51-52	EAHL	11	2	57	27	221	USAHA Champions	7	20,750
52-53	EAHL	8	7	38	49	190	EAHL Champions	9	19,159
53-54	IHL	6	4	21	22	87	Finals	6	16,609
54-55	IHL	Did Not Qualify for Playoffs							
55-56	EHL	1	3	15	17	16	Semifinals	2	5,783
56-57	EHL	2	4	13	30	85	Semifinals	3	12,147
57-58	EHL	2	4	13	20	46	Semifinals	3	10,436
58-59	EHL	7	6	36	38	68	Finals	6	18,987
59-60	EHL	9	4	39	25	169	EHL Champions	7	22,813
60-61	EHL	10	2	47	18	152	EHL Champions	5	10,936
61-62	EHL	10	5	55	34	82	EHL Champions	8	18,808
62-63	EHL	0	3	5	10	20	Division Semifinals	1	2,702
63-64	EHL	5	5	38	28	222	Division Finals	6	13,910
64-65	EHL	2	3	19	19	70	Division Semifinals	2	4,812
65-66	EHL	0	3	7	14	12	Division Semifinals	1	1,591
66-67	EHL	2	3	15	17	76	Division Semifinals	2	5,500
67-68	EHL	0	3	6	23	34	Division Semifinals	1	2,354
68-69	EHL	0	3	10	16	75	Division Semi-Finals	2	6,178
69-70	EHL	0	4	13	21	50	Division Semifinals	2	3,585
70-71	EHL	4	6	43	55	247	Division Finals	5	16,947
71-72	EHL	6	5	40	41	122	Division Finals	6	17,175
72-73	EHL	5	7	45	44	109	Semifinals	5	10,898
73-74	NAHL	4	8	33	43	137	Semifinals	5	9,027
74-75	NAHL	11	4	63	45	249	NAHL Champions	7	23,181
75-76	NAHL	4	6	46	47	208	Division Finals	4	11,908
76-77	NAHL	0	3	7	19	18	Quarterfinals	1	1,379
WINGS									
78-79		Did Not Qualify for Playoffs							
RED WINGS									
79-80		Did Not Qualify for Playoffs							
CHIEFS									
87-88	AAHL	0	3	10	15	101	Round Robin	2	7,782
88-89	ECHL	7	4	61	39	395	Finals	6	22,905
89-90	ECHL	Did Not Qualify for Playoffs							
90-91	ECHL	4	6	31	43	337	Semifinals	5	15,458
91-92	ECHL	3	3	18	24	212	Second Round	3	8,316
92-93	ECHL	2	3	14	17	140	Quarterfinals	3	7,567
93-94	ECHL	1	2	7	14	116	First Round	1	2,201
94-95	ECHL	2	3	20	25	116	1st Round	2	3,740
95-96	ECHL	Did Not Qualify for Playoffs							
96-97	ECHL	Did Not Qualify for Playoffs							
97-98	ECHL	Did Not Qualify for Playoffs							
98-99	ECHL	Did Not Qualify for Playoffs							
99-00	ECHL	3	4	2	18	208	Conf. Semifinals	3	5,995
00-01	ECHL	1	3	7	12	85	Conf. Quarterfinals	2	3,571
01-02	ECHL	3	5	19	17	180	Division Finals	3	6,818
02-03	ECHL	Did Not Qualify for Playoffs							
03-04	ECHL	0	1	1	2	10	Wild Card	1	1,941
04-05	ECHL	Did Not Qualify for Playoffs							
05-06	ECHL	2	3	12	16	70	Division Semifinals	2	2,346
06-07	ECHL	0	2	7	11	18	Preliminary Round	1	1,163
TOTALS		144	156	1008	1039	2047		147	386,626

NOTE: The statistics on these pages are the "Official" statistics put out by the Johnstown teams. Most have been confirmed through additional sources. A few changes were made where researchers had proof. A few have discrepancies where notated in the individual yearly statistics.

Sources: *The Sporting News: Hockey Guides & Registers; ECHL guides; EHL yearbooks; NAHL yearbooks; EHL press releases; The Tribune-Democrat.*